THE BIBLE IN CHURCH, ACADEMY, AND CULTURE

THE BIBLE IN CHURCH, ACADEMY & CULTURE

Essays in Honour of
the Reverend Dr. John Tudno Williams

Edited by
Alan P. F. Sell

◆PICKWICK *Publications* • Eugene, Oregon

THE BIBLE IN CHURCH, ACADMEY, AND CULTURE
Essays in Honour of the Reverend Dr. John Tudno Williams

Copyright © 2011 Wipf and Stock Publishers. All rights reserved. Except for brief quotations in critical publications or reviews, no part of this book may be reproduced in any manner without prior written permission from the publisher. Write: Permissions, Wipf and Stock Publishers, 199 W. 8th Ave., Suite 3, Eugene, OR 97401.

Pickwick Publications
A Division of Wipf and Stock Publishers
199 W. 8th Ave., Suite 3
Eugene, OR 97401

www.wipfandstock.com

ISBN 13: 978-1-60899-475-5

Cataloging-in-Publication data:

The Bible in church, academy, and culture : essays in honour of the Reverend Dr. John Tudno Williams / edited by Alan P. F. Sell.

xvi + 286 p.; 23 cm.—Includes bibliographical references and indexes.

ISBN 13: 978-1-60899-475-5

1. Williams, John Tudno (1938–). 2. Bible—Theology—History—20th Century. 3. Bible—Study and Teaching. 4. Wales—Religious Life and Customs—20th Century. I. Sell, Alan P. F. II. Title.

BS511.3 B53 2011

Manufactured in the USA.

Scripture quotations are from New Revised Standard Version Bible: Anglicized Edition, copyright © 1989, 1995 National Council of the Churches of Christ in the United States of America. Used by permission. All rights reserved.

Scripture quotations marked (CEV) are from the Contemporary English Version Copyright © 1991, 1992, 1995 by American Bible Society. Used by Permission.

Scripture quotations marked (ESV) are from The Holy Bible, English Standard Version® (ESV®), copyright © 2001 by Crossway, a publishing ministry of Good News Publishers. Used by permission. All rights reserved.

Scripture quotations marked (NASB) are taken from the New American Standard Bible®, Copyright © 1960, 1962, 1963, 1968, 1971, 1972, 1973, 1975, 1977, 1995 by The Lockman Foundation. Used by permission. (www.Lockman.org)

Scripture quotations marked (NLT) are taken from the Holy Bible, New Living Translation, copyright © 1996, 2004, 2007 by Tyndale House Foundation. Used by permission of Tyndale House Publishers, Inc., Carol Stream, Illinois 60188. All rights reserved.

Scripture quotations marked (RSV) are from Revised Standard Version of the Bible, copyright © 1946, 1952, and 1971 National Council of the Churches of Christ in the United States of America. Used by permission. All rights reserved.

Scripture quotations marked (TNIV) are taken from the Holy Bible, Today's New International Version®. TNIV®. Copyright© 2001, 2005 by Biblica, Inc.™ Used by permission of Zondervan. All rights reserved worldwide. www.zondervan.com

GOD'S WORD is a copyrighted work of God's Word to the Nations. Quotations are used by permission. Copyright 1995 by God's Word to the Nations. All rights reserved.

Contents

List of Contributors ix
Preface xiii
Abbreviations xv

1 Honouring John Tudno Williams: Minister, Scholar, Welshman · 1
  ALAN P. F. SELL

2 The Challenge of Being Biblical · 20
  GARETH LLOYD JONES

3 The Ethics of the Old Testament: Historical and Literary Approaches · 44
  ERYL W. DAVIES

4 "Let Us Maintain Peace" (Romans 5:2): Reconciliation and Social Responsibility · 58
  WILLIAM S. CAMPBELL

5 The Growth Motif in the Letter to the Philippians · 81
  ALLISON A. TRITES

6 Striving for Office and the Exercise of Power in the "House of God": Reading I Timothy 3: 1–16 in the Light of 1 Corinthians 4:1 · 104
  KATHY EHRENSPERGER

Contents

7 On Serving Two Masters · 124
OWEN E. EVANS

8 Hymns and Scripture: The Welsh Experience · 142
BRYNLEY F. ROBERTS

9 The Transmission of Biblical Visual Imagery in the Calvinistic Methodist/Presbyterian Church of Wales · 162
D. HUW OWEN

10 'From "Monastic Family" to Calvinistic Methodist Academy': Trefeca College (1842–1906) · 191
J. GWYNFOR JONES

11 A Chapter in the History of Welsh Theology · 227
D. DENSIL MORGAN

12 Divine Election: an Exercise in Bridge-Building · 254
STEPHEN N. WILLIAMS

Index of Persons · 275
Index of Subjects · 284

List of Contributors

Dr. William S. Campbell is Reader in Biblical Studies at the University of Wales Trinity St. David. His publications include *Paul's Gospel in an Intercultural Context: Jew and Gentile in the Letter to the Romans*, and *Paul and the Creation of Christian Identity*.

Dr. Eryl W. Davies is a Reader in the School of Theology and Religious Studies at Bangor University. He was educated at Bangor University and the University of Cambridge, and spent a year at the Ruprecht-Karls University in Heidelberg as an Alexander von Humboldt Scholar. His publications include *Prophecy and Ethics: Isaiah and the Ethical Traditions of Israel*; *Numbers* in *The New Century Bible Commentary*; *The Dissenting Reader: Feminist Approaches to the Hebrew Bible*; and *The Immoral Bible: Approaches to Biblical Interpretation* (forthcoming).

Dr. Kathy Ehrensperger is Senior Lecturer in New Testament Studies at the University of Wales Trinity St. David. Her publications include, *That We May Be Mutually Encouraged: Feminism and the New Perspective in Pauline Studies*, and *Paul and the Dynamics of Power: Communication and Interaction in the Early Christ-Movement*.

The Reverend Dr. Owen E. Evans taught at Wesley College, Headingly, Leeds, and Hartley Victoria Methodist College, Manchester, and at the Universities of Manchester and Bangor. He was Senior Lecturer in Biblical Studies and Dean of the Faculty of Theology at Bangor. He chaired the New Testament and Apocrypha Panel of *The New Welsh Bible* from 1974 to 1995, and from 1986–2001 was Director of the entire translation project. He has published a *Concordance* of the 1988 version of the Welsh Bible; *The Gospel according to St. John* in *Epworth*

List of Contributors

Preacher's Commentaries; *Saints in Christ Jesus: A Study of the Christian Life in the New Testament*; and *On Translating the Bible*.

Canon Professor Gareth Lloyd Jones is Emeritus Professor of Theology and Religious Studies at Bangor University and a former Chancellor of Bangor Cathedral. His published works include, *The Discovery of Hebrew in Tudor England: A Third Language*; *Lleisiau o'r Lludw: Her yr Holocost i'r Cristion*; *The Bones of Joseph: From the Ancient Texts to the Modern Church*; and *Hard Sayings: Difficult New Testament Texts for Jewish-Christian Dialogue*.

Professor John Gwynfor Jones was Professor of Welsh History at Cardiff University. His publications include *Aspects of Religious Life in Wales, c.1536–1660: Leadership, Opinion and the Local Community*; and *Crefydd a Chymdeithas: Astudiaethau ar Hanes y Ffydd Brostestannaidd yng Nghymru, c.1559–1750*.

Professor D. Densil Morgan is Head of the School of Theology, Religious Studies and Islamic Studies at the University of Wales Trinity St. David. His publications include *Wales and the Word: Historical Perspectives on Welsh Religion and Identity*; *Lewis Edwards*; *The SPCK Introduction to Karl Barth*; and *Barth Reception in Britain*.

Dr. D. Huw Owen was Keeper of Pictures and Maps at the National Library of Wales until his retirement in 2001. A professional archivist, he previously taught at the College of Librarianship, Aberystwyth, and at the University of Cardiff. His publications include, *Settlement and Society in Wales* (editor and contributor); *The Agrarian History of England and Wales, vol. iii, 1348–1500*, ed. E. Miller, (contributor); *Early Printed Maps in Wales*; *The Oxford Companion to Family and Local History*, ed. D. Hey, (contributor); *Capeli Cymru*; and *Olrhain Hanes Bro a Theulu* (editor and contributor).

Dr. Brynley F. Roberts was Librarian of the National Library of Wales from 1985 to 1994. He served as Chairman of The United Theological College Board from 1977 to 1998. He chaired the Interdenominational Committee which produced the Welsh hymnal, *Caneuon Ffydd* in 2001, and the Welsh Hymn Society from 1986 to 1997. His publications include *Gwassanaeth Meir*, a study of the Welsh translation of *Officium*

List of Contributors

parvum Beatae Virginis Mariae; *O Fab y Dyn*, an edition of the work of George Rees; a catalogue and study of Welsh translations of Latin and German hymns, and articles on the hymns of the Great Awakening, and on local Swansea hymnists.

The Reverend Professor Alan P. F. Sell is a philosopher-theologian and ecumenist with strong interests in the history of Christian thought, not least in its Reformed and Dissenting expressions. His most recent books are *Hinterland Theology: A Stimulus to Theological Construction*; and *Four Philosophical Anglicans: W. G. de Burgh, W. R. Matthews, O. C. Quick and H. A. Hodges*. He publishes and lectures widely at home and abroad.

Dr. Allison A. Trites is the Payzant Distinguished Professor Emeritus of New Testament at Acadia Divinity College, Acadia University, Nova Scotia, Canada. His publications include, *The New Testament Concept of Witness*; *The Gospel of Luke* in the *Cornerstone Bible Commentary*, vol. 12; and articles in *The New Interpreter's Dictionary of the Bible*, the *Encyclopedia of the Historical Jesus*, and the *NLT Study Bible*.

Professor Stephen N. Williams is Professor of Systematic Theology at Union Theological College, Belfast. His most recent publication is a commentary on *Joshua* in the *Two Horizons* series, co-authored with J. Gordon McConville.

Preface

The recipient of this *Festschrift* and the contents of the volume are introduced in the first chapter. It remains, therefore, to offer thanks to a number of people, and first to the authors of the papers. They are formally noted in the List of Contributors, but it is appropriate that their relationship to John Tudno Williams be spelled out in a little more detail. There are, first, those with whom he has had professional relations in the field of biblical scholarship: Owen E. Evans, Eryl W. Davies and Gareth Lloyd Jones of the University of Bangor; William S. Campbell and Kathy Ehrensperger of the University of Wales Trinity St. David; and Allison A. Trites of Acadia Divinity College, Nova Scotia, Canada. John has known the theologians D. Densil Morgan and Stephen N. Williams for many years. Indeed, the latter succeeded his father, R. Nantlais Williams, in the Chair of Christian Doctrine and Philosophy of Religion at The United Theological College, Aberystwyth, and was thus John's colleague from 1980 to 1991. In 1992 I myself succeeded to that Chair. The remaining three contributors, like John himself, are members of the Presbyterian Church of Wales. The historian, J. Gwynfor Jones, is editor of the *Journal of the Presbyterian Church of Wales Historical Society*; the authority on Welsh culture, D. Huw Owen, serves with John on the Board of the Davies Lecture; and Brynley F. Roberts, an authority on Welsh literature, chaired the Board of The United Theological College from 1977 to 1998. I could not have had a more enthusiastic, or a more dutiful, group of co-conspirators in this happy project.

    I am most grateful to Mrs. Ina Williams for her considerable help behind the scenes; to Dr. Eryn M. White for diligently and successfully

Preface

searching for a particularly elusive historical detail; and to Dr. Karen Sell for editorial assistance.

Thanks are due to the officers of the Publications Fund of the Guild of Graduates of the University of Wales for a generous grant towards the cost of publishing this book.

Lastly I thank both Dr. K. C. Hanson, the editor-in-chief at Wipf & Stock—himself a biblical scholar—for his eagerness to add this volume to his list; and all his editorial and production colleagues, with whom it has been, as ever, a pleasure to work.

Alan P. F. Sell
Milton Keynes, UK

Abbreviations

BibInt	*Biblical Interpretation*
BibIntSer	Biblical Interpretation Series
BZAW	Beihefte zur Zeitschrift für die alttestamentliche Wissenschaft
DWB	*Dictionary of Welsh Biography to 1940*
ExpT	*The Expository Times*
IDB	*The Interpreter's Dictionary of the Bible*, edited by G. A. Buttrick, New York: Abingdon, 1962
Int	*Interpretation*
IRT	Issues in Religion and Theology
JBL	*Journal of Biblical Literature*
Journal	*Journal of the Historical Society of the Presbyterian Church of Wales*
JSNT	*Journal for the Study of the New Testament*
JSNTSup	Journal for the Study of the New Testament Supplement Series
JSOT	*Journal for the Study of the Old Testament*
JSOTSup	Journal for the Study of the Old Testament Supplement Series
LNTS	Library of New Testament Studies
RHPhR	*Revue d'Histoire et de Philosophie Religieuse*
NTS	New Testament Studies

Abbreviations

OBS	Oxford Bible Series
ODNB	*Oxford Dictionary of National Biography*
OTS	Old Testament Studies
SNTSMS	Society for New Testament Studies Monograph Series
WMANT	Wissenschaftliche Monographien zum Alten und Neuen Testament
WUNT	Wissenschaftliche Untersuchungen zum Neuen Testament

1

Honouring John Tudno Williams: Minister, Scholar, Welshman

ALAN P. F. SELL

The three terms in the above subtitle go some way towards personalizing the overall theme of this *Festschrift*; for we are honouring one whose detailed knowledge of the Bible has permeated his faithful churchly and academic service, most of which has been offered, and continues to be offered, within Wales, to the culture of which nation he is deeply committed. In this paper I shall first attempt a biographical sketch of my friend and former colleague,[1] and I shall then briefly introduce the ensuing papers.

John was born on 31 December 1938 in Flint, where his father, Arthur Tudno Williams, an alumnus of Jesus College, Oxford, was minister of the Welsh Presbyterian Church. His mother, Primrose (née Hughes Parry), was raised on her father's farm, where she lived until

1. This task, though a privilege and a pleasure, is fraught with peril, for John has an eagle's eye for detail, and the secrecy surrounding the preparation of this volume has precluded access to the principal authority on his life, namely, himself. My own researches have, however, been supplemented by his wife, Ina, and by the Reverend Dr. Owen E. Evans. In addition, some alumni of The United Theological College, Aberystwyth, have, on the condition of anonymity, had their say concerning their former professor/principal. To all of these I am most grateful. The skeleton of John's career may be seen in *Who's Who* (London: A. & C. Black).

her marriage. Their family was completed with the arrival, two years after John, of his sister, Mair.

Evidence of the depth of John's roots in Welsh Presbyterianism is found on both sides of his family. His great-great grandfather on his mother's side was Robert Hughes (1811–1892).[2] The son of a tenant farmer, Robert had little schooling. In 1830 he joined a cattle drove to London, where he became a member of Jewin Street Calvinistic Methodist Church.[3] Three years later his father called him back to Wales to manage the large farm of Uwchlaw'r-ffynnon, Caernarfonshire. This was a daunting task, but in addition to his agricultural duties he became known for his wood carvings, and he began to write poems, for some of which he won prizes at eisteddfodau. He delivered his first sermon in 1838, and taught himself basic Greek, Latin and Hebrew. He received an offer of help to equip him as an Anglican clergyman, and another to study at University College, London, but his family and farming commitments would not permit him to leave. Ordained a Presbyterian minister in 1848, he went on preaching tours, and ministered without stipend at a chapel he built in 1857. At the age of sixty he took to painting with oils. In 1893 a volume containing his autobiography and some of his sermons was published.

In John's paternal line we find a succession of Presbyterian ministers. His grandfather, John Tudno Williams, held pastorates at Walham Green, West London (1896–1906), Fron and Brookhouse, Denbigh (1906–1912), and Bettws-y-Coed (1912–1921). His father was ordained in 1936, and during his Flint pastorate he spent some time as a tutor at Coleg Clwyd, Rhyl. From Flint he went in 1945 to Garston, Liverpool, where he remained until 1951, in which year he removed to Lewisham, London. He returned to Wales on accepting the call to the pastorate of Llansantffraid, Montgomeryshire in 1969, and in 1973 he retired to Ruthin, where he died in November 1994. Of him it is written that

> As a preacher he was a clear thinker and a strong reasoner, and the theologian and educationist would show through his ser-

---

2. For whom see R. T. Jenkins in *The Dictionary of Welsh Biography down to 1940* (London: The Honourable Society of Cymmrodorion, 1959); Geraint Jones. *Gŵr Hynod Uwchlaw'r-ffynnon* (Llanrwst: Gwasg Carreg Gwalch, 2008). The text is based upon a lecture given at the opening of an exhibition of Hughes's paintings in 2006.

3. The Presbyterian Church of Wales originated in the Calvinistic side of the Evangelical Revival of the eighteenth century.

mons. He would never miss a *Seiat* (the midweek fellowship), and his contribution would always be precise, if not rather abrupt, but never unrelated or hazy ... He was a keen ecumenist, an uncompromising pacifist, a warm-hearted nationalist, a great *eisteddfodwr* ... He had a sweet singing voice ... In Ruthin he supported all the events of the chapel, be it a service or a pantomime, concert or drama, the *Seiat* or the Literary Society ... He was not ashamed of the Gospel, and he testified to it with humility and enlightenment.[4]

Among John's early memories are those of German bombers flying over the family home towards Birkenhead and Liverpool, and of searchlights seeking to track them. Like many other children of his generation, John sat the 11 Plus examination at his primary school. This examination had been introduced nationally under the Butler Education Act of 1944, and it was the medium whereby children were selected for one of the available types of secondary education. Unlike most children of his generation John sat the examination at the age of ten, and earned his place at Liverpool Institute High School for Boys, then under the Headship of John Robert Edwards, M.A. This school, founded in 1825, was controversially closed in 1985, and the premises now house the Liverpool Institute of Performing Arts, the co-founder of which is an alumnus of the School, Paul McCartney.[5] Enrolled in 1949, it was at this school that John began to learn German, Latin and Classical Greek; and was here, too, that he was among the entire school of 921 boys who sang 'The Soldier's Chorus' from *Faust* on Prize Day in the Liverpool Philharmonic Hall, under the direction of Dr. J. E. Wallace, music master at the School and for forty years Chorus Master of the Liverpool Philharmonic Choir.

His father having accepted the call to Lewisham, John left the Liverpool Institute High School after five terms, and was enrolled at Colfe's Grammar School at Easter 1951. John Glyn had founded a school at Lewisham in 1574, but Colfe's was a more permanent institution: indeed, it continues to this day. Abraham Colfe (1580–1657), who founded the school in 1652, was Vicar of Lewisham from 1610

4. John Owen, obituary of A. T. Williams in *Year Book and Diary* of the Presbyterian Church of Wales, 1996, (Caernarfon: Gwasg Pantycelyn), 94.

5. For whom see *Who's Who*. He would have been a younger contemporary of John's at the School, had Arthur Tudno Williams not accepted the call to Lewisham in 1951.

until his death. In accordance with the terms of his will the school was placed in the custody of the Worshipful Company of Leathersellers, with which body it is still associated. The premises had sustained severe bomb damage in 1944, and during John's schooldays temporary accommodation was in use. In 1964 the school was re-opened on its present site. Its status had been that of a voluntary aided Grammar School, but in 1977 it became independent. The Headmaster from 1946 was Herbert Beardwood, M.Sc., J.P., who published an updated version of Leland Lewis Duncan's *The History of Colfe's Grammar School* to mark the school's tercentenary in 1952.[6] In further celebration of this event, approximately six hundred boys, John among them, were conveyed by double-decker buses to London's Mansion House for a reception. Among Duncan's other benefactions is the school song, "Carmen Colfanum," set to music in 1897 by the then–music master, Frederick Leeds. It is not difficult to imagine a particularly lusty rendering of it from the subject of this biography:

> Then gather, ye sons of Colfe around
> Your voices lend with a will:
> Here's jolly good luck to ev'ry man,
> And a cheer Hurrah! A cheer Hurrah!
> For the School from the Hill.[7]

It is not quite so easy to imagine John as Portia in *The Merchant of Venice*, but he trod the boards to this end with Colfe's Junior Players—before his voice changed. That change having occurred, in 1955 he began to sing solos accompanied by the school orchestra, and he appeared as the Grand Inquisitor in *The Gondoliers*, a joint production with the neighbouring girls' school, whence came his sister, Mair, in the role of the Duchess of Plaza Toro. Lest it be thought that John was entirely consumed by high culture, mention should be made of his

---

6. The first edition was published in 1912. Beardwood edited a third edition published in 1972. For the period of his own tenure as Headmaster see ch. 27. My references are to the third edition. For Duncan (1862–1923) see *Who Was Who*; Pernille Richards. "Leland Lewis Duncan and Colfe's Grammar School, Lewisham," *Kent Archaeological Society Newsletter* 79 (Winter 2008/09) 5. He was employed at the War Office from 1882 to 1922. His interests included medieval history and ecclesiology. He was a Fellow of the Society of Antiquaries of London.

7. H. Beardwood, ed., *The History of Colfe's Grammar School* (Christchurch: Christchurch Times, 1972), 184.

playing Rugby for the School, and of his emergence in his final years there as a champion sprinter. Academic pursuits were not neglected. On the contrary, John was among those able students who were permitted to accelerate their course. He was thus able to take his Ordinary Level examinations at the age of fourteen, thereby arriving young in the sixth form. The year thus gained enabled him to take five Advanced Level subjects: German, English Literature, Latin, Classical Greek and Ancient History, in all of which he succeeded. During his final year at Colfe's he was School Captain.[8]

John left Colfe's at the end of the summer term 1957, and in the autumn of that year, in the footsteps of his father, he began to read for the Honours Degree in Theology at Jesus College, Oxford. It would seem that John never considered any vocation other than that of Presbyterian minister, and he had begun preaching whilst still at school. But it was at Oxford that he laid his theological, and especially his biblical, foundations in earnest. Among his tutors were Denys Whiteley, the Pauline scholar, by whom John was greatly influenced; and David Jenkins, later Professor of Theology at Leeds University and thereafter Bishop of Durham. Whilst at Oxford John held offices in the University's Welsh Language Society, and also served as secretary of the University Branch of the Fellowship of Reconciliation. In 1960 he graduated with second class Honours in Theology.

With a view to preparing for the Presbyterian ministry, John immediately proceeded to The United Theological College, Aberystwyth, then led by Principal William Richard Williams, who served in that capacity from 1949 to 1962. The College was housed in the former Cambrian Hotel, which had been bought and donated to the Presbyterian Church in 1906. This was an imposing building, situated directly opposite the somewhat gaudier pier. The first students and staff were transferred there from Trevecca College, Breconshire. In 1922 the Presbyterian Theological College at Bala united with its Aberystwyth counterpart, hence the term "United" in the College's name. As time went on, significant developments affecting theological education occurred in the region. In 1971 St. David's College, Lampeter, an Anglican foundation dating from 1822, became a constituent college of the federal University of Wales, and thereafter the Aberystwyth and

---

8. H. Beardwood, *History*, 179.

Lampeter School of Theology of the University was constituted. Ten years later the Congregationalists transferred their Memorial College from Swansea to Aberystwyth, and in 1989 their Bala-Bangor College united with their Aberystwyth institution. These developments were of both ecumenical and educational significance. Teaching and other facilities could be shared, and there was a greater number of theological scholars in the town. As the colleges increasingly opened their doors to undergraduates who wished to read Theology but were not destined for the ministry (or were destined for the ministry of churches other than the Congregational and Presbyterian) this increase of resources proved invaluable, and it became more common to offer the full range of theological degrees. Students benefited not only from the libraries of the two colleges, but also from the University College Library and the copyright library, The National Library of Wales.

Like all Presbyterian ordinands, John experienced the challenge of preaching before church members, academic staff and, above all, fellow students, in Aberystwyth churches, and this with a view to ensuing criticism. A 1963 photograph of the staff and students of the College shows John and twenty-four other students, and the following Professors: Principal S. Ifor Enoch (New Testament), R. Nantlais Williams (Philosophy of Religion), Gwilym H. Jones (Old Testament) and R. Buick Knox (Church History). To his ministerial training John added a programme of research. He enrolled through the Department of Classics of the University College Aberystwyth (the senior College of the University of Wales), as a candidate for the University's Degree of Doctor of Philosophy. The Professor of Classics at the time was W. H. Davies,[9] but John's principal supervisor was Ifor Enoch of the Theological College. In 1976 he was awarded the PhD for his thesis entitled, "Cultic elements in the Fourth Gospel, with special reference to sacrificial and priestly ideas."

In the meantime John had been ordained in 1963, and inducted to the pastorate at Borth, Cardiganshire. At first he was responsible for four churches, to which two more were subsequently added. On 31 October 1964 John married Ina, the daughter of the Congregational minister, David Gwyn Evans and his wife Margaret Ann Evans. The wedding took place at Pencader, Carmarthenshire, where Ina's father

---

9. He held his Chair from 1947 to 1974.

was minister, and both he and Arthur Tudno Williams took part in the service. In due course Haf was born, to be followed four years later by Tomos. Ina's teaching career culminated in a period of twenty years as Primary Education Course Leader within the Department of Education of the University of Wales, Aberystwyth.

In 1966 John was appointed part-time lecturer in Biblical Studies at The United Theological College, and in 1973 he assumed the Chair in that discipline. Thus began a full-time teaching ministry that extended over thirty years until his retirement in 2003. During this time he travelled the length and breadth of Wales conducting worship in both Welsh and English. His published writings are largely in Welsh. They include *Problem Dioddefaint a Llyfr Job* (*The Problem of Suffering and the Book of Job*),[10] commentaries on 1 Corinthians, and Galatians and Philippians, and a number of articles and reviews in *Y Traethodydd* (*The Essayist*) and *Diwinyddiaeth* (*Theology*). Among English writings are articles and reviews in *The Expository Times*, *The Journal of Semitic Studies*, and the *Transactions of the Honourable Society of Cymmrodorion*. He has also contributed to a number of multi-author volumes,[11] and most recently he and Glyn Tudwal Jones jointly edited the bilingual volume, *A Book of Services*.[12]

For an authoritative judgment on John's contribution to biblical studies, with special reference to the new translation of the Bible into Welsh—a project in which John was involved from 1975 onwards—I turn to Dr. Owen E. Evans:

10. Caernarfon: Gwasg Pantycelyn, 1980.

11. "Bibliography of the works of C. H. Dodd," in F. W. Dillistone, *C. H. Dodd: Interpreter of the New Testament* (London: Hodder & Stoughton, 1977), 249–51; "Cultic Elements in the Fourth Gospel," in E. A. Livingstone, ed., *Studia Biblica 1978: Sixth International Conference on Biblical Studies, Oxford* (Journal for the Study of the New Testament Supplement Series 2; Sheffield, 1980), 2:339–50; "The Contribution of Protestant Nonconformists to biblical scholarship in the Twentieth Century," in Alan P. F. Sell and A. R. Cross, eds, *Protestant Nonconformity in the Twentieth Century* (Carlisle: Paternoster, 2000), 1–32; "Jesus the Servant— vicarious sufferer: a reappraisal," in R. Glenn Wooden, Timothy R. Ashley and Robert S. Wilson, eds, *You Will Be My Witnesses. A Festschrift in Honour of Allison A. Trites* (Macon, GA: Mercer University Press, 2003), 53–80; "C. H. Dodd and W. D. Davies: Two Welsh Congregationalists on the nature of the Church," in Anna M. Robbins, ed., *Ecumenical and Eclectic: Essays in Honour of Alan P. F. Sell* (Studies in Christian History and Thought; Milton Keynes: Paternoster, 2007), 159–71.

12. Caernarfon: Gwasg Pantycelyn, 2010.

> His biblical scholarship is founded on wide reading, sharp intellect and a thorough mastery of the original languages of the Bible (although his main field of expertise is the New Testament, for a considerable part of his teaching career he lectured on the Hebrew language and literature of the Old Testament as well as on the Greek language and literature of the New Testament. As a member of the Translation Panel for the N.T. and Apocrypha of *Y Beibl Cymraeg Newydd* (1988) and the Revised Edition thereof (O.T. and N.T., 2004; Apoc. 2008), his contribution was substantial and valuable, showing ample proof of his exact scholarship and balanced judgment. His appointment in 2001 to the Margaret and Ann Eilian Owen Fellowship of the National Library of Wales was further proof of his high standing as a biblical scholar.

A considerable variety of opportunities for academic and educational service came John's way, and to all of them he paid devoted and highly competent attention. He served two terms as Dean of the Aberystwyth and Lampeter School of Theology (1985–87, 1994–97); for almost twenty years he was the tutor in charge of the Religious Studies course for the external degree through the medium of Welsh at the University of Wales Aberystwyth; for some years he worked with Owen Evans as an examiner of A Level Religious Studies papers for the Welsh Joint Educational Committee, until in 1984 he succeeded Dr. Evans as Chief Examiner, holding the post until 1996; for thirty-six years he was secretary of the theological branch of the University of Wales Guild of Graduates, and the branch's representative on the Standing Committee of the Guild.

Any impression that John's interests were confined to Wales must immediately be dispelled. He attended Old and New Testament conferences far and wide; he served as external examiner to universities in England and Northern Ireland; and in 1997 he spent a semester as Visiting Professor at the Divinity College of Acadia University in Wolfville, Nova Scotia, whilst Professor Allison A. Trites filled his place at Aberystwyth. I have reason to know that both scholars thoroughly enjoyed the experience, and that both of them threw themselves not only into the teaching they were required to offer, but into the life of the churches and the wider communities. That their wives were able to enjoy something of the experience was a further delight to their hosts.

John's ecclesiastical experience has been equally diverse. From 1985 to 1998 he served on the Joint Churches' Committee on Education, the body that seeks to coordinate Christian responses and actions on matters concerning public education; and for some years he was a member of the Education Committee of the Free Church Federal Council of England and Wales. From 1990 to 1991 he served as Moderator of the latter body (only the second minister of his Church to do so), in succession to such notable ministers as John Scott Lidgett (Wesleyan), John S. Whale (Congregationalist), R. D. Whitehorn (Presbyterian) and Henry Townsend (Baptist). His year of office saw the fiftieth anniversary of the union of the National Council of the Evangelical Free Churches (1896) with the Federal Council of Evangelical Churches (1919).[13]

John's Induction Service as Moderator was held at Jewin Welsh Presbyterian Church, London. In his Moderatorial address he declared that the Free Churches still had an important role—not least a counter-cultural role—to play in the land. They were to be in the world, but not of it: "I venture to say unless we are aware of a tension between the demands of Christ and the demands of the world upon us we have let slip one of the basic precepts of our Christian Free Church calling."[14] He cited examples from Nonconformist history of those who had taken such a stand, and also referred to Christians in Eastern Europe and South Africa who were similarly challenging the *status quo* and striving for societal change. "Pietistic" voices notwithstanding, Christianity was not a private matter, and for the apostle Paul, to be "in Christ" was to be of Christ's body, the Church. There should be no dividing line between social witness and evangelical faith, a point exemplified in the lives of the Arminian Methodist Wesleys, the Calvinistic Methodist Howel Harris, the Baptist John Clifford and the Congregationalist P. T. Forsyth. But it was to the Lutheran, Dag Hammarskjold, that John turned for a concluding observation: "Never for the sake of peace and quiet deny your own experiences and convictions."[15]

During his year of office as Moderator, John attended the National Corrymeela Service in Birmingham. The Corrymela Community had

---

13. See further E. K. H. Jordan, *Free Church Unity. History of the Free Church Council Movement 1896-1941* (London: Lutterworth, 1956).

14. J. T. Williams, "Be Non-Conformists. (A summary of the address given by the Moderator at his Induction," *Free Church Chronicle* XLV no. 2 (Summer 1990) 2.

15. Ibid.

been established to work for reconciliation between Roman Catholics and Protestants in Northern Ireland, and the objective of the service was to acquaint people on the mainland with the situation in the Province, and to encourage practical and prayerful support of the Community's work. John visited Archbishop Robert Runcie at Lambeth Palace on two occasions, one such visit occurring on the day Margaret Thatcher resigned as Prime Minister; and he also visited Cardinal Basil Hume. He participated in An Observance for Commonwealth Day at Westminster Abbey, during which representatives of the major religions found in Commonwealth countries responded to five affirmations concerning respect for the natural world, justice, peace, the supremacy of love, and sacrificial service for the common good. He attended the concluding sessions of the British Council of Churches at Swanwick, Derbyshire: the prelude to the formation of Churches Together in Britain and Ireland. When the latter body was inaugurated in Liverpool, John was among those who processed from the Anglican Cathedral at one end of Hope Street to the Roman Catholic Cathedral at the other end of the street, to the jeers of supporters of the Protestant firebrand, Ian Paisley.[16]

John has served the Presbyterian Church of Wales in numerous ways. From 1979 to 2000 he was a member of the Church's Education Committee, and since 1983 he has served on the Board of Trustees of the prestigious Davies Lecture. In 1993 he delivered the Lecture himself, on "Welsh interpreters of Paul the apostle." Since 2003 John has been a member of the Church's Panel on Worship and Doctrine. He was Moderator of the Association of the South (2002–2003), and of the General Assembly of the Presbyterian Church (2006–07). During his year of office he attended the General Assemblies of the Church of Scotland and the Presbyterian Church of Ireland and, together with Ina, he visited Shillong in North-East India, where the Presbyterian Church owes its origin to the pioneering work of Thomas Jones of Berriew, Montgomeryshire.[17] Indeed, John's principal task there was to inaugurate a three-year programme of events marking the bicentenary of the birth of Jones. Among other things he unveiled a memorial to Thomas Jones, and preached to some 100,000 people at a Polo stadium. John's valedictory address as Moderator was based on 2 Corinthians 4:5, "It

---

16. For the details in this paragraph (supplemented by Ina Williams) see J. T. Williams, "From the Moderator," *Free Church Chronicle*, 1.

17. For Jones (1810–1849) see R. T. Jenkins in *The Dictionary of Welsh Biography*.

is not ourselves that we proclaim; we proclaim Jesus Christ as Lord, and ourselves as your servants for Christ's sake." He spoke of the challenge posed to the Church by an increasingly secular, atheistic, society, and of the need to proclaim the Lordship of Christ over all aspects of life. Christians must serve society in the name of "the man for others" (Bonhoeffer), he declared. His theme was echoed by words sung during the service by Cor Glannau Ystwyth, the rural choir of which John is a member. It is not fanciful to suppose that John ranks such impressive occasions as no more important than some twenty years of unofficial ministry he gave to his home chapel at Capel Seion, where Ina plays the organ, and serves as an elder, Sunday School superintendent and teacher, and church secretary.

Having served under Principals S. Ifor Enoch, who retired in 1979, Rheinallt Nantlais Williams, who served in that capacity from 1979–1980, and Elfed ap Nefydd Roberts, whose tenure ran from 1980 to 1997, when he accepted the call to Capel y Groes, Wrexham, John was appointed Principal of the College in 1998. None deserved this honour more than he, and he served with distinction until, for a variety of reasons the Church, which owned the premises, closed the College in 2003. The Congregational College having already closed, formal theological education to the highest level thus ceased in Aberystwyth. John faithfully superintended the winding down of the life of the institution to which he had devoted the major part of his ministerial career. For many years he had served as College Librarian, and not the least of his efforts were directed to the preservation, suitably housed, of the collections that he had so assiduously built up. The rarest books were deposited at the National Library of Wales, while the bulk of the collection was added to that at the University of Wales Lampeter, which institution awarded John an Honorary Fellowship in the Department of Theology and Religious Studies on his retirement.

In 2006 John's churchly, educational and scholarly contribution was recognized by the University of Wales, which awarded him the Degree of DD *honoris causa*. The ceremony took place in Swansea, and John was formally presented by his erstwhile colleague, W. Eifion Powell, a former Principal of the Congregational College in Aberystwyth.

The preceding account reveals a person who has faithfully and notably filled numerous roles, ecclesiastical, scholarly, and educational. But there is more to John than that. From his earliest years singing has been his delight. Reference has already been made to his schoolboy performances, and to his continuing membership of Cor Glannau Ystwyth. To these may be added his appearance on three occasions as a finalist in the bass competition of the National Eisteddfod of Wales; a number of Gilbert and Sullivan productions at the Theatr y Werin, Aberystwyth, and bass solo parts in Bach's *St. Matthew* Passion and Handel's *Messiah*. He and Ina sang with the Padarn Singers for many years.

A further interest of John's is politics. He has an encyclopaedic knowledge of Members of Parliament and their constituencies, and he exercised his own socio-political conscience as a Welsh Nationalist member of Aberystwyth Town Council from 1979 to 1987.

I should like to say what a very great pleasure it was to work alongside John at the Theological College for nine years. A person of great integrity, he was a most friendly and supportive colleague, ever willing to co-operate, not least in activities of the Centre for the Study of British Christian Thought which was established in order to provide a focus for the College's postgraduate studies. Among many happy memories are those of the Christmas Carol Services, where John would lead the choir, I would try to keep up on the organ, and Karen, my musician wife, would select special items from her extensive collection for the choir to perform. But nobody knows a professor in the way that students do. It is therefore fitting that the last word in this biographical sketch should go to them. A number of former students have shared their memories of John with me, and the following contributions are representative of others.

> The words that come to mind are scholarly, enthusiastic, knowledgeable. His lectures were detailed, as a tutor he was always fair, but a hard task master who did not suffer fools gladly. His greatest contribution was to commend scholarly pursuit, a great love of the biblical text and respect for its meaning and literary character. He once said that the mark of the scholar was not "having the answer" but knowing where to find the answer. Reference should also be made to his devotional contribution in the College chapel where he led worship with dignity and respect, enjoyed the singing and shared a personal and deep faith that was not always evident to more conservatively-minded [students] that attended his lectures.

John Tudno was infuriating if a student just wanted lecture notes to pass exams. He never stuck to a script. He was always willing to take up a student's ideas and digress. His lectures were inspiring—he succeeded in making biblical theology fascinating, even exciting at times. You always left his lectures with our mind in overdrive, full of new lines to investigate. The bell was ever an unwelcome interruption, even for a smoker! He taught almost on a one-to-one basis. If you expressed an opinion, he would encourage you to think it through, advise what books to read and even appear, an hour or two later, with a bundle of books from the library. He treated every opinion or question seriously, never dismissing a question as silly or trivial. I was warned by former students that JTW was liberal in theology and disliked evangelicals. However, I found him tolerant of a very wide range of opinions and each was respected. He only ever showed impatience with those who were not prepared to justify their opinions or expand their thinking by study or consider other people's stance. He did not seek to change anybody's theological convictions but rather to help them think it through. I shall ever be grateful to John Tudno for the kindness, tolerance, encouragement and, above all, enthusiasm with which he sought to teach my dim-witted self.

As a first year student I was slightly in awe of the sometimes stern-looking professor who had been part of the College fabric for decades, but by the time I was taught by JT (as he was affectionately known) I quickly learned that this warm-hearted scholar was keen to transfer a deep love of theology to his students. I remember going to see him in his study and being slightly surprised at the sheer mountain of books, papers and documents that filled the room, and even more overawed at the resources he quickly offered to assist my research. JT never gave hints for exams but fostered in his students a desire to discover and learn, something I now greatly appreciate. As a preacher my ongoing interest in the writings of the Apostle Paul is directly accreditable to JT. His singing voice as often put to good use and his comedy songs at Christmas concerts were something else! As a preacher, pastor and teacher he was a valuable member of the team that created such a happy place for ordinands and students to live and study.

∽

The Bible in Church, Academy, and Culture

It seemed clear from the outset that in view of John's long-standing commitment to studying, teaching, and writing about the Bible, the focus of this celebratory volume should be upon that collection of texts. The scholars who were approached for contributions had no difficulty in concurring: whether biblical scholars, theologians, historians or students of Welsh culture, they have all been able to write about, or at least with reference to, the Bible.

Professor Gareth Lloyd Jones offers the first of six papers by biblical scholars. In a lively and refreshingly honest way he faces "The challenge of being biblical." How easy is it, he asks, "to obey the Bible 'in its plain and canonical sense?'" Pertinent hermeneutical questions are raised concerning the characteristics and canonicity of Scripture, the variety of material within the Bible, and the varied cultural contexts depicted in the Bible—all of them so markedly different from our own. Interpretation and selective reading are unavoidable, as when lectionary compilers halt a reading at Joshua 6: 20, "because genocide in God's name [see verse 21] is not a practice which should be encouraged." We are thus led into Reception History, which is discussed with reference to Calvin's modification of the old prohibition of usury, and Mark Twain's denunciation of the activity of "the pulpit" in offering spurious justifications of the slave trade. Thus it is that changing times and circumstances make changing interpretations of, and attitudes towards, the Bible inevitable.

Dr. Eryl W. Davies' discussion of "The ethics of the Old Testament: historical and literary approaches", opens with the recognition of the quantity, variety and complexity of ethical writing in the Old Testament. For all that, Old Testament Ethics is emerging as a discipline in its own right, characterized by historical-critical and literary approaches to the text. Drawing upon insights from sociology, archaeology and anthropology, those who adopt the historical-critical method seek to delineate the social conditions and moral climate of Israel. This approach has been queried by some, owing to the dearth of hard evidence, the fact that the documents convey the perceptions not of Israel as a whole but of its intellectual and economic elite, and because the outcome is descriptive rather than normative ethics. Those who follow the literary-critical path seek to read biblical texts in their own terms, the emphasis falling upon the moral truths conveyed through a variety of literary genres. While cautioning that due attention must be paid to semantic changes and teminological ambiguities, Dr. Davies recommends the judicious blending of both approaches.

In his paper, "Let Us Maintain Peace (Rom 5:2): Reconciliation and Social Responsibility," Dr. William S. Campbell argues that for Paul, their new life in Christ notwithstanding, Jewish Christians remain Jews and gentile Christians remain gentiles. Their common unity in Christ is, however, contradicted by the enmity between them, and this is challenged by Christ's reconciling work: "Reconciliation presupposes enmity arising from difference but simultaneously demands its demise." There is a lesson here for Christians who claim to be at peace with God whilst being hostile towards one another. The theme of reconciliation with God and between Christians runs throughout Romans—a fact which calls into question the familiar division of the letter into eleven chapters of doctrine followed by five chapters of ethics. Paul is primarily concerned with "the relation of Jew and gentile both in theology and in life"; hence his peace language is synonymous with his reconciliation language, and doctrine and social ethics are inextricably interwoven in his thought.

Professor Allison Trites turns his attention to church growth, a subject upon which much has been written in recent years, not all of it to the author's liking: "Contemporary church growth writers," he declares, "often do not place their emphasis on biblical exegesis, and if they deal with the letters associated with Paul's name, they frequently do so in a disorderly, unsystematic fashion." Professor Trites seeks to redress the balance. He offers a detailed exegetical study of Philippians by way of revealing the fact of church growth, its Christocentricity, the necessity of qualitative church growth, its cost, relationships, prayerfulness and collegiality. There follows a topic by topic comparison of Paul's analysis of church growth in Philippians with than of Luke in Acts. While by no means suggesting that the whole of Paul's missionary activity can be classified under "church growth", Professor Trites shows that the apostle was deeply concerned with the subject, not least with the relevance of exemplary Christian character and lifestyle to the expansion of the Church.

In her contribution Dr. Kathy Ehrensperger proposes that in 1 Timothy the primary concern is "how to live in the house of God, the assembly of the living God." This theme takes precedence over the interest in establishing *quasi*-hierarchical offices in the infant church. *Pace* some scholars, such offices are not here introduced for the first time: hierarchies of authority were present in undisputed Pauline epistles, and they are not necessarily oppressive. The author of I Timothy is concerned with filling leadership roles appropriately, not with regulations as such. It should not be assumed that the structures and relationships within the house of God mirror those of imperial Rome. The patriarchal structure of the Christian "family" "did not inherently hinder" the contribution of women. Moreover, to pray for the state authorities is not tantamount to accommodating to their values: it is a survival strategy on the part of a minority group liable to persecution. Indeed, "I Tim 3: 1–16 appears to be a hidden transcript of resistance to the dominating powers rather than a call to accommodate to the ideology of the empire."

It is a particular pleasure to introduce "On serving two masters," a paper by the doyen of Welsh New Testament scholars, Dr. Owen E. Evans. First, I had the pleasure of sitting under Dr. Evans at the University of Manchester during the very period of which he writes, and I benefited from the extra load he bore when standing in for Professor T. W. Manson during the latter's periods of absence through ill health, and following his death. Secondly, almost forty years on I invited Dr. Evans to deliver a paper under this title at the Centre for the Study of British Christian Thought at The United Theological College, Aberystwyth, and this he gladly did. The sizeable audience included John Tudno Williams. I had long hoped that this paper would see the light of published day, for it can truly be said that Dr. Evans is the only person in the world who could have written it, since no one else was both a student under Vincent Taylor and an apprentice lecturer under T. W. Manson. We thus have an unique comparison of the characters and contributions of two giants of English New Testament scholarship of the mid-twentieth century. I take full responsibility for the notes added to this paper at Dr. Evans's request.

With Dr. Brynley F. Roberts's contribution, "Hymns and Scripture: The Welsh experience," we come to the first of four papers in which Welsh culture and history loom appropriately large. Dr. Roberts recalls medieval religious verse, finds the roots of modern Welsh hymnody in the metrical psalms of the sixteenth and seventeenth centuries, and refers to the popular Bible-based songs and carols of the period from 1662 to the first half of the eighteenth century. All of this notwithstanding, Dr. Roberts more than justifies his claim that "'Classical' Welsh hymnody has its roots in the Methodist societies of the eighteenth century." The Evangelical Awakening saw a flowering of hymnody fertilized by biblical allusions and language, and nurtured by doctrinal preaching and the experiential spirituality of local society meetings. The argument is illustrated by reference to Welsh hymnists. Dr. Roberts concludes by referring to recent changing styles and themes in hymnology, and suggests that just as the reading of the Bible can inspire modern hymnists, so if "the association of hymns and Bible in communal worship" is made explicit this "will be a means of making Bible reading central and full of meaning to today's congregations."

Dr. D. Huw Owen, writing on "The transmission of biblical imagery in the Calvinistic Methodist/Presbyterian Church of Wales," shows that while Calvin's prohibition of 'graven images' in worship had an inhibiting effect, things visual gradually came more and more to be tolerated and even welcomed. The prominent artists Hugh Hughes and S. Morris Jones were in the van in this matter. Portraits of prominent preachers became increasingly common—sometimes with the open Bible diplomatically shown; periodicals for children and adults were illustrated; portrait and group photography played its part; postcards were published; monuments to prominent Presbyterians were erected; and memorial tablets placed. The Connexion formally adopted its own badge and motto. Chapel architecture developed from the simple to the more ornate, with many chapels adopting and displaying biblical names outside and biblical texts within. Such texts also appeared on Sunday School banners. Dr. Owen concludes that the Calvinistic Methodists/Presbyterians have made a considerable contribution to the visual cultural heritage of Wales.

Professor J. Gwynfor Jones's paper, "From 'monastic family' to Calvinistic Methodist Academy: Trefeca College (1842–1906)," is concerned with the predecessor institutions of the College to which John Tudno Williams devoted most of his working life, and to Trefeca College in particular. It is a story which brings to the fore both the suspicions of those who think that the Bible, spiritual life and preaching suffer if formal theological education is offered; and the tensions engendered by vested interests in different sections of one denomination: neither of which phenomena are exclusive to Wales. As to the former, the Methodist leader Thomas Charles and the Anglican Griffith Jones appear as pioneers of the view that "biblical knowledge was far more beneficial to proclaim the gospel than inspired preaching."[18] As to the latter, neither supporters of Trefeca nor those of Bala were easily persuaded that their college should close in the interests of consolidated theological education. Professor Jones introduces us to the professors of Trefeca from 1842 onwards, notably Owen Prys, and his account ends with the transfer of ministerial training from Trefeca to Aberystwyth in 1906.

In "A Chapter in the History of Welsh Theology," Professor D. Densil Morgan provides an account of the way in which the theology of the Word, associated with the name of Karl Barth, found its way to Wales. He notes the importance of Mansfield College, the Congregational college at Oxford, in nurturing Welsh theologians. Some of these, like D. Miall Edwards, never departed from post-Hegelian immanentism, while others, among them J. D. Vernon Lewis, pioneered the reception of Barth in Wales in face of theological liberalism on the one hand and lingering scholastic Calvinism on the other. The most prominent early Welsh Barthian, John Edward Daniel, took his fellow Congregationalist, Miall Edwards, to task. In seeking to explain the "secret" of Barth's preaching, the Presbyterian Ivor Oswy Davies concluded that it was "Perhaps the absence of any apologetic note." This was consistent with Daniel's account of Barth's position: "There is no standard outside of revelation with which to judge God's truth." As the Second World War drew ever nearer, I. O. Davies' affirmation that God could bring light out of darkness as he had done at the Cross was a great encouragement to Welsh Christians.

In the concluding paper, "Divine election: an exercise in bridge-building", Professor Stephen N. Williams, sets out from Lesslie Newbigin's view that election confers not soteric privilege, but responsibility. Against this Professor Williams sets the view of H. H. Rowley,[19] that while election is primarily for service, "in the service of God is man's supreme privilege and honour." He proceeds to show the importance in the Old Testament of election as entailing communion with the living God both temporally and eternally. Indeed, "the greater the

18. In chapter 11, below, D. Densil Morgan quotes Lewis Edwards thus: "We are aware of the dangers of knowledge, but we think the dangers of ignorance to be greater."

19. The distinguished Old Testament scholar to whom Owen Evans refers in his paper as T. W. Manson's colleague at Manchester. By the same token this Baptist of wry humor and voluminous footnotes was another of my teachers.

privilege [conferred upon the faithful elect], the greater the penalty for unfaithfulness." Turning to the New Testament, Professor Williams laments that systematicians have too frequently "mapped questions of personal destiny onto biblical materials that do not deal with it." Thus divine election to life is improperly contrasted with preterition, rather than with the culpable rejection of life. Election, when viewed in relation to incarnation, concerns "Purposeful love towards humanity, getting as close as possible to the human race by becoming human, [and this] requires the particularity of space and time"; and it is all with a view to human salvation.

It may truly be said that the papers in this *Festschrift* gather around the central theme of the Bible. They severally concern the interpretation and exegesis of Scripture, and the Bible's place in hymns, in the visual culture of a particular Christian tradition, in institutions dedicated to the task of preparing those who shall preach the Word, and in theological reflection and construction. The volume is offered to John Tudno Williams with affection and esteem. It may confidently be asserted that if anything written in these pages were to stimulate a student, a scholar, a preacher, a hymnist, a craftsman or artist, or a theologian to turn with renewed zeal to the Bible—not the Bible conceived as simply a miscellany of antiquarian texts but as a compendium whose message needs to be heard and received in the present socio-cultural situation—none would be more delighted than John Tudno Williams.

2

The Challenge of Being Biblical

GARETH LLOYD JONES

Among the demands made on the Roman Catholic Church by the Second Vatican Council was that moral theology should be revitalized by closer contact with the Bible. In 1971 Charles Curran, a leading Roman Catholic scholar, listed and reflected on the benefits for the Church of what he called the "Scriptural renewal." But he then drew attention to certain "limitations" which, he said, were inherent in giving the Bible a special role in Christian morality. Vatican II, he asserted, had failed to notice the difficulty of taking Scripture as a guide in making ethical decisions.[1]

Despite Curran's caveat, we live in an age when much emphasis is placed within Christian circles on "being biblical." A current example is to be found in the literature produced by the Global Anglican Future Conference (GAFCON), which was convened in Jerusalem in June 2008. The participants were bishops, priests and laity from the world-wide Anglican Church. According to their publicity, they were responding to "the spread of erroneous theological teaching and practices within the Anglican Communion." In seeking to combat these

---

1. C. A. Curran and R. A. McCormick, SJ, eds., *The Use of Scripture in Moral Theology* (Readings in Moral Theology 4; Ramsey, NJ: Paulist, 1984), 178–212.

errors, they produced the 'Jerusalem Declaration' which lists fourteen points described as "tenets of orthodoxy which underpin our Anglican identity." The second and the fourth of the tenets read thus:

> We believe the Holy Scriptures of the Old and New Testaments to be the Word of God and to contain all things necessary for salvation. The Bible is to be translated, read, preached, taught and obeyed in its plain and canonical sense, respectful of the Church's historic and consensual reading.
>
> We uphold the Thirty-Nine Articles as containing the true doctrine of the Church agreeing with God's Word and as authoritative for Anglicans today.

Clearly, the Bible is at the centre of the current debate, and the debate is not confined to Anglicans. Obedience to its teachings implies belief in the literal truth of its narratives and in the binding nature of its laws.

In response to this call to obey the Bible "in its plain and canonical sense," I want to ask: How easy is it to do just that? Is it possible to live according to its prescriptions and examples without any qualification, or is such an undertaking far more problematic than we care to admit? In what way are we able to use a book which is, if we are honest, in many respects difficult and alien, as a foundation for our faith? In the words of the exiled psalmist as he sat by the waters of Babylon: "How can we sing the Lord's song in a strange land?"

In addressing these questions, it is not my intention to explore concepts such as inspiration, inerrancy, or the description of the Bible as the Word of God. These are beliefs *about* the Bible. Focussing primarily on the Old Testament, I propose to highlight some of the issues associated with what Curran calls the Bible's "inherent limitations," and consider how we respond to them. Identifying which prescriptions are relevant to us and knowing how to apply them in our everyday life is no simple matter. This is not a fruitless exercise because recognizing the obstacles we are likely to meet will assist us in seeking moral guidance in the Scriptures.

I begin by considering two features which, in the popular mind, distinguish the Bible from other books and give it an aura of sanctity.

Characteristics and Canonicity

The first is its physical characteristics. For many people the binding alone plays a not insignificant role in their perception of its authority and uniqueness. Though now available in paperback, the Bible is also bound in black leather, sometimes with a gold cross on the front cover. In many editions it is printed on thin, onion-skin paper. Its pages may be edged with gold or red. In some households it is still given a place of honour on the sideboard or coffee table, not necessarily to be read but to record the family history of hatches, matches and dispatches. Putting any object or book on top of it would amount to desecration. The way in which it is bound calls for deference and respect. Its outward appearance governs many people's response to it and confirms their belief that it is the Word of God, a repository of truths applicable to all people, at all times, in all places.

Another characteristic is the format of the printed page. Here two features which are common to both paperback and leather-bound editions are noteworthy. The first is the page set-up. Each page contains two columns of text, the space between them sometimes filled with cross-references to other verses. As far as the common run of books is concerned, this is unusual. The only others printed in double columns are reference books, books which are regarded as authoritative in that they provide accurate facts and detailed definitions.

The *Jerusalem Bible*, published in 1966, was the first major English version to abandon the two column format and use the full page. But when the *New English Bible* followed suit in 1970, the editors were severely taken to task by reviewers. Making the Word of God look like any other book displeased many people, presumably because it detracted from its authority. Combined with the binding, the double column format encourages its readers to regard the Bible in the same way as they would regard encyclopaedias and dictionaries—as a source of inerrant answers to perplexing questions.

The second distinguishing mark of the Bible's format is the use of chapter and verse. These divisions might appear to be a part of the text from the beginning, but in fact they were inserted during the late Middle Ages. Chapter numbers were put in by an Archbishop of Canterbury at the end of the twelfth century. The Old Testament verses were first numbered by a rabbi in the fifteenth century, and those of the New by the French printer, Robert Estienne, a century later. The first English Bible to have numbered chapters and verses was printed in 1560. So when the practice was adopted by the Authorized Version of King James in 1611, it was a relatively recent phenomenon.

While this particular format has obvious advantages, it has its limitations. It encourages readers to take a small segment of the text and quote it as universally authoritative without paying any attention to the context. The truth of the Bible is not sought in the narrative as a whole, but in an isolated text. Quoting specific verses in support of a particular cause or point of view is often an expression of power. Those who use "chapter and verse" or "proof text" theology do so in order to control Christians of a different persuasion and marginalize dissent. Speaking from what they perceive to be a watertight position, they proclaim a stringent certainty by supporting their beliefs with a string of biblical quotations. This method has brought many discussions about morality and ethics to a premature conclusion.

In addition to its appearance, its canonical status also sets the Bible apart from other books and gives it authority. The term 'canon' refers to the contents of the Bible, and defines them as authoritative. As a concept it came into Christianity from Judaism. By the end of the first century AD ancient Jewish writings fell into two groups: those written in Hebrew and those written in Greek. The Jews of Palestine wrote in Hebrew. But during this period more Jews lived outside Palestine than inside it and most of them spoke Greek, so they translated their sacred books into Greek. In addition, the Jews of the Diaspora composed new books of their own, such as Wisdom, Tobit, Judith, and Maccabees, which were greatly valued.

When the Palestinian Jews eventually decided which scrolls would be the basis of their faith, they opted only for those written in Hebrew. They chose 39 of them to form their canon of Scripture, what we call the Old Testament or the Hebrew Bible. However, the Diaspora Jews had far more than 39, but because these were written in Greek they were deemed unacceptable by the Palestinian authorities for inclusion in the canon. Nevertheless, the Greek speakers insisted that their extra books also should be regarded as authoritative. So in effect there were, for a while, two Jewish canons, one entirely in Hebrew and the other in Greek, the latter much longer than the former.

The Church opted for the Greek rather than the Hebrew canon as its version of the Old Testament. One reason for this was that whenever the New Testament writers quoted Scripture, they did so from the Greek Bible. But it could also be that rather than struggle with Hebrew, the early Christians chose the easier option of reading the Jewish writings in Greek, the *lingua franca* of the ancient world. So when the Christian canon was formally closed by the Church of the West at the end of the fourth century it was composed of the Greek Old Testament plus the 27 New Testament books which are in it today.

But like the Jews, Christians disagreed about the contents of the canon, and still do. Although defining it is important, inasmuch as it is the ultimate source of authority in any dispute, in the history of the Christian Church there has never been a single canon of Scripture. There are a number of different canons read in different Churches. For example, the New Testament of the Ethiopic Church contains 35 books. That of the Copts contains the two letters of Clement and the Apostolic Constitutions. The Syriac Bible omits the second and third letters of John, the letter to Philemon, and the second letter of Peter. The Greek Orthodox Old Testament adds 3 and 4 Maccabees.

The Roman Catholic canon contains many of the additions made to the Old Testament by the Greek-speaking Jews, such as Tobit, Judith, Wisdom and Ecclesiasticus, to name but a few. Although these books are referred to as "deutero-canonical," they are accorded the same authority as the rest of the Old Testament. But in the sixteenth century the Protestants rejected them and relegated them to the Apocrypha, a term used by the early Christians to describe heretical works which could in no way be considered scriptural. If printed at all in their bibles, these apocryphal books are placed in a kind of theological no man's land between the Old and the New Testaments.

According to the Thirty-Nine Articles, Anglicans may read the Apocrypha "for example of life and instruction of manners," but not "to establish any doctrine" because the books are not canonical. When Luther translated the Bible into German, he took it upon himself to exclude certain books from the canon. Though he translated them, he put Hebrews, James, Jude, and Revelation in an appendix, because they did not fit his theology. His successors, however, overturned his decision and reinstated them.

The significant point here is that the formation of "a canon of Scripture" is a human activity. The Bible derives its authority from the decision of the early Christians to recognize a collection of ancient writings as sacred texts and canonize them. The Churches created the bibles that we have. Whoever wrote or edited the various biblical books, the Churches drew up the contents page. The ecclesiastical authorities decided which books were to be included in the official list and which were not. So whether a specific book is canonical depends on which Bible one reads, "for historical methods can easily expose the variability through time of 'canon' and expose it as a fluctuating phenomenon."[2]

Because of this fluctuation, there is no consensus about what the word "Bible" means. Strictly speaking, there is no such thing as 'the Bible', only a number of bibles, because not every volume entitled "Holy Bible" contains the same books. It exists in different forms for the various faith communities. The Orthodox canon is different from the Catholic canon; the Catholic canon is different from that of the Protestants. For over a thousand years the Apocrypha was included in the canon; in the sixteenth century it was thrown out. Generalized references to the Bible as such can, therefore, be somewhat meaningless. If I am told to obey the Bible "in its plain and canonical sense," I may legitimately ask: "Which Bible?"

Distance and Diversity

Despite the aura of sanctity which surrounds the Bible, and to a certain extent conditions our response to it, we must recognize its otherness. In it we encounter a world very different and very far removed from the one we know. From the standpoint of Western Christians, it comes from a past not our own, and from cultures that are not ours. Distance and diversity must be regarded as "inherent limitations" when we seek to apply its teachings. Such a recognition involves attending to both history and culture before we can pronounce its teachings authoritative.

The biblical timeline takes us from the middle of the second millennium BC (1500) to the end of the first century AD. We go through six ancient empires starting with Egypt and ending with Rome. We

---

2. P. R. Davies, *Whose Bible Is It Anyway?* (JSOTSup 204; Sheffield: Sheffield Academic, 1995), 65.

start with wandering nomads and end with persecuted Christians. The historical background is important in that it reminds us that God does not speak in a social, political or religious vacuum. His self-revelation is anchored in the very human conditions of precise historical settings.

An appreciation of the original context is vital because we do not get any teaching which is independent of culture. Every story, every law, every poem, every proverb in Scripture belongs to one cultural setting or another—nomadic, settled, exilic, a time of oppression, or a period of prosperity. Though some texts are more obviously culture-bound than others, those referring to the practice of polygamy for example, even what we would regard as timeless truths have their origin in a specific culture.

The cultural gap that exists between us and the biblical world is stressed by James Barr: "Any work or text composed in an ancient time and an ancient culture has its meaning in that time and that culture, and in our time or culture may have a different meaning, or indeed may have no meaning at all."[3] The Bible cannot have the same meaning for us as it had for those who read it in its own cultural milieu. The limitations imposed upon it by the circumstances in which it was written must be recognized. That is not to say that there can be no bridges between one culture and another, but building them is not a straightforward matter. Because the cultural world of the Bible is so very different from our own, our ability to engage with it is limited. Two examples of this difficulty, one from the Old Testament and one from the New must suffice.

There are many aspects of ancient Israelite law which illustrate the cultural divide between the ancient world and ours. Consider Leviticus. Speaking from a Christian perspective, even a cursory reading of it will demonstrate that it is not possible to construct contemporary society in accordance with its regulations. It does not work for us as a historical text because the rules cannot be modernized. Taken literally, the vast majority of the laws cannot be regarded as divine commands intended for modern Christian believers; they can be appropriated only at a second level of meaning. For instance, Christians are able to respond to the instruction to sacrifice animals only in the light of the sacrifice of Christ. The injunctions must be transformed with reference to the New

---

3. James Barr, *The Bible in the Modern World* (The Croall Lectures, 1970; London: SCM, 1973), 39.

Testament and taken in a christological or allegorical sense if they are to have any significance.

Another example of cultural distance is eschatology. The early Christians expected the end of the world at any moment. In the words of St Paul, "The night is far spent, the day is at hand" (Rom 13.12). Consequently they had an understandable lack of interest in social justice and the rights of every human being. Rearranging the deckchairs is not high on the agenda of those who are convinced that the ship is sinking. Today most people do not believe that the world might end at tea-time tomorrow, witness the concern expressed by all the major Churches for human rights, the environment and the future of the planet. Given the issues which preoccupy us, it is not easy to relate to the apocalyptic mindset of first century Christians. We no longer relate to the world through this biblical framework.

It must be recognized that the Bible is a collection of documents formed in the distant past by and for a specific community. In seeking to apply any text to our own situation, discovering what the biblical writers were saying to their contemporaries is an important first step. We must ask what the text meant in its original setting before we determine what it means for us. Our primary task is reconstructing the situation which any given author was addressing there and then. Account must be taken of the distance, in both time and culture, that separates us from the world of the Bible. This is the only way we will give the text a fair hearing.

In addition to distance in terms of time and culture, we must also recognize the diversity which characterizes the contents of the canon. Christopher Evans points out that 'Christianity is unique among the great religions in being born with a Bible in its cradle.'[4] He is referring to what the New Testament writers call "the Scriptures." Another name for them was the Greek term *biblia*, meaning "Little Books," from which the word "Bible" is derived. The contents of the cradle was essentially a library, as the plural word *biblia* indicates, a collection of scrolls deemed authoritative by the Jews. As in every library, there were books from different periods, written by different authors, intended for different audiences, expressing different opinions. Though the Bible possesses an overarching unity, in that it comes from a single religious

---

4. P. R. Ackroyd and C. F. Evans, eds., *The Cambridge History of the Bible*, Vol. 1, *From the Beginnings to Jerome* (Cambridge: Cambridge University Press, 1975), 232.

tradition, its contents are marked by diversity. If there was a final editor, he did not try to unite the various traditions or obliterate the tensions between the many voices.

In his discussion of the way in which the Bible developed over a long period of time into a multi-vocal text, David Carr says: 'Within the Bible, as in the wider Ancient Near East, the *growth* of texts was the rule, not the exception. In our modern context, we would often just write a new text and discard the old if we felt the old did not address our needs. In contrast, we have many documented examples of ancient authors taking treasured traditions and adapting them, anonymously, to speak to new generations'. He cites the various editions of the Pentateuch and Jeremiah among the Dead Sea Scrolls, and Tatian's harmony of the canonical Gospels, before concluding: 'One might say that the ancients tended to change and supplement *the very texts they cherished most*, while leaving apparently irrelevant and unhelpful texts to gather dust . . . A mark of scripture was its multi-voiced character, *not* its alleged authorial unity.'[5]

Because of this diversity, the Bible is an uncomfortable book for anyone who maintains that there is only one kind of religious experience, and only one way of talking about God and doing his will. This is because if they read it carefully and honestly they are faced with conflicting opinions, which makes it increasingly difficult to claim that it has one clear and consistent meaning. Most people do not read it with that much care, or they read an expurgated version of it, so that the diversity inherent in a polyphonic or multivocal text is not taken into account.

But the many voices are there, discernible in the authors, the style and the theology. However we understand God's involvement in this collection of books, a vast array of people had a hand in telling, recording, editing, copying, and finally in canonizing the biblical story. The whole process spanned about a thousand years of theological enquiry. The finished product contains topics on which different positions were taken by competing voices over a long period of time within the same religion.

In the Old Testament there are inconsistencies and contradictions on several important issues. There are conflicting images of the divine.

---

5. David Carr, "Untamable Text of an Untamable God: Genesis and Rethinking the Character of Scripture," *Int* 54 (2000) 352.

God is portrayed as a wrathful and bloodthirsty warrior who engages in genocide and confiscation of land in some books, but as a loving and universal redeemer in others. Exclusive texts are to be found side by side with inclusive ones. The laws of Exodus and Leviticus are more humanitarian when they reappear in Deuteronomy. Next to texts of terror and ethnic cleansing, there are those of charity and tolerance. After reading about Joshua's xenophobia, read Ruth, Jonah and selections from the prophets, and you will find a very different attitude towards foreigners. The Wisdom Literature contains within itself two diverse views about the connection between sin and suffering. Israel's history as narrated in the books of Samuel and Kings is rewritten and interpreted from a very different perspective in Chronicles.

In order to grasp the implications of the Bible's polyphonic nature, compare and contrast it with the Koran. In the production of the Koran there were no lengthy periods of oral transmission, writing, and editing; the whole enterprise was completed in perhaps as little as 20 years. Because the text was dictated by God to an illiterate man, who was assisted by angels to write as instructed, there can be no dispute about what should or should not be included in it. The dictation was made in Arabic, which is why the text must be read and studied in Arabic. Of course there are translations, but they are referred to as "paraphrases"; they will give the reader a general sense of what is written, but not the true meaning. Though copied innumerable times, the Koran has miraculously been preserved from error; the scribes have never made a mistake. Therefore in Islam there can be nothing equivalent to Jewish and Christian biblical criticism.

There are religious communities, both Jewish and Christian, which treat the Bible in the same way that the Muslims treat the Koran—as a text exempt from critical scrutiny. But it is clear that Jehovah worked in a very different way from Allah. He seems to have been quite happy to use very many human collaborators over several centuries to achieve his purpose. The involvement of such a large company had a lasting effect on the content. It was inevitable that different voices from different periods would bring different perspectives to bear on many issues. Recognition of this variety is important, but it is obscured when we move from *biblia* to "bible," substituting a singular word for what was originally a plural.

Robert Alter, the distinguished scholar of Hebrew and comparative literature, draws attention to the fact that in Judaism there is a long tradition of reflecting on and interpreting the Scriptures. Although Jews are not exempt from claiming that absolute truth can be found in their sacred texts, the practice of critical inquiry keeps this dangerous inclination in check. With reference to the contents of the Old Testament he writes: 'Meaning, perhaps for the first time in narrative literature, was conceived as a *process*, requiring continual revision—both in the ordinary sense and in the etymological sense of seeing-again—continual suspension of judgement, weighing of multiple possibilities, brooding over gaps in information provided'.[6] Such a process militates against finding an unambiguous answer to every question in the back of the book.

One contribution of modern biblical study has been to highlight this literary and theological diversity and draw attention to the contradictory nature of the text. It has shown us how often authors were inspired not by a zeal for pure truth, or accurate theology, but by polemics against other writers whose emphasis they sought to correct. Surely if God had wanted to give us a single, definitive account of revealed truth, he should have inspired those who closed the canon to favour one side of a debate or the other. Instead we have multiple voices giving us their own account of crucial events and their significance. The expectation of consistency, which the concept of a canon produces, is one which cannot be fulfilled because the Bible is not a book. The more seriously one takes it, the more problematic become its contradictory voices.

We can of course ignore the issue of diversity and claim a unity which is not there. But if we recognize a deliberate diversity in its contents, it may mean that the Bible should be regarded not as a textbook of right belief, to be quoted as the final authority to clinch every argument, but as a sourcebook. For as Mark Brettler points out: "Sourcebooks are multiperspectival, and thus offer a suitable image for the Bible as a complex anthology, reflecting different interests, time periods, geographical settings, classes, and perhaps genders. But it is hard to give a sourcebook authority, precisely because it is multivocal rather than univocal."[7] If the Bible is seen as a sourcebook, and therefore as representing different

---

6. Robert Alter, *The Art of Biblical Narrative* (London: Allen & Unwin, 1981), 12.

7. Marc Brettler, "Biblical Authority: A Jewish Pluralist View," in W. P. Brown, ed., *Engaging Biblical Authority* (Louisville: Westminster John Knox, 2007), 5.

points of view, may it not be regarded as the starting point for discussion and debate rather than the last word; not an end but a beginning?

Picking and Choosing

Assuming that we recognize distance and diversity among the Bible's limitations, how do we deal with its contents? One answer is: by picking and choosing. Many interpreters choose one biblical perspective as being more authoritative than others, and thereby create a "canon within the canon." Fundamentalist Christians accuse their liberal or moderate counterparts of practising "Cafeteria Christianity," by which they mean that they select what biblical teachings they want to follow. For instance, they take a substantial helping of love and compassion, but leave the ban on homosexuality untouched.

But as Robert Davidson points out, in handling Scripture "selectivity is the name of the game we all play . . . and the selectivity we employ tells us something about ourselves, the cultural assumptions we make and the theology we profess."[8] Our selection of texts can even indicate what colour or gender we are, the Church of which we are members, and the family in which we have been nurtured. We select from the Scriptures that which is in keeping with our own presuppositions. If you are a regular reader of a copy of the Bible which you have had for many years, I can tell a lot about you simply by noting which parts of it are well-worn. Like everyone else, you will have favourite passages which will invariably give the game away.

I offer two examples of picking and choosing from the Old Testament, one relating to the laws of the Pentateuch, the other to offensive passages.

Assuming that we look to the Old Testament, and many Christians do, for guidance on ethical matters, we should have no difficulty finding something appropriate in the prophetic books. The social ethic of Israel's prophets has given hope and strength to struggling societies, ask the developing countries. But what of the legal parts of the Torah, the many laws enshrined in the five books of Moses? Starting from the premise that all of us are inevitably selective, how do we choose be-

---

8. R. Davidson, "In Honesty of Preaching 5: The Old Testament Dilemma and Challenge," *ExpT* 111 (2000) 365.

tween one commandment and another? By what criteria do we select out of that mass of material what is important and relevant to us?

This question faced Thomas Aquinas in the thirteenth century. He answered it by classifying Old Testament law into ceremonial, civil and moral. While the moral laws were to be kept by everyone, because they were judged to be timeless and prescriptive, the other two groups were specific to the Israelites and had no claim on the Christian. The same distinction is made in the Anglican Church's Thirty-Nine Articles. Article 7, entitled *Of the Old Testament*, reads: "Although the laws given from God by Moses regarding ceremonies do not bind Christian men, nor should its civil precepts of necessity be received in any commonwealth; nevertheless, no Christian man whatsoever is free from the commandments which are called moral." Clearly, according to those criteria, there were vast tracts of the Old Testament for which Christians had no use at all. It was only by distinguishing different types of law (civil, ceremonial, moral) that the Jewish Torah could be meaningful and authoritative for a Christian society.

For many this still seems to be an acceptable and obvious way of reading the Mosaic regulations. It is, presumably, what the members of GAFCOM do, since they "uphold the Thirty-Nine Articles as . . . authoritative for Anglicans today." But most modern theologians will reject this traditional division because the Bible provides no justification for holding it. In the Torah the so-called moral laws are mixed in with ceremonial regulations. Anyone who reads the small print of the Sinai covenant found in Exodus and Deuteronomy (and not just the Decalogue) will find both types of law appearing indiscriminately.

Furthermore, there is nothing in the text to indicate that some parts of the Torah are more important than others. All biblical commands are attributed to the divine imperative; they are not to be confused with recommendations or requests. In an interpreted and enhanced form both contributed equally to the development of Orthodox Judaism. For the Orthodox Jew it is just as important to keep the Sabbath as it is to refrain from stealing. In his commentary on the Thirty-Nine Articles, E. J. Bicknell writes: "The distinction (moral/ceremonial) is useful, but we need to remember that it is utterly alien to the Jewish mind. There is not one trace of it in the Old Testament itself. To the Jew all alike was the law of God; each part was equally divine and equally sacred."[9]

Even within the ceremonial law our Anglican forefathers were guilty of picking and choosing. For example, the prohibitions against shaving the beard, having a tattoo, and eating pork were disregarded. But the law stating that women were ritually impure after the birth of a child was observed. The 1662 *Book of Common Prayer* has a service entitled: "The Thanksgiving of Women after Child-birth, commonly called The Churching of Women." Churching 'cleansed' a woman of her impurity and rendered her suitable to attend church services. In the 1549 prayer book it was called "The Order of the Purification of Women," reflecting even more closely a practice which goes back to the primitive church, and is obviously based on Jewish ceremonial law (see Lev 12:1-8; 15:25-32). Though they ignored the ban on tattoos and bacon sandwiches, our revered forefathers kept the law relating to the ritual state of a woman after childbirth, despite Article 7.

Another aspect of selectivity is the omission from public reading of texts, especially from the Old Testament, which offend our moral sensibilities. This happens not infrequently in the Church's liturgical calendar. For example, the story of the capture of Jericho in many lectionaries stops at 6:20: "The trumpets were blown, and when the army heard the trumpets they raised a great shout, and the wall collapsed. The army advanced on the city and captured it." The next verse, which completes the paragraph, is omitted. It reads: "They destroyed everything. They put everyone to the sword, men and women, young and old, as well as the cattle, the sheep and the donkeys." The lectionary reading ends at verse 20 because genocide in God's name is not a practice which should be encouraged.

Psalm 137 is a beautiful and poignant little song. In vv. 1-6 the spiritual sensitivity of the author is moving. But by the end he is not in a good mood. He engages in a savage and gloating hatred of the Babylonians and concludes by wishing that someone would take their infants by the heels and beat their heads against the rocks. In the 1984 Church in Wales *Prayer Book* the last 3 verses of the psalm, where this wish is expressed, are in square brackets. We are discouraged from us-

---

9. E. J. Bicknell, *Theological Introduction to the Thirty-Nine Articles of the Church of England* (3rd rev. ed.; London: Longmans, 1955), 146.

ing them in the liturgy because no one wants to recognize that the Bible condones infanticide.

There are many other texts which we find offensive. But does that mean we have the right to airbrush them out of the Bible? Is it acceptable to omit from public reading and bible study passages which are deemed unedifying? In my opinion deliberate omission of such texts is not a practice which should be encouraged, and I say that for this reason: offensive passages make an important point about the nature of religion which we should heed. They remind us that religion is a fire which warms but also burns. As a cause of controversy it far surpasses education, politics, climate change, and even the health service. The most committed people within our faith communities can be very judgemental towards those whom they consider a threat to their beliefs, and they will quote the Bible in justification. Atrocities have happened and still happen in the name of one god or another.

Biblical texts which demonstrate the havoc religion can cause should not be omitted from our consideration but kept within our purview, so that we may challenge and refute them. In discussing whether or not to exclude from the liturgy what are described as "anti-Semitic" passages in the Gospel Passion Narratives, R. E. Brown concludes: "Accounts 'improved' by excision perpetuate the fallacy that what one hears in the Bible is always to be imitated because it is 'revealed' by God, and the fallacy that every position taken by an author of Scripture is inerrant." Those who read the Bible "must reckon with the implications inherent in the fact that God revealed *in words of men*."[10] Those who believe that God gave us the biblical books as a guide should recognize that part of the guidance is to learn from the dangers attested in them, as well as from their great insights.

Selectivity is forced upon us by the polyphonic nature of the text, and has been a constant characteristic of the Christian Church throughout history. We select those texts which give us the sort of God to whom we can relate, or provide us with a moral code which we find acceptable. We choose what we like and ignore the rest. So when you hear people claim, "The Bible says," what they mean is "My selection from the Bible says." Picking and choosing applies to us all. But we are reluctant to admit it because, as Davidson says, whereas it is "easy to see

---

10. Raymond E. Brown, *A Crucified Christ in Holy Week: Essays on the Four Gospel Passion Narratives* (Collegeville, MN: Liturgical, 1986), 15–16.

selectivity at work in other people, it is far harder to face the selectivity we use, and the assumptions which lie behind it."[11]

Fixed Texts and Changed Minds

Given that selectivity is the game we all play, how do we make that selection? How do we decide what is authoritative for us and what is not? There are doubtless several ways of making a judgement. But whatever view we hold, we cannot ignore two vital questions asked of the commandments and values expressed in the Bible: Are they timeless or time-bound? Are they prescriptive or descriptive? In other words, are they to be regarded as universal, prescribed for all people at all times, or, because they belong to a particular culture, are they limited to a certain period and place?

With these questions in mind, we will focus briefly on the way in which texts have been used or abused by Christians over the centuries. This will take us into the history of the interpretation of the Bible, which is known by the technical term "Reception History." This major aspect of modern biblical scholarship is based on the premise that the reader's situation and background govern the search for meaning. The interest of its practitioners centres on the impact of Scripture on belief and practice. In their view, the way people have interpreted biblical texts and transformed their meaning to suit a different social context is as historically important as what the texts originally meant. The focus is on discovering how the call to be 'biblical' has influenced political and social developments for good or ill, and to learn from that discovery. It is an examination not of the Bible itself but of the way in which it has been read and understood over the centuries.

The observations of Mark Twain in an essay entitled "Bible Teaching and Religious Practice," written in the 1890s, contain a good example of Reception History and provide a suitable starting point for considering specific texts:

> The Christian's Bible is a drug store. Its contents remain the same; but the medical practice changes. For 1800 years these changes were slight—scarcely noticeable. The practice was allopathic—allopathic in its rudest and crudest form. The ignorant

11. Davidson, "In Honesty of Preaching 5," 365.

> physician drenched his patient with hideous doses of the most repulsive drugs. He bled him, purged him, puked him, salivated him, never gave his system a chance to rally, nor nature a chance to help. He kept him religion sick for eighteen centuries, and allowed him not a well day during all that time. The stock in the store was made up of about equal portions of baleful and debilitating poisons, and healing and comforting medicines. But the practice of the time confined the physician to use the former; by consequence he could only damage his patient, and that is what he did.
>
> Not until our century was any considerable change in practice introduced... The patient fell to doctoring himself, and the physician's practice began to fall off. He modified his method to get back his trade. At first he relinquished the daily dose of hell and damnation, and administered it every other day only; next he allowed another day to pass; then another and presently another. When he had restricted it at last to Sundays, and imagined that now there would surely be a truce, the homeopath arrived and made him abandon hell and damnation altogether, and administered Christ's love and comfort, and charity and compassion in its stead. These had been in the drug store all the time, gold labelled and conspicuous among the long shelfloads of repulsive purges and poisons, and so the practice was to blame that they were unused, not the pharmacy. To the ecclesiastical physician of fifty years ago, his predecessor for eighteen centuries was a quack.[12]

Twain is referring here to 1800 years of ecclesiastical control over biblical interpretation. The Bible meant what the Church, the allopathic physician, said it meant. It was only with the advent of biblical criticism that the text could legitimately be understood in ways very different from those found in traditional Christian teaching. Today we would describe what Twain wrote as an essay on Reception History. The emphasis is on the practice not on the pharmacy. Let us consider two examples of how the historical and cultural contexts in which biblical texts were read and received have influenced their interpretation.

The first is the prohibition of usury. In modern parlance "usury" is normally taken to mean exorbitant interest. But in the Bible, the word signifies no more than the practice of charging interest on loans.

---

12. Mark Twain, *Europe and Elsewhere* (New York: Harper & Brothers, 1923), 387–88.

The Challenge of Being Biblical

It refers to any amount of money above the principal sum borrowed, however small. Judging from the attention it receives, in biblical times lending at interest was a pervasive misdemeanour which was regarded with the utmost seriousness. In the Torah, an Israelite is forbidden from charging interest on a fellow Israelite (Exod 22:25; Lev 25:35). Deuteronomy 23:19 repeats the same prohibition, but adds that the charging of Gentiles is permitted. The practice is condemned severely in Ezekiel 18:8-17, and the banning of it is commended in Psalm 15:5, though neither of these texts mentions the Gentile exception.

The reason given for the prohibition reflects the widespread concern for the poor found in the Old Testament. In a predominantly peasant society, the borrower might never get out of debt if he had to pay interest. The only solution would be for him to sell himself into slavery. However, charging interest on Gentiles could be justified because they were usually merchants and traders who could afford to pay.

A study of other ancient Middle Eastern law codes indicates that Israel was unique in prohibiting interest on loans. Since it has not been found anywhere else, Cyril Rodd suggests that this prohibition, "more than any other law deserves to be regarded as part of the divine revelation to Israel."[13] Although the New Testament makes no explicit comment on the subject, the Early Church Fathers adopted the Old Testament law. No Christian was permitted to lend to another Christian with interest. The fact that this practice was debated in several ecumenical councils indicates that enforcing the prohibition was not a hole in the corner affair. Admittedly the rule applied only to the clergy initially, but by the High Middle Ages it was universal. For a Christian, seeking to profit from a loan constituted the mortal sin of usury.

Though Luther and Zwingli followed the Roman Catholic Church and upheld the ban, John Calvin did not. He was the first of the Reformers to give a theological defence of lending at interest. In a letter to a friend, he puts forward his case for reworking the tradition and ignoring the law of Moses.[14] (14) His approach is to consider the historical and cultural context in which interest was originally banned. This leads him to the conclusion that the relevant biblical passages made

---

13. Cyril Rodd, *Glimpses of a Strange Land: Studies in Old Testament Ethics* (OTS; Edinburgh: T. & T. Clark, 2001), 156.

14. For the following quotations, see Mary Beaty and Benjamin W. Farley, trans., *Calvin's Ecclesiastical Advice* (Edinburgh: T. & T. Clark, 1991), 141-42.

sense when they were written, but not in the sixteenth century. "The situation in which God brought the Jews together . . . made commerce without usury apt among them. Our situation is quite different. For that reason, I am unwilling to condemn it, so long as it is practiced with equity and charity."

The end of the Middle Ages had brought about social and economic change; it was no longer a predominantly peasant society. The sophisticated world of finance had started to make an impact on the great European cities, and Calvin soon realized that the biblical texts could not be applied to the new realities of financial life. What was once intended to stop the poor falling into debt now prevented people from borrowing to finance business enterprises.

He recommends that a direct biblical command, even though it was part of the divine revelation, should be disregarded in favour of something which seems to be much vaguer. "I conclude that we ought not to judge usury according to a few passages of scripture, but in accordance with the principle of equity." Opposing usury because of the biblical ban is to "play with God in a childish manner, preferring words over the truth itself." This from a man who holds the Bible in very high regard and wrote a commentary on almost every biblical book.

What he is saying is: do not condemn the practice just because the Bible does, but open it up for debate. Accept that lending at interest is a necessary part of life, whatever Scripture says. Consider it in the context of the need for a level playing field. Spend time not legislating against it, but making sure that it is equitable. To support his case he invokes a hierarchy of moral values. He explains that equity implies fair dealing, charity is the Golden Rule.

This attitude freed people to discuss the real issues connected with usury: How do you protect the vulnerable from the loan sharks? What levels of interest are appropriate? What about the poor who are not able even to repay a loan, to say nothing of paying interest? By declaring that the general moral principles of equity and the Golden Rule take precedence over the prohibition of usury, Calvin affected a major breakthrough. He did not allow a specific text to have the last word, but reinterpreted it in the light of the underlying message of the Bible. By appealing to deeper biblical principles he overturned a Christian tradition which was based on the revealed will of God as found in Scripture, a tradition which had been utterly consistent for 1500 years. His justification was that financiers were now all equals, and that we should treat others as we would wish to be treated ourselves. He began a process which eventually resulted in the economic development of Europe and led to prosperity on a previously unimagined scale.

Calvin's interpretation of the usury law provides a good example of the reception history of the Bible by demonstrating the impact changed circumstances can have on the significance of a fixed text. For another example, let us return to Mark Twain. In developing his point about the pharmacy remaining the same but the medical practice changing, he says this about the Church's involvement in the slave trade:

> In all the ages the Roman Catholic church has owned slaves, bought and sold slaves, authorized and encouraged her children to trade in them . . . If any could know, to absolute certainty, that all this was right, and according to God's will, surely it was she, since she was God's specially appointed representative in the earth, and sole authorized and infallible expounder of his Bible. There were texts; there was no mistaking their meaning; she was doing in this thing what the Bible had mapped out for her to do. So unassailable was her position that in all the centuries she had no word to say against human slavery.
>
> Yet now at last we hear a Pope saying that slave trading is wrong, and we see him sending an expedition to Africa to stop it. The texts remain; it is the practice that has changed. Why? Because the world has corrected the Bible. The Church never corrects it; and also never fails to drop in at the tail end of the procession—and take the credit for the correction.
>
> Christian England supported slavery and encouraged it for 250 years, and her Church's consecrated ministers looked on, sometimes taking an active hand, the rest of the time indifferent. England's interest in the business may be called a Christian interest, a Christian industry . . . The first regular English slave hunter was Sir John Hawkins who named his ship *The Jesus*. But at last in England, an illegitimate Christian rose against slavery. It is curious that when a Christian rises against a rooted wrong at all, he is usually an illegitimate Christian. There was a bitter struggle, but in the end the slave trade had to go—and went. The biblical authorization remained, but the practice changed.
>
> Our own conversion came at last. We began to stir against slavery. There was no place in the land where the seeker could not find some small budding sign of pity for the slave. No place in all the land but one—the pulpit. It yielded at last; it always

does. It fought a strong and stubborn fight, and then did what it always does, joined the procession—at the tail end. Slavery fell. The slavery text remained; the practice changed, that was all.[15]

Twain gives us a glimpse of how the Bible was read and interpreted in relation to a burning issue of the early nineteenth-century. If we take Scripture as our guide we must conclude that slavery is ordained by God, sanctioned by the patriarchs, tolerated by Jesus, approved of by Paul. Although the Torah has many laws which deal with the proper treatment of slaves, the practice is never rejected, or even called into question in the Old Testament. Likewise New Testament teaching fails to liberate slaves or to mitigate their lot in life, although Paul instructs masters to deal kindly with them. In a nutshell, the biblical world did not regard slavery as a moral problem. It was part of the culture, it was regarded as the status quo, it did not need fixing.

In Britain the ecclesiastical authorities sided with the slave owners and used the biblical account of Noah's drunkenness and his curse of Canaan (Gen 9:24–27) as a definitive text to justify the enslavement of black people. At home and in the colonies the Church of England was at the heart of it all. The Society for the Propagation of the Gospel owned slaves; they were branded with the word "Society." When abolition was achieved, compensation was given not to the slaves but to their owners, including the then Bishop of Exeter.

In America slavery remained firmly established in the southern states well into the nineteenth century, in spite of the fact that it had troubled the conscience of prominent individuals such as George Washington. Thriving cotton plantations made slave labour essential. Here again biblical arguments were put forward to justify slaveholding. For example, a Virginia Baptist, Thornton Stringfellow, published a sermon in 1856 entitled *A Scriptural View of Slavery*. In it he claimed that God had sanctioned the practice, that it was incorporated into the Mosaic Law, and that Jesus and the apostles regarded it as a lawful institution.

For centuries Christians sincerely believed that slavery and racism were based on a correct understanding of Scripture. They worked on the principle that what is not proscribed is permitted. In keeping slaves they were living in accordance with biblical precepts. So those

---

15. Twain, *Europe and Elsewhere*, 391–92.

who challenged the trade found that they were challenging the authority and interpretation of Scripture. But eventually the tide turned. In Britain the 1807 Act for the Abolition of the Slave Trade was the first step in bringing the practice to an end. In America the victory of the Union armies half a century later had the same effect. Slavery still exists in the world, but no one today will defend it on the basis of the biblical laws and customs which were once quoted to support it.

The history of the way in which the Bible was interpreted indicates that over time the meaning of a biblical passage, and the use made of it by the reader, can change radically. Our perception has been influenced by the climate in which Scripture is read and interpreted. For centuries usury was considered to be a mortal sin, and slavery was practised with equanimity because it was perceived to be in accordance with God's will. In both cases the biblical authorization stands. No new translation has altered what we read in the Bible. No change has been made in the contents of whatever form of the canon we accept as authoritative. No lost manuscript has been found permitting usury. No archaeological discoveries have discredited the practice of slavery in the ancient world. The written word remains fixed and unaltered. "What has changed," writes Peter Gomes, "is the climate of interpretation, indeed, the lenses with which we read the texts and tell the tales. The texts have not changed, but we have, and the world with us."[16]

In Conclusion

In this essay specific attention has been given to usury and slavery. We have seen that although the text is fixed, 'the climate of interpretation' has changed. Do the same criteria apply to other ethical issues? Should we assume that texts which are confidently used to settle arguments and end debates have a plain, objective meaning which is immediately apparent, and applicable to everyone, everywhere, at all times? Or does an appreciation of a text's reception history lead us to conclude that the contemporary socio-political context in which it is read is as important as the historical context in which it was written? Furthermore, if the

---

16. Peter J. Gomes, *The Good Book* (New York: Morrow, 1996), 99. For further reflection on the 'lenses' through which we read the Scriptures see Marcus J. Borg, *Reading the Bible Again for the First Time* (New York: HarperOne, 2002), 3-53.

Church is deemed to have been wrong on the clear biblical warrant for banning the charging of interest on loans and supporting slavery, on what else could it have been wrong?

The issue is essentially one of authority. The central question is: May we legitimately stand in judgement on Scripture? Are we justified in repudiating certain biblical passages because of their disastrous reception history? Most believers are not encouraged to ask critical questions of their own religious tradition in this way. But Elizabeth Schüssler Fiorenza, a leading feminist theologian, maintains that they are. In her presidential address to the Society of Biblical Literature in 1988 she called on scholars to accept responsibility for "the ethical consequences of the biblical text and its subsequent interpretations. If scriptural texts have served—and still do—to support not only noble causes but also to legitimate war, to nurture anti-Judaism and misogyny, to justify the exploitation of slavery, and to promote colonial dehumanization, then biblical scholarship must take responsibility not only to interpret biblical texts in their historical contexts but also to evaluate the construction of their historical worlds."[17] (17) We must recognize the ideological nature of the Bible and decide whether or not its contents are capable of promoting violence and injustice.

Changed situations require a rethinking of the meaning and significance of a biblical passage. As we consider our attitude towards usury, slavery, racism, apartheid, divorce, and sexual orientation, to name only some of the issues which have caused controversy and division within Christendom, we must recognize that we have altered, even corrected, the lenses with which we read the Bible. We have done so in the light of new knowledge. Human nature may not change, but human situations do. It is quite irresponsible to interpret scriptural teaching about, for example, homosexuality without taking into account what has been learned about sexual identity during the past century. Because the situation or experience of the reader is a fundamental ingredient in any interpretation, new knowledge can mean that some texts not only require reinterpretation, but must be regarded as irrelevant. Some attitudes found in the Bible, however explicable in the age they were written, may be wrong attitudes if repeated today.

---

17. Elisabeth Schüssler Fiorenza, *Rhetoric and Ethic: The Politics of Biblical Studies* (Minneapolis: Fortress, 1999), 28.

There is an ancient Scottish prayer which goes something like this: "O God, we pray that we will never have to do battle on foreign soil. But if we do, and our maps do not match the terrain, help us to believe the terrain." Surely John Calvin would have said "Amen" to that.

3

The Ethics of the Old Testament: Historical and Literary Approaches

ERYL W. DAVIES

Scholars who have been concerned to analyze the ethics of the Old Testament have had to contend with the fact that they are engaged in a difficult and highly complex enterprise.[1] The most obvious problem, of course, is the sheer amount of information that needs to be examined, evaluated and discussed, for moral considerations occupy a major place in biblical law and feature prominently in the biblical narratives and Psalms, as well as in the oracles of the prophets and in the sayings of the wise. So the first question that faces the biblical scholar intent upon writing an 'ethics of the Old Testament' is, quite simply, where should one begin? How should the vast amount of material relating to moral and ethical issues be arranged and organized?

Scholars have long recognized that to write a full-blown 'ethics of the Old Testament' would be an awesome task, and it is hardly surprising that great differences of opinion exist as to how the enterprise should proceed. Some have sought to arrange the biblical material in chronological order and to trace an evolution in the ethical values

---

1. B. S. Childs, *Biblical Theology of the Old and New Testaments* (London: SCM, 1992), 674, notes that the "study of Old Testament ethics has frequently been paralysed by the sheer complexity of the methodological problems."

The Ethics of the Old Testament

embraced in Israel, from the primitive ideas of the pre-monarchic period down to the more sophisticated concepts of exilic and post-exilic times.[2] Other scholars, aware that a comprehensive discussion of the ethical teaching of the entire Old Testament might run into several volumes, have preferred to focus on particular literary genres, such as the biblical narratives,[3] or the legal,[4] prophetic[5] or wisdom traditions.[6] Still others have opted for a thematic approach and have sought to analyze what the Old Testament has to say on a variety of ethical issues, such as wealth and poverty, war and peace, marriage and divorce.[7]

It is, perhaps, owing to the extent and complexity of the subject-matter that the ethics of the Old Testament has remained a relatively neglected area of biblical research throughout much of the twentieth century.[8] Earlier scholars tended to regard it either as a modest and

---

2. This approach is exemplified in the volumes by H. G. Mitchell, *The Ethics of the Old Testament* (Handbooks of Ethics and Religion; Chicago: University of Chicago Press, 1912); and J. M. Powis Smith, *The Moral Life of the Hebrews* (University of Chicago Publications in Religious Education. Handbooks of Ethics and Religion; Chicago: University of Chicago Press, 1923). For a discussion of these and other writings which advocated a 'chronological approach' to Old Testament ethics, see Eryl W. Davies, *The Immoral Bible: Approaches to Biblical Interpretation* (London: T. & T. Clark, 2010), 22–43.

3. See, for example, W. Janzen, *Old Testament Ethics: A Paradigmatic Approach* (Louisville: Westminster John Knox, 1994); G. J. Wenham, *Story as Torah: Reading the Old Testament Ethically* (Edinburgh: T. & T. Clark, 2000); M. E. Mills, *Biblical Morality: Moral Perspectives in Old Testament Narratives* (Aldershot, UK: Ashgate, 2001).

4. See W. Harrelson, *The Ten Commandments and Human Rights* (Overtures to Biblical Theology; Philadelphia: Fortress, 1980); A. Phillips, *Ancient Israel's Criminal Law: A New Approach to the Decalogue* (Oxford: Blackwell, 1970); W. H. Schmidt et al., *Die Zehn Gebote im Rahmen alttestamentlicher Ethik* (Darmstadt: Wissenschaftliche Buchgesellschaft, 1993).

5. A. Davies, *Double Standards in Isaiah: Re-evaluating Prophetic Ethics and Divine Justice* (BibIntSer 46; Leiden: Brill, 2000); Eryl W. Davies, *Prophecy and Ethics: Isaiah and the Ethical Traditions of Israel* (JSOTSup 16; Sheffield: JSOT Press, 1981); A. Mein, *Ezekiel and the Ethics of Exile* (Oxford Theological Monographs; Oxford: Oxford University Press, 2001).

6. See J. Blenkinsopp, *Wisdom and Law in the Old Testament: The Ordering of Life in Israel and Early Judaism* (rev. ed.; Oxford: Oxford University Press, 1995).

7. Cf. C. S. Rodd, *Glimpses of a Strange Land: Studies in Old Testament Ethics* (OTS; Edinburgh: T. & T. Clark, 2001).

8. W. C. Kaiser, *Toward Old Testament Ethics* (Grand Rapids: Zondervan, 1983), xi, notes that it was with some trepidation that he attempted to write a volume on the ethics of the Old Testament, given "the magnitude of the field, the complexity of the

restrictive enterprise within the larger field of biblical theology,[9] or as a non-subject that could conveniently be shunted to the academic sidelines and palmed off to interested lay readers of Scripture with time on their hands.[10] In recent years, however, the tide has turned, and the subject of the 'ethics of the Old Testament' is now regarded as a valid discipline in its own right, and has quite properly been restored to a position of full respectability within the academic community. Indeed, since the 1980s there has appeared a veritable flood of articles, monographs and symposia examining various aspects of the ethical principles encoded in the Old Testament.[11]

Broadly speaking two approaches have dominated the study of the ethics of the Old Testament, namely, the historical-critical approach

---

issues, and my frustration at finding all too few guides who have blazed the trail before me." B.S. Childs, *Biblical Theology in Crisis* (Philadelphia: Westminster, 1970), 124, notes that "in spite of the great interest in ethics, to our knowledge, there is no outstanding modern work written in English that even attempts to deal adequately with the Biblical material as it relates to ethics." In the preface of the original edition of his volume *Living as the People of God: The Relevance of Old Testament Ethics* (Leicester: Inter-Varsity, 1983), Christopher J. H. Wright felt no need to apologize for adding yet another volume to the literature on the subject since "the subject of Old Testament ethics has scarcely any literature to add to" (9).

9. So, for example, W. Eichrodt, *Theology of the Old Testament II* (trans. J. A. Baker; London: SCM, 1967), 316–79. Eichrodt's subsuming of ethics under the broader category of "biblical theology" was not without its justification, however; for biblical ethics is nothing if not theologically grounded, and the Old Testament itself draws no sharp distinction between religion and morality. As B. S. Childs has observed, "in the Old Testament, religion and ethics are not identical, but neither can they be separated" (*Old Testament Theology in a Canonical Context* [London: SCM, 1985], 201). For a staunch defence of the view that biblical theology and biblical ethics are inseparable, see C. J. H. Wright, *Old Testament Ethics for the People of God* (Leicester: Inter-Varsity Press, 2004), 23–47.

10. As Cyril Rodd observes, there was a time when some called in question the very existence and viability of the subject, and he recalls that in 1956 he was discouraged from writing on the ethics of the Old Testament because there was no future in it (*Glimpses*, ix). As M. Tsevat noted with regard to the theology of the Old Testament for Judaism, the study of the ethics of the Old Testament was regarded as something akin to a "zoology of the unicorn"—a non-existent science about a non-existent subject ("Theologie des Alten Testaments—eine jüdische Sicht," in M. Klopfenstein, ed., *Mitte der Schrift? Ein jüdisch-christliches Gespräch* [Berne: Lang, 1987], 329).

11. Christopher J. H. Wright provided a useful survey of the relevant literature in an article published in 1993 ("Biblical Ethics: A Survey of the Last Decade," *Themelios* 18:2, 15–19), and in chapter 13 of his volume *Old Testament Ethics*, he brings the research up to date, noting in his bibliography (481–99) some four hundred titles, nearly three hundred of which appeared after 1983.

and the literary-critical approach. Although the two approaches are not necessarily mutually exclusive,[12] they do represent two quite separate methods, each with its own distinctive goals and procedures.

The Historical-Critical Approach

The 'historical-critical' method has dominated biblical scholarship for much of twentieth century. The historical-critical approach, of course, covers a range of different methods of studying the Old Testament, but they all share a common assumption, namely, that the biblical text should be interpreted in the light of the historical context and geographical and social setting in which it supposedly arose.[13] Great efforts were expended in an attempt to understand the social conditions and moral climate of ancient Israel in order to illuminate the matrix of beliefs, values and assumptions that helped to shape the Israelite nation. In effect, the Old Testament was regarded as a window through which the perceptive observer might view the social world and daily experiences of the people of Israel, and the task which faced biblical scholars was to reach behind the biblical text in an attempt to anchor their discussion of the ethics of ancient Israel in historical reality.[14] This approach naturally welcomed insights from other disciplines, such as sociology,[15]

12. John Barton, *Understanding Old Testament Ethics* (Louisville: Westminster John Knox, 2003), 54-64, commends the type of approach exemplified by Martha Nussbaum, who was both a historical and literary critic, and who advocated a 'both/and' rather than 'either/or' approach. She argues that historical critics may well appreciate the aesthetic qualities of a text, while literary critics may not necessarily want to detach a particular text from its cultural and historical moorings (see M. Nussbaum, *Love's Knowledge: Essays on Philosophy and Literature* [Oxford: Oxford University Press, 1990]). Nevertheless, Barton concedes that the battle lines are drawn between the two camps, and biblical scholars tend to regard themselves as either historical or literary critics. J. D. Pleins's volume, *The Social Visions of the Hebrew Bible: A Theological Introduction* (Louisville: Westminster John Knox, 2001), is an attempt to examine how the institutions and social structures of ancient Israel intersect with the literary compilation encountered in the Old Testament.

13. This approach is exemplified, for instance, in the work of J. Hempel, *Das Ethos des Alten Testaments* (BZAW 67; Berlin: Töpelmann, 1964).

14. The image of the 'window' is one that frequently recurs in Rodd's examination of the ethical values of ancient Israel (*Glimpses*, 3-4, 271, etc.).

15. Among earlier sociologists who made a significant contribution to our understanding of the Old Testament, reference may be made to Max Weber, who examined

archaeology,[16] and anthropology,[17] and much use was made of the wealth of information from the neighbouring cultures of the ancient Near East, which provided valuable comparative data to illuminate the biblical text.[18] Any information that could be gleaned, from whatever

the social and economic conditions presupposed by the biblical laws (*Ancient Judaism*, trans. H. H. Gerth and D. Martindale; New York: Free Press, 1952). N. K. Gottwald (*The Tribes of Yahweh: A Sociology of the Religion of Liberated Israel 1250-1050 B.C.E.* [Maryknoll, NY: Orbis, 1979]) describes his sociological approach as a cultural-materialistic reading of the Old Testament. Another important sociological study of the Old Testament is that by D. L. Smith, *The Religion of the Landless: The Social Context of the Babylonian Exile* (Bloomington, IN: Meyer-Stone, 1989), who examines the sociological context of the Babylonian exile. See, further, B. J. Malina, "The Social Sciences and Biblical Interpretation," *Int* 36 (1982) 229-42; Malina, *Christian Origins and Cultural Anthropology: Practical Models for Biblical Interpretation* (Atlanta: John Knox, 1986); R. E. Clements, ed., *The World of Ancient Israel: Sociological, Anthropological and Political Perspectives* (Cambridge: Cambridge University Press, 1989). Earlier sociological studies, such as those of Max Weber (*Ancient Judaism*) and A. Causse ("Les Prophetes et la crise sociologique de la religion d'Israel," *RHPhR* 12 (1932) 97-140; idem, *Du Groupe ethnique à la communauté Religieuse*, Paris: Alcan, 1937) raised important questions regarding the relation between ethics and the economic and social structures of ancient Israel. See Pleins (*Social Visions*, 9-16) and Davies (*Prophecy and Ethics*, 15-16) for a brief discussion of the contribution of these scholars, and for a more detailed study of Causse's contribution in particular, see S. T. Kimbrough, *Israelite Religion in Sociological Perspective: The Work of Antonin Causse* (Wiesbaden: Harrassowitz, 1978). R. R. Wilson has also made a significant contribution to the sociological analysis of the Old Testament; see, in particular, his volume called *Sociological Approaches to the Old Testament* (Philadelphia: Fortress, 1984).

16. Archaeological discoveries in Israel and throughout the ancient Near East were thought to illuminate the general environment which gave rise to the religious ideas and ethical practices of ancient Israel; see G. E. Wright, *The Old Testament against Its Environment* (SBT 1/2; London: SCM, 1950); T. Levy, *The Archaeology of Society in the Holy Land* (New York: Facts on File, 1995); A. Mazar, *Archaeology of the Land of the Bible 10,000-586 B.C.E.* (Anchor Bible Reference Library; New York: Doubleday, 1990).

17. See H. W. Wolff, *Anthropology of the Old Testament* (trans. Margaret Kohl; London: SCM, 1974), which is considered by some to be the definitive discussion of the anthropological approach to the Old Testament; see also B. Lang, ed., *Anthropological Approaches to the Old Testament* (IRT 8; London: SPCK, 1985); J. W. Rogerson, *Anthropology and the Old Testament* (Oxford: Blackwell, 1978); Rogerson, "Anthropology and the Old Testament," in R. E. Clements, ed., *The World of Ancient Israel*, 17-37. Mary Douglas is a noted cultural anthropologist who has made a significant contribution to clarifying the social significance of purity in ancient culture; see M. Douglas, *Purity and Danger: An Analysis of Concepts of Pollution and Taboo* (London: Routledge & Kegan Paul, 1966).

18. John Bright's reconstruction of Israel's history made much use of the richly informative sources from the ancient Near East (*A History of Israel* [2nd ed.; Westminster Aids to the Study of the Scriptures; London: SCM, 1972]). See also L. Epsztein,

source, about the economic and social situation that obtained at the time might provide helpful insights into the interpretation of particular passages. Thus, for example, the information gathered about the social, political and economic conditions that prevailed in Israel and Judah during the eighth century BCE might be helpful in illuminating the passages in Isaiah, Amos and Micah which deplore the unjust and oppressive treatment of the poor and vulnerable in society. The oracles of the prophets and their ethical pronouncements could only be properly appreciated when it was recognized that they were addressed to specific situations and were occasioned by specific circumstances. Indeed, such texts could not adequately be understood without a knowledge of the socio-economic structures that gave rise to the text in the first place. For example, Jeremiah 22:13–19, where the prophet denounces the king for underpaying the labourers involved with royal construction projects— a passage which has clear ethical import—could only be properly understood against the background of a political and economic system of monarchical authority that permitted the state to rely on forced labour to carry out its building projects (cf. 1 Kgs 5:13–18; 9:15–22; 12:1–7).[19] Moreover, the application of the social-scientific method to the study of the Old Testament was regarded as a means of illuminating the ethical values of particular groups in particular periods, and this served to provide a fuller and more nuanced portrait of the ethical values of ancient Israelite society.

Although the historical-critical method has dominated biblical scholarship during much of the twentieth century, in more recent years there has been an increasing awareness of the limitations of such an approach, not least when applied to the ethics of the Old Testament. Adherents of this approach were criticised for presuming to know far more about the ethics of ancient Israel than was actually the case[20], and

---

Social Justice in the Ancient Near East and the People of the Bible (London: SCM, 1986).

19. See Pleins, *Social Visions*, 4–8.

20. Although Rodd in his volume on the ethics of the Old Testament regularly warns against over-confident and over-simplistic assumptions about our ability to understand the actual ethical values and beliefs of ancient Israel, he himself falls into the same trap by making sweeping generalizations which are totally unwarranted by the extant evidence (cf., e.g., his comment that, in all probability, "the priestly understanding of ethics and purity was that of ancient Israel in general"; *Glimpses*, 18). Christopher Wright criticises Rodd for stating that certain issues "did not enter the thinking" of the ancient Israelites or "did not occur to anyone in Israel." As Wright remarks,

doubts were expressed concerning the reliability of the biblical sources and the extent to which it was possible to recover the ethical beliefs, outlooks and norms of a people who could no longer be observed at first hand.[21] It was argued that to study the ethical values of *contemporary* society would be a difficult enough undertaking; how much more so the ethical values of a society which existed between two and three thousand years ago. It was often impossible to place particular texts in their original historical setting, and the fact that practitioners of the historical-critical approach often failed to reach a consensus regarding the date and origin of particular passages did little to enhance confidence in their results. The questions raised by the historical critics were seldom susceptible of definitive answers, and it was emphasized that historical facts that had seemed obvious and irrefutable to one generation of scholars had often been challenged or questioned by the next.

Moreover, even the most ardent adherents of the historical-critical approach could not claim to provide a comprehensive overview of the ethics of ancient Israel, for the requisite evidence was simply not available. Little was known, for example, of the views of those whom the prophets condemned, or of the views of the priestly groups in the pre-exilic period. A detailed, comprehensive study of the ethics of the ancient Israelites would have to attempt to include all of the central and distinctive moral insights represented by all groups in all periods,[22] but since the evidence for this was no longer available, the picture provided by the historical-critical approach was, inevitably, regarded as fragmentary and incomplete.

---

how can he possibly *know*? (*Old Testament Ethics for the People of God*, 104 n2). See, further, E. W. Davies, *The Immoral Bible*, 51n17.

21. The historical reliability of the evidence contained in the Old Testament remains a contentious issue, and recent trends to question the date of the biblical sources, such as the Yahwist, has served to cast doubt on the historical events which they record. See J. Blenkinsopp, "The Pentateuch," in J. Barton, ed., *The Cambridge Companion to Biblical Interpretation* (Cambridge Companions to Religion; Cambridge: Cambridge University Press, 1998), 181–97.

22. Such an undertaking was attempted by Hempel (*Das Ethos*), who recognized that the Old Testament was the product of different groups within ancient Israel scattered over a long period of time, and who sought to investigate their different social contexts (peasants, urban dwellers etc.) and their different historical contexts (nomadic, tribal, monarchic, exilic, etc.).

Furthermore, it was increasingly recognized that the literature of the Old Testament was probably the product of an intellectual and economic elite who had their own particular agendas to promote, and the views which they advocated may not have been representative of the period in which they wrote. Indeed, their view of reality was almost certainly partial and perspectival, and consequently it was necessary to examine the way in which the social, cultural, class, gender and racial issues of the time had influenced the biblical text. It was thus impossible to examine the view of a particular biblical author and abstract from it what was normative for the period in which he was writing, and it was wrong to assume that the extant evidence of the biblical sources necessarily represented the complete or typical evidence. This, in turn, led to an important methodological observation, namely, that the ethics of the Old Testament should be distinguished from the ethics of ancient Israel, for the former may not necessarily have been synonymous with the latter.[23] What the Old Testament contained for the most part was merely an account of the 'official' religion of Israel, and the thoughts, beliefs and practices of the 'ordinary' Israelite may not always have coincided with the perspective of those who had a hand in producing the biblical canon. In order to overcome this difficulty, some scholars tried, albeit tentatively, to read between the lines of the biblical text and to present an account of the moral beliefs and practices of the person-in-the-street in biblical times;[24] however, serious doubts were raised

23. John Barton criticises Eichrodt for his failure to distinguish between the norms and values of the ancient Israelites and the morality revealed in the biblical text, and he emphasizes that the "Old Testament is evidence for, not coterminous with, the life and thought of ancient Israel" (*Understanding Old Testament Ethics*, 17). Childs comments favourably on Barton's criticisms of Eichrodt, though he draws very different methodological implications from Barton's critique (*Biblical Theology of the Old and New Testaments*, 675–76).

24. Barton believes that some idea of the nature of popular morality in Israel between the eighth and the sixth centuries BCE can be gleaned, in part, from the quotations in the prophets that allude to the beliefs of the people ("Understanding Old Testament Ethics," *JSOT* 9 [1978] 57–59). But, as Barton himself recognizes, this evidence must be used with considerable caution, for although some of the prophetic quotations may have a ring of authenticity about them, which might justify their acceptance as the genuine popular views of the people at large, there can be little doubt that in many such sayings the prophets were presenting a caricature of the beliefs of those whom they opposed. See, further, E.W. Davies, "Ethics of the Hebrew Bible: The Problem of Methodology," in D. A. Knight, ed., *Semeia 66: Ethics and Politics in the Hebrew Bible* (Atlanta: Scholars, 1995), 48.

concerning such hypothetical reconstructions, for the evidence at our disposal was hardly complete and it was most improbable that anything but a general and impressionistic picture of Israel's 'popular morality' would emerge.[25]

Moreover, the very concept of the 'ordinary' Israelite was itself rather vague and ambiguous, for the fact was that Israelite society consisted of diverse groups (peasant and elite, rural and urban, male and female etc.), and it could not be assumed that all groups (or even all members within a single group) shared the same ethical values and concerns. To embark upon a study of Israel's 'popular morality' was thus bound to be an endeavour fraught with difficulties, for Israelite society almost certainly spoke on the moral issues of the day with a divided voice.

The distinction between the 'ethics of the Old Testament' and the 'ethics of ancient Israel' leads to a further methodological consideration, namely, the ultimate purpose of our ethical inquiry. Is it intended to delineate the actual behaviour of a given society or the ideals of behaviour to which that society subscribes? In the context of Old Testament studies, are we to be concerned with how the Israelites *did* behave in practice or how they believed they *ought* to behave in principle? Moreover, care must be taken to distinguish between the different levels at which moral norms operate within the Old Testament, for the official norms set out, for example, in the law codes may have been different from the actual implementation of those laws in practice.

A further weakness of the historical-critical approach was that it failed to make the Old Testament ethically relevant to the present. Limiting the study to an examination of how ancient Israel viewed moral matters had the effect of locking the teaching of the Old Testament into the remote past; what it singularly failed to do was to provide a basis for ethical reflection for subsequent communities that regarded these texts as Scripture. The historian's reconstruction of ancient Israel's ethics, however informative and constructive it might be, could never claim the same normative status as the canonical accounts. The fact was that modern believers based their ethical values on 'what Scripture says' not on 'what ancient Israel was like.' In brief, no attempt was made to

---

25. B. C. Birch, "Old Testament Ethics," in L. G. Perdue, ed., *The Blackwell Companion to the Hebrew Bible* (Blackwell Companions to Religion 3; Oxford: Blackwell, 2001), 294.

move from *Israel's* story to *our* story. The historical-critical approach to the biblical text was primarily a descriptive discipline concerned with what the text 'meant' rather than what it 'means,' to use the famous distinction of Stendahl.[26] The text was seen primarily as historically informative, and biblical scholars seemed oblivious to questions concerning its significance to readers of the text in the modern world, and little effort was expended to discover the meaning of the text for life here and now. Of course, in their defence, historical-critical scholars would argue that this was never within their remit: they were concerned with descriptive not normative ethics, and they conceived their task as being to describe the ethics of the people of Israel, not to explain and expound ways in which the norms and directives of the Bible could be applied to contemporary concerns. Nevertheless, the effect of the historical-critical approach was to alienate the text from the modern reader and make it an object of merely antiquarian interest.

The Literary-Critical Approach

In view of the difficulties inherent in the historical-critical method, many scholars in recent years have favoured a literary approach to the biblical text.[27] A significant development in this regard was James Muilenburg's presidential address to the Society of Biblical Literature meeting in 1968;[28] his call to move beyond the earlier, largely historical, interest in the Old Testament represented something of a watershed in critical approaches to the Bible. Extrinsic factors such as historical background, archaeological data, and compositional history were to be set to one side, and the text was to be interpreted in its own terms. Adherents of the literary approach to the Bible did not minimize or disparage the importance of past efforts to understand the original histori-

---

26. See K. Stendahl, "Biblical Theology, Contemporary," in *IDB* 1:418–32.

27. The term "literary approach" actually encompasses a broad range of scholarly approaches to the text, including rhetorical criticism, reader-response criticism, structuralism, and deconstruction, and their goals and strategies differ from each other. But inherent in all these approaches is the assumption that the biblical text can be interpreted with little or no knowledge of its historical or social setting. For an appraisal of these different approaches, see J. Barton, *Reading the Old Testament: Method in Biblical Study* (new ed.; London: Darton, Longman and Todd, 1996).

28. See J. Muilenburg, "Form Criticism and Beyond," *JBL* 88 (1969) 1–18.

cal setting of the ethical teaching of the Old Testament;[29] they merely believed that such research had probably taken us as far as we are able to go and that the time had come to move on and explore the text from a different perspective. Thus, for example, whether the story of David and Bathsheba in 2 Samuel 11 reflected an actual event in the life of the monarch was regarded as a secondary (and perhaps irrelevant) consideration, for there was much ethical food for thought in this narrative even if David's reign could be proved never to have existed, or could be shown to be merely the product of a later ideological construction. The point was that reading the narrative as 'story' was different from reading it as '*hi*story,' for its interest lay not in the factual events which it purported to record but in the moral truths to which it bore witness. According to this view, the task of understanding the meaning of a text should not be reduced to establishing the historical facts which underlie it; indeed, such preoccupation with the historical background of a narrative may prove an unnecessary distraction, and prevent the reader from viewing it as a vehicle for moral and theological reflection.

The literary approach to biblical ethics, therefore, largely dispenses with questions of historicity and focuses, instead, on the plot of the narrative, the development of its themes, and the recurrence of certain patterns, motifs and imagery. What is of particular interest is the way in which the story unfolds, the way in which its characters relate to one another, and the way in which conflicts and tensions within the narrative are resolved. Attention is given to the dynamics of the text, its ironies and ambiguities, and to the hidden structures of power- and gender-relations to which it often bears witness. Such an approach clearly involves a detailed exegesis and sustained examination of the text itself, and ethical insights are developed not only from its content but from careful scrutiny of its language and structure. Of course, the literary approach must, above all, respect the particularity of the literary form in which the ethical values appear, and the conventions governing each genre must be duly recognized and observed.[30] Thus, for example, it would be misguided to regard the ethical principles of a narrative as if they were legally binding prescriptions; similarly, it would be mis-

---

29. Cf. D. M. Gunn, and D. N. Fewell, *Narrative in the Hebrew Bible* (OBS; Oxford: Oxford University Press, 1993), 11.

30. To complicate matters, some books (such as the prophetic corpus) contain a wide variety of literary forms, each requiring its own canons of interpretation.

The Ethics of the Old Testament

leading to view particular moral directions intended for a particular time and place as though they were intended to be timeless, universal principles.

Adherents of the literary approach are aware of the dangers inherent in viewing the texts in isolation, and they recognize that a reading of a particular passage is often enriched by attention to its inter-textual allusions and to the larger ethical themes to which it relates. It may be, for example, that a particular story is part of a larger meta-narrative and, if so, it is often helpful to consider how it resonates with its wider canonical context. Sometimes it is by no means clear why a particular narrative was placed in its present context within the canon. Why, for example, was the story of Jacob and Tamar located in the middle of the Joseph story in Gen. 38?[31] How does its present context affect its interpretation and the ethical insights to which it bears witness?

Just as particular texts need to be considered in their wider context so, too, must individual ethical terms and phrases.[32] There have been studies of key ethical concepts such as 'holiness' and 'righteousness', and there can be no doubt that clarifying of the meaning of such terms is a significant aspect of any ethical inquiry. But even these studies have not always exhibited an appreciation of the complexity of the task involved, for what these words may mean in one context may be quite different from what they mean in another. Writers on the ethics of the Old Testament have constantly to be sensitive to the fact that many of the words with which they deal may have a wide variety of connotations, and that it simply will not do to abstract a word from its contextual background and make sweeping and unwarranted generalizations.[33] The Hebrew term *mišpaṭ*, for example, is open to a range of meanings, depending on the specific context in which it occurs; in some texts it simply signifies 'justice' in an abstract sense, but in other passages it has a more technical connotation of 'lawsuit', 'legal claim' or 'legal decisions/

---

31. R. Alter has made a compelling case based on theme motif and language for connecting this episode with the story of Joseph (*The Art of Biblical Narrative* [London: Allen & Unwin, 1981], 3-12).

32. Norman Snaith's *The Distinctive Ideas of the Old Testament* (London: Epworth, 1944) is sometimes criticised precisely because it tends to study individual terms in isolation instead of viewing them in their broader context. See B. S. Childs, *Old Testament Theology in a Canonical Context* (London: SCM, 1985), 205-6.

33. Cf. Davies, "Ethics of the Hebrew Bible," 44.

proceedings.' Similarly, the noun *ṣedeq* carries a wide range of semantic meanings. Sometimes the word is associated with legal procedures, and is used with reference to the settling of a controversy or the adjudication of guilt; at other times the word is an expression of covenant loyalty and, in such contexts, is seen primarily as a relational term.[34] Texts take on new and expanded meanings by nature of their alignment with other texts, and the meaning assigned to Hebrew words must be settled by appeal not only to the literary context in which they appear but to their use in other settings too. As Gerstenberger has observed, words are in perpetual motion; they are vehicles of meaning, and as they travel from one context to another they accumulate a surplus of meanings on their journey.[35] As words shift form one context to another they often undergo subtle transmutations of meaning; consequently, the transmission history of key terms must form an important aspect of any scholarly study of the ethics of the Old Testament.

Of particular relevance in this regard is the issue of translation. Do Hebrew ethical terms such as 'sin' or 'abomination' have the same semantic resonance as their equivalents in English? The problem is that Hebrew words are often open to a plurality of interpretative options, and the biblical translator and interpreter must be sensitive to the ambiguity and multiplicity of meanings that a particular word may have. One obvious example is the Hebrew word *torah*, the ethical significance of which may well depend upon how the word is translated into English. If it is rendered as 'law', it may well be adjudged to have negative connotations (being associated with authority, lawsuits, legal decisions etc.), but if the term is translated as 'teaching' or 'direction' it is likely to be viewed more positively.[36] A further example may be cited from the Decalogue. Does the sixth commandment mean 'you shall not kill' or 'you shall not murder' (Exod 20:13)? Its meaning ostensibly seems straightforward and clear-cut, but the commandment requires interpretation. Does it

---

34. See G. von Rad, "'Righteousness' and 'Life' in the Cultic Language of the Psalms," in *The Problem of the Hexateuch and Other Essays* (trans. E. W. Trueman Dicken; Edinburgh: Oliver & Boyd, 1966), 243–66.

35. See E. S. Gerstenberger, "Canon Criticism and the Meaning of *Sitz im Leben*," in G. M. Tucker et al., eds., *Canon, Theology, and Old Testament Interpretation: Essays in Honor of Brevard S. Childs* (Philadelphia: Fortress, 1988), 21.

36. See G. von Rad, *Old Testament Theology*, vol. 2 (trans. D. M. G. Stalker; Edinburgh: Oliver & Boyd), 388–409.

refer to all taking of human life, including war and self-defence, or does it refer to the narrower range of offences implied by the translation 'murder'. Does it apply to animals? Does it forbid capital punishment? Clearly, the commandment needs to be carefully nuanced, for the Old Testament elsewhere commands the killing of animals (for sacrifice) and criminals (for various offences).[37] Words are often ambiguous and multivalent, and we must always be sensitive to the linguistic possibilities encoded within the language of the Bible.

Conclusion

Although the literary approach to the ethics of the Old Testament may appear opposed to the historical approach, it is arguable that both approaches should be used together for an adequate understanding of the moral values enshrined in Scripture. Historical criticism aims to reconstruct the ethical principles and moral values embraced by the peoples who inhabited the land of Israel during the first millennium BCE, and although the evidence adduced by this approach is sometimes a matter of speculation and hypothetical reconstruction, it does help to clarify the nature and character of biblical ethics, and to set it in the context of the culture out of which it arose. On the other hand, the techniques of literary criticism enable us to appreciate the way in which the material as it stands has been organized, and to appreciate the ideas it embodies and the message it was intended to convey. There has sometimes been a tendency for those who adopt the historical-critical approach to look with disdain at methods which pay attention to the narrative qualities of the text, and for those taking a literary approach to seek to discredit the practitioners of historical criticism. Reading the Old Testament as 'story' is undoubtedly different from reading it as 'history', but this does not mean that the latter can be dispensed with. The fact is that neither the historical-critical nor the literary-critical method is without its difficulties and potential drawbacks, but a judicious use of both approaches together will undoubtedly help us to appreciate more fully the rich possibilities of the biblical text.

---

37. Cf. S. Moyise, *Introduction to Biblical Studies* (2nd ed.; London: T. & T. Clark, 2004), 5.

4

'Let Us Maintain Peace' (Romans 5:2): Reconciliation and Social Responsibility

WILLIAM S. CAMPBELL

Introduction: Why Focus on Reconciliation in Paul?

In my book on Christian identity[1] and in a subsequent article on Ephesians 2,[2] I argue that the retention of Jewish identity in Christ is not only tolerated by Paul but explicitly commanded as in 1 Cor 7:17ff.[3] Despite the use of anthropological terms such as hybrid identity,[4] and despite my acknowledgement that this hybridity may well represent a useful categorization in recent or contemporary society, I wish to emphasize that as I understand Paul, in Christ Jews remain Jews and likewise gentiles, (though no longer pagans in that they are obliged to give up idolatry), remain gentiles, related to the family of Abraham as gentiles, but not as hybrid Jews or Jewish other than in sharing a Jewish

---

1. Campbell, *Paul and the Creation of Christian Identity*.

2. Campbell, "Unity and Diversity in the Church: Transformed Identities and the Peace of Christ in Ephesians."

3. Augustine was one of the first to recognize the right of Jews to retain their Jewishness, cf. Fredriksen, "Judaizing the Nations."

4. Cf. for example Johnson Hodge, *If Sons, Then Heirs*, esp. 134–35 and 149–51.

symbolic universe.⁵ The recognition that gentiles in Christ are related to Abraham *via* Christ does not mean that they become Israelites or lose their status as gentiles. It is only as *gentiles*, that is, as non-Jews in Christ that these have access to God's grace. It is in and through their identity as believing gentiles that they are simultaneously related to, but also differentiated from, the people of Israel. Paul and other first century Jews saw the maintenance of clear boundaries between Jew and gentile as essential for the identity of Judaism.⁶ As Pamela Eisenbaum asserts, "All will be kin; none will be strangers, but the gentile will not become Jew, and the Jew will not become gentile."⁷

My view is that Romans addresses the gentile Christ-following groups in Rome with greetings to other groups added in chapter 16.⁸ However, an objection could be raised against my proposal concerning the retention of particular identity in that this could be read as support for some kind of ethnic apartheid or ethnic cleansing.⁹ I take this very seriously, just as seriously as I do the prejudice against any retention of Jewishness in Paul's theology. I was particularly attracted by the notion of Christ depicted as removing hostility¹⁰ in Ephesians where the three essential elements of the discussion, identity difference, the work

---

5. To share the Jewish symbolic universe is to view the world from the perspective of God's promises to Abraham, rather than to become identical with Israel, and should mean that gentiles are brought near to God and also to Israel, cf. Fowl, "Learning to Be a Gentile," 28–32.

6. But Paul's perspective was lost to a great extent when the Christ-movement changed rapidly towards the end of the First Century due to the fall of the Temple, growth in the number of gentile adherents and other social and political factors. Paul's letters must not be anachronistically interpreted from the perspective of the texts of this later period as is frequently done, particularly when identity issues are discussed in relation to texts only without due contextual correlation, Cf. Holmberg on "Identity as a Textual Phenomenon" in his essay, "Understanding the First Hundred Years of Christian Identity," 7–10.

7. Eisenbaum, *Paul Was not a Christian*, 254–55, cf. also 98.

8. For a detailed argument see my "The Addressees of Paul's Letter to the Romans: Assemblies of God in House Churches and Synagogues?"

9. On this issue see esp. Miroslav Volf, "Exclusion and Embrace: Theological Reflections in the Wake of 'Ethnic Cleansing'"; see also his extended study, *Exclusion and Embrace*.

10. As Fowl asserts in relation to Ephesians 2:14-15, "the best theological option will require us to take the term 'hostility' as the direct object of the verb 'nullify'" ("Learning to Be a Gentile," 29). It is not the erasure of particular identities that is demanded but of the hostility resulting from these.

of Christ, and reconciliation in face of hostility are interlinked. Here I found the connection I needed to make between retaining one's identity in Christ and the necessary corollary to ensure a cessation of hostility against those who are and who remain different. In the world of the first century, where Paul lived and worked, this meant above all the hostility between Jew and gentile.[11] If one believes that one's identity in Christ is subsumed into a new identity that is neither Jewish nor gentile, it would seem that the problem of hostility resulting from abiding difference is solved only by the escape from particular identities. I am not convinced that it is a real existential option to leave behind one's actual social identity in order to take on this new "in Christ identity," but in any case, the posited new identity, supposedly surpassing all earthly identities, no more resolves the problem of abiding differences than does the retention of one's identity in Christ, because these real differences do still abide despite the rhetoric, and are all the more serious because it is claimed that their effects are somehow overcome. Idealism offers no solution here.

Thus I realized that alongside the claim to retain one's identity in Christ, there must be a necessary link with the demand for an ongoing life of reconciliation. In the case of Ernst Käsemann, stressing justification by faith, he argued that the gifts of God through justification cannot be enjoyed in Christ apart from his lordship; the gift cannot be separated from the giver.[12] The advantage however of using the image of reconciliation is that the work of Christ is described in such a way that there cannot remain any ground whatsoever for the inconsistency of claiming to be in Christ and simultaneously being at enmity with one's brother or sister, (and that means all humans, not merely those in one's own denomination). *Reconciliation presupposes enmity arising from difference but simultaneously demands its demise.* Indeed the demand for Christ-followers to be conciliatory towards those who differ from them is basic to the gospel—"blessed are the peacemakers."[13] Yet sadly our contemporary society offers abundant evidence to the con-

---

11. Cf. my article, "Unity and Diversity in the Church," 20–23.Cf also Heckel, "Das Bild der Heiden und die Identität der Christen bei Paulus," 282.

12. Käsemann, "The Righteousness of God in Paul," 174.

13. Davina Lopez maintains that theological reflection on justification by faith should be re-imagined as "reconciliatory justice-making through solidarity," *Apostle to the Conquered*, 168.

trary, evidence, that is, of "conflictual" Christians rather that conciliatory. This I think is associated with a sectarian attitude to life and to the world: "I alone am left, and they seek my life" (Rom 11:3). But God never leaves himself without thousands who have not bowed the knee to Baal and, in any case, such a negative "conflictual" attitude is detrimental in the extreme for Christian witness. Of course the Gospel may lead to conflict, but conflict by itself is no proof of grace but often only of its absence. In the UK as in North America, the fragmentation of Christian faith into innumerable splinter groups with ongoing hostility and in-fighting, coupled with the Western world's confrontation with Islam, has rightly led some thoughtful people to question the connection between current "Christianity" and the crucified Christ.

Militant, and aggressive in many of its forms, contemporary Christianity needs to look afresh at the gospel of reconciliation, and consider carefully what has produced such paradoxical expressions of its gospel of good news for the world. Irrespective of whether or not reconciliation can be claimed as significant as justification faith, I nevertheless embrace the emphasis on reconciliation as a most appropriate metaphor for proclaiming and promoting the gospel without compromise both by conciliatory attitude and example. In how many parts of the world today does it not sound ironic when Christian groups claim to have peace with God even when they are hostile to one another, to people of other faiths (or none), and to those who dare to disagree with them? Surely the claim to have peace with God ought to mean something in terms of human relations, a peace that is with God alone has, I suggest, no earthly or social significance. The peace we are speaking of in Paul's letters has real social and political significance, its roots are in the Hebrew term *shalom*, in which there is a posited harmony throughout the world, with God as well as neighbour.[14]

If we view the differing images of atonement and redemption as simply differing ways to express what God in Christ has done for the

14. The politicization of religion in Northern Ireland has resulted in ongoing community conflict so tragic in communities where religion historically has held such a significant status. Cf. Megahey, *The Irish Protestant Churches in the Twentieth Century*. It is to be hoped that the reconciliation process so seriously undertaken in South Africa will provide a model for the ongoing resolution of conflict in Northern Ireland, and that current visits by Northern Irish politicians to South Africa will prove fruitful, cf. Michael Battle, *Reconciliation: The Ubuntu Theology of Desmond Tutu* (Cleveland: Pilgrim, 1997).

world, then these ought not to be seen as in opposition, but as parallel images which, unlike differing concepts, can coexist side by side without contradiction. Thus I do not see the metaphor of reconciliation as subsidiary to justification, even though the latter precedes it in Romans, there is no necessary exegetical reason to subordinate reconciliation to justification. The chapters of Romans are not written in ascending order, and some excellent interpreters have suggested a reverse order reading starting with the concluding chapters and reading the rest of the letter in the light of these.[15] Paul went to great lengths to relate his gospel to the particular needs of his communities, and today in the contemporary world there is a need for a conciliatory brand of Christianity so great that reconciliation should become the dominant image. As Ralph Martin has noted, whereas Paul employs traditional atonement language without explanation in Rom 3:24–5 and 5:6–8 it is only with the introduction of the word καταλλάσσω in 5:10 that he moves into an explanatory mode, thus providing a larger context for righteousness, one that easily extends to the reconciliation with fellow human beings.[16]

The Source of Paul's Imagery of Reconciliation

The roots of the reconciliation motif lie in the vision of Isaiah who saw a time of universal *shalom* when the lion would lie down with the lamb, when the nations would be reconciled to God and to one another. The restoration of Israel from exile will usher in a new era, described symbolically in Isaiah 43:18–19 and Isaiah 65:17 in terms of a new creation. In my view it is not a serious problem that scholars have found it difficult

---

15. K. Stendahl's innovation in his *Paul among Jews and Gentiles,* was to argue for chapters 9–11 as "the real centre of gravity" (28), if not the climax to Paul's argument in Romans, a stance similar to that which I had proposed in my unpublished PhD thesis, "The Purpose of Paul in the Letter to the Romans," submitted to the University of Edinburgh, 1972. The older more traditional view had meant in practice that chapters 1–8 were considered the core of the letter and that 9–11 were by one means or another effectively marginalized. This perception, coupled with a view of chapters 12–16 as general parenesis, produced an interpretation of the letter, amenable to theological reflection, but divorced from and immune to many of the real issues with which Paul had to wrestle in his mission. Stendahl challenged the tendency of contemporary scholarship by questioning whether chapters 1–8 were in essence a preface to the central revelation of chapters 9–11 (29).

16. *Reconciliation: A Study of Paul's Theology,* 148 and 152.

to link Paul's thought with *precise* texts of scripture, since there is here a clear connection with the Isaiah context in Paul's thought, suggesting this is the source of Paul's imagery. As Gregory Beale has demonstrated, what is especially striking in 2 Cor.5:17 is the unique contrast in the New Testament between τα ἀρχαῖα and καινά, connected by ἰδού plus creation vocabulary. [17] It appears that prior to writing Romans, Paul had found an understanding of Christ's death as reconciliatory which he uses in a revised form to address problems in Rome. This is in keeping with Beale's conclusion that both in 2 Corinthians, Ephesians and most likely also in Romans, "the emphasis of reconciliation is upon both the restoration of alienated human relationships and the reconciliation of alienated people to God."[18]

It is quite probable that Paul's use of reconciliation language has a specific link with his own experience of Christ on the Damascus road. He was at that time zealously persecuting the followers of the fledgling Christ movement. He was their enemy prior to joining the movement himself. It makes good sense for Paul, reflecting later on his earlier behaviour, to describe himself from his new perspective as having formerly behaved as an enemy of God. Kim argues that Paul's conversion provides the likely location for the development of the concept of reconciliation and therefore of his experience of Christ.[19] Through his vision of the risen Christ, Paul discovered that God had taken the initiative and overcome this enmity by reconciling Paul to himself through Christ. And even those who still are enemies not of God (despite the RSV and NRSV readings of Rom.11:28) but of the gospel can be reconciled by divine initiative.

We are seeking at this point to give some coherence to Paul's theologizing by avoiding a dichotomy between belief and experience.[20]

17. "Reconciliation in 2 Corinthians 5-7," 553-55.

18. Ibid., 579; similarly see Lambrecht, "Reconcile Yourselves . . . A Reading of 2 Corinthians 5:11-21."

19. Cf. Kim, *The Origin of Paul's Gospel*, 13-20. Christian Wolff claims that, "this experience of reconciliation shaped Paul's apostolic existence," "True Apostolic Knowledge of Christ:Exegetical Reflections on 2 Cor.5:14ff," 93.

20. I have argued earlier on the problems in interpreting Romans arising from reading chapters such as Romans 9 as consisting primarily of abstract theological language without a concrete contextual setting.

"Divergent Images of Paul and His Mission." Cf. also S. J. Kraftchick, "Death's Parsing: Experience as a Mode of Theology in Paul."

Thus Paul's own personal experience on the Damascus road and even during his mission work,[21] may have combined with his reading of the Isaiah passage, *to provide a vivid understanding of divine activity,* first with Israel at the time of exile, and then also in the mission to the gentiles, which in turn would lead to the restoration of Israel. It is of great significance that all of these items occur together in Romans chapter 11, especially since Paul's own mission activity is included at a point where it might not have been anticipated (vv.13–14).

This step in the argument is strengthened by Cilliers Breytenbach's thesis that Paul drew the reconciliation language from the political sphere of creating peace between warring parties showing that diplomacy in particular employed such terminology.[22]

Moreover, John T. Fitzgerald argues that Paul, in a radical paradigm shift, in contrast to the normal view that the offending party must take the first step toward peace, makes God the offended party, the one who takes the initiative in reconciliation.[23] Both of these insights fit with our understanding of Paul who sees himself, particularly in the context of chapters 9–11, like the prophets of old, exercising his ministry among the leaders of nations rather than just in reconciling individual Jews or gentiles to God.[24]

Locating Reconciliation Language within the Structure of Romans

The fact that reconciliation terminology tends to be regarded as located primarily in chapter 5 of Romans can be very misleading. The stance taken in this paper is that the motif of reconciliation is much more prevalent in Romans than the frequency of occurrence of spe-

---

21. Although I do not agree with C. H. Dodd's view of the nature of Paul's radical spiritual crisis as a result of his illness combined with the problems at Corinth, it is important to note that the apostle, like other humans, had to learn by experiences, both good and bad, and that it makes good sense to view Paul as becoming increasingly conciliatory in his human relations. Cf. Kraftchick, "Death's Parsing," 152–54.

22. Breytenbach, *Versöhnung: Eine Studie in Paulinischer Soteriologie,* 40–104.

23. Fitzgerald, "Paul and Paradigm Shifts: Reconciliation and Its Linkage Group," 241–62.

24. On collective identity see Reckwitz, "Der Identitätsdiskurs: Zur Bedeutung einer sozialwissenschaftlichen Semantik."

'Let Us Maintain Peace' (Romans 5:2)

cific terminology might suggest. Thus the explicit use of reconciliation language in 5:10-11 is taken up again in 11:15, but recurs in differing form in 15:7 with the call to accept one another as Christ accepted you. If reconciliation terminology is meant to convey to gentiles the meaning of atonement—this would help to explain why this terminology is not used previously in Romans, but only introduced in Romans 5.[25] It is possible that the atonement language of chapter 3 represents a more Jewish understanding of the work of Christ expressed in justification terminology, whereas the reconciliation terms in chapters 5 and 11 represent Paul's way of expressing the gospel to gentiles. This is explicit at least in ch.11 where the ἀποβολή of the Jews results in the reconciliation of the kosmos, here clearly referring primarily to the gentile world. It is also now no longer necessary to separate the doctrinal and paraenetic sections of the letter as earlier scholarship insisted. As recent scholarship has demonstrated as, for example, in the work of Dunn[26] and Haacker,[27] the pastoral and doctrinal sections are closely inter-linked and inter-related. This allows a much more flexible understanding of the letter and enables a more coherent interlinking of all its parts. It is also now more recognized that the actual explicit occurrence of specific terminology cannot be the sole carrier of meaning in a letter since the same meaning can be transmitted implicitly as well as explicitly and without being limited to the same choice of words. Thus the terminology of righteousness, peace and joy in Romans 14, as well as of life and peace *via* the Spirit in Romans 8 are to be taken into account alongside the explicit references to the reconciliation word group in Romans chapters 5 and 11. I will argue therefore that the theme of reconciliation re-emerges in chapters 12-15 and thereby connects back to chapters 5-11, and that it is by no means unwarranted to describe Romans as a letter about reconciliation of differing groups as well as reconciliation to God.

---

25. Cf. Paul Achtemeier's suggestion that it is another dimension of God's righteousness, *Romans*, 91-92.

26. *Romans*, lv-lviii.

27. "Der Römerbrief als Friedensmemorandum," 25-41.

Inner-Group Conflict among the Roman Christ-Followers

I have dealt at length with this understanding elsewhere.[28] My view is that the text of the letter, especially chapters 12–15, read in light of what can be known of the history of the Roman congregations in this period, requires for its explanation, the posited existence of some measure of inter-group hostility and conflict. It seems there was much diversity among the Christ-followers at Rome, and that Paul is seeking to persuade them to accept one another despite their abiding difference (15:8). We stress the continuing difference here, rather than as sometimes has been the case, a temporary tolerance of the other who is different until such times as they give up their differing patterns or gradually grow out of these. But true reconciliation cannot occur where either or any of those requiring reconciliation is unable to retain their own identity and integrity.[29] Reconciliation occurs not by the removal of the offending differences but by their acceptance and a willingness, where possible, to accommodate to the other in their abiding difference.[30] If we take Paul's exhortation for mutual acceptance individualistically, then there would seem to have been an easy solution if individuals in their diversity would simply acknowledge the right of others who differ to, as it were, do their own thing, provided each was fully persuaded in their own mind that this was right for them (14:5b). But Paul was speaking to groups of Christ-followers, and addressing the problem that some individuals amongst them were being seriously damaged by inter-group division (14:15). This was possibly accentuated by leaders who were putting pressure on individuals to conform to group norms of behaviour, including differing eating patterns (14:15–23). A typical feature of human activity when people act as members of groups, is that they tend to take sides stressing the differences that constitute each group rather

---

28. Cf. "The Rule of Faith in Romans 12:1—15:13: The Obligation of Humble Obedience to Christ as the Only Adequate Response to the Mercies of God," 259–86.

29. Cf. Jae Won Lee, "Paul and Reconciliation in Romans: From A Korean Postcolonial Perspective" paper read at the Romans Through History and Cultures seminar SBL annual meeting, New Orleans, November 2009.

30. Cf Dieter Georgi's claim, "Biblical identity means solidarity with all other creatures, the respect for their otherness included. Their otherness is an essential part of their integrity, their independent and equal worth, and only in respecting that do we retain and maintain our own integrity and identity." See "The Early Church: Internal Jewish Migration or New Religion," 68.

than what is held in common.[31] One central issue in these disputes concerned what it means to live Jewishly in Christ (14:1–6). What is to be retained of Jewish life patterns in relation to hospitality with outsiders etc, and should gentile Christ-followers take on or even recognize anything revered by their Jewish brothers and sisters in Christ?

Paul's solution here, as it was already in 1 Corinthians 7 is that everyone remain in the state in which they were called whether as Jewish or gentile. Thus the Roman Christ-followers should keep their patterns of life except in those cases where these might injure a weaker person: in this case the stronger and more powerful should relinquish their freedom out of love for those at risk. Thus we are not positing only two groups in the congregations at Rome, for example a Jewish and a gentile only.

As noted, whilst the issue of living or not living Jewishly and the compatibility of this with being in Christ was central, there was greater diversity than this. The letter as a whole is primarily addressed to gentiles, but gentiles who were (initially Rome had been a Jewish foundation), and almost certainly still are, in close contact with other Christ-followers of Jewish background. An earlier Jewish form of the faith is now probably in the process of evolving into a more diverse phenomenon in which differing patterns of life-style may be partially in conflict. Part of the complication may have also resulted from powerful leaders, possibly a minority of these being of higher social status, or from meeting separately in differing venues whether in basement workshops or members homes, or in differing areas of the city with only occasional joint meetings. It is apparent that the most powerful and possibly the more numerous were those of gentile life-patterns who needed persuasion that rather than continuing to please themselves, they should please their weaker colleagues just as Christ did not please himself. The use and application of Christ's example demonstrates the seriousness with which Paul regards the divisions affecting the Christ-following groups at Rome (15:1–3). Paul's prayer for the disparate Roman congregations is that they will live in harmony with one another in accord with Christ Jesus so that with one voice—the one voice of har-

---

31. This tendency is typical of group dynamics today and reminds Christians and others not to be needlessly divisive but to acknowledge and to promote our common historical heritage.

monious existence between those who are and remain different- they may glorify God (15:5–6).

Such a scenario fits well with recent research which suggests that instead of looking at particular models such as synagogues, house-churches, trade guilds or philosophical schools to help us understand the issues Paul addresses in his letters, and since there is also a certain amount of overlap between these comparative models, we ought perhaps rather to focus on such generic features of first-century groups as that each involves the coming together of people on a regular basis; each is a distinct unit with a sense of social identity; in each members have or develop relatively close ties with each other; each has its own norms and ethos; each meeting takes place in a regular physical setting, relevant to the groups activities; each imitates to some extent patterns in the wider civic area.[32] Adams concludes that "If the most telling similarities between the Pauline churches and the different comparative models are at the generic level, the quest for the most appropriate first- century analogy may be somewhat misguided."[33] Our conclusion on this issue is that groups following the Pauline patterns of the Christ-movement have encountered at Rome differing patterns of life with resultant conflict such as might be anticipated in the dynamics generic to group activity in Rome at this period in history.

It is not just individuals who are called upon to accept one another but groups who differ substantially in their group norms and possibly behaviour patterns.[34] This is my envisaged context to which Paul addresses his Roman letter, and to which his call for reconciliation is directed

Reconciliation in Practice

Thus the outcome of Paul's argument ending in 5:11 is that if God shows his love in that Christ died for us while we were yet sinners, then

---

32. Cf. Edward Adams, "First-Century Models for Paul's Churches: Selected Scholarly Developments since Meeks," 77–78.

33. Ibid., 78.

34. Thus Jewett's view of Paul as an ambassador ("Ambassadorial Letter") and Breytenbach's emphasis on Paul's use of the language of diplomacy (see n. 22 above) point to the communal and political significance Paul accords to his concept of reconciliation.

Christ followers are secure because through Christ they have received reconciliation. But this leads into a call for obedience following the example of Christ with whose death his followers are now united. "So you also must consider yourselves dead to sin and alive to God in Christ Jesus." Both exhortation and command call for a cessation of yielding ones limbs as instruments of sin. So Romans ought not to be artificially subdivided into doctrine in the first part-chapters 1–8and ethics, chapters 12–16 with chapters 9–11 in brackets about the Jewish issue. To allow later doctrinal formulations to determine the reading of Romans by interpreting it thematically rather than exegetically is clearly anachronistic. This means that the ethical demands of being in Christ begin at the latest with the reconciliation language in ch.5:1 ff. Read in this way, Romans has as its essential agenda the reconciliation of Jew and gentile to God and to his kingdom through Christ, both theologically and socially, through the obedience that faith demands.

But that raises the issue as to why Paul does not specifically apply καταλάσσω / καταλλαγή language in Romans as he does in the more personal and direct manner of 2 Corinthians. It cannot be because Romans may be viewed as a doctrinal treatise with only general parenesis which has no specific connection with the situation at Rome. This outdated and unlikely view has, I believe, been partly responsible for reconciliation not being accorded the significance in Paul's thought that it rightly deserves. I believe there are two main reasons for Paul's presentation of reconciliation in Romans.

The first is that Paul's primary focus in Romans is on the relation of Jew and gentile both in theology and in life. Thus reconciliation is explicit in chapter 11 where it is structured again as it was already in chapter 5 in a *qal wachomer*, lesser/greater type of argument. Grammar and content together indicate specific continuity between these two chapters. At this point the reconciliation of God in Christ of chapter 5 is combined with the reconciliation of Jew and gentile in God's purpose— i.e., how the coming of Christ has reconfigured the operation of God in relation to these peoples, and thus their relation to one another. The basis for good relations in chs.12–15 and especially in chapters 14–15 is argued already in explicit reconciliation terms in chapter 11. Instead of pessimism over the emerging fact that only some of the Jewish people have as yet responded positively to the Christ-movement, Paul in a brilliant refusal to accept the apparent failure of God's covenant promises and the resultant mistaken boasting of gentile over Jew, turns the situation on its head by arguing that since from Israel's failure, a positive outcome has emerged in the gospel going to the gentile world, how much more blessing is guaranteed when the final acceptance of the rest of Israel takes place. (11:15). Thus gentiles in Christ must not boast over the apparently faithless Jews but humbly stand in awe of God's plan for them to share in the richness of the olive tree (11:17–20). Then in the later chapters, the semantic field of reconciliation continues to be explicitly fed into the conversation.

Secondly the reasons why Paul is not so explicit in using reconciliation terminology as in 2 Corinthians is that he does not know the Romans so well, that he has been slow in coming to visit them, that he is presently going instead in the opposite direction to Jerusalem, and thus they might feel that it is they who need to be reconciled with him. Also he does not want to be too explicit because there are differing views of himself and possibly also concerning the nature and scope of his mission in circulation at Rome to which he does not want to add and thus contribute to further tension.[35]

Paul in 2 Corinthians is estranged from this community, and he uses the Hebrew Bible background to enforce his argument that the readership needs to be restored or reconciled to him as God's authoritative representative, which amounts to a reconciliation to God himself[36]. But here, in this case with the Romans, unlike in 2 Corinthians, Paul cannot include himself along with the Romans as ambassadors for peace. The problem arises amongst the Romans themselves, and from their context in the centre of the Empire rather than being mainly the result of Paul's reception by the Romans. So he approaches the conflicts indirectly rather than head-on as he did in 2 Corinthians. The emphasis in Romans is not so much on the process of reconciliation itself as on its desired outcome in unity and peace in place of conflict. This becomes apparent in the manner in which peace becomes a recurring theme in the letter, reaching its explicit climax in chapters 14–15 as Haacker has strongly asserted.[37] Whether we maintain that Romans is a letter that stresses reconciliation or, alternatively, peace there can be no doubt that

---

35. Cf, my "Divergent Images of Paul and his Mission" (n20 above)
36. Cf. Beale, "Reconciliation in 2 Corinthians 5–7," 579.
37. See note 27 above.

'Let Us Maintain Peace' (Romans 5:2)

in it the kingdom of God is presented as closely linked to both righteousness and peace as well as to the outcome of these in everyday life (joy in the Holy Spirit, Rom.14:17).

After the normal introductory "grace and peace" in 1:7, εἰρήνη first occurs in a general reference in 2:10 "glory and honour and peace to all those doing good" etc., then in a negative reference in a scripture citation in 3:17, "the way of peace they did not know." But it comes centre stage at 5:1 "we have peace" or more appropriately as we shall argue "let us have peace" or better still "let us maintain peace." Then in chapter 8 the contrast is made between the mind (φρόνημα) of the σάρξ which is death, and the mind of the Spirit which is life and peace.

Most significantly in 12:18 the exhortation emerges, "If possible inasmuch as you are able, live peaceably with all." The present participle form of the verb εἰρηνεύω appears here and the second person present imperative of the same verb occurs in the other reconciliation letter, 2 Corinthians, at 13:11 (τὸ αὐτὸ φρονεῖτε εἰρηνεύετε.) and similarly also in 1 Thessalonians 5:13. Interestingly in the latter passage, the command to "be at peace amongst yourselves," occurs immediately after a call to respect those who are over you and who labour among you, suggesting that the possibility for peace was related to acknowledgement of the leaders.

What could well be regarded as the most important reference to εἰρήνη occurs in the powerful summarizing statement in 14:17, "for the kingdom of God is righteousness and peace and joy in the Spirit" followed in 14:19 by the programmatic exhortation, "Let us then pursue what makes for peace and for mutual upbuilding." The recommended pursuit of peace has as its fruit and desired outcome, the edification of the other and the up-building of the community. After this point we find three significant occurrences of similar peace terminology in 15:13 firstly at the end of a sub-section, "May the God of hope fill you with all joy and peace in believing" and then two important final references in 15:33 to "the God of peace" (which we interpret as "the God who promotes peace"), " May the God of peace be with you all" and in 16:20, "Then the God of peace will soon crush Satan under your feet."

Indirect evidence concerning reconciliation and peace is to be noted in the references to enmity, hostility at 8:7,[38] i.e. the opposite

---

38. As Jewett notes, the nominal form φρονέω (be minded) is used here for the first time in Paul's letters and indeed in the NT—φρόνημα has the same meaning as

71

of peace occurs here in relation to the mind of the sarx. Jewett finds it rather puzzling that a reference to peace occurs in 8:6 where one would anticipate life to occur in contrast with death. Jewett goes on to acknowledge however that peace is extremely relevant for the congregations. Thus, he asserts, Paul draws stark distinctions so that it can become clear in 11:17–25 and 14:1—15:13 that the habits of the old age of the flesh, still visible in the arrogant and discriminatory behaviour of competitive congregations, entails serious consequences.[39] Thus the explicit reconciliation language of 11:13–15, is followed by the warning against competitive boasting of gentile over Jew, and the effects of this arrogance on relations between differing groups at Rome.

Even in this contrast with its opposites, the theme of living in peace and the semantic connection with this is still implicit. As Joseph Fitzmyer reminds us, in thinking of reconciliation we must bear in mind that "the notions of enmity, hostility, estrangement and alienation, as well as their counterparts, reconciliation, atonement, friendship and intimacy are derived from social intercourse of human persons or from the relations of ethnic and national groups, such as Jews and Greeks."[40] Thus we cannot make a firm separation between the vertical and horizontal dimensions of Paul's thought. The horizontal presupposes the vertical and the two are inseparable images of divine activity and its impact on human behaviour.[41] From this we conclude that peace language in Romans is nothing other than reconciliation language.

Since the majority of manuscripts support the subjunctive both here and in καυχώηεθα in 5:3, I follow the proposal of Erich Dinkler to translate 5:1 as "let us maintain peace," putting the emphasis upon

---

the infinitive—to be minded—namely, the mindset or orientation itself. Note that in the use of ἔχθρα in 8:7 the φρόνημα of the flesh is hostile to God whereas the mind of the Spirit is life and peace (8:6) (*Romans*, 487–88).

39. Ibid.

40. Hay and Johnson, *Pauline Theology*, 162, Cf. similarly Beker, *Paul the Apostle: The Triumph of God in Life and Thought*. Beker argues that despite differing metaphors, "the levels of symbolic interaction do not justify a view that there is a dichotomy between juridical and mystical language, or an emphasis on one as opposed to the other." On the contrary, he maintains that "Paul interprets the coherent apocalyptic core of the gospel in a variety of metaphors that interact and interweave to form an organic whole, so that a developmental or atomistic analysis of the various metaphors bypasses his hermeneutical intent" (259–60).

41. Martin, *Reconciliation*, 229.

the anticipated outcome of reconciliation with God as reconciliation with those who differ.[42] Jewett makes an excellent case for the subjunctive reading. "Rather than a triumphalist argument about the current possession of peace and hope by Christian believers that the indicative interpretation has traditionally assumed, the subjunctive produces an admonition about the correct embodiment of faith in the life of the congregation. The formulation in the first person plural includes all the members of Paul's audience as well as Paul and his colleagues in a common obligation."[43] What is more, their common corporate experience of living as a community of reconciliation is how they learn together its meaning, not only for themselves, but also for those who disagree with them , whether about forms of corporate activity in house-congregations or synagogue groups. It is here that the meaning of reconciliation becomes intelligible and understandable in *the experience of striving to live peaceably*, not just with everyone individually, but particularly with differing groups divided by strong opinions and equally strong practices. In the obligation to live peaceably, the link between the doctrine of reconciliation with God and Christian social ethics is bridged, and the body of Christ becomes recognizable and effective in a world where enemies co-exist side by side with Christ-followers.[44]

Reconciliation and Paul's Purpose in Romans

Paul asserts he is not ashamed of the gospel for it is the power of God to everyone who believes, but then surprisingly adds to the Jew first, and only then "and also to the Greek." This suggests that there are some gentiles in Rome—since they are the addressees—who are criticizing Paul, claiming that he is ashamed of the gospel for gentiles 'apart from

42. For Dinkler's proposals see Jewett, *Romans*, 345–50. Jewett also interprets 5:1 as subjunctive, "let us have peace"; S Porter also has made a good defence of this reading, "The Argument of Romans 5: Can a Rhetorical Question Make a Difference?"

43. Jewett, *Romans,* 348, cf. also Schütz's emphasis that for Paul the 'singularity of the gospel' and the 'unity of the church' are the top priorities, *Paul and the Anatomy of Apostolic Authority.*

44. Thus faith and politics cannot be separated, and despite its failings the attempt at political reconciliation of differing peoples in South Africa must be recognized as a valid experiment in communal reconciliation. Cf. Tutu, *No Future without Forgiveness*; Battle, *The Ubuntu Theology of Desmond Tutu*; Volf, "Forgiveness, Reconciliation and Justice."

the law' and that he still wants to retain his troubled association with Judaism. But this image of the apostle is unwarranted in that although Paul will not permit gentiles to become Jews, this does not mean that they are to separate from all things Jewish or from all relations with Jews and Judaism.[45] So Paul gives the standard Jewish view of gentile society in Romans 1:18–32, stressing that God gave up the gentiles to their idolatry. After a discussion of judging one another, Paul turns in 2:17 to the question of who is a true Jew: simply to call oneself a Jew will not do. So here is reflected the dilemma of those gentiles who had acquired a Jewish pattern of life. Some gentile Christ-followers in Rome ask a question, implying they will receive a negative answer: What then is the advantage, if any, of being a Jew? "Much in every way" is Paul's answer. There is no need to be ashamed of being a Jew or of being related to Jews as children of Abraham. Abraham is not someone to be despised for the sake of Aenaeas or other Roman forefathers. Abraham is ultimately unique in Paul's genealogy. He is the bearer of the promise; he left his pagan origins and after believing the promise God gave him, accepted circumcision, thereby making him truly the father of many nations. Thus Abraham is a uniting figure for believing Jews and gentiles, because he has become the model for all those believing without circumcision and likewise also of those believing and being circumcised. There is now no need for hostility and enmity between circumcised and uncircumcised in Christ because of this shared ancestry. The atonement through the life and death of Christ, explicit in 3:21–26 is implicit here. The promise to Abraham and to his descendants did not come through the law but through Christ and the words "it was reckoned to him as righteousness" were written also for those who trust in Christ in whom the promises were confirmed (4:22–25). We can paraphrase Paul's emphasis as follows: 'having obtained access to this grace in which you as gentiles stand, let us then seek to maintain peace and to live peaceably with all those who are different' (whether they are Christ-followers or not).

45. See Fredriksen, "Judaizing the Nations." Fredriksen argues against the concept of Paul's gospel being described as a "law-free" gospel, since he imposes Jewish ritual demands of no worship to native gods, thus "Judaizing the nations." Only common usage prohibited Paul from using the term "Judaizing" positively. But Fredriksen still insists as I do that Paul strongly maintained the division of humanity into Jew and gentile, and that this perception was not done away even in Christ.

This grace in which we stand is moreover the obedience that faith enables. Christ is contrasted with the disobedience of Adam, and then Gentile believers are exhorted and commanded in 6:1–7:6 to live a life of obedience, following the leading of the spirit into peace and righteousness in chapter 8.

Then in chapters 9–11 the relation of gentile Christ-followers to the *whole of Israel* is explicitly considered. This suggests that some gentile Christ-followers in Rome were hostile to Jews and Judaism generally, not just to those gentile Christ-followers who choose to continue to live a Jewish life pattern. Thus it seems that the question of eating and drinking-of the weak and the strong, an issue in my view among gentile Christ-followers in particular, becomes centre-stage. However it is not just a matter of food and drink but rather of *food and drink as perceived symbols of Judaism* that some Christ-followers in Rome were keen to leave behind them. They were mistakenly beginning to despise the heritage of Abraham, but Paul overturns their gentile view of the world by depicting them as wild olives receiving their enrichment not from the Greek world but from Abraham.[46] There is possibly real hostility from some gentile radicals as is glimpsed briefly in 16:17 "I appeal to you, brethren, to take note of those who create dissensions and difficulties, in opposition to the doctrine (διδαχή) which you have been taught; avoid them."

Note the echo here of 6:17, "the standard of teaching" (τύπον διδαχῆς). If the Petrine mission from Jerusalem led to the foundation of the church at Rome, then that Jewish foundation would have taught its first converts a Jewish Christian pattern of life-that is why Paul is so careful how he builds on another's foundation- he has learnt from Antioch, and he desires peace, not the hasty martyrdom brought on by conflict between Jew and gentile, or by the refusal to pay one's taxes.[47]

Conclusion: The Pursuit of Peace

The quest for peace must not be confused with a sentimental aspiration. In Paul, it is a powerful exhortation "pursue what makes for peace" (14:19) or as in 1 Corinthians 14:1, "pursue love" (cf. Rom 12:13 "pursue

---

46. Cf. W. D. Davies, "A Suggestion concerning Romans 11:13–24."
47. Cf. my *Paul and the Creation of Christian Identity*, 77–79.

hospitality," and of Paul's own testimony concerning what he himself 'pursues' according to Phil 3:12–16). This denotes not just a passive pious acceptance of what might be termed the peace principle, but active and self-conscious living by the "mindset" of the Spirit. "To set the mind on the flesh is death, (τὸ φρόνημα τῆς σαρκὸς) but to set the mind on the Spirit (τὸ φρόνημα τοῦ πνεύματος) is life and peace" (8:6). Paul's goal is that the minds of the Romans should be transformed so that groups do not think of themselves more highly than they ought to think, but to think with sober judgment, each according to the measure of faith which God has assigned (12:2–3). The emphasis on the mindset already introduced in chapter 8, is now related back to the pride of gentile Christ-followers noted in 11:17–24, indicating that it is the super or hyper-mindedness of some gentiles that is causing conflict between the groups. Such an attitude corresponds to the mindset of the flesh denounced in 8:6 as contrary to the mindset of the Spirit that brings life and peace.[48] "Live in harmony with one another; do not be highminded, but associate with the lowly; never be conceited."(12:16—note here the recurrence of φρόνιμοι). The renewal of the mind in Christ is Paul's response to community conflict. So the response to persecution, to those who do evil, is never to avenge or retaliate but in "so far as it depends upon you, to live peaceably with all" and thus "overcome evil with good" (12:14–21). Thus Paul links life and peace indicating that the latter is a prerequisite for the former and essential to the well-being and growth of the communities.[49]

So whilst Paul acknowledges that he teaches freedom in Christ as some of his gentile followers in Rome were confident he would, yet at the same time, he actually takes the side of the weak: "associate with the lowly" and "stop being conceited." He commands those in power not to destroy the weak persons caught between conflicting life patterns and between differing factions at Rome. His advice is reconciliation and full acceptance of each other's differing stance. "Accept one another as Christ has accepted you," freely, with no qualifications, no reservations, no limitations as to Jewish affiliation or lack of it. His warning is that 'you who have power in your gentile Christ-following groups, do not endanger the brother' (who is not able or willing to renounce his previ-

---

48. Cf. Jewett *Romans*, 487–88.
49. Cf. Schütz as in n. 38 above.

ous pattern of living in Christ after a Jewish fashion). Thus difference is not the cause of the perpetuation of hostility but rather the refusal to accept the other in his/her difference and to be reconciled to them as they are.

This is because contrary to what some gentile Christ-followers think, Judaism is not annulled, nor are the branches lost that were apparently broken. God has plans still for all Israel, and *gentile obedience can assist or hinder those plans*. That is why, says Paul, I plan to visit Jerusalem prior to coming to see you because I need to witness still to the order of the gospel, to the Jew first and also to the Greek. You gentiles have obtained the riches of the God of Israel and the gospel of his son the messiah of Israel, so it is necessary for you as gentiles to share your material blessings with those through whom the promises of Abraham were transmitted to the world. So Paul invites the Roman gentiles to follow his example of a reconciliation offering to the Jews in Jerusalem as evidence that the offering of Christ had brought reconciliation to the gentile world and still held out hope for the salvation of all Israel. Paul himself was no stranger to conflict and for the sake of Christ would not shirk to oppose anyone, but despite this, his advice to all is to pursue peace "pleasing his neighbour for his good" in a reconciling pattern of life even as Christ did not live to please himself (Rom.15:2–3). It is most fitting therefore that in Ephesians Paul is depicted not only as the champion of the gentiles, but significantly also as an apostle of peace, "eager to maintain the unity of the Spirit in the bond of peace" (4:13).

I offer this study of reconciliation and peace in a world of diverse identities and much conflict in appreciation particularly of the biblical contribution of John T. Williams but also of his deep and abiding respect for the Reformed and cultural traditions of his native Wales.

BIBLIOGRAPHY

Achtemeier, Paul J. *Romans*. Interpretation. Atlanta: John Knox, 1985.

Adams, Edward. "First-Century Models for Paul's Churches: Selected Scholarly Developments since Meeks." In *After "The First Urban Christians": The Social-Scientific Study of Pauline Christianity Twenty-Five Years Later*, edited by Todd D Still and David Horrell, 60–78. London: T. & T. Clark, 2009.

Battle, Michael. *Reconciliation: The Ubuntu Theology of Desmond Tutu*. Cleveland: Pilgrim, 1997.

Beale, Gregory. "The Old Testament Background of Reconciliation in 2 Corinthians 5–7 and Its Bearing on the Literary Problem of 2 Corinthians 6:14—7:1." *NTS* 35 (1989) 550–81.

Beker, J.Christiaan. *Paul the Apostle: The Triumph of God in Life and Thought*. Philadelphia: Fortress, 1980.

Breytenbach, Cilliers. *Versöhnung: Eine Studie in Paulinischer Soteriologie*. WMANT 60. Neukirchen-Vluyn: Neukirchener, 1989.

Campbell, William S. "The Rule of Faith in Romans 12:1—15:13: The Obligation of Humble Obedience to Christ as the Only Adequate Response to the Mercies of God." In *Pauline Theology*. Vol. 3, *Romans*, edited by D. M. Hay and E. E. Johnson, 259–86. Minneapolis: Fortress, 1995.

———. "Divergent Images of Paul and His Mission." In *Reading Israel in Romans: Legitimacy and Plausibility of Divergent Interpretations*, edited by Cristina Grenholm and Daniel Patte, 187–211. Romans through History and Cultures Series. Harrisburg PA: Trinity, 2000.

———. *Paul and the Creation of Christian Identity*. London: T. & T. Clark, 2006.

———. "Unity and Diversity in the Church: Transformed Identities and the Peace of Christ in Ephesians." *Transformation: An International Journal of Holistic Mission Studies* 25 (January 2008) 15–31.

———. 'The Addressees of Paul's Letter to the Romans: Assemblies of God in House Churches and Synagogues?' In *Between Gospel and Election: Explorations in the Interpretation of Romans 9–11*, edited by Florian Wilk and J. Ross Wagner, 171–95. WUNT 257. Tübingen: Mohr/Siebeck, 2010.

Davies, W. D. "A Suggestion concerning Romans 11:13–24." In *Jewish and Pauline Studies*, 153–63. Philadelphia: Fortress, 1985.

Dunn, James D. G. *Romans*. Word Bible Commentary 38A–38B. Dallas: Word 1988.

Eisenbaum, Pamela. *Paul Was Not a Christian: The Real Message of a Misunderstood Apostle*. New York: HarperOne, 2009.

Fitzgerald, John T. "Paul and Paradigm Shifts: Reconciliation and Its Linkage Group." In *Paul beyond the Judaism/Hellenism Divide*, edited by Troels Engberg-Pedersen, 241–62. Louisville: Westminster John Knox, 2001.

Fitzmyer Joseph A. *Pauline Theology: A Brief Sketch*. Englewood Cliffs, NJ: Prentice-Hall 1967.

Fowl, Stephen E. "Learning to Be a Gentile: Christ's Transformation and Redemption of Our Past." In *Christology and Scripture: Interdisciplinary Perspectives*, edited by Andrew T Lincoln and Angus Paddison, 22–40. LNTS 348. London: T. & T. Clark, 2007.

Fredriksen, Paula. "Judaizing the Nations: The Ritual Demands of Paul's Gospel." *New Testament Studies* 56 (2010) 232–52.
Georgi, Dieter. "The Early Church: Internal Jewish Migration or New Religion?" *Harvard Theological Review* 88 (1995) 35–68.
Haacker, Klaus. "Der Römerbrief als Friedensmemorandum." *NTS* 36 (1990) 25–41.
Hay, David M. and E. Elizabeth Johnson, eds. *Pauline Theology, Volume 3: Romans*. Reprinted Atlanta: SBL, 2002.
Heckel Ulrich. "Das Bild der Heiden und Die Identität der Christen bei Paulus." In *Die Heiden: Juden, Christen, und das Problem des Fremden*, edited by Reinhard Feldmeier and Ulrich Heckel, 269–96. WUNT 1/70. Tübingen: Mohr/Siebeck, 1994.
Hodge, Caroline Johnson. *If Sons, Then Heirs: A Study of Kinship and Ethnicity in the Letters of Paul*. Oxford: Oxford University Press, 2007.
Holmberg, Bengt. "Understanding the First Hundred Years of Christian Identity." In *Exploring Early Christian Identity*, edited by Bengt Holmberg, 1–32. WUNT 226. Tübingen: Mohr/Siebeck, 2008.
Jewett, Robert. "Romans as an Ambassadorial Letter." *Int* 36 (1982) 5–20.
———. *Romans: A Commentary*. Hermeneia. Minneapolis: Fortress, 2006.
Käsemann, Ernst. "The Righteousness of God in Paul." In *New Testament Questions of Today*, 168–82. New Testament Library. London: SCM, 1969.
Kim, Seyoon. *The Origin of Paul's Gospel*. Tübingen: Mohr, 1981.
Kraftchick, S. J. "Death's Parsing: Experience as a Mode of Theology in Paul." In *Pauline Conversations in Context: Essays in Honour of Calvin J Roetzel*, edited by J. C. Anderson et al., 144–66. JSNTSup 221. Sheffield: Sheffield Academic, 2002.
Lambrecht, Jan. "Reconcile Yourselves . . . : A Reading of 2 Corinthians 5:11–21." In *Studies on 2 Corinthians*, edited by R. Bieringer and J. Lambrecht, 263–68. Bibliotheca Ephemeridum theologicarum Lovaniensium 112. Leuven: Leuven University Press, 1994.
Lee, Jae Won. "Paul and Reconciliation in Romans: From a Korean Postcolonial Perspective." Paper read at the Romans through History and Cultures seminar at the Society of Biblical Literature annual meeting, New Orleans, LA, November 2009.
Lopez. Davina C. *Apostle to the Conquered: Reimagining Paul's Mission*. Minneapolis: Fortress, 2008.
Martin, Ralph. *Reconciliation: A Study of Paul's Theology*. New Foundations Theological Library. Atlanta: John Knox, 1981.
Megahey, Alan. *The Irish Protestant Churches in the Twentieth Century*. Basingstoke: Macmillan, 2000.
Porter, Stanley. "The Argument of Romans 5: Can a Rhetorical Question Make a Difference?" *JBL* 110 (1991) 655–77.
Reckwitz, Andreas. "Der Identitätsdiskurs: Zur Bedeutung einer sozialwissenschaftlichen Semantik." In *Kollektive Identitäten und kulturelle Innovationen. Ethnologische, soziologische und historische Studien*, edited by Werner Rammert et al., 21–38. Leipzig: Leipziger Universitätsverlag 2001.
Schütz, John H. *Paul and the Anatomy of Apostolic Authority*. New Testament Library. Louisville: Westminster John Knox, 2007.
Stendahl, Krister. *Paul among Jews and Gentiles*. Philadelphia: Fortress, 1976.
Tutu, Desmond. *No Future without Forgiveness*. London: Rider 1999.

Volf, Miroslav. "Exclusion and Embrace: Theological Reflections in the Wake of 'Ethnic Cleansing.'" *Journal of Ecumenical Studies* 29 (1992) 230–48.

———. *Exclusion and Embrace: A Theological Exploration of Identity, Otherness and Reconciliation*. Nashville: Abingdon, 1996.

———. "Forgiveness, Reconciliation and Justice: A Theological Contribution to a More Peaceful Environment." *Millennium: Journal of International Studies* 29 (2000) 861–77.

Wolff, Christian. "True Apostolic Knowledge of Christ: Exegetical Reflections on 2 Cor.5:14ff." In *Paul and Jesus: Collected Essays*, edited by A. J. M. Wedderburn. JSNTSup 37. Sheffield: Sheffield Academic, 1989.

5

The Growth Motif in the Letter to the Philippians

ALLISON A. TRITES

Professor John Tudno Williams has had a long and distinguished record, teaching students in Biblical Studies and working in both Old and New Testaments. He has published articles in Welsh and English, as well as two commentaries in Welsh, and has served on the translating panel for the New Welsh Bible. In addition, he was secretary of the Theological Branch of the University of Wales's Guild of Graduates for 36 years. On his retirement in 2003, he was recognized for 37 years of faithful service with a D.D. by the University of Wales. In addition, during the last five years of his tenure he provided leadership as Principal of the United Theological College, Aberystwyth.

Among his many responsibilities he served as Moderator of the General Assembly of the Presbyterian Church of Wales and of the National Free Church Federal Council. It was my privilege to teach in his place for the autumn term in 1997 while he taught New Testament in my stead at Acadia Divinity College, Acadia University. It is thus a distinct honour for me to contribute to this *Festschrift*.

The purpose of this paper is to take a careful look at the whole subject of church growth from a biblical perspective. For reasons of time and space, this attempt will largely focus on one of the New Testament letters traditionally attributed to the Apostle Paul,[1] thereby hoping to gain an insight into the motifs of church growth which have guided believers in sharing their faith through the centuries.

Accordingly, this study begins with an examination of church growth in the letter to the Philippians. Then for comparative purposes these observations will be checked and contrasted with the place given to church growth in the book of Acts, where obviously the growth motif assumes a place of major importance. Perhaps the widespread decline of the church in many segments of western society and the paradoxical growth of the church in many parts of the Third World make this study timely and appropriate today.

Paul is presented as in chains (Phil 1:7), and is writing from prison (1:12–14) to his friends in Philippi, whose financial support and encouragement he has appreciated (4:10, 14–16). The place of imprisonment has been frequently debated, but as it is of no consequence for this study, it will not be explored.[2] A study of the church growth motif here is of value because some of the recent literature on the subject is rather unsatisfactory from an exegetical point of view.[3] Contemporary

---

1. The question of Pauline authorship of Philippians is not widely debated by New Testament scholars. As Leander Keck has noted, "There is virtual unanimity" that Philippians is to be included in the letters that have been correctly ascribed to the apostle Paul (*Paul and His Letters* [Philadelphia: Fortress, 1979], 3). The following abbreviations are used in this chapter: AV : Authorised Version; CEV: Contemporary English Version; ESV: English Standard Version; Goodspeed: *The Complete Bible: An American Translation* (Chicago: University of Chicago Press), 1929; GWT: God's Word Translation; NASB: New American Standard Bible; NEB: New English Bible; NIV: New International Version; NLT: New Living Translation; NRSV: New Revised Standard Version; RSV: Revised Standard Version; TNIV: Today's New International Version.

2. While several locations have been advanced as the site of Paul's imprisonment, including Ephesus, Caesarea, or even Corinth, a reasonable case can still be made for the traditional view that Paul was writing while in prison in Rome. So McDonald and Porter, *Early Christianity and Its Sacred Literature* (Peabody, MA: Hendrickson, 2000), 372–76. There is evidence from the early second century that points to the continued growth of the church. For example, Pliny the Younger, the governor of the Roman province of Pontus-Bithynia, writing about 111 AD, informed the Emperor Trajan that he found Christianity to be spreading and noted that formal charges had been raised against them (Epistle 10:96–97).

3. Donald McGavran has been called the father of the growth movement. In 1957 he created the Institute of Church Growth in Eugene, Oregon, and established the School of World Mission at Fuller Theological Seminary in Pasadena, California. He

church growth writers often do not place their emphasis on biblical exegesis, and if they deal with the letters associated with Paul's name, they frequently do so in a disorderly, unsystematic fashion, showing a greater concern for contemporary relevance than a detailed study of the text itself.[4]

The Fact of Church Growth

First of all, the fact of church growth, in some measure, is indicated by the letter itself. Paul wants to assure his friends in Philippi that his incarceration has not closed the doors for an effective witness to the gospel of Christ. In fact, he asserts to the contrary that "what has happened to me has actually helped to spread the gospel" (1:12). Paul views his time in prison as having a providential outcome, "so that it has become known throughout the whole imperial guard and to everyone else that

---

placed great stress on evangelism and church planting, and also underscored the place of the social and behavioural sciences to detect the factors that either impede or facilitate church growth. His major work, *Understanding Church Growth* (1970) has been edited and revised in a third edition by C. Peter Wagner, Grand Rapids: Eerdmans, 1990. Win Arn introduced church growth principles to North America; see Arn and McGavran, *Back to Basics in Church Growth* (Wheaton, IL: Tyndale, 1981). For popular expositions related to North American church life see Rick Warren, *The Purpose Driven Church* (Grand Rapids: Zondervan, 1995); and Aubrey Malphurs, *Planting Growing Churches for the 21st Century* (3rd ed.; Grand Rapids: Baker, 2004). For a critical appraisal of the motivation behind programs of church growth in the newly emerging megachurches see D. Neal MacPherson, *Church at a Crossroads* (Eugene, OR: Wipf & Stock, 2008), 6–7; and in greater detail, Os Guinness, *Dining with the Devil: The Megachurch Movement Flirts with Modernity* (Grand Rapids: Baker, 1993).

4. On the general framework of the church growth movement, see Wayne Weld and Donald McGavran, *Principles of Church Growth* (2nd ed.; South Pasadena, CA: William Carey Library, 1974); Roy D. Pointer, *How Do Churches Grow?* (Basingstoke, UK: Marshalls, 1984); G. Edwin Bontrager and Nathan D. Showalter, *It Can Happen Today! Principles of Church Growth from the Book of Acts* (Scottdale, PA: Herald, 1986); Loren B. Mead, *More Than Numbers: The Ways Churches Grow* (Washington DC: Alban Institute, 1993); C. Peter Wagner, *Strategies for Church Growth* (Ventura, CA: Regal, 1987); Eddie Gibbs, *I Believe in Church Growth* (Grand Rapids: Eerdmans, 1982); Ebbie B. Smith, *Balanced Church Growth* (Nashville: Broadman, 1984). George Peters, *A Theology of Church Growth* (Grand Rapids: Zondervan, 1981), makes more extensive use of the Bible but does not attempt a systematic analysis of Paul or Luke. For other references to the literature see Allison A. Trites, "A Study of Church Growth in Colossians and Philemon," in *From Biblical Criticism to Biblical Faith: Essays in Honor of Lee Martin McDonald*, edited by William H. Brackney and Craig A. Evans (Macon, GA: Mercer University Press, 2007), 103–4.

my imprisonment is for Christ" (1:13; cf. v.22, "fruitful labor for me").[5] Paul sees his own experience behind bars as having a productive effect on the Philippian believers, for "most of the brothers and sisters, having been made confident by my imprisonment, dare to speak the word with greater boldness and without fear" (1:14) He sets a challenging example to his friends in Philippi, unabashedly declaring his faith in Christ by speaking "with all boldness," even in a prison cell (1:20).

Paul acknowledges not only the development of Christian work in Philippi, but also the help of the Philippians in supporting him financially when he left the province of Macedonia "to spread the Good News" (1:12, GOD'S WORD).[6] While Paul certainly does not concentrate on the statistical side of growth in the manner of the book of Acts,[7] the letter to the Philippians is not lacking in indicating several aspects of church growth. The Christian faith was expanding geographically, and Philippi clearly served as the launching pad for the gospel's westward advance into Europe. It is significant that in the letter to the Philippians specific mention is made of the "advance" of the gospel (*prokopē*, 1:12, TNIV). But the development of Christianity was more than numbers and extending its frontiers, for it also included the spiritual development and cultivation of the lives of its adherents. Thus Paul could use the same Greek word to suggest his willingness to remain in Philippi for the "progress"(*prokopē*) and "joy in faith" of his converts (l: 25; cf. 1 Tim.4:15, where a similar pastoral concern is expressed for Timothy).

---

5. Unless otherwise indicated, all references will be cited from the New Revised Standard Version (1989). On the issue of fruitlessness, Jesus noted the possibility of producing no fruit in his famous parable of the sower and the seeds (Mark 4:19; Matt 13:22; cf. John 15:5). Paul cautioned about praying in a tongue but with one's mind being unproductive (1 Cor 14:14). It was vitally important for him that believers "be productive" (note the use of *karpophoreō* in Rom 7:4, 5; cf. Col 1:6, 10). Elsewhere the New Testament epistles castigate "the unfruitful works of darkness" (Eph 5:11) and point out the danger of "unfruitful" or "unproductive" activity (Tit 3:14). 2 Peter warns against things that make the Christian "ineffective and unfruitful" (2 Pet 1:8), and Jude notes the false teachers who "pervert the grace of our God into licentiousness" (v. 4) and are "without fruit" (*akarpos* is used in Jude 12, as in the other passages cited).

6. God's Word to the Nations, *God's Word Translation* (Holiday, FL: Green Key, 2003).

7. For the evidence of Acts see Allison A. Trites, "Church Growth in the Acts of the Apostles," *McMaster Journal of Theology* 1/1 (1990) 1–18.

The Christocentricity of Church Growth

For Paul there could be no genuine church growth without a high Christology. This comes to striking expression in the second chapter, where he speaks so passionately and poetically of the self-emptying of Christ in the incarnation, in his servant ministry, and ultimately, in his death on the cross, followed by his divine exaltation to the highest place of honor in his resurrection, ascension, and glorification (2:5–11).[8] With this comprehensive view of Christ, Paul identified completely, not only by accepting it as a series of propositions to be believed, but also as setting a pattern for his own life and that of his converts. He had been completely "captured by Jesus Christ" (3:12, Goodspeed), and expected them to be similarly captured, so he instructed them: "Have the same attitude that Christ Jesus had" (2:5, Goodspeed). Despite his confinement to a prison cell where he faced the real possibility of martyrdom, he expressed his fervent desire that Christ might "be exalted now as always in my body, whether by life or by death" (1:20). As Paul declared on the basis of his own personal experience, "Living is Christ and dying is gain" (1:21).

The "Good News" or gospel that Paul had discovered in Jesus Christ was vitally important to him, and he plainly depicted his life in terms of his relation to it. This is repeatedly underscored in the letter to the Philippians. Thus his relation to the Philippian church is described as "the fellowship of the gospel" (1:5, AV), and his preaching is viewed as the "confirmation of the gospel" (1:7). Paul's work as an ambassador and apostle of Christ is noted as "the progress of the gospel" (1:12), and his clashes with his opponents are seen as "the defense (*apologia*) of the gospel" (1:16; cf. v.7). His message is presented as "the faith of the gospel" (1:27), and others labor with him "in the work of the gospel" (Timothy, 2:22; Euodia and Syntyche, 4:3). In sum, Paul's campaign in Macedonia and Achaia is viewed as "the beginning of the gospel" (4:15, AV; or "the early days of the gospel," NRSV). Clearly, Paul saw the es-

---

8. On this subject see Ralph P. Martin, "The Christology of the Prison Epistles," in Richard N. Longenecker, ed. *Contours of Christology in the New Testament* (McMaster New Testament Studies; Grand Rapids: Eerdmans, 2005), 193–218. After carefully discussing the strophic structure of Phil 2:5–11, Martin observes that in Philippians the story of Jesus presents the Lordship of Christ as a compelling "ethical stimulus" (195-98).

tablishment and growth of the first church that he planted on European soil in very Christ-centered terms.

Paul lived with eternity's values in view. He saw himself as a citizen of heaven, and preached an eschatological message, "expecting a Savior, the Lord Jesus Christ" at the climax of history (3:20-21; note the use of *politeuma* in 3:20). The "day of Christ" was the eschatological horizon that Paul kept ever before him (1:6, 10; 2:16; cf. 1 Cor 1:8; 5:5; 2 Cor 1:14; 1 Thess 5:2, 4). That was the future time when all believers were to share in Christ's eternal glory (1 Cor 1:8; Phil 3:20-21; 1 Thess 4: 13-18; 5:9-10; cf. 2 Thess 1:10). He believed that he, in common with all Christians, was personally accountable to his Lord and would answer for his actions at the judgment seat of Christ (cf. Rom 14:10; 2 Cor 5:10). He claimed that he acted consistently on this principle and accordingly urged his fellow believers to act ethically, never forgetting that as "stewards" of the gospel they were responsible to their Lord for their faithfulness in handling the Christian message and living in accord with its precepts (1 Cor 4:1-2; cf. Rom 12:6-7; 1 Pet 4:10). So he challenged the Philippians: "Whatever happens, as citizens of heaven live in a manner worthy of the gospel of Christ" (Phil 1:27, TNIV). Closely related to this emphasis on Christ is a real concern for corresponding growth in Christian character.

The Necessity of Qualitative Church Growth

Thirdly, there is a strong interest in *qualitative* church growth. Here, as elsewhere in his letters, Paul was concerned that his missionary efforts should not prove futile or "in vain" (*eis kenon*, Phil 2:16[twice]; see also 2 Cor 6:1; Gal 2:2; 1 Thess 3:5; note similarly the double use of *eikē* in Gal 3: 4). Manifestly he was interested in their full development as Christian believers, truly "mature" in their faith (*teleioi*, 3:15; cf. 1 Cor 2:6; 14:20; Eph 4:13; Col 1:28; 4:12; note similarly the reference to "firmness [*stereōma*] of faith" in Col 2:5).[9] The apostle's earnest concern

---

9. Note also Col 1: 9-10, where the apostle continually prays that "you may be filled with the knowledge of God's will in all spiritual wisdom and *understanding*" (*synesis* is used here, as in 2:2). Similarly, Paul reminds Philemon he is concerned that "your partnership (*koinōnia*) in the faith may be effective (*energēs*, "powerful, active") in deepening your understanding of every good thing we share for the sake of Christ" (Philem 6, TNIV). In addition, observe the commendation of the Thessalonians "be-

for the genuine spiritual growth of the Philippians is explicitly stated. While acknowledging their gifts with gratitude (4:10–20), he declares that he seeks not their gifts but "the profit (lit., 'fruit,' *karpos*) which increases to your account" (4:17).He lovingly admonishes them to "stand firm (*stēkete*) in the Lord" (4:1).

It must be remembered that Paul is writing here to a church that had experienced tensions and divisions (2: 2–4; 4: 1–3). Grumbling and arguing were present in the church (2:14). In such circumstances it would be natural for Christians to divide on controversial issues like circumcision (3:2–3). Paul acknowledges that differences of opinion have affected their internal cohesion, so he urges them to pull together as a community of faith, "standing firm in one spirit, striving side by side with one mind for the faith of the gospel" (1:27).They were to be "united in mind" (*sympsychoi*, 2:2). He earnestly pleads with his two hard-working co-labourers Syntyche and Euodia to overcome their quarrelling, close ranks, and "be of the same mind in the Lord" (*to autō phronein*, 4:2). Moreover he asks Clement to "help" or "assist" these women in resolving their disagreement (*syllambanō* is used here in 4:2).

Quality control was important in the growth and development of Christian character and also in the extension of the Christian mission in a credible way; therefore Paul prayed fervently for the whole Christian community "that your love may overflow more and more with knowledge and full *insight* (this is the only use of *aesthēsis* in the NT, a word meaning "perception" or "discernment") to help you determine what is best" (1:9,10a). It was vital for their effectiveness as Christian workers

cause your faith is 'growing abundantly'" (2 Thess 1:3, where the rare verb *hyperauxanō* is used to describe the wonderful growth in their faith).

Spiritual maturity was clearly valued as an indispensable condition for fruitfulness and growth. On the importance of spiritual "fruit" (*karpos*) in Paul's epistles see Trites, "A Study of Church Growth in Colossians and Philemon," cited in endnote 4, 105; and David J. Williams, *Paul's Metaphors: Their Context and Character* (Peabody, MA: Hendrickson, 1999), 40–41. Similarly note in the preaching of John the Baptist the strong ethical insistence on bearing "good fruit" and "fruit worthy of repentance" (Matt 3:10, 8; Luke 3:9, 8) and the teaching of Jesus about a tree being known by its fruit (Matt 7:16–20; 12:33–37; Luke 6:43–44; cf. John 15:1–10, with its emphasis on bearing "much fruit"). Jesus spoke of the great effort required to enter the kingdom "through the narrow gate" (Luke 13:24; cf. Matt 7:13–14). Also Jesus' parable about the barren fig tree pointed to the continuing patience of God with those who had not yet provided evidence of repentance (Luke 13:6–9). Note also that James sees true wisdom expressed in "good fruits" and speaks of "the fruit of righteousness" as "sown in peace for those who cultivate peace" (Jas 3:18, 19).

and leaders to heed Paul's admonition, "Only let us hold fast to what we have attained" (3:16). Paul asked of them only what he demanded of himself, for his stated aim was clear—an unremitting commitment to excellence (4:8-9). Using Greek athletic metaphors drawn from the popular foot races, Paul described the great effort that was called for, the finishing line to be crossed, and the award given to the victor: "I press on toward the goal for the prize of the heavenly call of God in Christ Jesus" (3:14). His life was "straining forward to what lies ahead" (3:13), and as their mentor he expected no less of his converts: "Keep on doing the things that you have learned and heard and seen in me, and the God of peace will be with you" (4:9).

Paul's letter of friendship is not a formal theological treatise, but it is directed to appeal to the Philippians' experience of genuine life in Christ: "If there is any encouragement in Christ, any consolation from love, any sharing in the Spirit, any compassion and sympathy, make my joy complete: be of the same mind, having the same love, being in full accord and of one mind" (2:1-2). Here in this letter Paul pours out his heart in fervent concern for the spiritual welfare of this much treasured church that he called "my joy and crown" (4:1; cf.1:8). The love and support of this Christian community meant a great deal to him (4:10, 14).

The Cost of Church Growth

The gospel Paul had offered to the Philippians presented both *gift* and *demand*. On the gift side, they had received salvation as a free unearned blessing from God, obtaining a divine righteousness "that comes through faith in Christ, the righteousness from God based on faith" (3:9; cf. Rom 1:16—4:25 for a fuller treatment). On the demand side, the apostle reminded them of their obligations and responsibilities as believers: "Work out your own salvation with fear and trembling; for it is God who is at work in you, enabling you both to will and to work for his good pleasure" (2:12b-13). This was not "cheap grace," but costly discipleship that would enable the young church to make its impact on the surrounding society: "For he (God) has graciously granted you the privilege not only of believing in Christ, but of suffering for him as well" (1:29). They were called to join Paul in "the same struggle" in which he himself was still engaged (*agōn* is used to describe this "conflict," 1:30, cf. Col 2:1; 1 Thess 2:2).

Their wholehearted response to God's grace was vital to make this impact for the Christian faith possible, and Paul reminded them of it: "With reverence and awe make every effort to insure your salvation" (2:12, Goodspeed). Their lifestyle was to be so transparent and wholesome as they lived innocent and blameless lives, demonstrating the reality of their faith publicly as "children of God without blemish in the midst of a crooked and perverse generation, in which you shine like stars in the world" (2:15; cf. Matt 5:14) . For this ideal of an attractive, winsome discipleship to become a functional reality, the quarrelling, arguing, and other expressions of disunity had to be honestly faced and put aside (2:14; 4:1–3; cf. 1:27). No wonder Paul includes a digression in his letter concerning those who advocate the necessity of circumcision, thus demanding that Christians observe the laws of Judaism (3:1b–3). These Judaizers were Paul's bitter foes elsewhere, particularly in Galatia, and their tactics are exposed and criticized here (cf. Gal 5:2–12).

Since the Damascus road experience, Paul's whole life had been dedicated to Christ, and his supreme desire is summed up in 3:10, where he says: "I want to know Christ and the power of his resurrection and the sharing of his sufferings by becoming like him in his death." In fact, Paul likened his possible death to a temple sacrifice which he gladly was prepared to make to establish the Philippians in their faith (2:17, using *spendomai*, meaning "offer one's life in sacrifice;" cf. 2 Tim 4:6; Ex 29:38–40). In stressing the costliness of discipleship and Christian commitment, Paul stated what was expected: "Brothers and sisters, join in imitating us, and observe those who live according to the example (*typos*) you have in us" (Phil 3:17; similarly 1 Cor 10: 6; 1 Thess 1:7; cf. 2 Thess 3: 9; 1 Tim 4:12; Tit 2: 7; 1 Pet 5:3).

The Relationships of Church Growth

In view of his close relationship with them Paul had no need to stress his apostolic authority, as he did in addressing the churches of Corinth and Galatia (1 Cor 1:1; 2 Cor 1:1; Gal 1:1; cf. Col 1:1). Instead he emphasizes the fact that he is their friend and companion in proclaiming the gospel and advancing the work of Christ in Philippi. They share with him the task of acting "in the defense and confirmation of the gospel" (Phil 1:7, 16).

Here it is evident that Christian growth was to be expressed in healthy relationships. Nowhere else in Paul's letters to the churches, with the possible exception of 1 Thessalonians,[10] does this close sense of relationship to his converts come to sharper focus than in Philippians. Over and over again Paul speaks of them "all" in terms of real affection, endearment, and pastoral concern. At the beginning of the epistle the apostle writes to "all the saints in Christ Jesus who are in Philippi" (1:1). Personally he admits that he thinks "about all of you" (1:7), indeed, he yearns for his Philippian friends—"how I long for all of you" (1:8). He delights in the fact that their corporate solidarity is in Christ: "for all of you share in God's grace with me" (1:7). While Paul's own future may be uncertain, he sees himself as probably remaining alive to make a contribution to the Christian community in Philippi--"since I am convinced of this, I know I will remain and continue with all of you . . . so that I may share abundantly in your boasting in Christ Jesus when I come to you again" (1:25-26). Their welfare mattered profoundly to Paul, and he gladly would do whatever he could to foster healthy relationships with them.

None of this Pauline affection can obscure the fact that there were real difficulties in this local community of believers. Paul grieves over the disunity created by envy (*phthonos*) and rivalry (*eris*). Their destructive effects on the church's ongoing mission and outreach were apparent.[11] For this reason the apostle offered his hard-hitting counsel:

---

10. Edward P. Blair, *Illustrated Bible Handbook* (Nashville: Abingdon, 1987), 310, argues the case for 1 Thessalonians (e.g., 1 Thess 2:8): "Here he is a tender shepherd of newborn lambs—a pastor—who lovingly feeds, protects, and encourages the young. To use the letter's own figure of speech, Paul is a nurse caring for children (2:7), a father gently encouraging his little ones (2:11)." In addition, observe the commendation of the Thessalonians "because your faith is 'growing abundantly,'" (2 Thess 1:3, where the unique verb *hyperauxanō* is used to describe the wonderful growth). For other examples of feminine images used by Paul see Beverly Roberts Gaventa, *Our Mother Saint Paul* (Louisville: Westminster John Knox, 2007).

11. *Phthonos* in Phil 1:15 points to "the feeling of displeasure produced by witnessing or hearing of the advantage or prosperity of others" (W. E. Vine, *Expository Dictionary of New Testament Words* [London: Oliphants, 1967], 37); similarly the chief priests are said to have delivered Jesus to Pilate "out of envy" (Mark 15:10// Matt 27:18). Note also the comment of H. Giessen in *Exegetical Dictionary of the New Testament*, eds. H. Balz and G. Schneider (Grand Rapids: Eerdmans, 1991), 2:52: "*eris* is always used of *disputes* that endanger the Church . . . The context [Phil l] (vv.16-18) suggests that the concern here is with the danger to the unity and peace of the Church." Thus G. B. Caird, *Paul's Letters from Prison* (New Clarendon Bible; Oxford: Oxford University

"Do nothing from selfish ambition (*eritheia*, used also in 1:17) or conceit (*kenodoxia*, a rare word used only here in the NT, but cf. *kenodoxoi* is used in Gal 5:26 of conceited people) but in humility regard others as better than yourselves" (Phil 2:3). This was necessary instruction in a church where it was all too common for folk to "look after their own interests, not those of Jesus Christ" (2:21, RSV).

In contrast with such a self-seeking spirit, Paul singled out for special praise his own understudy in the faith, Timothy, whose genuine, unselfish commitment to the cause of Christ was well known to the community: "But Timothy's worth you know, how like a son with a father he has served with me in the work of the gospel" (2:22). Paul pays tribute to Timothy's deep loyalty and partnership, declaring, "I have no one like him" (2:20, using the unusual word *isopsychos*, found only here in the NT!). No wonder Paul was anxious to dispatch Timothy to the Philippian church as soon as possible. Such a stalwart, magnanimous and dedicated worker was certainly worthy of emulation, and Paul could commend a man of his calibre to their attention. Similarly he notes the loving, sacrificial lifestyle of Epaphroditus and sets him up as a model worthy of imitation: "Welcome him then in the Lord with all joy, and honor such people" (2:29; cf. 3:17).

The Prayerfulness of Church Growth

Paul had a strong conviction about the importance of prayer that led him to remind the Philippians what they already knew as a remedy for anxiety and a recommended approach to all issues: "Do not worry about anything, but in everything by prayer and supplication with thanksgiving let your requests be made known to God" (4:6). The promised blessing was "the peace of God, which surpasses all understanding, will guard your hearts and your minds in Christ Jesus" (4:7).

Like Luke (Acts 14:27; 15:4, 12),[12] Paul believed that God was sovereign and therefore ultimately in charge of the development and

---

Press, 1976), 98, in drawing attention to the close connection that Paul felt with the church he founded in Philippi has probably overstated the warmth of the relationship when he finds "hardly a hint of criticism" of the Philippian church in the letter. There are serious relational issues that Paul feels called upon to address, and he does so in the letter to his much loved church.

12. Allison A. Trites, "Church Growth in the Acts of the Apostles," *McMaster*

expansion of the church (Phil 2:13; similarly, 2 Cor 3:5-6; cf. Col.4:3, where prayer is sought that God may open a "door" for the word "to declare the mystery of Christ" and also Rev 3:8). It was this conviction in large measure that led the apostle to the Gentiles elsewhere to attach such major importance to intercession for the Christian mission (see Rom 15:30; 2 Cor 1:11; 1 Thess 5:25; cf. Eph 6:18-20; Col 4:2-4,12; Phlm 22; 2 Thess 3:1). Paul was conscious of God's power to bless the church and extend its missionary thrust into the world, and he knew that church members could play a vital part in advancing that mission.

Accordingly, Paul was profoundly thankful to the Philippians for "your partnership in the gospel from the first day until now" (1:5, RSV). This had been expressed in practical ways by both their loving act of sending Epaphroditus to minister to him on their behalf when he was in prison (note 2:25, "your messenger and minister to my need"), and certainly through their generous financial contributions which the apostle gratefully acknowledges (4:10-20). But just as important for the advancement of the gospel was the fact that he could count on them for prayer support: "I know that through your *prayers* and the help of the Spirit of Jesus Christ this will turn out for my deliverance (1:19; the term used here is *deēsis*, "petition," "request," "entreaty"—the same word Paul used twice in describing his own intercessory prayers for the Philippians, 1:4). Paul was confident that whatever happened to him, God was in charge of the mission and would use him to further it, whether by life or by death (1:20-26); nevertheless, he relied on their prayers to help him face whatever lay in store for him (cf. 1 Thess 5:25; Col 4:3).

In this epistle it is interesting that it is principally Paul who repeatedly prays for the Philippians rather than requesting their prayers for him (1:3-4, 9-11). They were in need of spiritual help, and Paul, their spiritual mentor, was prepared to give it in whatever form it was required, including prayer (so also Rom 1:8,9; 1 Thess 1:2; cf. Eph 1:16-19; 3:14-19; Col 1:9; 2 Thess 1:11-12; 2 Tim 1:3). Evidently Paul

---

Journal of Theology 1/1(Spring 1990) 6-8. Cf. Wayne G. Rollins, *The Gospels: Portraits of Christ* (Philadelphia: Westminster,1963), 88-89, who describes Luke as "the God-intoxicated Evangelist... God alone is the central actor in history... The line between theology and Christology, between God and Christ, is essential to Luke's theology of history... For Luke, God is the eternal subject of history and Christ is a moment in his self-revelation." For examples of this theocentric element in the book of Acts note Acts 14:27; 15:4, 12; 21:19.

believed, like James and Luke, that "the prayer of the righteous is powerful and effective" (Jas 5:16; cf. 2 Cor 1:11; 1 Thess 5:17; Luke 18:1; Acts 4:24-31; 12:5).

The Collegiality of Church Growth

Another distinctive feature of this epistle is its sense of collegiality. Paul frequently drew attention to its importance (Phil 1:1, 14, 27; 2:25; 3:17; 4:3,21; cf. 1 Cor 1:1; 3:1-9; 2 Cor 1:1,19; Col 1:1; Phlm 1-2; 1 Thess 1:1; 2 Thess 1:1). While Paul might serve as one of the principal spokesmen and architects of church growth (cf. Paul's own comparative description of himself as "like a skilled master builder" in 1 Cor 3:10), he certainly was no "lone ranger"! In fact, he took great pains to affirm his appreciation of those who worked with him as his "co-partners" (*synkoinōnoi*, Phil 1:7; cf. 1 Cor 9:23) in the gospel. Thus he thanked God for the longstanding generous "sharing" (*koinōnia*, Phil 1:5) of the Philippian Christians that had clearly persisted from their own initial experience of Christian faith right up to the time of writing. He regarded his friends in Philippi as his colleagues in presenting the gospel—"holding forth the word of life (2:16 [KJV, RV; cf. NIV, "hold out"; NEB, REB, "proffer"], taking the verb *epechō* to mean "offer" as in Barclay's translation: "You must go on offering them the word of life."[13] On the other hand, if *epechō* means, as seems more probable, "hold fast" (so RSV, NRSV, NASB, ESV; cf. CEV, NLT, TNIV, "hold firmly to"), then the steadfast commitment and perseverance of the Philippians in the face of opposi-

---

13. William Barclay, *The New Testament: A New Translation* (London: Collins, 1968-1969), 2:143. So also Goodspeed: "offering men the message of life." Cf. NIV: "as you hold out the word of life"; or GNB: "as you offer them the message of life." This interpretation has also been recently defended by Mark J. Keown, *Congregational Evangelism in Philippians* (Paternoster Biblical Monographs; Milton Keynes, UK: Paternoster, 2008). Keown argues that Paul wanted the Philippian church to continue an "evangelistic proclamatory mission" (1). While some exegetes have opposed this view (e.g., the recent commentary of John Reumann, *Philippians: A New Translation with Introduction* (Anchor Yale Bible 33B; New Haven: Yale University Press, 2008), 393-94, 413, what is clear in Philippians is that Paul concentrated his attention on fostering harmonious relations among the believers in his audience, an emphasis present also in his other epistles (Rom 12:16; 1 Cor 1:10; 12:12-26; 2 Cor 13:11; 1 Thess 5:13; cf. Eph 4:1-6).

tion and persecution would point to the reality and genuineness of their faith and be evidence of the gospel's transforming power (1:28).

That collegiality was important to Paul is also clear in other parts of his correspondence. There is a fondness for Greek nouns that are combined with the preposition *syn* meaning "with," "together with" (for example, note the double use of the verb *synchairō* to express his joy: "I am glad and 'rejoice with' all of you" (2:17f.). Additionally, Paul counts Epaphroditus as a "brother" (*adelphos*, a popular term in Paul used well over 100 times and 9 times in Philippians: 1:12,14; 2:25; 3:1,13,17; 4: 1, 8,21),[14] and then goes on to describe him as a "fellow-worker" (*synergos*, 2:25;[15] also used in 4:3 of "Clement and the rest of my fellow-workers," RSV; cf. 1 Cor 3:9; 2 Cor 1:24; 8:23; Col 4:11; 1 Thess 3:2; Phlm 1, 24) and fellow soldier" (*systratiōtēs*, Phil 2:25; cf. Phlm 2, where it is used of Archippus). Besides Clement, an apparently unnamed but influential person is noted as a "loyal companion" (it is possible that the Greek word for "companion" here could be a man's proper name Syzygus in 4:3, but this is unlikely). In addition, note that the Christians in Philippi are asked to be "imitators" of Paul (using *symmimētai*, 3: 17; cf. 1 Cor 4:16; 11:1; Eph 5:1; 1 Thess 1:6; 2:14).

Similarly, a number of Greek verbs are formed with the prefix *syn*. The Philippians "shared in" Paul's distress (*synkoinōneō*, Phil 4:14; cf. Eph 5:11), and were called to become "like him in his death" (*symmorphizō* means "share the likeness of," 3:10). They were asked by Paul to act as spiritual athletes, "striving side by side" (*synathleō* means "fight together with," "work together with" in Phil 1:27; the same verb is used again in 4:3, where Paul notes the women co-workers "who have struggled beside me in the work of the gospel"; note the similar use of *athleō* twice in 2 Tim 2:5).[16] Partnership was supremely important to

---

14. "Brother" is a very important term for both Luke and Paul Outside the Gospels, it is generally used figuratively, and often refers to believers who work together in the cause of Christ e.g., Acts 6:3; 9:17,30; 11:1; 14:2; 15:22; Rom 1:13; 7:1,4; 1 Cor 1:1,10,11; 2:1; 2 Cor 1:8; 2:13; 8:1; Gal 1:2,11; 3:15; 1 Thess 1:4; 2:1,9,14). For details see J. Beutler, "*adelphos*," in Horst Balz and Gerhard Schneider, eds., *Exegetical Dictionary of the New Testament* (Grand Rapids: Eerdmans, 1994), 1:28–30.

15. Cf. the similar term *symmathētēs* (a *hapax legomenon* for "fellow disciple"), used to describe the original disciples of Jesus in John 11:16. *Synergos* "is a common term found in the epistles, usually in the Pauline writings: Rom 16:3, 9; 1 Cor 3:9; 2 Cor 1:24; 8:23; Phil 2:25; 4:3; Col 4:11; 1 Thess 3:2; cf. 3 John 8)." See Trites, "A Study of Church Growth in Colossians and Philemon," 116.

16. This fondness for *syn* words is also found in the Pastoral Epistles (e.g.,

Paul, and he never tired of mentioning and affirming its value, as has been noted in his other epistles.[17] In passing, it may be noted that Luke also notes the importance of collegiality to Paul in the book of Acts (note, for instance, Acts 13:3,5,13; 15:40; 16:3,15,25; 20:3-6; 21:16).

The idea of partners in team ministry is indicated in other ways. Paul mentions in Philippians Timothy in the opening salutation and associates him with the writing of the letter (1:1). This is characteristic of Paul's real sense of collegiality (note also 2:19-22) and is found in other letters, where he refers to Sosthenes (1 Cor 1:1), Timothy (1 Cor 4:17; 16:10; 2 Cor 1:1), "all the members of God's family who are with me" (Gal 1:2), and Silvanus and Timothy (1 Thess 1:1; cf. 2 Thess 1:1). Their sharing in leadership and service was a valuable contribution to the furtherance of the gospel, and it is frequently recognized and appreciated.

Conclusion

It is appropriate that one should ask how Paul's analysis of church growth in Philippians compares to Luke's treatment of the same theme

---

synkakopatheō in 2 Tim 1:8 and 2:3; *synapothnēskō* and *syzaō* in 2 Tim 2:11 [also in Rom 6:8; 2 Cor 7:3]; *symbasileuō* in 2 Tim 2:12 [also in 1 Cor 4:8]. Elsewhere Paul speaks of other Christians "working together" for the kingdom of God (note the use of *synergeō* in 1 Cor 16:16; 2 Cor 6:1; cf. Rom 8:28, which speaks of God "working with" human agents). The epistles note that believers have been "buried" and "raised together" with Christ (using the verbs *synthaptō* and *synegeirō* respectively in Col 2:12; they talk of being "crucified with" Christ (*systauroō*, Rom 6:6; Gal 2:19), and observe that God had "made" them "alive together with him" (using *syzōopoieō* in Col 2:13; cf. Eph 2:5). Paul makes a striking request for collegiality in prayer on behalf of his evangelistic and missionary work in Rom 15:30, where the unique verb *synagōnizomai* (a *hapax legomeonon*) is used to invite the Romans to join Paul in the struggle by prayer. Similarly Paul recognizes the support of the Corinthians believers "as you join in helping us by your prayers" (2 Cor 1:11, where another *hapax* is used, *synypourgeō* meaning "aid along with another, help together, support together").

On the other hand, Paul hopes "to experience refreshment " in company " with" his fellow Christians (note the singular use of *synanapauomai* in Rom 15:32).

17. For instance, Paul describes believers as "co-heirs" with Christ (*synklēronomoi*, Rom 8:17; cf. Eph 3:6, where the Gentiles are called "heirs together with Israel") and speaks of their service as *syndouloi* of Christ (Col 1:7; 4:7; cf. Rev 6: 11; 19:10; 22:9). Observe the similar use of *syn* in compound terms in Ephesians noted in Allison A. Trites, "Proclaiming Ephesians: God's Order in a Needy World" (*Southwestern Journal of Theology* 39 [1996] 47); for Colossians and Philemon see Allison A. Trites, "A Study of Church Growth in Colossians and Philemon," cited in note 4, 102-21, esp. 114-16.

in the book of Acts, where the subject is more prominent.[18] Several provisional observations can be made, though it is quite possible that they may require some revision and refinement when the rest of Paul's letters are carefully examined.[19]

First, it is clear that Luke and Paul are both interested in the growth of the church (Acts 2:41, 47; 4:4; 5:14; 6:7; 9:31; 11:24;14:1; 16:5; Phil 1:12-14; 2:16; 4:13; cf. Col 1:6, 10, 23; 2:6-7, 19; Phlm 6; note also 1 Cor 3:6, 7; 2 Cor 9:10; 10:15, 16). The missionary journeys of Paul are striking evidence of this in the book of Acts (Acts 13:1—14:28; 15:36—18:21; 18:22—21:16).

Second, both Luke and Paul are conscious that it is God's work in which believers are engaged (Acts 1:24-25; 9:15; 13:2-4; 22:10; 26:15-18), and therefore God must make the "progress" of the gospel possible (Phil 1:12, 25). As Paul notes elsewhere, God must open the "door" (*thyra*) to make fruitful mission possible (1 Cor 16:9; 2 Cor 2:12; cf. Col 4:3; Rev 3:8). Luke also underscores the importance of the "door" which only God opens (Acts 14:27; cf. 11:18; 13:47-48). Luke and Paul are alike in emphasizing the point that the growth really comes from God, and is to be attributed to the divine initiative (Acts 2:47; 5:14; 11:21; 14:27; 15:4, 12; 16:14; 21:19; 22:10, 14, 15; Phil 1:12, 13, 20-24; 2:9-11; 4:13, 19; cf. 1 Cor 3:5-9; 2 Cor 9:10; 10:15-18; Col 1:12-14, 19-20, 22, 25-27; 2:13, 19; 4:3). This marked sense of dependence on God for the success of the mission and its extension is a feature common to both men (Acts 6:6; 9:15; 13:2-3; 14:23, 26-27; 15:4, 12; 20:32; Phil 1:27-28; 4:13; cf. 1 Cor 16:13; 2 Cor 3:4-5; 12:9-10; 1 Thess 1:5; 2:13).

Third, Luke considers the geographical aspects of church growth more thoroughly than Paul (note his frequent references to Roman provinces such as Achaia, Bithynia, Cilicia, Mysia, Cappodoccia, Macedonia, Pontus, Asia, Pamphylia, etc.). As noted elsewhere, "This is to be expected, given the length of Acts and the historical nature of Paul's epistles . . . Luke has space to explore the spread of the gospel from Jerusalem through Judea, Samaria, Galilee and into the larger Roman world, where Paul, concerned principally with pastoral matters in the churches, can only mention such growth in passing (note

---

18. Allison A. Trites, "Church Growth in the Book of Acts," in Roy B. Zuck, ed., *Vital New Testament Issues* (Vital Issues Series 8; Grand Rapids: Kregel, 1996), 44-54.

19. For a previous study see Trites, "A Study of Church Growth in Colossians and Philemon," 102-21.

Acts 1:8; 2:47; 9:15, 31; 11:24; Col 1:6, 23; cf. 1 Thess 1:7-8; Rom 1:8; 10:18; 15:19-20)."[20] By contrast, Paul in Philippians only mentions the Roman province of Macedonia (Phil 4:15, though he also mentions the Macedonian city of Thessalonica, 4:16).

Fourth, Luke places far greater emphasis on the numerical growth of the church than Paul does (notice, for instance, Luke's repeated use of *prostithēmi* ["add"] in Acts 2:41, 47; 5:14; 11:24). Thus he uses the word "number" (*arithmos*) in several passages that clearly refer to church growth (Acts 4: 4; 6:7; 11:21; 16:5; 21:20 mention a vast multitude, *myriades*). Paul is evidently not as concerned with such matters.[21] Luke writes as an early church historian, and is naturally concerned with the increase in numbers. Thus he explores this feature at greater length than Paul, who only touches on such growth incidentally (see Acts 1:15; 2:41, 47; 4:4; 5:14; 9:31, 35; 11:24; 12:24; 16:5; 19:20; 21:20; Phil 1:12-13; 4:22; cf. Rom 1:8; 10:18; 15:18-20; 1 Cor 3:6; 15:6; 1 Thess 1:7-8).

Fifth, Luke and Paul alike consider both personal and corporate prayer as indispensable elements in the life of Christian people and also a vital feature in the execution of the Christian mission (Acts 1:14; 2:42; 4:24-31; 6:4; 12:5; 13:3; 16:25; 20:36; 21:5; Luke 18:l; Phil 1:3-5, 9-11, 19; 4:6, 7; cf. Rom 1:8-10; 15:30; 1 Cor 7:5; 2 Cor 1:11; Eph 3:14-21; 6:18-19; Col 1:3, 9, 10; 4:2-4,12; Phlm 4, 22; 1 Thess 5:17).[22]

Sixth, praise, thanksgiving and rejoicing are prominent features in both Luke (Luke 1:47; 2:13, 14, 20; 5:25, 26; 7:16; 10:20, 21; 13:13; 17:15-18; 18:43; 19:37-38; 24:52-53; Acts 5:41; 8:39; 16:34) and Paul (Phil 1:3-5, 18, 19; 2:17-18; 3:1a; 4:4, 6, 10; cf. Rom 5: 2, 3; 15:6, 9-11; 2 Cor 6:10; 9:13; Gal 4:27; Col 1:3, 24). These expressions of doxology

---

20. Ibid., 117.

21. For example, Paul uses *arithmos* only once, in Rom 9:27, in loosely citing Isa 10:22-23 (LXX), where only a "remnant" of Israel is to be saved. Luke also uses the term to refer to the "number" of four hundred men slaughtered in the rebellion against Roman authority led by Theudas in AD 44 (Acts 5:36), an incident also mentioned by Josephus (*Ant.* 20.97-98). In addition, Luke frequently uses the noun *plēthos* ("great number," "crowd") to describe the large number of disciples in the Christian community (Acts 4: 32; 5:14; 6:2, 5; 14:1; 17:4); Paul does not use the term at all in his epistles.

22. On Luke's strong interest in prayer see Allison A. Trites, "The Prayer Motif in Luke-Acts," in Charles H. Talbert, ed., *Perspectives on Luke-Acts* (Perspectives in Religious Studies: Special Studies Series 5; Danville, VA: Association of Baptist Professors of Religion, 1978), 168-86.

and spiritual vibrancy communicated a buoyancy in lifestyle that made the Christian way of life attractive to "outsiders" (the *hoi exō*, noted in Col 4:5 and 1 Thess 4: 12), despite the fact that believers were often persecuted or attacked by their enemies (e.g., Acts 5:40; 7:54, 58; 11:19; 14:19; 16:23-25; Phil 1:27-30; 3:2, 10).

Seventh, qualitative spiritual growth in both individuals and in the church community was important to both writers (Acts 6:8; 7:59-60; 13:1-3; 14:23; Phil 1:5-7; 2:12-16; 4:1-3, 15-18; cf. 1 Cor 3:5-9; 12:4-11; Gal 6:5-6; Col 1:7, 28-29; 2:6-7; 4:12-13, 17). Luke repeatedly stresses the unfailing diligence of Paul and his colleagues in strengthening the church and edifying its members (Acts 11:23; 13:43; 14:22; 15:32, 41; 16:4-5; 18:23). Similarly, Paul holds a high ideal of Christian discipleship before his converts, and challenges them to uphold it (Phil 1:3-11, 27; 2:1-4, 16; 3:15-17; 4:8-9). He sets before them the peerless example of Christ (2:5-11), and also cites Epaphroditus, Timothy, and himself as examples known to them personally of faithful, sacrificial discipleship worthy of emulation (2:19-30; 3:17). This setting of elevated moral standards is common elsewhere in the Pauline corpus (Rom 8:2-6, 12-17; 12:1-2; 1 Cor 6:9-11; Gal 5:16-26; 6:7-10; Col 1:28-29; 2:6-7; 3:1-3, 12-17; Phlm 9-14; 1 Thess 2:10-12; 4:1-8). The building up of believers and the buttressing of the life of the church were vital matters for both men.

Eighth, collegiality is an observable feature in both Luke and Paul (Acts 1:13-14; 2:14; 11:30; 13:1-3; 14:23; 15:22, 28; 20:4-5; Phil 1:1, 5, 27; 2:25; 4:3, 14; cf. Rom 16:1-16; 1 Cor 1:1; 3:9; 2 Cor 1:1; 8:23; Gal 2:7-10; Col 4:7-15; 1 Thess 1:1; 3:2; Phlm 1, 2, 24; Tit 1:5).[23] For

---

23. A particularly interesting example of Paul's collegiality is cited by Luke in the book of Acts. It concerns the delivery of a special collection taken from the Gentile churches for the relief of poor Christians in Jerusalem, an offering noted several times by Paul himself (Rom 15:25-29; 1 Cor 16:1-4; 2 Cor 8-9; Gal 2:10). Paul, Luke tells his readers, brought his friends with him to the holy city to provide maximum accountability of his financial stewardship: "He was accompanied by Sopater son of Pyrrhus from Beroea, by Aristarchus and Secundus from Thessalonica, by Gaius from Derbe, and by Timothy, as well as by Tychicus and Trophimus from [the Roman province of] Asia" (Acts 20:4-5). Evidently the principle of multiple witness, often mentioned throughout the Bible (Deut 17:6; 19:15; John 8:17; 15:26-27; 2 Cor 13: l; 1 Tim 5:19) was considered important to avoid any charges of misappropriation of funds. For other examples of collegiality in Acts see Darin H. Land, *The Diffusion of Ecclesiastical Authority : Sociological Dimensions of Leadership in the Book of Acts* (Princeton Theological Monograph Series 90; Eugene, OR: Pickwick Publications, 2008), who

instance, both Luke and Paul mention gospel "travelling companions," fellow-travellers who helped them carry the gospel to other communities (note the use of *synekdēmos* in Acts 19:29 and 2 Cor 8:19), and Paul is happy to "send with" Titus two other Christian brothers who are unnamed (2 Cor 8:18, 22-23, where the verb *sympempō* is used). Previously Luke had called attention to the method used by Jesus himself, first in sending out the twelve apostles (Luke 9:1-6), and then subsequently the seventy or seventy-two (Luke 10:1).[24] The great importance of cooperative effort in establishing churches and maintaining healthy, vigorous Christian communities was repeatedly noted by both Luke and Paul.

Ninth, a Christocentric perspective appears in both Luke and Paul (Acts 2:32-36; 4:12; 5:31; 10:36-42; 16:30-32; Phil 1:20-21, 27; 2:5-11; 3:20-21; 4:4-5, 7, 10, 13, 19; cf. Eph 1:15-23). This strong, prominent emphasis on the place of Christ is a common feature of the Pauline corpus (1 Cor 1:23-24, 30-31; 11:23-32; 15:3-8; 2 Cor 1:18-21; 2:14-17; Gal 2:19-20; 5:1; 6:14; Col 1:15-20, 28; 2:9; 1 Thess 1:9-10; 4:13-18; Phlm 5, 6, 25).

Tenth, Luke and Paul alike see church growth as radical and costly, and in consequence note the place of suffering, persecution, and even martyrdom in the development and expansion of their mission (Acts 6:11-14; 7:54-58; 8:1; 11:23; 13:43, 50; 14:4-7,22; 15:26; Phil 1:20, 27-30; 2:17, 30; 3:15, 17; 4:10, 14; cf. Rom 12:1, 9-20; 2 Cor 10:3-6; Col 1:22-24; 2:1; 3:1-3, 5-17; Phlm 8-10; 2 Tim 1:8, 11-12; 3:12). Both men perceive a providential dimension in Christians enduring suffering and persecution. Paul declares that his imprisonment has served to spread the gospel throughout the whole imperial guard and to encourage his fellow believers with the result that they shared their faith "with greater boldness and without fear" (Phil 1:12-14; cf. Rom 1:15-16). In a similar fashion Luke calls attention to the remarkable growth of the church in Judea and Samaria following severe persecution (note the three significant uses he makes of the verb *diaspeirō* in Acts 8:1, 4; 11:19 [where the persecuted believers were "scattered" "as far as Phoenicia, Cyprus, and Antioch"]). The buoyancy of believers in the face of their opponents

---

studies in detail Acts 13:1-3; 15:1-35; 20:17-38; 21:17-26 as examples of ecclesiastical authority in a Diaspora setting.

24. On the delicate textual issues see Roger L. Omanson, *A Textual Guide to the Greek New Testament* (Stuttgart: Deutsche Bibelgesellschaft, 2006), 127-28.

was a glowing testimony to the reality of their faith and served to advance it (Acts 4:20, 29–31; 5:40–42; 6:15; 14:14–19; 16:11–40).

Finally, both Luke and Paul recognize the reality of spiritual warfare. In Luke's Gospel, as in the other Synoptic Gospels, Jesus, although "full of the Holy Spirit," was subject to temptation: he was unmistakably "tempted by the devil" (Luke 4:1–13; cf. Matt 4:1–11; Mark 1:12–13; similarly Heb 2:18; 4:15). In addition, Luke noted the presence of satanic activity in Judas Iscariot (Luke 22:3–6; Acts 1:15–26; cf. Matt 26:14–16; Mark 14:10–11; John 13:2). Even Peter, who later became such a key leader in the early church, was tested by Satan, a sombre point noted by Luke (Luke 22:31–32; cf. 1 Pet 5:8–9).

This opposition from hostile forces is present in the book of Acts, where persecutions were often the lot of the early Christians (Acts 4:3; 7:54–8:1; 14:19–20; 21:30–36). The ministry of Jesus proclaimed in the apostolic *kerygma* included not only "doing good" but also healing "all who were oppressed by the devil" (10:38, note the use of the rare verb *katadynasteuō* ["exploit," "oppress"] here; cf. Jas 2:6). Other indications of spiritual conflict are observable in Acts, such as Satan filling the heart of Ananias (5:1–11), the spiritual battle noted in the life of Elymas the sorcerer (13:10), the exploited fortune-telling girl with "the spirit of divination" (Gk., *pneuma pythōna*, 16:16–18), and the devilish ways of Simon the sorcerer in his power encounter with Peter (8:9–24; cf. 19:11–17, the conflict of Paul with the sons of Sceva).

In like manner Paul speaks of this spiritual warfare in his writings (e.g., observe his use of *strateuomai*, "wage war, battle" and *strateia* to refer to the Christian "warfare" in 2 Cor 10:3–4; and note a similar play on words in 1 Tim 1:18; 2 Tim 2:4). A believer is called to "struggle" or "fight" in a spiritual battle (note the use of *agōnizomai* in Col 1:29; 4:12; 1 Tim 4:10; 6:12; 2 Tim 4:7; cf. the similar use of *antagōnizomai* in Heb 12:4 and *epagōnizomai* in Jude 3), and this entailed strenuous effort against stiff opposing forces (note the double use of the verb *athleō* in 2 Tim 2:5 to refer to competing as an athlete in a spiritual contest). This conflict, noted in several places (Rom 7:23; 8:38–39; 2 Cor 2:11; 4:4; 11:14; Gal 5:17; Eph 6:10–20; cf. Jas 4:1; 1 Pet 2:11; and Heb 10:32, where the author uses a *hapax legomenon* [*athlēsis*] to describe the contest, combat or struggle), is prominent in Colossians, where believers are put in mind of Christ's victory over the hostile forces of the universe in the cross (Col 2:15). A battle must be fought with evil (note the use of *agōn* meaning "struggle, fight" [Phil 1:30; 1 Thess 2:2; cf. Col 2:1; 1 Tim 6:12; 2 Tim 4:7]). Christians were summoned to "fight together," working cooperatively with other believers as they contended against hostile forces (note the use of *synathleō* in Phil 1:27 and 4:3; cf. Paul's use of *synagōnizomai* in soliciting the prayers of his fellow believers in Rom 15:30).The conflict was real (note the reference to "Satan hindered us" in 1 Thess 2:18), but in principle Jesus had delivered Christians from the "dominion of darkness" and had "transferred" them to "the kingdom of his beloved Son" (Col 1:13, ERV). The divine resources were available for a victorious conflict (Phil 4:19; Rom 16:25; 2 Cor 2:14; Eph 3:20; cf. Jude 24).

Similarly in Philippians Epaphroditus is recognized as a "fellow soldier" (*systratiōtēs*, Phil 2:25); the same word is used to describe Archippus, who is mentioned in the letter to Philemon as engaged in spiritual warfare as a "fellow soldier" (Phlm 2). The spiritual battle was a genuine one, and honestly faced and recognized by both Luke and Paul. Incontestably Paul was deeply concerned that his missionary efforts should not prove fruitless or unproductive (Phil 2:16; cf. 1 Cor 15:10, 14, 58; 1 Thess 2:1).

In reviewing our findings we observe in Philippians and in other Pauline writings, as in Luke, a considerable interest in church growth. Note, for instance, the common theme of thanksgiving for the growth of the gospel and for the local spiritual community addressed (Phil 1:9–11; 1 Thess 1:5; Phlm 1:6; cf. 2 Thess 1:3, 11). Again, we may observe that elsewhere the verbs "to grow" (*auxanein*) and "to bear fruit" (*karpophorein*) are employed by Paul several times in connection with the gospel and the development of spiritual life (Rom 7:4–5; 1 Cor 3:6–7; 2 Cor 9:10; 10:15; cf. Col 1:6, 10). Of course it would be unfair and inaccurate to suggest that church growth provides a comprehensive category to cover all aspects of Paul's missionary activity. There are plainly other factors to be taken into account in any judicious overall assessment. There is much struggle, pain and suffering that Paul faces, and inevitably there are many setbacks, disappointments, and difficulties. "Yet through it all Paul persists, toiling on even when things go badly and there is no growth, but rather opposition, strife, and division."[25] In

---

25. Carl R. Holladay, "Church Growth in the New Testament: Some Historical Considerations and Theological Perspective," *Restoration Quarterly* 26/2 (1983) 85–102. See also the helpful comments of Martin J. J. Menken, review of Christopher A.

faithfulness he endures, "as seeing him who is invisible" (Heb 11:27). He presses on unremittingly, believing that God will honor his efforts in the long run and produce abiding fruit for the kingdom of God.

But when all due qualifications have been made, it remains true that Paul in Philippians, as in other epistles,[26] was concerned with *bona fide* church growth expressed pre-eminently in exemplary Christian character and lifestyle and issuing in a life "filled with the fruits of righteousness which come through Jesus Christ, to the glory and praise of God" (1:11, RSV; cf. Jas 3:17). Paul was writing to the Philippians from prison (1:7, 13; 4:22), and it was by no means certain that he would escape martyrdom (1: 20, 21).

In any case, Paul recognized that being a disciple of Jesus was a costly thing for him personally, and the same would be true of his converts (cf. 1 Thess 3:2-4; 2 Tim 3:12). They too were called to share in the struggle with him, fighting in the same spiritual conflict in which he was engaged (Phil 1:27-30), and using the same weapons of faith, prayer, and perseverance. They were "brothers and sisters" (Phil 1:12; 2:25; 3:17; 4:1, etc.), called to be united in the service of Christ (2:1-5, 12-16). Their past interventions on Paul's behalf had been appreciated (4:10-12). Now they were urged to continue steadfast in their Christian commitment (4:1-3), knowing that they would ultimately be accountable for their stewardship of the gospel on "the day of Christ" (1:6, 10; 2:16; cf. Rom 14:10; 1 Cor 1:8; 2 Cor 5:10; 1 Thess 5:2; 2 Pet 3:10).

With all the talk today of the need for community in a postmodern situation, there is a message here for an increasingly broken, fragmented world that is threatened with disintegration. The growth of the church in some parts of the third world is in striking contrast to its decline in many parts of the west. Yet the characteristics of church growth presented by Paul and observable also in Luke-Acts remain

---

Beetham, *Echoes of Scripture in the Letter of Paul to the Colossians, Review of Biblical Literature* (2009) online: http://www.book reviews.org.

26. See notes 4, 16. Recently James H. Howard, *Paul, the Community, and Progressive Sanctification: An Exploration into Community-Based Transformation within Pauline Theology* (Studies in Biblical Literature 90; New York: Lang, 2007), has argued that in Pauline theology the redeemed community must be considered an indispensable factor. His book attempts to provide a corrective to the individualized approach to church growth, so that the focus of God's transformative activity culminates in the community rather than the individual, the goal of which is the revealing of God's glory to the broader creation.

as a challenge to the contemporary church. Christocentricity must be matched by a corresponding lifestyle in believers that will give credibility to the truth claims of the gospel. Accordingly, church growth can be expected to be costly, and marked by difficulties, problems and reverses. Relationships within the faith community will still be vitally important, and prayer will continue to be a major force in propelling any advance in outreach. Partnership in mission will be essential, and will involve putting aside all bickering and self-seeking. A purified, united community of believers may still be expected to make a difference in the expansion of the church.

6

Striving for Office and the Exercise of Power in the "House of God": Reading 1 Timothy 3:1–16 in the Light of 1 Corinthians 4:1[1]

KATHY EHRENSPERGER

Introducing Hierarchies?

What seems to drive the first letter addressed to Timothy is a concern for how to live in the house of God, the assembly of the living God. The concern seems motivated as indicated in several passages (1:3–7; 4:1–3) by people/forces which confuse the brothers and sisters in this respect, and the letter claims to provide guidance in this confusion. The emphasis in the verses with which this chapter is concerned seems to be on the introduction of some hierarchical church order which should support stability within the assembly,[2] counter disruption by internal

---

1. It is a great honour for me to dedicate this contribution to John T. Williams, a warm colleague and distinguished scholar who in his contribution to church life and scholarship, his rootedness in the great Welsh tradition of biblical scholarship and his international presence is an excellent example of fruitful local and global networking. Earlier versions of this article were presented at the SBL Annual Meeting 2009, New Orleans, and the Research Seminar of the Department of Theology and Religious Studies, University of Wales, Lampeter.

2. MacDonald, "Exhortations concerning leadership roles in the Pastorals provide

struggles,³ and maintain peace with the surrounding society (1 Tim 2:1–2).⁴ A significant number of scholars see in this the intention to accommodate the assemblies to the norms of the dominating Graeco-Roman society, its values and patterns of life. The labels used for this process range from "catholicising,"⁵ introducing church order,⁶ promoting a process of institutionalization,⁷ introducing the episcopate and hierarchical structures, to promoting a process of "patriarchalisation," including the introduction of misogyny into the assemblies of God.⁸ Depending on the perspective of the interpreter this is either negative or positive, a necessary evolution from the earliest days of the movement, the logical sequel to Paul's undisputed letters, or a distortion of the original Jesus movement's intentions.⁹ In whatever sense the letter is interpreted there seems to exist a widely held consensus that what we find in this letter are instructions to accommodate to the values of the surrounding society, a kind of appeasement policy at the expense of the challenging dimension of the gospel.¹⁰

When it comes to the interpretation of the verses in question, scholars have often assumed that the introduction of hierarchical offices in the assemblies of God is advocated here.¹¹ The fact that the function of the ἐπισκοπή is closely associated with the role of the head

---

evidence of a prevailing domestic ideal which apparently acts as an important means of stabilizing community life" (*The Pauline Churches*, 220).

3. Cf. Marshall notes that "If anything about the circumstances of the PE is clear, it is that their immediate occasion is the development of groups within the churches which are regarded as opposed to the authority and teaching of Paul." *The Pastoral Epistles*, 41.

4. D'Angelo, "'Knowing How to Preside over His Own Household,'" 294.

5. Käsemann, "Ministry and Community in the New Testament," 5–9.

6. Schlier, "Ordnung der Kirche."

7. Cf. Horrell, "From ἀδελφοί to οἶκος θεοῦ," 310; also Macdonald, *Pauline Churches*, 164, 220.

8. Schüssler Fiorenza, *In Memory of Her*, 347–51; Schottroff, *Lydia's Impatient Sisters*, 104–19.

9. Schottroff, *Lydia's Impatient Sisters*, 112.

10. As, e.g., James W. Aageson maintains, "Deeply embedded in the thought world of 1 Timothy is the image of a natural order to which people in the household of God ought to conform, the result of which is a tendency towards consolidation and conformity, rather than novelty and innovation" (*Paul, the Pastoral Epistles and the Early Church*, 35).

11. Bassler, *1 Timothy, 2 Timothy, Titus*.

of a household is interpreted as pointing clearly in that direction. In addition e.g. the order in which the two named functions are presented in these "prescriptions" (not descriptions) is taken as an indication that the relationship between the two functions is hierarchical, the episcopate being the superior function over against the διάκονοι because it is mentioned first and the list of qualities required of an ἐπίσκοπος is longer.[12] In addition the episcopate is perceived to have some superiority also over the 'elders' mentioned in 4:14; 5:17. This assumption is accompanied in some interpretations with a reading of these verses in conjunction with 2:11–15 which are then seen as intending to silence and subordinate women generally under the authority of men.[13] To summarize, most interpreters perceive the focus of 1 Tim 3:1–17, as of the letter as a whole, to be the *introduction or affirmation* of an hierarchical church order, this being actually the main purpose of the letter.[14] Thus the perception of 1 Timothy (and in most interpretations of the Pastorals as a whole) is that of a document which demonstrates the process of development in a new movement from being charismatic and thus following a charismatic leadership style to the institutionalization of power in hierarchical structures at the later stage of the movement.[15]

Hierarchical from the Beginning

However, recently some scholars have questioned this consensus and proposed alternative readings of 1 Timothy.[16] In my own research I have

---

12. See, e.g., Marshall, *Pastoral Epistles*, 488.

13. Schottroff, *Lydia's Impatient Sisters*, 106–7.

14. This seems to be the emphasis even when it is acknowledged that this is part of a wider goal, namely the missionary enterprise of the church as, e.g., by Towner, *The Goal of Our Instruction*, 256–57.

15. Cf., e.g., Schweizer, *Church Order in the New Testament*. Horrell, "From ἀδελφοί," 306–09, and to some extent also MacDonald: "It is indisputable that we find a more established or institutionalized church in the Pastorals than can be traced in other Pauline or deutero-Pauline writings" (*Pauline Churches*, 164). Approaches which argue for such a development in some form or another are based on Max Weber's paradigm "from charismatic leadership to institution building," *Economy and Society*, 1:246, which is critically discussed by Schütz, *Anatomy of Apostolic Authority*, 264–73.

16. Marshall sees a change reflected in the Pastorals which has to do with the absence of the first leadership generation, rather than the introduction of a hierarchical church order. Cf. *Pastoral Epistles*, 175.

demonstrated that the existence of asymmetrical relationships within the Christ-movement, and of hierarchies of authority is not a development of a later more institutionalized "church," but is present also in the undisputed Pauline epistles. It is evident that Paul presupposes the existence of clear leadership roles with different degrees of hierarchies between these; there is, for example, an hierarchical difference between apostles and other workers in the gospel, and between these and the communities.[17] Already at this early stage there seem to exist certain named functions within the ἐκκλησίαι. In addition to the specific role of apostles[18] different terms are used for these leadership functions, such as συνέργοι, διάκονοι, ἀδελφος, although the specific task associated with such labels remains difficult to ascertain for sure.[19] Thus in 1 Cor 4:1 Paul refers to himself and other apostles, in this case to Apollos in particular, also as ὑπηρέται and οἰκονόμοι which implies a perception of leadership roles as being in a subservient position in relation to an authority. This perception of leadership roles in the Christ-movement is supported by the use of διάκονοι for Paul's own service at various points as well (e.g.1 Cor 3:5). The clearest reference to specific functions within the ἐκκλησίαι can be found in 1 Cor 12:28–29 where in addition to apostles a whole range of functions is listed: prophets, teachers, miracle workers, healers, helpers, administrators, speakers in tongues, and interpreters play specific but different roles within the group.[20] This is hardly a description of a spontaneous group which meets without any kind of structured order! Although the precise characteristics of this order and of hierarchies within it cannot be identified it can hardly be denied that there were members in these groups who in specific contexts claimed power over others. Different functions, including leadership roles, are characteristic of the earliest Christ movement. [21] However,

17. Cf. Ehrensperger, *Paul and the Dynamics of Power*, 35–62.

18. Ibid., 37–45.

19. Ibid., 46–55.

20. With reference to the terms with which Timothy (and Titus) is addressed Marshall notes that they "do not significantly diverge from the picture of the apostolic coworker that emerges in the main Pauline letters" (*Pastoral Epistles*, 172).

21. As, e.g., in 1 Cor 3:5–7; 12:28–29. See also Clarke, who affirms that "irrespective of the absence of official titles in the early Pauline epistles, there is clear evidence that there were leaders in each of these communities" (*Pauline Theology of Church Leadership*, 16).

asymmetrical relationships and hierarchies need not be inherently expressions of dominating power structures. A number of factors contribute to dominating hierarchical structures, among them are the means to exercise force over against others and static arrangements of superiority and subordination. As long as they remain flexible and open to the members of the group in question hierarchies need not necessarily lead to domination and oppression.[22] Thus hierarchical relationships as such need not be detrimental to a movement which emphasizes equality for all its members. Groups need to organize themselves and attribute certain functions to members in order for them to function. There is evidence for this already in the earliest Christ-movement and certainly in the undisputed Pauline letters. However, it is not possible to identify specific tasks for each of the named leadership roles, and certainly not the same task set for each role across all the undisputed Pauline letters. As with other topics, each occurrence of such named roles needs to be evaluated in its specific literary and social context rather than assuming identical tasks for these roles across the letters.[23] From this brief survey it can thus be concluded that neither hierarchies nor specific terms for certain leadership functions within the Christ-movement could have been later introduced to what were formerly so-called charismatic assemblies in a process of institutionalization.[24] The model for such a development relies too uncritically on the paradigm set out by F. C. Baur which, combined with the sociological model of Weber, resulted in the perceived "dichotomy between the early charismatic community of faith and incipient institutionalization."[25]

---

22. On flexible hierarchies see Derrida, *Negotiations,* 20–21.

23. Clarke in his fine study acknowledges the diverse contexts and the potential difference in tasks for the same named roles but tries to identify common themes for all the named leadership roles in the corpus Paulinum, thus claiming that "there was remarkable consistency across the Pauline congregations during the New Testament period" (*Pauline Theology of Church Leadership,* 73).

24. Cf. also Marshall, *Pastoral Epistles,* who maintains that "the distinction sometimes drawn between an earlier charismatic ministry and a later institutional system of 'office' is inappropriate and should be dropped from the discussion" (176). Also Clarke, *A Pauline Theology of Church Leadership,* 71–73.

25. Meeks, "Introduction," xx.

Striving for Office and the Exercise of Power in the "House of God"

Puzzling Hierarchical Relationships

It should thus come as no surprise that evidence for the *existence* rather than the *introduction* of specific leadership roles can be found within 1 Timothy itself. The guidance given to "Timothy" by the author presupposes the existence of the roles of an ἐπίσκοπος and of διάκονοι, rather than arguing for the necessity of introducing such roles. As J. Herzer has argued convincingly "the letter does not seek to establish a certain hierarchy in the community. Instead, the way the author speaks about these offices suggests that they are already established and structured." [26] The issue the author addresses is how to find appropriate candidates for these roles, not the roles as such. This may explain the absence of any description of what these roles actually encompassed, what their duties and tasks were within the assemblies.[27] A role description would be required if the letter intended to *introduce* these functions, but if they are already established the addressee/s would know what they encompass. If the issue is *who* would be an appropriate candidate for such a role then it seems natural that what follows are characteristics a person should have rather than what they are supposed to do.[28] The role seems to be so established that it is apparently superfluous to explain its function to the addressee. Unfortunately this means that it remains unclear to contemporary readers what these functions actually encompassed precisely. In this article I deliberately do not use any of the possible translations for these terms, as there is so much history attached to them that I think they obscure rather than help to uncover potential meanings at the time of writing.

Despite this obvious lack of information interpreters have tried to find hints in the text which may shed some light on the nature of, and the relationships between these roles. As mentioned above it has been argued that the order in which the roles are dealt with gives an indication of the hierarchy between these: since the epsicopate is mentioned first this must be the superior role over against διάκονοι.[29] This is not convincing in my view as apart from later history there is no indication

---

26. Herzer, "Rearranging the House of God," 558

27. Also Clarke, *Pauline Theology of Church Leadership*, 43.

28. Cf. Marshall, *The Pastoral Epistles*, 487, Aageson, *Paul, the Pastoral Epistles, and the Early Church*, 22.

29. Marshall, *Pastoral Epistles*, 488.

in the text which would lend itself as a basis for such a conclusion. The relationship between the two functions is not addressed at all (nor is the role of the elders, and the relation between episcopate and elders is an issue later in the letter). It does not emerge conclusively that the episcopate implies superiority over the group of elders or over the διάκονοι. In addition it is significant to note that "Timothy" and the author are referred to as διάκονοι—rather than as ἐπίσκοποι,[30] whilst clearly claiming a leadership role probably even superior to the ἐπίσκοπος. There is an interesting dimension one could derive from the use of the terms οἰκονόμος in 1 Cor 4:1 and of ἐπίσκοπος in 1 Timothy—their range of meaning seems to cover roughly the same role/function in a group, organization or institution. As a term which denoted the function of supervisors or leaders in diverse contexts in Greek societies it was used in the LXX in relation to civil and military leadership roles, including some which involved religious leadership (Num 31:14; Judg 9:28; Neh 9:11; Isa 60:17).[31] There seem at least to be some similarities in that the οἰκονόμοι have to be trustworthy—a requirement which seems to be referred to in more detail in 1 Tim 3:2-4. Whilst there is no way by which a direct link between 1 Cor 4:1 and 1 Timothy 3 could be established it is worth noting the similarity.

Whilst "Timothy" is clearly perceived and addressed as one who is in a leadership position this is not identified with the episcopate and the internal relationship between the specific functions mentioned in the letter, ἐπίσκοπος, διάκονοι, πρεσβύτεροι, and widows remains mainly unclear. Thus an hierarchical relationship between ἐπίσκοπος and διάκονοι cannot be established beyond doubt. Although there is a concern with the functioning of the community life and thus the relationships between its members, there are only fragmentary indications as to what these relationships actually imply. What emerges from this is that the relationship and thus the hierarchy between the terms and roles mentioned in 1 Timothy is impossible to establish. Thus the question arises whether the characteristics of these relationships were presumed

---

30. Cf. ibid., 171

31. Kathleen Corley recently argued that leadership roles in voluntary associations are the most likely source for these functions within the early Christ-movement; cf. *Marantha*, 13–14; also Ascough, "Voluntary Associations and the Formation of Pauline Christian Communities," 162–69; however, Corley's argument is based on Phil 1:1 and does not take "house" terminology into account.

to be self-evident for the audience –or whether they were of no interest or importance to the writer and the addressee/s. Some scholars presume the first in that they assume that the reference to the "house" inherently implies that the relationships are more or less structured hierarchies according to the pattern prevalent in the Graeco-Roman household.[32] However, if the latter is assumed could this mean that we have here a glimpse of an insight into hierarchies on the one hand and the handling of these in a flexible way ? To me this seems a plausible option which requires further research although I cannot pursue this in this article. However, it should be noted that the absence of clear references one way or another leaves room for interpretive explorations in more than one way.

Managing the House

If an obvious hierarchy is seen as present here, with the ἐπίσκοπος in the key leadership role, this is based on a combined reading of the description of this role in 3:1–7and the reference to the οἶκος θεοῦ in 3:15.[33] Thus Andrew Clarke maintains that "The overseer has been the most neglected of the offices in Pauline studies, and yet it emerges that this is the essential post of leadership in all communities . . . the essential requirement that an overseer is able to 'manage his household' is precisely because this is a fundamental element of the job description —and not merely evidence of the potential overseer's character."[34] It has further been argued that the characteristics required of ἐπίοσκοποι and διάκονοι in conjunction with the reference in 1 Tim 3:15–16 of the assembly as the house of God is evidence for the accommodation of the church to the Graeco-Roman household structure, even to Roman imperial family values, as, for example, Jouette Bassler emphasizes "when the author conceptualizes the social structure of the church as

---

32. Aageson, *Paul, the Pastoral Epistles*, 21–22; Clarke, *Pauline Theology of Church Leadership*, 87–88.

33. Thus I. H. Marshall maintains, "The conceptual link between church and household is clear in v. 5; the church/household analogy is not in itself an innovation . . . but new ground is broken in developing the implications of the analogy into a concept of leadership" (*Pastoral Epistles*, 480); also Clarke, *Pauline Theology of Church Leadership*, 137.

34. Clarke, *Pauline Theology of Church Leadership*, 185.

household, he is following a familiar pattern, for Greek and Roman philosophers viewed the family as the microcosm of the empire."[35]

There can be no doubt that the "house" meaning the "family" is the most important social unit of societies in antiquity.[36] But it needs to be noted that this not only applied to the Roman empire but to societies in antiquity and beyond in general. To emphasize the importance of this unit and to present certain values and characteristics of good "management" of the "house" as of relevance beyond the "house" is neither unique to Graeco-Roman societies nor is it exceptional as such.[37] To refer to it as an organisational unit meant to refer to the most important and widespread social structure known by the addressee/s. It is not *per se* a reference to Roman imperial values despite the fact that the "house" and family values as the key to the stability of the Empire were promoted in a particular way in support of imperial ideology since Augustus' ascent to power. They could only become an instrument of imperial power because all groups in the realm of the empire recognized their importance without any doubt. The construction of an ideology which required loyalty to the empire in the form of loyalty to the house of the emperor and the house deities associated with him was built on the strength of this omnipresent "institution" in societies subjugated by Roman power. This was done in a particular way with the emperor as the *pater patriae*—the Father of the House of the Roman Empire who guarded over the loyalty/πίστις of the members of the house and through his own piety/εὐσέβεια to the ancestral gods guaranteed the success of the "house," that is, the domination of the imperial house/Rome over the "nations."[38]

That this common social unit was used as an instrument in support of Roman imperial ideology and power cannot be doubted. Whether this renders this unit inherently and necessarily an instrument of imperial domination is another question. In my view the two aspects are frequently not dealt with separately and it is assumed that wherever reference to the "house," "household" or family values and

---

35. Bassler, *1 Timothy, 2 Timothy, Titus*, 73.

36. Cf., e.g., Osiek and Balch, *Families in the New Testament World*.

37. Cf. references to the house of Jacob (Isa 2:5; 48:1), the house of David (2 Sam 7:16), etc.

38. Cf. Lacey, *Augustus and the Principate*, 169–89; also Elliott, *Arrogance of Nations*, 122–35.

structures are made this must be an indication for the introduction of, or accommodation to, Roman imperial domination structures.[39] Without a critical review of the evidence it cannot be assumed that the references to "houses" in the Pauline tradition are universally accountable for replicating and stabilizing the imperial order of domination. And although the structure of the "house" or "family" was patriarchal throughout this did not inherently hinder women from playing a significant and by no means subservient role in the "house," this being a "women's place,"[40] the place where power was exercised by women as e.g. the term οἰκοδεσποτεῖν (1 Tim 5:14) indicates. What I wish to challenge here is the assumption that the reference to τοῦ ἰδίου οἴκου προϊστάμενον (manage one's own house) provides explicit or implicit evidence for the accommodation to Roman imperial family ideology in the early Christ-movement. In addition to the noted general importance of the "house"/family in societies in antiquity I should like to highlight some further aspects on which my challenge is based. It has been noted that the characteristics which render someone a candidate either for the episcopate or as a διάκονος are for the most part "virtues lauded in the Greco-Roman world";[41] they represent "the ideal of moderation promoted broadly in Greco-Roman moral teaching."[42] Bassler also notes the absence of certain aspects she seems to expect to be mentioned in these lists "There is no theological grounding of these positions, no list of duties associated with them . . . no spiritual requirements for them."[43] This may be not so surprising if it is taken into account that inherent to the "house" as the most important social unit was its role as a worshipping group. "The oikos/domus was a center of worship with its male head (kyrios/pater familias) as head of the unit, the wife (kyria/mater familias) also playing an important role."[44] Thus

39. Cf., e.g., Fatum, "Christ Domesticated."

40. Cf. MacDonald and Osiek, who maintain, "This constant theme tells us that, in spite of a veneer of male supervision in the household, it was really a system run by women. The household was women's space" (*A Woman's Place*, 152).

41. Bassler, *1 Timothy, 2 Timothy, Titus*, 63, cf. also Söding, "1 Timotheus 3," 77–79.

42. Bassler, *1 Timothy, 2 Timothy, Titus*, 67.

43. Ibid., 71

44. Osiek and Balch, *Families in the New Testament World*, 82; cf. also ibid., 83: "Everyone in the familia belonged to the family cult, including children and slaves, and in the Roman religion the whole household gathered daily to invoke the protection of its special deities and ancestors."

the "religious" dimension was an inherent part of the "house" and there seemed to be no necessity to mention any special aspect in relation to this. However, there is something more remarkably absent from the list, that is, noble birth, wealth, power and education, the characteristics expected from a leader of the Roman elite![45]

If the intention of this list were to introduce Roman imperial values of domination into the assemblies of God it would be strange not to find the most important expectations of a leader according to this ideology mentioned.[46] This in my view is an indication that what is intended here is not accommodation to the Roman imperial ideology and domination system but something else. In addition, the reference to the admonition in 2:2 to pray for "kings and all in high positions, that we may lead a quiet and peaceable life" has been perceived to support the argument for accommodation as being the driving issue in 1 Timothy. However, from the perspective of a tiny minority group at the margins and threatened if not by open persecution, nevertheless regarded with suspicion and in danger of being accused of disloyalty at any moment in time, this admonition rather than being an indication for accommodation to imperial values can be seen as a mere survival strategy. It is a possible strategy of minority groups when open resistance and rebellion would merely lead to destruction and bloodshed. [47]

The focus on the "house" as a reference to Roman family ideology and thus issues of hierarchical structures within the "church" in my view misses a decisive point made in this passage in the context of the letter as a whole. As mentioned above the introduction of an hierarchical structure and thus accommodation to Roman imperial leadership values cannot be the purpose of the letter as evidence for hierarchical structures can already be found in the undisputed Pauline letters.[48]

---

45. Bartchy, "When I am Weak I am Strong," 54–55, also Ehrensperger, *Paul and the Dynamics of Power*, 114–16.

46. Clarke notes the absence of certain titles (such as ἄρχων, ἀρχηγός, ἡγούμενος) but does not draw conclusions with regard to the potential political implications, cf. *Pauline Theology of Church Leadership*, 75–76.

47. Cf. Kar-Yong Lim, "Reading Romans 13:1–7 with Multiple Lenses," Also Herzer, "Rearranging the House of God," 556–68 although he does not see the political implications of this.

48. Cf also Herzer, "Rearranging the House of God," 559.

Striving for Office and the Exercise of Power in the "House of God"

Ὀικος Θεοῦ

There is this specific focus on the "house" in this passage, but rather than paying special attention to the Graeco-Roman "house" it is a focus on the "house of God" which is further characterized as "the assembly of the living God," followed by a piece of early hymnic Christ tradition. The significance of this subscript has been noted by Bassler among others: "This brief passage contains two of the most significant theological passages in this letter: the description of the church and the fragmentary Christian hymn."[49] However, Bassler does not attest any significance to this in conjunction with the references to the leadership functions in the immediate context of the passage, and any particular significance to the term "the living God" is dismissed as being irrelevant here.[50]

Jens Herzer and Thomas Söding in two recent articles attribute high theological significance to 1 Tim 3:15–16 as the decisive part for understanding of 1 Timothy 3,(which possibly begins even earlier with chapter 2:1).[51] Söding maintains that the key aspect in 3:15–16 is the emphasis on the "house of God" understood as a reference to the temple. The author of 1 Timothy thus not only applies the term metaphorically to the ἐκκλησία but in Söding's view actually perceives the ἐκκλησία as being the temple of God. In claiming that what is found here is a distinction between the profane (the actual household of 3:4–5) and the sacred, he emphasizes that what is in view in this passage is not the individual congregation but the church as a whole, the una sancta. As such the ἐκκλησία is the temple of the living God and as such represents the divine presence in the world. This temple ecclesiology is perceived as being present throughout the Corpus Paulinum.[52] In arguing for such an exclusive identity between the ἐκκλησία and the presence of God, there can hardly be an room for the Jerusalem temple which moves this interpretation close to a replacement ecclesiology.[53]

---

49. Bassler, *1 Timothy, 2 Timothy, Titus*, 77.

50. Ibid., 74.

51. I. H.Marshall has emphasized the significance of this passage as follows: "The theology of the church given in 3.15 is central to the instruction of the letter ... In connection with vv. 14 and 16, it indicates that what has been said in the letter is in effect an instruction about the behaviour in the house of God." *Pastorals*, 498.

52. Söding, "1 Timothy 3," 80

53. As is evident in the explanatory note 70 (p.82) in Söding's article. Donfried also

Herzer more cautiously maintains that "with regard to the semantic field . . . οἶκος θεοῦ primarily evokes the idea of the congregation as God's temple."⁵⁴ I have some reservations against an interpretation which perceives this reference as invoking God's temple as directly as Söding, and to some extent also Herzer imply, but I agree that the focus of the passage is on the presence of God in this "house," and among this "assembly."⁵⁵ The reference to the ἐκκλησία as "temple of God" in 2 Cor 6:16 is already evidence of a metaphorical use of the temple image in relation to the ἐκκλησία in the undisputed Pauline epistles; but rather than being an implicit criticism of the Jerusalem temple this metaphor only makes sense when a positive appreciation of the temple is associated with it.⁵⁶ It is worth noting that the temple in the Corinthian passage is characterized as the "temple of the living God," the same characterization found in 1 Tim 3:15 for the ἐκκλησία. The context of the Corinthian passage makes it clear that to be part of an assembly of the "living God" requires the active dissociation of the members from certain practices of the Graeco-Roman society they live in. In view of this I share to some extent Herzer's doubt "that the lexeme οἶκος θεοῦ in this particular context functions as a metaphor of the community structured according to ancient household codes and that in the semantic framework the common translation of οἶκος as "household" is appropriate at all."⁵⁷ However, both Söding and Herzer consider the significance of this passage to lie in the clear distinction it draws between the profane and the religious or sacred realm. This is a significant insight but at the same time a rather narrow perception of the passage, and it raises the question whether such a distinction actually can be claimed for the period in question given the fact that the "house" was a

---

argues that "There is sufficient linguistic evidence in the Pauline letters to suggest that Paul viewed his communities as being replacements for the Temple . . ." and claims that this is "the emphasis in 1 Timothy as well." See "Rethinking," 177.

54. Herzer, "Rearranging the House of God," 560

55. Cf. the convincing references to "house of God" as temple in Söding, "1 Timothy 3," 81n64.

56. Thus I cannot see any "new temple" image used here by the author nor any indication that the temple image which is invoked refers to a new dwelling place of God which would replace the "old" temple. There is no old/new terminology inherent in this passage.

57. Herzer, "Rearranging the House of God," 559.

social as well as a "religious" unit.⁵⁸ Thus to draw a distinction between the two aspects according to the parameters proposed by Herzer and Söding is problematic in my view. However, their caution against the assumption that οἶκος here primarily invokes the household structures of Graeco-Roman society is commendable. It draws attention to the fact that this house is referred to as οἶκος θεοῦ.

The two aspects present in this passage, the "house" as the fundamental social unit of society and the "house of God" as a metaphor for the ἐκκλησία of the living God indicate that there is something going on here which could possibly be described as a process of negotiation between accommodation and resistance. ⁵⁹ Mary Rose d'Angelo has argued that the distinction between accommodation to the dominating ideological discourse and social structures and dissociation from, or resistance to, these are "mutually dependent reactions"⁶⁰. As mentioned above, the fundamental significance of the social unit of the "house," that is, the "family" throughout societies in antiquity and the "family values campaigns mounted by successive emperors from Augustus to Hadrian"⁶¹ cannot be entirely irrelevant with regard to 1 Timothy 3. Thus the emphasis on leadership characteristics which conform to Graeco-Roman values could be seen as an accommodating move within the Christ-movement, although I doubt that it actually introduces something entirely new to the movement. But to see this as *the* emphasis of the passage actually misses the point which the author makes here in my view. The subscription vv.14–16 explicitly states the purpose of the passage and in my view clearly indicates its key focus—the admonitions (which I think start actually in 2:1ff.) provide guidance for the life of "the assembly of the living God" which is actually the "house of God."⁶² They provide guidance for life in the realm of the presence of God. Clearly this is not any kind of "house" in Graeco-Roman society, despite some shared features with such a "house," this is actually the "house of God." The fact that subsequent interpretation and its impact in the history of the church emphasized the aspect of accommodation according to Graeco-Roman household codes and thus contributed,

---

58. Cf. n. 45 above.
59. D'Angelo, "Roman Imperial Family Values," 163.
60. Ibid., 164
61. Ibid., 162; also Glancy, "Protocols of Masculinity," 240.
62. Marshall noted this as the key emphasis here as well, cf. *Pastoral Epistles*, 508.

as some scholars have argued to the "domestication of faith in Christ," cannot mean that an alternative reading is not viable, more likely even closer to the historical context. The least that can be asserted is that there is a tension between the more accommodating admonitions and the urge to lead a "quiet and peaceable life" (2:2) and the emphasis on this "house" as the "house of God" followed by a creedal hymn which in no uncertain terms talks of the Epiphany and the justification of someone other than any of the deities or rulers of the Empire. The implicit contrast between this "house" and the "house of Caesar" present in the public representation of Roman rule can hardly be incidental.[63] This is the "house" not of Caesar or any other power or authority but solely and exclusively the house of God—who is further characterized as the 'living God'. In the context of imperial ideology which presented the Emperor as the *pater patriae* and thus implied that the empire was a "house"/family with the emperor as the *pater familias*, who required loyalty and *pietas* to himself and the deities of the empire[64], this establishes a loyalty claim which constitutes not an open but nevertheless a hidden form of resistance.[65]

The peculiar term "living God" supports the drive of this argument in that it has been demonstrated that this term specifically occurs in scriptural contexts where a distinction or contrast between the "living God" of Israel and other deities/idols is made.[66] This is noted by Bassler, but dismissed as not significant here and Goodwin, although working out the significance of the concept, considers it only relevant for missionary purposes. The key element of the alternative claim of power, which actually constitutes a hidden transcript of resistance is not in view in Goodwin's monograph.[67] But he clearly notes that the term is used as a marker in the Scriptures to distinguish the God of Israel from other deities which are thus characterized as dead.[68] If it is taken into account that in the passage which immediately follows 1 Tim 3:15–16

---

63. N. Elliott makes this claim with regard to Romans—the application of his insights in the *Arrogance of Nations* has informed my reading of 1 Timothy; cf. 72.

64. D'Angelo, "Roman Imperial Family Values" 142.

65. Scott, *Domination and the Art of Resistance*.

66. I am indebted here to my PhD student Edward Pillar, who has alerted me to the significance of the term in 1 Thess 1:9b.

67. Goodwin, *Paul: Apostle of the Living God*, 204–6.

68. For references, see ibid., 3–5.

the danger of "departing from faith" is addressed the emphasis on the ἐκκλησία as the "ἐκκλησία of the living God" again is hardly incidental.

The passage concluding the guidance on how to live as the ἐκκλησία of the living God (vv.15–16) can be seen as evidence that 1 Timothy 3 is an attempt to negotiate life in the Christ-movement in the "shadow of empire" by arguing for the necessity to try to live in peace as a means to survive in a more or less hostile environment but at the same time to emphasize that this does not mean that the loyalty of this group should be directed to the parameters of the dominating ideology of this society. To keep the peace is a means of protection but not at the expense of accommodation. The hidden transcript of resistance is inscribed into the seemingly accommodating sections in no uncertain terms. And the primary loyalty and parameters of orientation are set in clear distinction from the "powers of this world." The piety/εὐσεβεία owed to the empire in the form of *pietas*/εὐσεβεία devoted to the emperor who was presented as the personification of true piety to the deities of Rome was all prevailing in the empire.[69] The reference to τῆς εὐσεβείας μυστήριον in v16 maintains that the loyalty of this "assembly of the living God" is to the one confessed in the subsequent hymn, one who was ἐδικαιώθη ἐν πνεύματι, that is, vindicated, which implies that he had suffered a previous act of injustice against him. From the perspective of imperial ideology and practice these "assemblies of the living God" were impious/ἀσέβεια. However, through the consistent emphasis on true εὐσέβεια/*pietas* throughout the letter the author insists that the implicit refusal to devote *pietas*/εὐσεβεία to the Emperor, does not mean that these assemblies are ἀσεβεια but to the contrary they are truly pious/εὐσεβής in their exclusive loyalty to the "living God."

Conclusion

It has been demonstrated that although the passage 1 Timothy 3 does build on the significance of the "house" in societies in antiquity, and resonates with the "family values" campaigns of successive emperors, this does not provide evidence for the introduction of hierarchical structures into the Christ-movement as such are already evident in the undisputed Pauline letters. Thus the emphasis of the passage cannot be

---

69. Cf. Elliott, *Arrogance of Nations*, 121–28.

on accommodation to the Graeco-Roman ideology as has often been claimed, nor is it evidence for the institutionalization of a previously charismatic movement. The key to the purpose of the passage is seen in vv. 14–16 which clarify that the "house" for which some guidance concerning the choice of leaders is given in vv. 1–13 is the house which owes piety/εὐσέβεια not to the emperor but to the "living God." To strive for office or be prepared to serve in a leadership role and exercise power in this movement does not inherently imply to strive for honour and office as understood among the Roman elite of the time. Rather shaping leadership roles in accordance with ideal leaders of the dominating society the paradigm for leaders in this movement would come from Jewish scriptural tradition and earliest Jesus traditions. Paul's reference to the gentleness and humbleness of Christ in 2 Cor 10:1 seems to be early Jesus tradition and is probably an indication for the presence of such a paradigm in the early Christ movement.[70] Read in light of the hymn in v. 16, the reference to the danger of departure from faith in 4:1, and the hope to live a life in peace and quiet (2:2), 1 Tim 3:1–16 appears to be a hidden transcript of resistance to the dominating powers rather than a call to accommodate to the ideology of the empire. Read in this vein the passage 1 Tim 3:1–16 provides insight into the attempt of early Christ-followers to negotiate their life as participation in Christ[71] "in the shadow of the empire" between accommodation and resistance.

---

70. See also my *Paul and the Dynamics of Power*, 111–14 and 187–91.
71. Cf. Campbell, "Covenantal Nomism and Participation in Christ."

BIBLIOGRAPHY

Aageson, James W. *Paul, the Pastoral Epistles, and the Early Church*. Library of Pauline Studies. Peabody, MA: Hendrickson, 2008.

Ascough, Richard S. "Voluntary Associations and the Formation of Pauline Christian Communities: Overcoming Objections." In *Vereine, Synagogen und Gemeinden im kaiserzeitlichen Kleinasien*, edited by A. Gutsfeld and D.-A. Koch editors, 146–83. Studien und Texte zu Antike und Christentum 25. Tübingen: Mohr/Siebeck, 2006.

Balch, David L. "Paul, Families, and Households." In *Paul in the Greco-Roman World: A Handbook*, edited by J. Paul Sampley, 258–92. Harrisburg, PA: Trinity, 2003.

Bartchy, S. Scott. "'When I Am Weak I Am Strong': A Pauline Paradox in Cultural Context." In *Kontexte der Schrift*. Vol. 2, *Kultur, Politik, Religion, Sprache, Text. Wolfgang Stegemann zum 60. Geburtstag*, edited by Christian Strecker, 49–60. Stuttgart: Kohlhammer, 2005.

Bassler, Jouette M. *1 Timothy, 2 Timothy, Titus*. Abingdon New Testament Commentaries. Nashville: Abingdon, 1996.

Campbell, William S. "Covenantal Nomism and Participation in Christ: Pauline Perspectives on Transformation." In *New Perspectives on Paul and the Jews*, edited by R. Bieringer and D. Pollefeyt. Leuven: Peeters, forthcoming.

Clarke, Andrew, *A Pauline Theology of Church Leadership*. LNTS 362. London: T. & T. Clark, 2008

Corley, Kathleen C. *Maranatha: Women's Funerary Rituals and Christian Origins*. Minneapolis: Fortress, 2010.

Davies, Margaret, *The Pastoral Epistles*. New Testament Guides. Sheffield: Sheffield Academic, 1996.

D'Angelo, Mary Rose, "'Knowing How to Preside over His Own Household': Imperial Masculinity and Christian Asceticism in the Pastorals, *Hermas*, and Luke-Acts." In *Semeia 45: New Testament Masculinities*, edited by Stephen D. Moore and Janice C. Anderson, 265–95. Atlanta: SBL 2003.

D'Angelo, Mary Rose. "Roman Imperial Family Values and the Sexual Politics of 4 Maccabees and the Pastorals." *BibInt* 11 (2003) 139–65.

Derrida, Jacques. *Negotiations: Interventions and Interviews 1971–2000*. Edited, translated, with an introduction by Elizabeth Rottenberg Cultural Memory in the Present. Stanford: Stanford University Press, 2002.

Donfried, Karl P., editor. *1 Timothy Reconsidered*. Monographische Reihe von "Benedictina." Biblisch-Ökumenische Abteilung 18. Leuven: Peeters, 2008.

———. "Rethinking Scholarly Approaches to 1 Timothy." In *1 Timothy Reconsidered*, edited by Karl P. Donfried, 153–82. Monographische Reihe von "Benedictina." Biblisch-Ökumenische Abteilung 18. Leuven: Peeters, 2008.

Ehrensperger, Kathy. *Paul and the Dynamics of Power: Communication and Interaction in the Early Christ-Movement*. Library of New Testament Studies 325. London: T. & T. Clark, 2008.

Elliott, Neil. *The Arrogance of Nations: Reading Romans in the Shadow of Empire*. Paul in Critical Contexts. Minneapolis: Fortress, 2008.

Fatum, Lone, "Christ Domesticated: The Household Theology of the Pastorals as Political Strategy." In *The Formation of the Early Church*, edited by J. Adna, 175–207. WUNT 183. Tübingen: Mohr/Siebeck, 2005.

Glancy, Jennifer. "Protocols of Masculinity in the Pastoral Epistles." In *Semeia* 45: *New Testament Masculinities*, edited by Moore Steven D. Anderson Janice C. Anderson, 235–64. Atlanta: Society of Biblical Literature, 2003.

Goodwin, Mark J. "The Pauline Background of the Living God as Interpretive Context for 1 Timothy 4.10." *JSNT* 61 (1996) 65–85.

———. *Paul, Apostle of the Living God: Kerygma and Conversion in 2 Corinthians*. Harrisburg, PA: Trinity, 2001.

Herzer, Jens, "Rearranging the 'House of God: A New Perspective on the Pastoral Epistles." In *Empsychoi Logoi: Religious Innovations in Antiquity; Studies in Honour of Pieter Willem van der Horst*, edited by Alberdina Houtman et al., 547–66. Ancient Judaism and Early Christianity. Leiden: Brill, 2008.

Horrell, David. "From αδελφοί to οικος θεοῦ: Social Transformation in Pauline Christianity." *JBL* 20 (2001) 293–311.

Johnson, E. Elizabeth. "Life Together in the Household of God." In *Shaking Heaven and Earth: Essays on Honor of Walter Brueggemann and Charles B. Cousar*, edited by Christine Roy Yoder, 89–103. Louisville: Westminster John Knox, 2005.

Käsemann, Ernst. "Ministry and Community in the New Testament." In *Essays on New Testament Themes*, 63–94. Translated by W. J. Montague. SBT 1/41. London: SCM, 1964.

Lacey, W. K. *Augustus and the Principate: The Evolution of a System*. ARCA, Classical and Medieval Texts, Papers, and Monographs 35. Leeds: Cairns, 1996.

Lim, Kar-Yong. "Reading Romans 13:1–7 with Multiple Lenses: Some Reflections from a Mulit-Faith Context with Malaysia as a Test Case." A paper presented at the SBL International Meeting, Rome 2009.

MacDonald, Margaret Y. *The Pauline Churches: A Socio-historical Study of Institutionalization in the Pauline and Deutero-Pauline Writings*. SNTSMS 60. Cambridge: Cambridge University Press, 1988.

Marshall, I. Howard. *A Critical and Exegetical Commentary on the Pastoral Epistles*. International Critical Commentary. Edinburgh: T. & T. Clark, 1999.

Meeks, Wayne A. "Introduction to the Westminster John Knox Edition." In *Paul and the Anatomy of Apostolic Authority*, by John H. Schütz, xiii–xxiv. Westminster John Knox, 2007.

Osiek, Carolyn, and David L. Balch. *Families in the New Testament World: Households and House Churches*. Family, Religion, and Culture. Louisville: Westminster John Knox, 1997.

Osiek, Carolyn, and Margaret Y. MacDonald, with Janet H. Tulloch. *A Woman's Place: House Churches in Earliest Christianity*. Minneapolis: Fortress, 2006.

Schlier, Heinrich. "Die Ordnung der Kirche nach den Pastoralbriefen." In *Die Zeit der Kirche: Exegetische Aufsätze und Vorträge*, 129–47. Freiburg: Herder, 1968.

Schottroff, Luise. *Lydia's Impatient Sisters: A Feminist Social History of Early Christianity*. Translated by Barbara and Martin Rumscheidt. Louisville: Westminster John Knox, 1995.

Schussler Fiorenza, Elisabeth. *In Memory of Her: A Feminist Theological Reconstruction of Christian Origins*. New York: Crossroad, 1983.

Schütz, John H. *Paul and the Anatomy of Apostolic Authority*. Louisville: Westminster John Knox, 2007.

Schweizer, Eduard. *Church Order in the New Testament*. Translated by Frank Clark. SBT 1/32. London: SCM, 1961.

Scott, James C. *Domination and the Arts of Resistance: Hidden Transcripts.* New Haven: Yale University Press, 1990.
Söding, Thomas. "1 Timotheus 3: Der Episkopos und die Diakone in der Kirche." In *1 Timothy Reconsidered*, edited by Karl P. Donfried, 63–86. Monographische Reihe von "Benedictina." Biblisch-Ökumenische Abteilung 18. Leuven: Peeters, 2008.
Towner, Philip H. *The Goal of Our Instruction: The Structure of Theology and Ethics in the Pastoral Epistles.* JSNTSup 34. Sheffield: JSOT Press, 1989.
VanderKam, James C. *The Book of Jubilees.* Guides to Apocrypha and Psuedepigrapha. Sheffield: Sheffield Academic, 2001.
Weber Max. *Economy and Society: An Outline of Interpretative Sociology.* Vol. 1. Edited by Guenther Roth and Claus Wittich. New York: Bedminster, 1968.

7

On Serving Two Masters[1]

Owen E. Evans

Exactly fifty years ago I was an accepted candidate for the Methodist ministry waiting to be allocated to one of the connexional theological colleges for training. I had expressed a preference for Hartley Victoria College in Manchester,[2] where it would be possible to take a degree course in the Faculty of Theology at Manchester University.[3] There were

1. A paper delivered under the auspices of the Centre for the Study of British Christian Thought, The United Theological College, Aberystwyth, on 1 March 1996. The original manuscript is among the Owen E. Evans papers at the National Library of Wales. It is reproduced here by kind permission of Llyfrgell Genedlaethol Cymru/ The National Library of Wales. At the author's request the notes have been supplied by the editor.

2. In the wake of the Methodist union of 1932, Hartley College (Primitive Methodist, 1881) amalgamated with Victoria Park College (United Methodist, 1871) in 1934 to form Hartley Victoria College. See W. Bardsley Brash, *The Story of Our Colleges 1835–1935* (London: Epworth, 1935), chs. 11, 12; *Hartley Victoria Methodist College: The First Hundred* Years (Manchester: published by the College, 1981); Geoffrey E. Milburn, *A School for the Prophets. The Origins of Ministerial Education in the Primitive Methodist Church. Published to Mark the Centenary 1881–1981 of Hartley Victoria College, Manchester* (Manchester: published by the College, 1982).

3. The Faculty of Theology at Manchester was founded in 1904, and from the outset professors of the local theological colleges were involved in its teaching and organization. See T. W. Manson et al., *Manchester University: Faculty of Theology. Theological Essays in Commemoration of the Jubilee* (Manchester: Manchester University Press,

several reasons for my opting for Manchester, but not the least of them was my awareness that the Faculty there boasted among its staff two of the most distinguished of contemporary biblical scholars, namely, Professors H. H. Rowley[4] and T. W. Manson.[5]

As things turned out, the Methodist Ministerial Training Department decided, for perfectly genuine reasons which need not concern us here, to send me to Wesley College, Headingley, Leeds — on the other side of the Pennines from Manchester.[6] Though disappointed at being denied the college of my choice, I consented without demur and comforted myself with the thought that Headingley College also boasted among its staff two very distinguished biblical scholars in Drs. Vincent Taylor[7] and Norman Snaith.[8] So it was to Leeds that I made my way in September 1946, confident in the knowledge that, though deprived of the chance to sit at the feet of Rowley and Manson, my education in the languages and contents of the Bible as a whole would nevertheless be in expert hands, those of Snaith and Taylor.

1954); David A. Pailin, ed., *University of Manchester Faculty of Theology. Seventy-fifth Anniversary Papers 1979* (Manchester: published by the Faculty, 1980).

4. For the Baptist, Rowley (1890-1969), see ODNB; R. E. Clements, "The Biblical Scholarship of H. H. Rowley (1890-1969)," *Baptist Quarterly* 38.2 (1999) 70-82; D. E. Gowan, "Harold Henry Rowley," in Donald K. McKim, ed., *Dictionary of Major Biblical Interpreters* (Downers Grove, IL: IVP, 2007), 877-80.

5. For the Presbyterian, Manson (1893-1958), see ODNB; Matthew Black, "Theologians of our time: Thomas Walter Manson," *Expository Times* 75.7 (1964) 208-11; R. P. Martin and M. W. Linder, "Thomas Walter Manson," in D. K. McKim, *Dictionary*, 699-702; Morna D. Hooker, "T. W. Manson and the twentieth-century search for Jesus," in Timothy Larsen, ed., *Biblical Scholarship in the Twentieth Century: The Rylands Chair of Biblical Criticism and Exegesis at the University of Manchester, 1904-1994*, being the *Bulletin of the John Rylands University Library of Manchester* 86.3 (2004) 77-98.

6. For Headingley College (1868-1967) see W. B. Brash, *The Story of Our Colleges*, ch. 7; Kenneth B. Garlick, "The Headingley branch of the Wesleyan Theological Institution," *Proceedings of the Wesley Historical Society*, XXXVIII pt. 1, May 1971, pp. 16-20; A. Raymond George, "Ministerial training at Headingley," in *Preachers All. Essays to Celebrate the Silver Jubilee of the Yorkshire Branch of the Wesley Historical Society* (published by the Yorkshire Branch, 1987), 1-10.

7. For Taylor (1887-1968) see ODNB; Owen E. Evans, "Theologians of our time: Vincent Taylor," *Expository Times* 75.6, (1964) 164-68; R. Brawley, "Vincent Taylor" in McKim, ed., *Dictionary*, 960-63.

8. For Snaith (1898-1982) see R. E. Clements, "Norman Henry Snaith," in McKim, ed., *Dictionary*, 929-33.

Little did I dream, however, as I entered Headingley College in September 1946, that exactly seven years later, in September 1953, I should arrive in Manchester to take up an appointment as Tutor in New Testament Language and Literature at the very college which earlier I had hoped to enter as a student, and to begin an association with the University Faculty in which I had hoped to sit at the feet of Rowley and Manson—an association, indeed, which would bring me into a close relationship with those very scholars, not as a student but as a very junior colleague. And so, in due course, and by a circuitous route, the ambition which I had cherished in 1946 was *more* than amply fulfilled.

Moreover, the more I recall the experiences of those early years of my career as a student and teacher of the New Testament, the more convinced I become that it was precisely *because* I was led to Leeds rather than to Manchester in 1946 that the ambition which seemed at that time to have been frustrated was eventually fulfilled in such fuller measure than I could ever have imagined to be possible. For it was in fact entirely due to Vincent Taylor, the mentor and master to whom unexpectedly I became discipled in 1946, that my ministerial career developed in a way that I had never intended or anticipated that it would, with the result that within a few short years I was privileged to become discipled to the second of the two mentors and masters who are the subject of this talk.

By any reckoning Vincent Taylor and T. W. Manson must be included in the Premier League (so to speak) of twentieth-century British—and, indeed, *world*—New Testament scholars. They were, roughly speaking, contemporaries, Manson being born some six years later than Taylor and predeceasing him by some ten years. In background and temperament they were strikingly different. Nevertheless they had a great deal in common as regards their understanding of their ministerial and scholarly vocations, as regards the scholarly methods which they practised, and as regards the conclusions to which their studies led them concerning some of the most burning issues of contemporary New Testament scholarship. They were both products of the liberal school of biblical scholarship, believing that the biblical documents, like all works of literature, must be subjected to the most honest and searching criticism (both "higher" and "lower"). Neither, however, succumbed to the more radical tendencies which had already become fashionable in their own day, especially in Germany, and which have since their day become even more widely fashionable. From the point of view of such radicalism, Taylor and Manson, for all their liberalism, would no doubt be regarded as conservatives. They themselves would—justifiably to my mind—regard themselves as representatives of a sane and balanced middle-of-the-road position.

Taylor and Manson both came to New Testament scholarship by way of an early vocation to the Christian ministry, and it is true of each of them that the scholarly eminence they achieved never obscured their primary vocation as ministers of the Gospel. Their respective careers, however—as I have already hinted—developed in very different ways, as the following "potted biographies" will show.

Vincent Taylor was a Lancastrian born and bred. At Accrington Grammar School he gained the matriculation of the Northern Universities and became a pupil teacher. But, having been brought up in a devout Wesleyan Methodist home, the son of a lay preacher, his heart was set on becoming a minister, and having been accepted as a candidate at the age of nineteen in 1906 he was sent to Richmond College, London, for training.[9] London University did not recognize the Northern matriculation, so in addition to his theological studies he prepared for and passed the London matriculation examination in order to qualify for the London BD course. This meant that when he left college after three years he had advanced, so far as academic honours were concerned, no further than the Intermediate BD examination, less than half a degree. But he was determined to succeed academically and continued to study for the Final BD as an external student, whilst serving as a full-time Methodist circuit minister. He gained the BD after two years, in 1911, but at no small cost to himself, for he suffered a serious breakdown in health, entailing a period of six months in a sanatorium. I never heard him talk about that anxious period, but his wife (who was his fiancée at the time, and had been so ever since they were pupil teachers together in Lancashire) told me more than once that he had assured her that he *would* get well again because he knew God had work for him to do which no one else could do. That reminds me of a story that used to be handed down from one generation of students to another at Headingley, that when V. T.'s turn came to preach in College Chapel as a student at Richmond he had taken as his text the words

---

9. For Richmond College (1843–1972) see W. B. Brash, *The Story of Our Colleges*, ch. 5; E. S. Waterhouse, *Richmond College 1843–1943* (London: Epworth, 1943).

of John 16:12, "I have yet many things to say unto you, but you cannot bear them now." Whatever his hopes for the future, and whatever ambitions he may have cherished, he could hardly have imagined at that time, and certainly none of his hearers could have realised, how prophetically applicable to the preacher himself those words would in due course prove to be!

The young minister did recover and, resumed his studies as a part-time external student of London University. Without in any way neglecting his ministerial duties at Mansfield, Carmarthen and Bath respectively, he gained in turn the BD Honours (then a specialised post-graduate degree equivalent to the later MTh), then in 1920 the PhD, and finally the DD in 1926. Moreover, his doctoral theses, the PhD on *The Historical Evidence for the Virgin Birth* (1920), and the DD on *Behind the Third Gospel: A Study of the Proto-Luke Hypothesis* (1926), were both immediately published by no less prestigious a Press than that of Oxford University, and quickly became recognized as contributions of first importance on their respective subjects. Thus Vincent Taylor, without the benefits of a University education or the opportunity to enjoy years of leisurely full-time study in an academic environment, had before reaching his fortieth birthday established himself as a leading scholar—and to a very large extent a self-made scholar—in the field of New Testament studies. Thereafter his fame spread and further works of outstanding importance and influence continued to flow steadily from his pen for the remaining forty years of his life, especially during the twenty-three years (from 1930 to his retirement in 1953) of his association with Wesley College, Headingley, as Professor of New Testament Language and Literature and (for all but the first six of those years) Principal and Resident Tutor—offices which made considerable inroads into the time that was available for private study and research. The outstanding distinction of his contributions to scholarship was recognized by Honorary DDs from the Universities of Leeds, Glasgow and Dublin, by the Fellowship of the British Academy, and by the award of that Academy's Burkitt Medal (the "Victoria Cross," so to speak, of biblical scholarship). The fact that he never occupied a distinguished University Chair of New Testament studies was not for want of opportunity. All attempts to entice him in that direction were resisted (though he did confide to me more than once that he had been sorely tempted to accept one or two offers) because of his conviction that he had been called to the ministry of the Methodist Church and that that was where his duty lay.

By contrast the academic career of Thomas Walter Manson was a much more normal and conventional one. If Taylor was a Lancastrian through and through, Manson was a "Geordie" of Scottish origin (his roots through both his parents were in fact in Shetland). Born in Tynemouth, Northumberland in 1893, Manson's brilliance as a student was recognized at the Tynemouth Municipal High School. Although he too (an interesting partial parallel with Vincent Taylor) acted for a brief period as a pupil teacher, he was always marked out for a university education as a preparation for entering the ministry of the Presbyterian Church of England. He went up to Glasgow University in 1912, but his studies there were interrupted by army service during the First World War. After the war he returned to Glasgow and completed his MA degree in 1919 with First Class Honours in Mental and Moral Philosophy, gaining both the Clark and Ferguson Scholarships, the latter of which was regarded as the blue ribbon of Scottish philosophical awards. From Glasgow Manson proceeded to Cambridge, to be trained for the ministry at Westminster College,[10] and at the same time to become a research student at Christ's College, where he gained the BA by thesis on a philosophical subject, then read for the Oriental Tripos, obtaining a First in Oriental Languages (Part II: Hebrew and Aramaic). He stayed on at Cambridge, as a tutor in Westminster College until 1925, continuing his research and picking up prestigious Scholarships and Prizes in Hebrew, Greek and Septuagintal studies. Only then, at the age of thirty-two, was he ordained and inducted to his first charge at Bethnal Green in East London. Thus, by contrast with Taylor, Manson had enjoyed some ten years of full-time University life in the academic environment first of Glasgow and then of Cambridge, sitting at the feet of several of the most eminent scholars of the period, and serving a valuable apprenticeship

---

10. John Oman was on the staff of Westminster College when Manson arrived there, and he became Principal in 1922. The College was strongly represented in biblical studies. John Skinner, the first Nonconformist to receive the DD of the University of Oxford, held the Chair of Old Testament Literature and Apologetics; Charles Archibald Anderson Scott, the first Nonconformist to gain the DLitt of the University of Cambridge, held the Chair of New Testament Language, Literature and Theology. For the College see W. A. L. Elmslie (who followed Skinner in the Old Testament Chair) *Westminster College Cambridge 1899-1949* (London: Presbyterian Church of England, [1949]).

as tutor and lecturer. On the other hand, like Taylor, he refused to forsake his vocation to the ministry and his loyalty of his Church. After a brief period in London he became minister of the Presbyterian Church at Falstone in his native Northumberland in 1926, and remained there until 1932, turning down invitations to a lectureship in Philosophy at St. Andrews and an assistant professorship in the Oriental Institute of the University of Chicago. Like Taylor, again, it was in the manse of an active and busy minister of the Gospel that Manson produced the work that made his name known throughout the world of New Testament studies. This was *The Teaching of Jesus: Studies of its Form and Content*, which in 1931 was published (as were Taylor's first two books) by the distinguished Press of one of the ancient Universities—in Manson's case, naturally enough, the Cambridge University Press. In 1932 his *alma mater*, the University of Glasgow, recognized the book's author by the award of its DLitt degree, and in the same year Manson was appointed Yates Professor of New Testament Greek and Exegesis, not in his own denomination's college at Cambridge, but at Mansfield College, Oxford, a Congregational foundation.[11] When C. H. Dodd,[12] his predecessor in that Chair, left Mansfield in 1932 to become Rylands Professor of Biblical Criticism and Exegesis at the University of Manchester, the Congregationalists had no scruples about adopting the method that would nowadays be termed "head hunting" in order to ensure the most suitable possible successor to Dodd, namely, the Presbyterian Manson. They could hardly have anticipated that within four short years the University authorities at Manchester would be playing the same trick on them, when Dodd's comparatively brief tenure of the Rylands Chair was cut short by his appointment to the Norris-Hulse Chair at Cambridge, and Manchester in 1936 called Manson from Mansfield to the Rylands Chair, which he filled with the same distinction as his illustrious predecessors A. S. Peake[13] and C. H. Dodd, until his untimely death in 1958.

11. For this College see Elaine Kaye, *Mansfield College, Oxford: Its Origin, History and Significance* (Oxford: Oxford University Press, 1996).

12. For Dodd (1884-1973) see ODNB; John Tudno Williams, "Aspects of the Life and Work of C. H. Dodd," *Transactions of the Honourable Society of* Cymmrodorion, 1974/1975, 215-42; F. W. Dillistone, *C. H. Dodd: Interpreter of the New Testament* (London: Hodder & Stoughton, 1977); James D. G. Dunn, "C. H. Dodd and New Testament Studies," in T. Larsen, ed., *Biblical Scholarship*, 55-75; D. A. Hagner, "Charles Harold Dodd," in McKim, ed., *Dictionary*, 378-83.

13. A. S. Peake (1865-1929) was the first Rylands Professor at Manchester

That two such famous centres of theological learning should both in quick succession have shown such a strong desire and determination to avail themselves of his services is ample proof of Manson's standing and reputation as a biblical scholar and teacher.

Although, unlike Taylor, Manson did allow himself the luxury of occupying a University Chair, his adherence to his primary vocation was never in any doubt. During the Second World War he added the pastoral charge of St Aidan's Presbyterian Church in Manchester to his university duties, and for ten years from 1944 onwards he served as President of the Manchester Free Church Council. Then in 1953–54 he served the whole of his denomination as Moderator of the General Assembly of the Presbyterian Church of England.

Manson, like Taylor, was the recipient of many outstanding academic honours. Two of the universities which conferred Honorary DDs on Vincent Taylor also honoured T. W. Manson in the same way: Glasgow and Dublin. Similar honours came to the latter from Cambridge, Durham, Strasbourg, and Halifax, Nova Scotia. Both scholars became Fellows of the British Academy, and both were awarded the Burkitt Medal for Biblical Studies. As a University Professor, Manson had more freedom than Taylor to accept invitations to lecture abroad and to participate in international conferences of biblical scholars. Consequently he was much more widely known in a personal sense (as distinct from knowledge by reason of reputation and from his writings) to the international community of scholars than was Taylor, who never crossed the Atlantic until after his retirement when, in 1955–56

(1904–1929). From 1892 he had taught at Hartley College, and from 1895 also at Lancashire Independent College, whence came two of his colleagues in the new University Faculty: W. F. Adeney, a mainstay of the Century Bible series of commentaries, and W. H. Bennett, the first President of the Society for Old Testament Study. Peake relinquished his college positions in 1912, continuing in his Chair until his death. For Peake see ODNB; Leslie S. Peake, *Arthur Samuel Peake. A Memoir* (London: Hodder and Stoughton, 1930); John T. Wilkinson [(1893–1980), who taught at Hartley Victoria College from 1946 to 1960, was Principal from 1953, and was one of the very few who have earned the rarely-awarded Manchester DD], *Arthur Samuel Peake. A Biography* (London: Epworth, 1971); T. Larsen, "A. S. Peake, the Free Churches and Modern Biblical Criticism," in T. Larsen, ed., *Biblical Scholarship*, 23–53; R. E. Clements, "Arthur Samuel Peake," in D. K. McKim, *Dictionary*, 801–4. For Adeney (1849–1920) see Alan P. F. Sell, *Hinterland Theology: A Stimulus to Theological Construction* (Milton Keynes: Paternoster, 2008), ch. 9 and passim; for Bennett (1855–1920) see ODNB. For Lancashire Independent College see Elaine Kaye, *For the Work of Ministry: A History of Northern College and Its Predecessors* (Edinburgh: T. & T. Clark, 1999).

he spent a year as Visiting Professor in New Testament Studies at Drew University in New Jersey. Manson was indeed one of the group of twelve scholars who were responsible for founding the international society of New Testament scholars, *Studiorum Novi Testamenti Societas* in 1938, and he became one of its earliest presidents and one of its leading and most popular members. Taylor was naturally elected to membership of the Society, but seldom attended its annual meetings; even when he was elected President in 1954 he excused himself from attending in person to deliver his Presidential Address on "The Origin of the Markan Passion Sayings," which had to be read on his behalf by his friend and great admirer, Professor Charles Kingsley Barrett.[14]

What I have just said illustrates as well as anything could the striking difference in temperament between the two great scholars we are considering. In a revealing memoir titled, "T. W. Manson: An Appreciation," printed as an introduction to the posthumous published collection of Manson's famous John Rylands Library Public Lectures,[15] his great friend and colleague Professor H. H. Rowley wrote of Manson,

> In the life of Staff House [where members of staff of all grades and of all faculties meet together, particularly after lunch] Manson took an active part, and usually joined a group that contained members of several faculties—Science, Arts, Law, Theology, Medicine, Economics—as well as members of the administrative staff. Here a lively conversation on a wide range of topics took place, and many good stories were told. Manson was himself a good raconteur, and his richly stored mind and ready wit enabled him to contribute to the discussion on most subjects, whether they concerned general affairs or the life and work of the University. He was always excellent company, and whether the conversation were grave or gay his versatility ensured him a part in it.

Elsewhere in the same memoir we read, "For twenty years [Manson] was the official Presenter for honorary degrees, and for this his skilful turn of phrase and never-failing wit were invaluable. His colleagues came to Founder's Day with high expectation that was never

---

14. For C. K. Barrett (1917-), prominent Methodist and Lightfoot Professor of Divinity at Durham University (1958-1982), see J. Painter, "Charles Kingsley Barrett," in McKim, *Dictionary*, 155-61.

15. T. W. Manson, *Studies in the Gospels and Epistles*, ed. Matthew Black (Manchester: Manchester University Press, 1960).

disappointed, and many an honorary graduate of the University must treasure the little gem of a speech with which he was presented to the Chancellor." And one further quotation to complete this thumb-nail sketch of the personality and temperament of T. W. M.—this time from a delightful obituary notice in *The Times* (I should explain that he was a well-known and well-loved figure at Printing House Square as he frequently reviewed books for the *Times Literary Supplement*. He was not less well known and popular at the offices of the *Manchester Guardian*, to which, over many years, he contributed regular brief articles on Free Church affairs): "If Chesterton had been a Presbyterian, he might have taken Dr. Manson as his model for Father Brown. Manson would not have minded this suggestion . . . Had he and Father Brown crossed swords on paper or in conversation, the duel would have been a lovely one to follow and fought cleanly and free from all animosity."

Now for all the warm affection in which I came to hold Vincent Taylor and with which I shall always remember him, I should be the first to admit that such words as I have just been quoting could never have been written about him. By comparison with Manson he was a much more solitary figure, much more reserved in temperament. He was not immediately at ease in the company of those who did not share his scholarly interests. The first impression he gave to colleagues—in scholarly and ministerial circles alike—and to students was one of a certain austerity and distance, which inspired a sense of respectful awe rather than of attraction. It took time for the ice to break and for the reserve to be penetrated; and I think it took also a certain amount of effort and courage on the part of the other person—or at least a willingness to dare to approach him and open one's heart to him. Those who did so came to discover that beneath the austere and rather forbidding outward shell there was a genuine warmth of humanity and sympathy and in due course friendliness at the heart of the man. In the Obituary Notice which he wrote for the *Proceedings of the British Academy* in 1970,[16] Kingsley Barrett, himself one of Taylor's succession of junior assistants at Headingley, wrote of him, "He was always at the service of his men, though not all of them found it easy to take the first steps in approaching him. Probably he was at his best with the best students"; and again, "There were many who found conversation with Taylor difficult,

---

16. See *Proceedings of the British Academy* 56 (1970) 283–92.

and even daunting, but willingness to speak, however incompetently, about New Testament criticism and theology was a ready passport to his confidence, and to those who knew him he would talk freely and entertainingly on many topics, though he never tired of returning to the themes that were both work and recreation to him."

My own experience, both as his student and as another of the succession of his junior assistants, confirms those judgments of Barrett's, and I too more than once heard from his lips the words which Barrett records that Taylor once spoke to him: "Do you not feel that, even if there were nothing more in it than a literary puzzle, New Testament scholarship would be the most fascinating pursuit in the world?" Such was his delight in and enthusiasm for the subject which claimed his single-minded devotion throughout his life, and which was, indeed, for him ,a very great deal more than "the most fascinating" of human pursuits; his devotion to the New Testament was the expression of his devotion to the Lord to whom the New Testament bears witness.

What I have just said about Taylor's attitude to, and understanding of, the significance of New Testament scholarship is, of course, no less true of Manson. The difference between them was simply that Manson did not allow his pursuit of New Testament scholarship to exclude him from other legitimate, healthy and enjoyable human pursuits such as trout fishing and swapping yarns with genial companions over a glass of claret. I cannot by any stretch of the imagination picture Taylor in waders beside a trout stream, although I do possess a snapshot taken by his wife during a holiday they spent, at my recommendation, in North Wales, showing V. T. and O. E. E. with their trousers rolled up paddling in the sea on the beach at Criccieth. Such recreations were, however, for him rare and uncharacteristic occurrences!

One of my most vivid and poignant memories is of a visit I paid to Dr. and Mrs. Taylor during the closing months of his life, which they spent together in a nursing home for the elderly near Winchester. It was in fact the last time I saw him in the flesh, which had become very frail, and the power of his great intellect had begun to fade. On the table beside the chair in which he sat lay a long line of volumes between two bookends—all his published works. He gazed at them lovingly and then turned to me with a smile and said in a weak croaky voice, "My children." One was aware of a man at peace, facing death with a deep sense of contentment at having lived to some purpose.

That experience reminded me of a letter he had once shown to me; I believe I was one of a select few privileged to see that letter, which had been written to Dr. Taylor by the brother of Dom Gregory Dix, the great Anglican liturgical scholar.[17] It told how Gregory Dix, on his deathbed, had lost all interest in reading even the paperback detective stories which he so much enjoyed, or in talking to other people. Then someone had given him a copy of Vincent Taylor's recently published *Commentary on St. Mark's Gospel*. As he looked at it, Dix's interest was aroused; he read it eagerly, and received fresh energy, so that he was stimulated to resume conversation with another patient, and actually led him to belief in Christ. I believe that letter meant more to V. T. than all the scholarly reviews which greeted his *Commentary* with such praise and appreciation.

In the closing years of his active life—after completing the memorable works of what might be called his theological maturity for which he will be primarily remembered: his two great trilogies on the Atonement and the Person of Christ respectively, and his monumental *Commentary on St. Mark*, which occupied him for ten years between the former trilogy and the latter (ten years during which he set himself, with rigid self-discipline, the goal of producing one quarto page of typescript per day—when I became his pupil he was about half-way through the task)—in these closing years of his life he returned to the theory that had first made his name famous among students of the New Testament, namely, the Proto-Luke Hypothesis, which he had never ceased tenaciously to defend in the face of much criticism. He had been much encouraged by very detailed studies of parts of the Lucan Passion Narrative by the German scholars Jeremias, Schürmann and Rehkopf, which supported his views on the non-Markan basis of Luke's account of the Passion and Death of Jesus.[18] And so he set himself the task of re-examining, and of re-writing in a fuller and completely up-to-date version, that part of his early book, *Behind the Third Gospel*, which dealt with the Passion Narrative. Sadly, the deterioration in his physical and

---

17. For George Eglinton Alston Dix (1901–1952), Benedictine monk (religious name, Gregory Dix) and liturgical scholar, see ODNB.

18. Taylor welcomed their work in an article entitled, "Theologians of our time: VII. Friedrich Rehkopf," *ExpT* 74.9 (1963) 262–66. He observed that they supported the Proto-Luke Hypothesis "very much in the form in which it was first presented by B. H. Streeter [1924]," 262.

mental powers to which I have already referred prevented him from revising his typescript of this work and preparing it for publication. On his death in 1968 the unrevised typescript was entrusted to my hands, and with the enthusiastic encouragement of the late Professor Matthew Black,[19] at that time editor of the New Testament Studies Monograph Series, I undertook the task of editing the work, which was published by the Cambridge University Press in the said series in 1970, under the title, *The Passion Narrative of St. Luke: A Critical and Historical Investigation*. This was a work of *pietas* which I felt very privileged to accomplish.

I have already referred to Professor Kingsley Barrett as one of the highly privileged succession of V. T.'s junior assistants at Headingley College. I now add one further quotation from Barrett's obituary in the *Proceedings of the British Academy*: "His junior assistants," he writes, "of whom the writer of this memoir is proud to have been one, found in him not only an example of exact scholarship, but forbearance with their early efforts as teachers and generous encouragement of their own attempts to write." The first of the above-mentioned junior assistants was Dr. Leslie Mitton,[20] who contributed a magnificent and comprehensive essay on "Vincent Taylor: New Testament scholar" to the memorial volume published in 1970. Writing out of the depth of his own experience, Mitton concludes his essay with the following paragraph, every word of which I myself can echo from my own experience:

> As well as his own writing and lecturing, he was constantly providing inspiration and encouragement to younger men in whom he discerned some promise of scholarly achievement. It was his confidence in them, his unfailing readiness to offer his help in most generous measure, his determined insistence on their perseverance, and his own splendid example, which

---

19. For Matthew Black (1908-1994) see ODNB; D. Garland, "Matthew Black," in McKim, ed., *Dictionary*, 197-201. From 1937 to 1939 he was Assistant Lecturer in Semitic languages at Manchester, where Manson encouraged him to explore the Jewish background to the New Testament. With this the foundation for Black's subsequent work was laid.

20. The memorial volume referred to is Vincent Taylor, *New Testament Essays* (London: Epworth, 1970). Mitton's essay is on pp. 5-30. Charles Leslie Mitton (1907-1998), a Manchester and Hartley College alumnus, later became Principal of Handsworth College, Birmingham (1881), from 1956 to 1970. He edited *The Expository Times* from 1965 to 1976. See C. S. Rodd in *ExpT* 109.9 (1998) 257. For Handsworth College see W. B. Brash, *Our Colleges*, ch. 8.

enabled many of them to achieve far more than would have been possible without his prompting and his guidance. These remember him with special veneration and gratitude [and] gratefully acknowledge the formative influence he has had upon their minds and their lives.

V. T. took a great risk by appointing me to fill an unexpected vacancy in the assistant tutorship at Headingley even before the result of my final London BD examination was known; he made me his protégé, giving me unstintingly the benefit of his personal tuition, guidance and encouragement. And I was never under any illusion that it was anything other than his advocacy that persuaded the Ministerial Training Committee and the Methodist Conference in 1953 to take the further risk of appointing me to another vacancy that had unexpectedly occurred in the New Testament Chair at Hartley Victoria College, which carried with it a part-time Lectureship in the Manchester University Faculty of Theology. It was thus Taylor, my first mentor and master, that introduced me to Manson, my second—in more ways than one, since Manson's *Teaching of Jesus* and his *Sayings of Jesus* were prominent among the books that he had long since insisted that I should become thoroughly acquainted with.

My personal relationship with Manson was inevitably much shorter and less intimate than that which I enjoyed with Taylor. Although I had heard him lecture once or twice, I had never met him personally before my arrival in Manchester in September 1953. By then his health was already causing concern; what he referred to with a wry smile as his "old ticker" was at times being troublesome; and he had already moved his residence to Milnthorpe in Westmorland, whence he commuted each week during term time for such days as his duties required his presence in Manchester. He died on May 1st 1958, so that my association with him lasted less than five years. It was long enough, however, for the great respect in which I had long held him as a scholar to be combined with a warm affection towards him as a man. It was—as I have indicated earlier—much easier to feel immediately at ease in the company of T. W. M. than it had initially been with V. T.

I remember how he rang me up from Milnthorpe a few days after my arrival in Manchester, and welcomed me with warm friendliness, saying that he was looking forward to meeting me and having me as a colleague, adding, however, that in my own interest and at the suggestion of my predecessor, Dr. H. G. Meecham,[21] he had agreed to allow me time to settle into my duties at Hartley Victoria before beginning to lecture at the University. In the meantime, Dr. Meecham, who had retired to Colwyn Bay, had agreed to hold the fort by travelling to Manchester on a couple of days each week to give the necessary lectures. Over the following months the Professor maintained his friendly interest in my progress and called me to his study from time to time to explain the way things worked in the Faculty, to put me at ease and to share with me something of his own vast experience as a teacher. My tasks would be to lecture each year on Mark and Galatians to the second year BA (Theology) class, and in alternate years on Luke, and 1 Corinthians and 1 Peter together to a joint class of third-year BA students and postgraduate BD students. Manson himself looked after the parallel course which included John (in the year when I was doing the Epistles) and Romans and I John (in the year when I was dealing with Luke). BD students, if they so opted, could take both sets of texts.[22] Manson confided to me that he himself, though making it abundantly clear that the students would be examined on the whole of the set texts, was never particularly bothered about how much of the text he covered in his lectures. The aim was to give them a clear idea of how to go about studying New Testament criticism and exegesis. He expected me, however, for my own part (and no doubt in my own interest as a raw beginner!) to read through the whole of the Greek texts with the classes, carefully explaining all the difficult bits of grammar and syntax

---

21. Henry George Meecham (1886–1955) was a tutor at Hartley College from 1930 to 1934, and Principal from 1948 to 1953. The Regulations for the earned Manchester DD were approved in 1905; it was first awarded in 1920. In 1944 Meecham became only the third successful candidate.

22. The curriculum of the postgraduate Manchester BD was in three sections: Biblical Studies; Doctrine, Philosophy and Ethics; and Ecclesiastical History and Comparative Religion. Candidates were required to specialize in one section, and to take courses from the other two. Hebrew and Greek were unavoidable; the degree had to be completed within seven years; examinations in a minimum of three subjects had to be sat each year; and if even one paper were failed it had to be retaken together with two others. It was a tough regime. At a time when 6% only of the age-group went to university in Britain, students worked hard to be admitted, and even harder to stay in; and in one not untypical Manchester theological college those training for the ministry had numerous additional tasks to attend to, not least pastoralia, sermon class, Bible examinations on the first and last Saturday (yes, Saturday!) of each term, and preaching far and wide on Sundays.

and drawing their attention briefly to the problems of exegesis on which they could consult the commentaries for themselves. No doubt he was anxious to reduce the amount of Greek that the poor students would have to work through unaided!

As it happened, H. G. Meecham died suddenly before completing the period for which he had agreed to hold the fort. So I had the responsibility thrust upon me sooner than either Manson or I had anticipated. I remember how kind, understanding and supportive he was, and how invaluable I found his advice and encouragement, and indeed his confidence in me. As I gradually found my feet I looked forward to years of immensely profitable association with and discipleship of my second mentor and master in the field of New Testament studies. My sense of privilege knew no bounds! Sadly, however, his absences from the University owing to his deteriorating health began to be lengthier and more frequent. I well remember the first occasion on which he rang me up from his sick-bed, complaining that his doctor had insisted that he must not think of going to the University for two or three weeks at least. He was deeply concerned about the effect of this on his students' course, and asked whether I could possibly arrange to take over his regular classes. The one on St. John in Greek he thought I could manage as I saw fit by going through the Greek text with them and referring them to the commentaries. As for the other course, on New Testament Theology, he told me his secretary would be able to hand me his own lecture notes, which were full enough for me to read at dictation speed to the class. I would find a date marked in pencil in the margin opposite the point which he had reached at the end of each lecture. "And you'll be perfectly free to add," he assured me with a chuckle, "any comments of your own that you may care to make."

I duly obtained the file of lecture notes, which I discovered to be written in the author's own beautifully neat and legible handwriting, with emendations and marginal glosses and occasional longer insertions on separate sheets, but always with the intended position clearly indicated; and every so often a pencilled date in the margin. I knew well enough that Manson did not himself lecture *at dictation speed*, but I discovered that I could cover at that speed the amount of material between one date and the next in much less than the fifty minutes of the lecture period. So it was obvious that students were missing all the *obiter dicta* and *ad lib* expansions of the written text that made his personally delivered lectures so fascinating and memorable. My own occasional comments—which I was always very careful to distinguish from the "authentic text"—were a very poor substitute.

So it was that I became, for two or three periods of varying length between 1956 and 1958, not the amanuensis but the classroom voice (so to speak) of T. W. Manson—though I hastily add that I never attempted to imitate his accent! The set of theological lecture notes that I dictated from was in two parts, Pauline and Johannine, the whole comprising a full year's course. After Manson's death they came into the hands of Professor Matthew Black who, having read them, decided that they were far too valuable to remain unpublished; so he prepared them for the press and they appeared in 1963 in the SCM series of Studies in Biblical Theology under the title, *On Paul and John: Some Selected Theological Themes*. "The book," wrote Black, "might well be described as a minor classic in theology: great themes are presented and developed with all their author's well-known clarity, felicity and pungency of expression, and illuminated by his own deep spiritual insights." This was one of three collections of Manson's works to be published posthumously. Manchester University Press published *Studies in the Gospels and Epistles* (1960), also edited by Matthew Black, with the memoir by H. H. Rowley from which I quoted earlier, and containing a selection of Manson's famous public lectures delivered over a period of years at the John Rylands Library. The other was a series of lectures given in the U.S.A. on *Ethics and the Gospel*, which was edited by Canon Ronald Preston, another friend of Manson's, who lectured in Christian Ethics in the Manchester Faculty.[23]

Time is running out, but I cannot conclude without mentioning one other work of Manson's that only saw the light of day posthumously. It was probably the last thing he wrote. This was his gem of a short commentary of Romans, written for the new *Peake's Commentary on the Bible* which was published under the editorship of H. H. Rowley and Matthew Black in 1962. Manson's commentary was, naturally enough, a condensation of the lectures on Romans which he had regularly delivered to his students. In his last academic session he was reading to his class, as the basis for his lectures, his own original draft of the commentary, written in his own hand (as methodically neat and legible as ever).

23. For Ronald Preston (1913–2001), who pioneered Christian Ethics at Manchester University, see ODNB.

Very early in the Spring of that session his condition weakened and it became obvious that he would be absent for a protracted period. Under his instructions, his secretary rang me to say that she had all his notes ready for me to act once more as his understudy. Accordingly I took up the reading of his commentary on Romans at the point—somewhere in chapter five if I remember rightly—at which he had left off. So it went on throughout the Spring term and into the Summer term.

It so happened that from 11.30 a.m. to 12.30 p.m. on 1 May 1958 I was taking the Romans class. At 12.30 I was hurriedly summoned to the room of the University Registrar[24]—a good friend of Manson's—who told me he had received a telephone message with the news that Professor Manson was sinking fast. Later the same day, on the BBC North regional news, I heard the sad news that Professor T. W. Manson had died at his home in Westmorland shortly after mid-day on that first day of May. And I realised that at the very moment of his passing I had been reading to his students his own commentary on the latter part of the thirteenth chapter of Romans, where the words occur, "Now is our salvation nearer than when we first believed; the night is far gone, the day is at hand."

So it was that for each of the two mentors and masters it was my inestimable privilege to know, to learn from, and to serve, I was given the opportunity—at the close of their earthly lives—to perform some little act of *pietas*.

---

24. This was Vincent Knowles (1912–2003), who became the doyen of university registrars. A classicist, he had gained Manchester's MA for a thesis on Euripides (on which subject he lectured to myself) when that degree was a rigorous research degree, and he continued to "keep his hand in" in the Classics department following his appointment as Registrar. Shortly before he died he told me, with mingled glee and regret, that when he started, the Vice-Chancellor, the Bursar and he would meet daily at 10.30 with a view to drinking coffee and tackling *The Times* crossword. He could not imagine that his sometimes harassed latter-day successors could enjoy such a privilege. See his obituary in *The Times*, 16 September 2003.

8

Hymns and Scripture: The Welsh Experience

BRYNLEY F. ROBERTS

The pleasure and privilege of being able to greet John Tudno as a contributor to this *Festschrift* is, however, somewhat unnerving as I find myself in the company of so many distinguished theologians and biblical scholars. But as one who has sat many times under John Tudno's Sunday ministry and appreciated not only his preaching but also his resonant singing, perhaps a few thoughts on Welsh hymns will not be out of place as a token of gratitude for his friendship and service.

'Classical' Welsh hymnody has its roots in the Methodist societies of the 'Great Awakening' of the eighteenth century. There is, of course, a difference between religious verse and hymns. One of the earliest Welsh religious poems, from the perhaps the eleventh century, is an original, exuberant 'Benedicite' which praises God in all his creation.[1] Rather later, in the fourteenth century, the Welsh translation of the Little Office of the Virgin, a devotion popular with lay folk, contains some five well known hymns as well as metrical psalms and versions of the *Te Deum* and of the *Benedicite*, but whether any of these were actually sung must be doubted and the Welsh Office was more probably read and recited

---

1. The poem reflects psalms such as 148, 150 and the *Benedicite* itself. It is printed with other examples of Welsh religious poetry throughout the ages in the Church in Wales's hymnary *Emynau'r Eglwys* (Cardiff: Western Mail & Echo, 1941), no. 722.

Hymns and Scripture

privately. Modern Welsh hymnody begins, as in so many other countries, with the Reformation and with sixteenth and seventeenth-century metrical versions of psalms. Archdeacon Edmwnd Prys's Welsh version of the complete psalter was published, together with twelve hymn tunes, in the 1621 edition of the Welsh *Book of Common Prayer*. With a few local exceptions, nonconformist congregations have made little use of psalm singing (chants) and some of Prys's psalms remained in popular use until the early twentieth century when their sometimes archaic language restricted the number that could be sung meaningfully. Interestingly, Revd. Gwynn ap Gwilym, an Anglican priest, has recently emulated Prys's efforts to give psalms a greater role in worship by translating the Psalter on a variety of well-known and easily recognisable hymn-tune metres.[2] Songs (*cwndidau*) and carols were being written throughout the sixteenth century in Glamorganshire, often, but not always, by priests, to instruct lay folk in the Decalogue, Creed and Pater Noster and parts of the Bible. These have a wide range of scriptural allusions and they have aptly been termed sermons in song but they are not hymns.[3] More akin to popular hymns are some of the homely verses written by vicar Rhys Pritchard of Llanymddyfri (1579–1644). These doctrinal sermons, moral precepts and exhortations, prayers for all occasions and a daily regimen of prayer, often based on primers and other devotional books, appeared first as loose sheets but were then published as a collection, *Cannwyll y Cymry*, in 1681. Rhys Pritchard's verses gained wide circulation and were reprinted many times. Many of them became part of the common folk memory up to the nineteenth century and beyond and though they may never have been used in church services, apart perhaps from some Christmas carols and selections of verses that have become hymns which are still used, they made the concept of popular hymn singing possible. More closely based on scripture were songs known as *halsingod*, characteristic of the literary culture of the Teifi valley in southwest Wales. These popular songs, written and copied from about 1662 to the first part of the eighteenth century and usually composed by recognised poets, use parts of the Bible as allegory to teach doctrine, scripture and morality and they have many of the same figures, and sometimes laboured typology, as appear

2. *Salmau Cân Newydd*, Llandysul: Gomer, 2008.
3. See 'Hopcyn' and 'Cadrawd,' eds, *Hen Gwndidau, Carolau a Chywydddau*, Bangor: Jarvis & Foster, 1910. Pages xxxvii–viii contain a long list of images and types.

in the later Methodist hymns; they are religious, moral, instructional verses or poems versifying portions of scripture for lay people. But an eighteenth-century description of the way in which they were used (or performed) allows us to recognise these as hymns even if they had no part formally in church services as such. In his *A View of the State of Religion in the Diocese of St. David's About the beginning of the 18th Century* (1721), the Anglican priest Erasmus Saunders congratulated 'the poor Inhabitants of these mountains' for their attachment to religious services:

> to make their private Instructions more agreeable and effectual, as they are naturally addicted to Poetry, so some of the more Skilful and knowing among them frequently compose a kind of Divine Hymns, or Songs, which they call *Halsingod*, or *Carolion*, which generally consist either of the Doctrinal, or Historical parts of Scripture, or of the Lives, and worthy Acts of some eminent Saints. The young people learn these by heart and sing them at home in their own Houses, as upon some Publick Occasions; such as at their Wakes and solemn Festivals, and Funerals, and very frequently in their Churches in the Winter Season, between *All Saints* and *Candlemass*; at which Times, before and after divine Service, upon *Sundays*, or *Holy-days*, Eight or ten will commonly divide themselves to Four or Five of a side, and so forming themselves, as it were into an imitation of our Cathedral, or Collegiate Choirs, one Party fist begins, and then by way of Alternate Responses, the other repeats the same *Stanzas*, and so proceed till they have finish'd their *Halsing*, and then coincide with a *Chorus*.[4]

In spite of some continuing objection to their use in public worship, some hymns, in the stricter sense, were written or translated by Puritans but, noting Bernard L. Manning's remark that the greatest hymns have a solid structure of historical dogma, the passionate thrill of present experience, and the glory of a mystic sunlight coming directly from another world, Garfield Hughes commented that the second

---

4. E. Saunders. *A View of the State of Religion in the Diocese of St. David's* (London, 1721; reprinted Cardiff: University of Wales Press, 1949), 33. For these *halsingod* see Garfield H. Hughes. 'Halsingau Dyffryn Teifi'. *Yr Eurgrawn*, 133. 1941, 58-63, 89-91, 126-27; Geraint Bowen. 'Yr Hasingod.' *Transactions of the Honourable Society of Cymmrodorion*. 1945, 83-108.

Hymns and Scripture

and third of these elements are rare or wholly missing from the early nonconformist hymns.[5]

Nevertheless, some of the more successful of these are still to be found in modern hymnals but they are not typical of what I have called 'classical' Welsh hymnody, that is, hymns that can now be regarded as characteristic of the (largely nonconformist) tradition of hymn writing in Wales. As has already been suggested, this has its origins in the Methodist societies and it maintained its creative vitality as a reflection of the ambience of the societies while they continued to be the focus of nonconformist church life.[6] The 'golden age' of Welsh hymnody, it is said, was between circa 1750 and circa 1850. Society meetings were central to the growth and structure of early Methodism and in Wales the *seiat* remained at the core of church life even after 1811 when the movement finally resolved to ordain its own ministers to administer the sacraments, thereby acknowledging what it had already become—a church entity separate from the Church of England. Church membership was expressed in terms of *seiat* membership and even as Sunday worship developed, it was normal that congregations would be larger in number than at *seiat* meetings and that the sacraments were reserved for members of the *seiat*. The importance of the *seiat* was more than a tradition of church order for these meetings fulfilled functions that were essential for vibrant church life and witness. Methodism laid stress on personal response to saving grace and on witness to Christ's atonement. The spirituality of the *seiat* was by its very nature intensely personal but it would not be correct to regard it as individualistic, for the society, as the name makes clear, was a group meeting. Members were questioned about their spiritual condition, they shared their experiences, recognising in others aspects of their own spiritual lives, be they of assurance or of doubt, and deriving support from one another under the guidance of the society leader. Edification and experience were, however, mediated in an atmosphere of worship, praise and thanksgiving. Society meetings commonly opened with praise and prayer and hymns were to be the affective expression of deeply held convictions and of shared communal experiences.

5. 'Emynyddiaeth gynnar yr Ymneilltuwyr,' *Llên Cymru*, 2 (3), 1951, 135–46, p. 146.

6. For a concise account see Eryn M. White, *'Praidd Bach y Bugail Mawr,'* Llandysul: Gomer, 1995, 125–27.

Howell Harris, the founder of the first societies in south Wales following his traumatic conversion on Palm Sunday 1735, soon introduced 'psalms, hymns and spiritual songs' into society meetings as a friend remarked when he sent him a few hymns. Presbyterians and Independents had published small collections of hymns in the early years of the eighteenth century. Some were used by Methodists, but in general their unemotional theology and lack of spontaneity, allied with uncertain metrical forms, did not ensure an enthusiastic reception. *Seiat* members shaped their own hymnody, soon to be adopted by the other nonconformist churches, with the result that the newly created hymn would become the typical literary form of the 'Great Awakening' and the years that followed. Society leaders, counsellors rather than preachers, were conscious of the dangers of unbridled experiential worship and meetings were always firmly grounded in Bible reading and study. Conviction and theology, worship and doctrine, inspiration and discipline, went hand in hand, the one confirming and validating the other. Hymns would be the voice of the *seiat* so that it was inevitable that their style should reflect the discourse of the *seiat* throughout its history. As Derec Llwyd Morgan stresses, Methodism was a religion founded in the scriptures; hymnists should be steeped in the poetry of the Bible, demanded William Williams, Pantycelyn.[7] Some hymns make unequivocal but joyous theological statements: *Cyn llunio'r byd* (527), *Cyfamod hedd* (207), *Rhagluniaeth fawr y nef* (114), *Cawn esgyn o'r dyrys anialwch* (747), *Daeth ffrydiau melys iawn* (524), *Mae Duw yn llond pob lle* (76). But the interaction of theology and worship is epitomised in the two stanzas of *Mae'n llond y nefoedd, llond y byd, Clyw, f'enaid tlawd, mae gennyt Dad* (215), as Edward Jones (1761–1836) stands in wonder that the majestic God whose presence fills heaven

---

7. See the discussion by Derec Llwyd Morgan, translated by Dyfnallt Morgan, *The Great Awakening in Wales* (London: Epworth, 1988), 279–80 and chapter 9. As my essay is not intended to be an historical survey, I have considered only hymns (but not translations), of any period, that appear in *Caneuon Ffydd*, the interdenominational hymnal published in January 2001. This is now in general use (it is in its fourth printing) and may be taken as an indication of the nature of the canon at the end of the twentieth century and the beginning of the twenty-first. Delyth G. Morgans, *Cydymaith Caneuon Ffydd*, 2nd ed., 2008, is an essential companion volume to the hymnal which I have found very useful in preparing this essay. For a convenient overview of Welsh hymnody see Alan Luff, *Welsh Hymns and Their Tunes* (London: Stainer & Bell, 1990).

and hell, the world and all eternity and whose essence is in himself, is, nevertheless, the compassionate and understanding Father and Brother. As ever, William Williams, Pantycelyn (1717–91) takes this to a higher level and his remarkable contemplation in wonder, awe and love of the presence of Christ offers a deeper insight into the worship of the *seiat*, *Os yw tegwch d'wyneb yma* (318, 'If your beauty in the here and now bring a host to love you, what will the effect of your beauty be in eternity?'). But the genial farmer and folk poet, John Thomas (1742–1818), would have recognised Pantycelyn's vision for he, too, found his solace in Christ's presence, *Pwy welaf fel f'Anwylyd* (334, 'Whom do I see like my Beloved'). For him, as for so many others throughout the ages, imagery to express adoration and love was at hand in the Song of Solomon, and Welsh phrases and epithets like *Gwyn a gwridog*, *Anwylyd*, *Rhosyn Saron* would become common, if not conventional. Pantycelyn, however, reminds us that adoration and scripture must be brought together in the Christian experience: *Gwyn a gwridog, hawddgar iawn, yw f'Anwylyd, ... Dyma sylfaen gadarn gref drwy fy mywyd; credu, ac edrych arno ef, yw fy ngwynfyd* (358, 'My Beloved is white and ruddy, very lovely ... Here is a firm and strong foundation throughout my life; to believe and gaze on him is my bliss').

The themes of the 'classical' Welsh hymn are familiar—e.g. the reality of continuing temptation and the conviction of sin, atonement and the scheme of salvation through the Cross, the Person of Christ, the mystery of Providence, thanksgiving, the work of grace, and prayer for faithfulness—and given the central role of the Bible, hymnists found their appropriate mode of expression in their reading of scripture. The hymns are full of phrases taken from the Bible, revealing how thoroughly biblical phraseology had permeated common speech. But beyond these commonplaces of everyday talk lie the host of biblical references and figures that characterise the 'classical' Welsh hymn. This is more than a literary style that used the Bible as a quarry for allusions and epithets for these Christians 'knew what typology meant'.[8] It was accepted that the Old Testament was to be read as a divine metaphor of Christ's work in the New so that passages such as Hebrews 9–10 set the keynote for both

---

8. Rowan Williams, 'Beyond Aesthetics: Theology and Hymnody,' *The Hymn Society of Great Britain and Ireland Bulletin*, 15:4 (1997) 73–78. p. 75. For a study of William Williams Pantycelyn's typology see Kathryn Jenkins, 'Williams Pantycelyn a'r Beibl,' *Y Traethodydd*, 143 (July, 1988) 159–70.

the broader understanding of the Bible and for the significance of specific words and images. This was not new for Welsh worshippers. Rhys Pritchard had prefaced one of his sets of verses, *Crist yn cael ei borteadu trwy y cysgodau Iuddewig* ('Christ portrayed through the Jewish shadows'), giving a four-line verse to names or images of Christ. Most are scriptural but others are excessively novel (and hardly Jewish) as when Christ is God's Privy Councillor and his Master of Horse or the flour crushed from the wheat to pay our ransom.[9] Dafydd William (1761–1844) not only regularly prefaced his hymns with scriptural references (the 'proof-texts' complied by so many hymnists from the Puritans onwards) but in one case he entitled a hymn *Crist y gwir Sylwedd yn rhagori ar yr holl gysgodau* ('Christ the true Essence excelling all the shadows'). The unknown author of the second stanza of 507 (which was familiar by 1806), not only used Hebrews 9, 10:1–14 but knew too that her/his congregation would understand what she/he was saying and what they were singing: *un aberth mawr yn sylwedd /yr holl gysgodau i gyd* ('the one great sacrifice the realisation (substance, effect[10]) of all the shadows'). This author was perhaps a woman, and therefore a lay person, and the hymn is a sign of how thoroughly versed *seiat* members were both in the content of the Bible and in the 'technique' of Bible reading which give their particular ethos to the work of many hymnists, none more so than Ann Griffiths (1776–1805). Her hymns are intensely personal but find their expression of deep longing for a fuller spiritual life and of the wonder of love and salvation in an interweaving of biblical allusions and imagery. *Dyma babell y cyfarfod* (338) derives its images from Leviticus, Numbers, Matthew, Exodus, Psalm 84, and Proverbs. *Rhyfedd, rhyfedd gan angylion* (446) is equally extensive in its allusions to Exodus, Luke, Revelation, Psalm 2 and the way that it fuses Luke 2:12 and Matthew 8:20b into one image.[11] Dafydd William in the hymn referred to above (326; this has only one of the four original stanzas) has been accused of mixing an abundance of metaphors as he progresses from the proclamation that the fountain of healing is opened to urge his soul to pass through the open door; a ladder whose rungs are promises

---

9. Excesses such as these would be of concern to later Methodist counsellors as they sought to instruct *seiat* leaders and lay preachers.

10. Cf. Ezekiel 12:23, 'the effect of every vision' (*sylwedd pob gweledigaeth*).

11. For studies and analyses of these two hymns see John Ryan, *The Hymns of Ann Griffiths* (Caernarfon: Tŷ ar y Graig, 1980), 88–91, 148–55.

lies before him and the sun of righteousness has risen; he sees the altar with its precious sacrifice and hears the song to the Lamb on the golden harps of heaven, echoed upon our small earthly harps. To list references and sources in this way is to suggest confused bewilderment and to give an impression that biblical allusions are being flung together, but these hymns derive from a shared environment and systematic faith gives a structure to the hymns. The worshipper progresses from despair to the joy of salvation and that this is expressed in the hymns is all too often hidden in the truncated versions in modern hymnals: Morgan Rhys's *Peraidd ganodd sêr y bore* (439) is a striking example of what is lost in the process. The mental cross-referencing serves to enrich the singing (or reading) of words for the worshipper as it did for the hymnists themselves as scripture both engenders experience and deepens it. John Gwilym Jones observed how difficult it is to find a hymn by Pantycelyn that is not overflowing with biblical imagery,[12] and T. H. Parry-Williams, in a famous passage written in 1955, sought to reduce the emphasis on the 'uniqueness' of Ann Griffiths's style and claimed that this was the normal and characteristic language of *seiat* members even in his own youth: 'Their way of expressing themselves, their images and figures of speech, their religious aspirations were the same as hers. They did their theology in pictures, prayed in parables, argued in allegories, quoting and using phrases from scripture and spinning themes the one through the other had become second nature to them and they had the terms of denominational doctrine on the tips of their tongues.'[13] Whatever of his thesis, this is a good description of *seiat* language. But for a generation less attuned to biblical language and imagery, and unfamiliar with the life of the *seiat*, the rhetoric of these hymns is strange, disturbing perhaps, and the response to her hymns and those of other hymnists of the 'Golden Age' must surely be significantly the poorer.[14]

More common is the use of single images—life as a pilgrimage, or journey, through an arid wilderness led a column of fire or cloud, to a promised land where Christ reigns, or the release from captivity and bondage (through an open door) to restored freedom from sin;

12. 'Yr emyn fel llenyddiaeth,' *Bwletin Cymeithas Emynau Cymru*, 1:5 (1972) 113–32, p. 128.

13. Translated from 'Ann,' in *Myfyrdodau*, Aberystwyth: Gwasg Aberystwyth, 1957, 50–56, p. 51.

14. Examples are 191, 192, 193, 263, 524, 730.

life may be a voyage in stormy seas to a safe haven guided by the Christ who walked on the waters; the sinner is washed, the price of his sins paid, in the blood (of the Cross or the Lamb). Always the journey is homewards, to holy Salem, that better city, the fair inheritance, to the rising of the sun of righteousness, and images of pilgrims and voyagers, of prisoners freed, of crossing Jordan safely, of a path through the sea, of a fiery furnace and the stone removed abound. Hope resides in the Friend and Brother, the Shepherd of Israel, the Author of Salvation, the Second Adam, the Bread of Life; rock, tower and shield, streams of living water or the river of life ('from under the threshold of the house' or 'out of the throne of the Lamb'), the Woman's seed and the crushing of the Dragon's head underfoot, praising the Lamb—all these, and many more, were novel and daring images but all were recognised as the language of scripture as expounded in the teaching and instruction of the *seiat*. Their sources, most commonly in Exodus, the Prophets, Job, Song of Solomon, the Psalms, the Gospels and Revelation, would have been familiar.

Psalms, it has already been noted, are not a feature of nonconformist 'liturgy' but they have always been a much used medium of personal devotion. This is reflected in the hymnals not so much in metrical translations as in the paraphrases of a few psalms based on the 1588–1620 Welsh Bible. This was the standard translation in general use until the new translation, *Beibl Cymraeg Newydd*, appeared in 1988 and many portions of it, psalms especially and single verses, are familiar to churchgoers thanks to the Sunday school emphasis on learning by memory and recitation. As might be expected, psalm 23 has proved to be the most popular to be paraphrased and there are 25 versions dating from 1603 to the twentieth century in the collection published by the Welsh Hymn Society in 1991.[15] Edmwnd Prys's translation remained popular and was used in most hymnals, but *Caneuon Ffydd* chose to use two more recent versions, both of which follow the text closely, though that (62) by Ieuan S. Jones (1918–2004) contains more verbal echoes of the Bible text than the version (112) by J. J. Williams (1869–1954). The only two of Prys's psalms that have been retained in *Caneuon Ffydd* are 75, his version of Psalm 100 (now most often sung to the Jimmy Owen's 'Doxology' of 1972) and 120, a truncated version

---

15. Rhidian Grifiths, ed., *Salm 23: detholiad o fersiynau Cymraeg*.

of Psalm 121. Another well loved psalm is 103, verses 1–5,8,9,13, 22b, closely paraphrased (102) by W. Nantlais Williams (1874–1959) who succeeded in retaining the words, phrases and rhythms of the original text. Another close paraphrase (of Psalm 19, 1, 2, 8, 14) is 4 (Evan Griffiths, 1795–1873) who, like Isaac Watts, makes this a Christian hymn by relating reconciliation though the Law to the sacrifice of the Son. Part of the appeal of hymns such as these is that congregations recognise that they are, in fact, singing the psalm but the selection of verses is what makes them structured hymns. Paraphrases of other portions of the Bible are not uncommon and these are sometimes used as the basis of hymns of further meditation. The first stanza of hymn 188 by W. Rhys Nicholas (1914–96) is another reflection of Psalm 103:1–4, though with fewer verbal correspondences than in Nantlais Williams's version. But in his two following stanzas Rhys Nicholas departs from the psalm and develops his own meditation on God's blessings. These stanzas are not based on a particular portion of scripture but in the style of the classical Welsh hymn he uses, or echoes, scriptural phrases used by many other hymnists—peace like the river, justice like the sea, the moving of the '(earthly) tabernacle'. Siôn Aled, a young contemporary poet, has written a metrical paraphrase of Romans 8:37–39 (564) which is full of echoes of the 1588–1620 Welsh Bible, but sung to the tune 'To God be the glory' (W. H. Doane), it has its own power and character as a hymn of confidence in the unconquerable strength of the love of Christ, epitomised in the chorus, 'Praise him! Praise him! The battle has turned . . .'. Similarly, Peter M. Thomas (279) paraphrases Christ's 'manifesto' in the synagogue at Nazareth (Luke 4:18–19) and uses it as a prayer for the power of Christ's love in us. Richard Jones (1772–1833) seems less concerned with paraphrasing a familiar passage of scripture for its own sake (as it were) than with presenting the gracious invitation to enjoy the blessings of God's presence and enabling his congregation to respond in song. His hymn (237) is an extended paraphrase in three stanzas of Isaiah 55:1 but in the fourth and final stanza, the invitation to the feast, the hymnist turns to Luke 14:16–24, signalled, and recognised by his audience, by the words *Mae'r wledd yn barod* ('the feast is prepared'), so that the paraphrase becomes a hymn that has an immediacy which calls for a willing response.

Paraphrases become new hymns and this may be developed even further. A hymn that begins by using a New Testament episode and then gives it a more general application is 375 (John Roberts, 1910–84). The first stanza is the hymnist's appeal to the risen Christ to come, bearing his peace, as he came to the fearful disciples behind the locked doors of the upper room. It is not a paraphrase of John 20:19-21 but its force relies on the congregation recognising the reference. The hymn then takes a different direction. The prayer that He should come showing 'the scars of your sacrifice' leads to a meditation on Christ's sacrifice and to a prayer that His reconciliation between God and man should be the means of reconciliation and peace between man and man, nation and nation.

Hymnists and congregations alike would have been brought up to memorize portions of the Bible, extended passages or single verses, so that these would have been part of their common and normal religious language, but other passages would have been learnt in an involuntary way through their frequent use in services. The closest nonconformist services come to adopting an established liturgy is in the communion service. This has been heightened in recent years as the use of service books has increased but even previously the communion service had an acknowledged pattern and used the appropriate readings which became deeply engrained in the minds of worshippers. Hymns of the passion of Christ and the anguish of Gethsemane, whether designed for use in the communion service or more generally, naturally turn to scripture for words to convey these most significant moments of His earthly ministry. The hymnist's own words in this context above all others become not only inadequate but almost sacrilegious; congregations appropriate the hymnist's words as they share in worship and hymns become a truly communal experience. One of the best known communion hymns is 500 where each stanza opens starkly with the single accented syllable, *Cof* ('memory'), which loses its power as we attempt to convey its meaning—'we remember,' 'let us recall'. William Lewis, the weaver of Llangloffan in Pembrokeshire (died 1794), leads his congregation to contemplate vividly the scene at Gethsemane but he can find no words to describe what he sees except those of Luke 22:44, and as he follows Christ to Calvary and to the horrors of the flagellation, Psalm 129:3, 'The plowers plowed upon my back; they made long their furrows,' gives him the words that he needs. William Lewis makes the scene a more immediate experience as he quotes Christ's words directly from the Welsh Bible, '*Gadewch i'r rhain fynd ymaith*' (John 18:8), but then adds Christ's appeal, implicit in John, 'take me in their place'. The hymn is testimony to Lewis's poetic skills but it is also testimony to the worship of the *seiat*. Thomas Lewis (1760–1842), the blacksmith of Talley (Talyllychau) in Carmarthenshire, uses the same imagery from Luke and Psalm 129 in his reflection on the passion in his single stanza (519) and Thomas William of Bethesda'r Fro in the Vale of Glamorgan (1761–1844) uses the phrase 'take me in their place,' though not in identical words, in one of his hymns (497). The three hymns give us some idea of the nature of *seiat* worship not so much in the similarity of words and images but even more so in the way that they all have an appeal that the contemplation of the suffering that reveals the power of Christ's love should melt the hardest of hearts and become repentance. In a very different setting, Jesus's words in Matthew 19:14, 'forbid them not to come … for of such is the kingdom of heaven' are quoted more or less verbatim in a baptismal hymn (642) by Thomas Williams (1771–1845).

Many other passages and verses were capable of less specific application and, without their biblical context being retained, might come to mind in a variety of personal or general circumstances. Poets were quick to recognise that some verses or sentences formed perfect metrical units and being in natural language they could be quoted as they stood. J. G. Moelwyn Hughes (1866–1944) in a famous account related how his eyes fell upon the words *Pwy a'm dwg i'r ddinas gadarn?* ('Who will bring me into the strong city?'), Psalm 60:9, or Psalm 108:10, and used this rhetorical question as the opening line of each of the first three stanzas of a hymn (699) that sets out to describe the holy city. The last stanza answers the question, *Iesu a'm dwg i'r ddinas gadarn*, as Jesus brings him home after the wandering in the wilderness, to the city 'whose walls are salvation' ('Thou shalt call thy walls Salvation,' Isaiah 60:18). The hymn was written by the nineteen-year-old Moelwyn Hughes, at the time a solicitor's clerk, while the family with whom he was lodging were at Sunday service (toothache had prevented his joining them), and the facility with which he turns so readily to other parts of scripture relating to the Christian's journey and to the holy city (with echoes of Isaiah 33:20, Hebrews 11:13, 1 Peter 2:11) is a clear indication not merely of familiarity with the Bible and its language but of an ability, probably typical of church members, to use allusions creatively, as he draws upon Isaiah's vision of the restored Jerusalem (60) and its golden roads (Revelation 21:21). Zecharias 14:7, 'At evening time it shall be light' (*Bydd goleuni yn yr hwyr*) spoke more forcibly to E. Herber Evans (1836–96) in his personal circumstances than did the biblical context. The metaphor, which had a real application for him from his house in Caernarfon overlooking the sunset across the Menai Straits and Anglesey, was particularly meaningful at a time of great personal and family difficulties, and he used the verse as the closing line of each of the three stanzas of a hymn (726) that proclaims (with an echo of Psalm 23) the continuing strength and comfort of God's love in Jesus. In the same way, Psalm 73:28, *(Minnau), nesáu at Dduw sy dda imi* ('But it is good for me to draw near to God') became especially meaningful for David Jones (1805–68) following the death of his daughter and it was used as the final line of each of the three stanzas of his majestic hymn on the unchanging ever present Father (76). In these two cases, the verses speak directly to worshippers in normal language so that their context is not of the essence of the appeal of the hymns. This is true also of a line in the popular hymn 791, *Tydi a wnaeth y wyrth, O Grist, Fab Duw* (W. Rhys Nicholas), a hymn of praise for the blessings of full life in Christ. The second stanza expresses this as light scattering the shadows and in natural language the hymnist rejoices, *lle'r oeddwn gynt yn ddall 'rwy'n gweld yn awr*, an almost word for word quotation of John 9:25, 'whereas I was blind, now I see'. It is clear that the biblical episode has inspired the stanza but realising this is not central to the significance of the line. A verse that became the first line of each of three stanzas is Psalm 31:15, *Yn dy law di y mae fy amserau* ('My times are in thy hand'). The English and Welsh sentences construe differently and have different rhythms. The English AV is a statement but the Welsh uses syntax which lays stress on the first phrase to expresses differential emphasis so that the verse becomes a proclamation of confidence in God's unmatched sovereignty. Nantlais Williams uses the verse (without the affixed pronoun) to compose a hymn (71) that reflects the psalmist's trust in God but in the context of facing the unknown of a New Year as the Christian commits herself/himself to the God who is Lord of all seasons in the natural world and also in the believer's circumstances. The preferred custom of teaching and learning single verses, often with little regard for their context and so long a feature of Sunday school and family practice, has been criticised, but individual verses have their own autonomous strength as responses to events and as the source of meditation. This has been (more accurately, perhaps, 'was') the experience of generations of church people and perhaps the most familiar role of scripture in the lives of many.[16] Welsh hymnals have long been books read in private devotion and there is no doubt that part of this appeal lies in the recognition of biblical phrases and allusions.

In the 'Golden Age' of Welsh hymnody, scripture and hymns were in a symbiotic relationship, the one enriching the understanding of the other. This is deeper than the use of literary imagery, akin to the classical allusions that English writers of the eighteenth and nineteenth centuries were so fond of or even the religious and church life allusions used by Welsh writers in the nineteenth century and the first part of the twentieth. Allusions such as these do, of course, enrich our reading as a single word or reference brings to mind other allusions and contexts so that the reader creates for himself a many-layered text, beyond perhaps what the author himself had envisaged. But the intertextuality of the hymn is different, for what is produced is not a literary or cultural experience but the expression of a shared conviction. Notwithstanding their valued private use, hymns are essentially communal and are a central element in corporate worship[17]—is there not something paradoxical about solo hymn singing as a concert or eisteddfod item?—and scriptural allusions, quotations and typology are part of the life that members of congregations, and indeed of the broader church, have in common. From the mid-nineteenth century to the period of World War II (and even to some extent beyond), nonconformity, in spite of the name, was to all intents and purposes the established form of Christianity in Wales. The great majority of church adherents were nonconformist, the leaders, both national and local, were leaders in many aspects of public life, both cultural and political, and there was a broad consensus of general attitudes; theological differences were on particular issues—

16. D. Gwenallt Jones (1899–1968) expressed the part that hymns played in his spiritual journey in his poem, 'Yr hen emynau' ('The old hymns'), *Gwreiddiau*, Aberystwyth: Gwasg Aberystwyth, 1959, 12–13. They sang as birds above his cradle and in the communal life of his youth but he banished them from the trees with the cudgel and gun of materialistic philosophy and science. Unknown to him, they continued their song, and when the light returned to the woods they rose again, their song having matured in the dark night and bringing to him the manger and the empty grave in a new brilliant brightness.

17. For the performative aspect of hymns, see Kathryn Jenkins, 'Ailddiffinio'r emyn: y cyd-destun perfformiadol,' in *Cân y ffydd: ysgrifau ar emynyddiaeth* (ed. Rhidian Grifiths, forthcoming).

Calvinism, baptism, church government among them—and frequently had as much to so with denominational rivalry as conviction. To all appearances, churches were thriving, their life characterised by popular preaching, large congregations and a full programme of activities, but familiar hymns were losing their appropriate context and in a predominately nonconformist society they were in danger of becoming the popular songs of the day to be used in non-religious environments as well as in worship. Astute observers like the novelist Daniel Owen could see the dry rot in the woodwork. His novel, *Hunangofiant Rhys Lewis* (1882–85), describes the tension between the old generation of devout believers and the younger more questioning generation forced to bring their Christianity face to face with new industrialism, and his later novel, *Profedigaethau Enoc Huws* (1890–91), is a sustained satirical criticism of the hypocrisy of chapel life in a small town and of the weakening of the convictions professed. What Daniel Owen had seen was that established church life had begun to feed off itself and that it was losing its external inspiration. In the context of hymnody, what had been vital scriptural allusions and images, an adventurous interweaving of themes, verses and words understood and capable of invoking a response, became the stereotypes of hymn writing. One senses not so much a lack of conviction but a conventionalised theology expressed in a tired style and vocabulary. Granted the danger of generalisations, it appears that Welsh hymns, apart from some 'social witness' hymns, have not achieved the 'directness and normality of language'[18] that characterises many modern English hymns. Indeed, it has been said that many Welsh hymns of the twentieth century could have been written any time since the eighteenth, one critic going so far as to term them 'imitations', written in the style of and reflecting the ideas of a past age.[19]

More positively, many twentieth-century hymns, though not overtly theological or directly bible-based, are hymns of social action and compassionate response to the plight of society across the world. They comfort and exhort and are conscious of the injustices and inequalities of life worldwide. (The Welsh Methodist hymnal of 1927 in a section on social issues had 21 hymns out of a total of 767, *Caneuon*

---

18. Richard Watson and Kenneth Trickett, eds., *Companion to 'Hymns & Psalms'* (London: Methodist Publishing House, 1988), 29.

19. D. Tecwyn Lloyd, 'Canu emyn a chanu crefydd', *Y Goleuad* 31/3/1989, 1, 8, 7/4/1989, 6–7, p. 6.

Ffydd contains 69 out of a total of 873.). This is not to say that they are not inspired by Christian conviction and theology, or by the prophets and the Jesus of the Bible but it is true that hymns of the second part of the twentieth century tend to be less obviously scriptural in imagery and language, a reflection of the less than central role of Bible reading among today's Welsh Christians perhaps. One should note here that the rhetoric of the 1988 Welsh translation of the Bible is different from that of the 1588–1620 version which was designed more for public reading, but, nevertheless, decline in Bible study in the chapels began long before 1988. There is a danger that classical Welsh hymns become intellectually (and culturally) unintelligible. Scriptural referents are not literary allusions, for they must be touched by the spark of the faith and conviction both of the hymnist and the worshipper. Losing their field of scriptural reference, allusions tend to be comprehended literally and may in some cases be unacceptable, aesthetically ('washed in blood,' 'a lake of blood,' and the like) or socially (Williams Pantycelyn's *cannu'r Ethiop*, 'to blanch the Ethiopean,' based on Jeremiah 13:23 and Acts 8, was changed in *Caneuon Ffydd* (730) to 'blanch the darkest,' the metaphor of the darkness of sin being more acceptable, by most, than an unfamiliar biblical reference). Even as experienced a literary critic as D.Tecwyn Lloyd felt uncomfortable that Williams Pantycelyn should address Christ as *Anwylyd* ('Beloved'), *Priod* ('Spouse'), *rhosyn Saron* ('rose of Sharon'), though his actual comment would, today, be unacceptable to many (*Yng ngenau ac yn llên gŵr, mae ymadroddion fel hyn am ŵr arall yn annaturiol ac, yn fy marn i, yn afiach*: 'On the lips and in the writing of a man, phrases like these about another man are unnatural and, in my opinion, unhealthy')[20]—so are we all children of our culture. Even if the biblical reference is lost, or at least hazy, some allusions may have a residue of literal significance or a recognised literary quality and thus retain some meaning; to take a few examples, the prayers of the saints ascend 'with their windows open to Salem,' 'the balm of Gilead,' the bitter waters of Marah, 'the voice of the turtledove,' water 'from the well of Bethlehem,' the valley of the dry bones, and though the image is not familiar, the import of the hymn, *Wele'n sefyll rhwng y myrtwydd* ('Lo, standing among the myrtle trees' 319, Zechariah 1:10) is clear enough. There is no doubt, however that in

---

20. Tecwyn Lloyd, art. cit, 6.

cases such as these the image is impoverished and the strength of the reference reduced. Tecwyn Lloyd[21] asserted some twenty years ago that he doubted whether anyone under the age of twenty-five would understand the allusion to *Preswylydd mawr y berth* (763, cf.119,600). These hymnists were not simply quoting Deuteronomy 33:16 ('of him that dwelt in the bush') but they had in mind the whole field of reference to the burning bush in Exodus 3:2 so that what is being lost is not a title for God but the value of an important episode, for Moses and for us, in the awareness of His nature.

Hymns also contain 'hidden' allusions, that is, the content derives from a specific event that remains un-named. J. Edward Williams (1931–2005) opens, 'Thou who walked the path to Emaus' (633) and the reference and its application are clear enough, but one wonders whether congregations gain the deepest understanding of Elfed's evening hymn (43) which is wholly based on the (unspoken) encounter of the two disciples and the risen Christ. Similarly, Nantlais Williams's hymn 'Who is this who walked the waters' (377) reflects Mark 6:45–56 in some detail while J. T. Job's Ascension hymn (577) is a rich tapestry of allusions from Acts 1:9, 2:6, Psalm 24:7, Revelation 14:1 and even 2 Kings 2:11. Typology is both allusion to and interpretation of God's Word, and as our comprehension of hymns becomes attenuated so, too, is the medium of our communal worship. This is broader than our hymnody, for we may be losing the grammar of religious language which is of necessity full of biblical imagery and find ourselves once more, like the woman at Jacob's well, like Nicodemus, like the disciples in John 6, especially 54–58, having to learn the words so that we may recognise the concepts. The loss of imagery may, indeed, be more far reaching than uncertainty about technical terms, e.g. 'grace,' 'salvation,' 'covenant,' 'reconciliation,' that are used in the more theologically driven hymns.

If scriptural references tend to pass us by, it does not follow that the Bible cannot continue to be a vital source for our worship. Some hymnists have taken passages of the Bible, rather than single verses, as the basis of extended mediation. The application of scripture to contemporary situations is, of course, central to much preaching so that it is not difficult to imagine that these hymnists have drawn on their ex-

---

21. Tecwyn Lloyd, art. cit. 6; cf. J. Gwilym Jones, 'Yr emyn fel llenyddiaeth,' 128.

perience as preachers and pastors in writing some of their hymns. The allegory of the True Vine (John 15:1-6) is one such passage that lends itself as a vehicle to consider church life. Morgan D. Jones is concerned with the fragmented witness of the church in contemporary Wales (620). Christ the True Vine is the first of the scriptural metaphors that he uses in this prayer for Christian unity and in each of the following stanzas he has a different figure who is addressed—the Shepherd calling his scattered flock together to the same fold, Christ, the Head, healing His bruised body and ridding us of our petty differences, the Architect and Builder creating a firm edifice of 'lively stones' to raise up Zion once again. Arthur Williams (1910-83) takes the familiar passage of the vine and its branches portraying the life of the church as life in Christ. In his hymn (285) it becomes a prayer that we, barren branches as we are, may be spared and not cut away as utterly worthless but that the merciful hand of the Gardener may cleanse and dress us so that Christ's sap may rise in these withered branches and so that we may bear fruit (calling to mind, no doubt, that other vine that was spared and given an opportunity to respond to God's active mercy). The hymn is a pastoral reading of the allegory.

Another of the sayings of Jesus, the structure of which invites the composition of a hymn, is John 14:6, 'I am the way, the truth and the life: no man cometh unto the Father, but by me'. Both W. Rhys Nicholas and Tudor Davies, two of the most productive and most popular hymn writers in Wales today, have been drawn to this verse but in different ways. In three stanzas Rhys Nicholas (342) develops each of the three phrases to be prayers for grace to withstand the temptations of the negatives to Christ's metaphors: that we depart from the paths that have led to weary disappointment and seek the unchanging and incomparable way of Christ and that we are rescued from the deceit of cynical words and wealth that denigrate life. Christ, the everlasting life, is the fountain of strength that overcomes the world and the hymn ends on a note of exultant praise for the life that is full of grace and mercy. It is not difficult here to be aware of a hymnist speaking directly to his congregation in plain words that are immediately meaningful and without any biblical allusions other than the three phrases (that do not rely on recognition of their source for their significance).[22]

22. For a study of Rhys Nicholas's hymns, see Cynthia and Saunders Davies, 'Emynydd o'r Fro: W. Rhys Nicholas (1914-96),' *Bwletin Cymdeithas Emynau Cymru,*

Tudor Davies (386) offers his congregation a more personal response to the three phrases but, interestingly, in four stanzas; worshippers are invited to share the hymnist's meditation on the Person of Christ and to make it their own. Tudor Davies has frequently emphasised that he writes his hymns with specific tunes in mind, and this is particularly clear here where he uses a tune hitherto uniquely associated with a hymn of thanksgiving for the light of the gospel. *Diolch i ti, yr hollalluog Dduw* (49, attributed to David Charles, 1762–1834, and perhaps a translation) remains popular, especially so in the former 'mission fields' of the Presbyterian Church in north-east India, modern Meghalya and Mizoram. Each stanza of Tudor Davies's hymn opens with an address, *O Grist*, a statement—you are the way to God the Father, the truth of the meaning of life, life in its fullness for all who believe, the door to your world of peace and grace; each second line is an expression of thanksgiving, of worship, a prayer for trust and for the coming of the kingdom within us. Each stanza closes, as does the 'mission' hymn, with 'Halelwia, Amen'. The hymn is deceptively simple, for its very directness and restraint guide the meditation of the congregation effectively while they sing, and here again, recognition of the context of the saying in John is not crucial for the understanding of the hymn. Tudor Davies has used the same simple structure in his stanzas as the well known *Diolch i ti*, so that in its singing congregations are inevitably reminded by the tune of the wider setting of the new words and their spiritual (or ecclesiastical) experience deepened.

In 1971, greatly moved by scenes of starvation and suffering that he had seen on television news, Tudor Davies was inspired (a word to be understood in its full meaning) to write a hymn that he entitled simply *Cymorth Cristnogol* ('Christian Aid'). In five powerful stanzas (always sung to the tune 'Arizona') he commits to God the starving millions dragging out an existence in the shadow of the grave and whose death looks us in the face. He prays that we may be granted God's compassion to recognise these as our brothers and sisters and not turn away from their plight but rather to become Samaritans to them. 'Grant that we may learn how to minister joyfully to those in need, bringing real hope

---

4:1–2 (2008–2009) 14–32. Cf. also Kathryn Jenkins, 'W.Rhys Nicholas a'r emynau,' *Cristion*, 93 (Mawrth/Ebrill 1999), 5–6. For Tudor Davies's work see Kathryn Jenkins, 'Rhai agweddau ar yr Emyn Gymraeg Ddiweddar' (sic), *Y Traethodydd*, 156 (2000) 102–11.

Hymns and Scripture

and a desire for the nourishment of faith'. The hymn closes with the conviction that the gospel alone can meet all the needs of the mankind; 'even all is not enough without you: bread of our life, sustain us'. Like all Tudor Davies's hymns, this is well crafted, written in natural language and immediate in its point, as it moves from unmistakable physical suffering to spiritual need. But what makes the transition interesting, as a biblically based hymn, is the way that Tudor Davies has used the account of the feeding of the five thousand in St. John's Gospel in its fullest context as his meditation. This 'sign' is frequently read as the account of a single miraculous event. But nothing in this Gospel is to be taken at face value and the narrative has to be read through John 6 to 6:58 as it progresses from the feeding of the 5000 at the time of the Passover to the second encounter with the multitude the following day. At verse 26 it becomes clear that the 'sign' is not only of physical hunger but of spiritual need. Jesus proclaims himself the Bread of Life, which alone can bring 'life unto the world' and satisfy the deepest hunger and thirst. The path of meditation in John 6 is mirrored in Tudor Davies's hymn and the two are brought together in the final words of the hymn, *bara ein bywyd, cynnal ni*.

We have moved some distance from biblical quotations, allusions and imagery. If the style and diction of traditional Welsh hymnody are a language to be learned, paraphrases of portions of the Bible in natural language can become hymns, while meditating creatively on extended passages of scripture through the medium of hymns, and making explicit the association of hymns and Bible in communal worship, will be a means of making Bible reading central and full of meaning to today's congregations.

9

The Transmission of Biblical Visual Imagery in the Calvinistic Methodist / Presbyterian Church of Wales

D. Huw Owen

A number of comparatively recent publications have corrected the erroneous view that the Welsh Calvinistic Methodists, the forerunners of the Presbyterian Church of Wales, together with the other Nonconformist denominations of Wales, were fiercely opposed to the use of biblical visual imagery in their religious activities.[1] It is certainly true that they were influenced by the views expressed during the Reformation forbidding the use of images in worship. John Calvin, who was a dominant influence on the Welsh church which bears his name, placed great emphasis on the injunction in the Second Commandment: "You shall not make a carved image for yourself nor the likeness of anything

---

1. Peter Lord, *Hugh Hughes, Arlunydd Gwlad, 1790–1863* (Llandysul: Gomer. 1995); Peter Lord, *Imaging the Nation. The Visual Culture of Wales* (Cardiff: University of Wales Press, 2000); John Harvey, *The Art of Piety. The Visual Culture of Welsh Nonconformity* (Cardiff: University of Wales Press. 1995; Harvey, John. *Image of the Invisible: The Visualization of Religion in the Welsh Nonconformist Tradition* (Cardiff: University of Wales Press. 1999); O'Kane, Martin, and John Morgan-Guy, eds. *Biblical Art from Wales* (Sheffield: Phoenix, 2010).

The Transmission of Biblical Visual Imagery

in the heavens above, or on the earth below, or in the waters under the earth."[2]

This led Calvin to argue that God 'rejects, without exception, all shapes and pictures, and other symbols by which the superstitious imagine they can bring Him near them.'[3] Any attempt to visually represent God was condemned by Calvin, who emphasised the dangers of images, even though they might have been intended to assist believers becoming themselves objects of idolatry. He was especially critical of the portrayal of religious leaders, including prophets, saints and martyrs, as frequently found in churches.[4] Calvin's views were echoed in the catechism by Alexander Nowell, the English Puritan, published in 1570 which enacted that portraits and paintings were not forbidden provided that they played no part in the worship of God, and stated that images and pictures were considered to be "very perilous" in churches.[5] The English translation of Calvin's catechism for children, 1594, stated that God did not forbid the making of any image, but he did forbid any image to either represent Him or to be used to worship him.[6] The early Calvinistic Methodist 'Fathers' may well have been aware not only of the determined efforts to remove images and paintings from churches during the sixteenth and seventeenth centuries, but also a reluctance to obey the instructions issued to enforce their removal.[7] The Welsh people were generally considered to have been superstitious in the early seventeenth century, and in the reign of James I they were described as "an idolatrous nation and worshippers of Devils."[8] John Calvin had accepted that works of art, which he considered to be gifts from God, were permissible in certain circumstances, and these included the depiction

---

2. Exodus 20: 4 (NEB).

3. John Calvin, *Institutes of the Christian Religion* (trans. Henry Beveridge; 3 vols.; Edinburgh: Calvin Translation Society, 1845), I, 120–21.

4. Harvey, *Art of Piety*, 5–6; Calvin, *Institutes*, I, 133.

5. Alexander Nowell. *A Catechism Written in Latin by Alexander Nowell* (ed. G. E. Corrie; Cambridge, 1853), 123–24.

6. Margaret Ashton, *England's Iconoclasts* (Oxford: Oxford University Press, 1998), I, 447–48.

7. Glanmor Williams, *Wales and the Reformation* (Cardiff: University of Wales Press, 1997), 299–301, 319–20.

8. Jenkins, Geraint H. *The Foundations of Modern Wales, 1642–1780* (Oxford: Oxford University Press, 1987); J. Gwyn Williams, "Witchcraft in Seventeenth-century Flintshire," *Flintshire Historical Society Journal* 26–27 (1975–76) 22.

of historical events which could be valuable for teaching purposes. However, in places of worship the significant media for the instruction of Christian believers was through "the preaching of the Word and the administration of the sacraments."[9]

This continues to be a basic tenet of the Presbyterian Church of Wales, but yet the Church, through the medium of a number of significant artists and photographers, has made a considerable contribution to the visual cultural heritage of Wales. At the same time there has been an occasional reluctance to be involved in artistic activities and an awareness of the need to defend the use of visual material. These trends are illustrated in various incidents relating to the activities of two prominent artists, Hugh Hughes and S. Maurice Jones, who were active Calvinistic Methodist members. One of the Calvinistic Methodist leaders who became the subject of a portrait by Hugh Hughes was Robert Dafydd, Brynengan, a weaver and Methodist counsellor, originally from Cwmbychan, near Nantmor. In a tribute by Henry Hughes, Bryncir, published in 1893, he was described as six foot tall, with a very strong body, large head and wide face, with his white hair, like wool, for thirty years before his death, falling over his shoulders. Having come under the influence of Robert Jones, Rhos-lan, and attended his school, he had travelled approximately 12 to 15 miles to services held at Brynengan, before deciding to reside there. It was suggested that Robert Dafydd had expressed considerable reluctance to be portrayed, as he was aware that the danger of the attention to himself might lead to idolatry, thereby remind us of Calvin's writings on this subject. However, he agreed to the portrait as the completed portrait would be a correct depiction and not an imaginary image.[10] This also seems to have been the attitude of the other leaders of the Calvinistic Methodist Connexion portrayed by Hugh Hughes. The artist was also obliged to present a defence for the inclusion of visual material in the children's periodical *Yr Addysgydd*, 1823, whose significance is discussed below. He therefore referred to their entertainment value, their ability to assist in the understanding of the events portrayed, and the opportunity

---

9. Harvey, *Art of Piety*, 5-6; Calvin, *Institutes*, I, 127.

10. Henry Hughes, "Robert Dafydd, Brynengan," *Y Traethodydd* 48 (1893) 111-22; John Aaron, *The Calvinistic Methodist Fathers of Wales* [translation of J. Morgan Jones and William Morgan, *Y Tadau Methodistaidd* (Swansea, 1895-97; reprinted, Edinburgh: The Banner of Truth Trust, 2008), 2:95-105.

The Transmission of Biblical Visual Imagery

to illustrate the extraordinary events in the Scriptures.[11] Later in the century, about the year 1870, the artist Samuel Maurice Jones recalled the difficulties experienced when an 'old saint' was evidently troubled by his intention to study the arts and had called for the church authorities to investigate the matter. Despite this incident, the artist made a notable contribution to the history of Welsh visual culture, and also was a prominent member of the Connexion.[12]

Two events in 1811 had made a considerable impression on Hugh Hughes. In August 1811, 343 pictures and sculptures were displayed in the large exhibition held in Liverpool. The exhibits included works by the famous sculptor John Gibson who, with his brother Solomon hailed from the Llandudno area, as also did Hugh Hughes, and the three young men attended the same Sunday School in the Pall Mall chapel, Liverpool.[13] Earlier in the same summer, on 19–20 June. Hugh Hughes was present at the historic *Sasiwn* [Association] held at Bala when eight individuals from the north, were ordained as ministers of religion. The result of this action, followed by the ordination of eleven ministers from the south, was the separation of the Calvinistic Methodists from the Anglican Church and their establishment as a separate denomination.[14] Attendance at the *Sasiwn* inspired Hugh Hughes to plan the execution of portraits, in the form of miniatures, of the more prominent Methodist leaders of north Wales, whose roles as "men of the Word" was undoubtedly fully appreciated by the artist. The undoubted leader of the Calvinistic Methodists in 1811 was Thomas Charles, who had reluctantly agreed to the momentous action taken at Bala in spite of his earlier opposition to the ordination of ministers, as he was fully aware of the implications involved. A naïve and crude portrait, in the form of a watercolour drawing on a card, was produced, c. 1812, and this was the source of the image which became very popular in Wales during the course of the nineteenth century on the basis of a number of engravings and photographs, with the naïve drawing transformed into a

---

11. Peter Lord, "The Bible in the Artisan Tradition of Welsh Visual Culture," in *Biblical Art from Wales*, 103.

12. Ibid., 103.

13. Peter Lord, "John Gibson and Hugh Hughes: British attitudes and Welsh Art," in *Gwenllian: Essays on Visual Culture* (Llandysul: Gomer, 1994), 9–35; Lord, *Hugh Hughes*, 9–21.

14. Aaron, *Calvinistic Methodist Fathers of Wales*, 378–431.

mirror-image of the respectable middle-class Methodist establishment. A pen and book were added to the portrait by J. Collyer in the first engraving, in 1812, and thereby conform to the contemporary convention. The portrait was adapted for a new print, c. 1838, by the engraver Bailey in response to a request by Robert Saunderson, the Bala publisher, "instead of a pen, he [Thomas Charles] had better appear in the act of preaching—and to have the Bible before him, and a Reading Glass in his right hand… you will also please to tell him to put as much benevolence as he can in Mr. Charles's countenance-for he certainly had a most benign smile when animated by his subject."[15] The addition of the open Bible in this portrait was appropriate, in view of Thomas Charles's activities in the period which witnessed the establishment of the British and Foreign Bible Society. Other versions of the Hugh Hughes portrait which circulated widely throughout Wales were John Thomas's *carte de visite* photograph, c.1870, and the engravings by E. Pick, c. 1880, and Edward Jones, Bala, c. 1900. The original naïve portrait was also the basis for the oil portrait by William Roos, the artisan painter from Anglesey, c. 1835, and also for the statue by William Davies (Mynorydd) which was unveiled outside Capel Tegid, Bala, in 1872.[16]

A Bible was also significantly placed in a prominent position in Hugh Hughes's portrait of John Roberts, with the Methodist leader from Llangwm depicted as reading part of the Gospel of St. John.[17] Two of the other original Methodist ministers from north Wales were portrayed by Hugh Hughes, and again extremely-popular engravings were widely-distributed. Thomas Jones, Denbigh had argued forcefully in favour of the ordination of ministers before 1811, and in 1820, an engraving by R. Burt, based on a watercolour drawing, was published in 1820 on the frontispiece of a biography of him. It is probable that Hugh Hughes was responsible for the engraving in 1812 of John Elias, who became the leader of the Methodists after the deaths of Thomas Charles and Thomas Jones. Hugh Hughes also portrayed Mary Lloyd, Llanrwst and Mrs. Lloyd, Llangwm, the wives respectively of John Elias and John Roberts, and also John Evans, who had worked as a weaver

---

15. Lord, "The Popular Iconography of the Preacher," in Lord, *Gwenllian: Essays on Visual Culture* (Llandysul: Gomer, 1994), 47–49; Lord, *Hugh Hughes*, 24–27, 30–32; Lord, *Imaging the Nation*, 206–7.

16. Lord, *Imaging the Nation*, 278.

17. Lord, *The Bible in the Artisan Tradition*, 99.

and as a leadminer in the Coed-poeth area before moving to Bala. A friend and co-worker of Thomas Charles, he had led the devotion at the Bala *Sasiwn*, 1811, and was described as 'the embodiment, as it were, of the Methodist tradition in the North'.[18] An engraving of the portrait, painted in oil on canvas in 1812, was published in the denominational magazine, *Trysorfa Ysbrydiol* (1819) and widely distributed.[19] This painting is regarded as one of the "classics of our visual art", with Hugh Hughes having succeeded in producing "an image of remarkable presence."[20]

Another highly-regarded work was Hugh Hughes's painting in 1813 of the family of Huw Griffith, Bodwrda, at their home near Aberdaron in the Lleyn peninsula. Huw Griffith, a successful farmer and tenant on the Nanhoron estate of the Edwards family, was an elder in the Penycaerau chapel for over 30 years and was one of the most prominent Methodists on the Lleyn peninsula.[21] Pwllheli was one of the main centres associated with Hugh Hughes, who distributed leaflets and posters publicising his work in the town and among the members of Penmount chapel, whose leader was Michael Roberts, the son of the Rev. John Roberts, and his wife, who had been the subject of his early portraits.[22] Hugh Hughes had completed the greater part of his series of the Methodist fathers by 1814 when he moved to London. By 1817 he had established himself as an independent engraver in Wilderness Road, Clerkenwell. He had probably carefully selected this location as his work-shop was very near to the Calvinistic Methodist chapel in the same road. He continued to visit Wales, and, having previously concentrated on the Methodist leaders, the popular appeal of the movement was illustrated by his engraving of the 1816 *Sasiwn* at Bala with a large number of common people attracted to the Association meeting.[23] He

---

18. Lord, *Hugh Hughes*, 27–29.

19. Lord, Catalog Arddangosfa/Exhibition Catalogue, *Hugh Hughes: 1790–1863, Arlunydd Gwlad, Artisan Painter* (Aberystwyth: The National Library of Wales. 1990), 14.

20. Ibid., 14; Lord. *Imaging the Nation*, 205.

21. Lord. *Hugh Hughes*, opposite p. 32; Lord, *Imaging the Nation*, 182.

22. Further information on Michael Roberts and Penmount Church is available in Hughes, D. G. Lloyd. *Hanes Eglwys Penmount Pwllheli* (Pwllheli: Pwyllgor Dathlu. 1981), 32–34, 39.

23. Lord, *Imaging the Nation*, 206–7.

returned again to Bala in 1820, and recorded with amazement the large congregations which assembled for the meetings. He referred to nine thousand present one evening in a service with two preachers, "most excellent and impressive", and, the following morning, he listened to "seven sermons of the same class, the congregation swelled to seventeen or eighteen thousand."[24]

Hugh Hughes's activities had tended to concentrate on north Wales, Liverpool and London before 1821, but Carmarthen became increasingly significant to him following his visit to the town in that year. As a result of his contact with John Evans, a successful printer and publisher of several volumes, together with the *Carmarthen Journal*, he painted John Evans 's family at breakfast, c. 1822-4. This has been considered to have been one of the masterpieces of Welsh visual culture, and the most important Welsh painting in the first half of the nineteenth century.[25] Hugh Hughes and John Evans co-operated on a number of projects, including the preparation of visual material in Welsh for children. One of these was *Yr Addysgydd* (1823) the first original Welsh-language publication for children to include pictures illustrating events from the Old Testament and the New Testament, such as the ones of *The Flood, Jonah and the Whale* and *The Healing of the Lame Man*. This periodical only survived for one year, but yet it is regarded as an important one as it was a model for several denominational periodicals produced for the use of Sunday schools.[26]

Hugh Hughes was responsible for the pictures, and he was also the co-editor of the periodical with another Carmarthen man, namely David Charles the younger. He was the son of David Charles, senior, the brother of Thomas Charles, a ropemaker in Carmarthen and one of the first group of ministers ordained in south Wales in 1811. David Charles was portrayed by Hugh Hughes, c. 1827, and the artist was responsible for two published versions of his sermons, one edited in Welsh in 1840 and the other, together with a memoir, in English in 1846.[27] In the

24. Lord, *Hugh Hughes*, 35-6.

25. Ibid., 111; Lord, "The Family of John Evans at Breakfast and the Concept of Quality in Painting," *Planet*, 114 (December–January 1995-96) 70; and in Lord, *The Meaning of Pictures: Images of Personal, Social and Political Identity* (Cardiff: University of Wales Press. 2009), 60.

26. Lord, *Hugh Hughes*, 112-15.

27. Ibid., 130, 217-19, 247, 249-50.

memoir, reference was made to his impressive appearance and his gifts as a preacher: "His countenance was fine, and possessed of extraordinary power of expression, particularly when lit up by the light of the truths which occupied his contemplation, and fired the powers of his soul."[28] Also, his continuing influence on the artist when administering the Communion: "Some instances witnessed by the writer, wherein Mr. Charles administered the Lord's supper were so remarkable, that the remembrance can never be effaced . . . to enjoy such a treat once in an age is enough to balance much of life's labours and sorrows."[29] Hugh Hughes depicted several members of David Charles's family. Two of his daughters who may be seen in the oil painting of his family, 1822–1827, were Sarah, who married Hugh Hughes and appeared with her husband and daughter in a picture, c.1830; and Eliza, who married the merchant Robert Davies, and who, together with their children, David Charles and Sarah, were painted as a family, c. 1833–4.[30] This family was again significant in the history of the Presbyterian Church of Wales. The *Cyffes Ffydd* [Confession of Faith] of the Calvinistic Methodists was prepared at their home in Aberystwyth in 1823, and David Charles Davies became a minister and principal of the Connexional college at Trefeca.[31]

The need for a chapel in a more central location led to the opening of the Jewin Crescent chapel in 1823. The new chapel was painted by Robert Owen who had moved to London in 1824 from Caernarfon where he had been trained as a painter, and was praised for his work of placing the arms of the family on a set of chairs at Glynllifon Park, the home of Lord Newborough.[32] He was described as an enthusiastic member, and one of the pillars of the Sunday school.[33] He co-operated with Hugh Hughes on the compilation of *Canau Duwiol*, 1826, a Welsh translation of Isaac Watts's hymns for children in the Sunday school,

28. Ibid., 250; Hugh Hughes, *Sermons of the Rev. David Charles, Carmarthen, with a Memoir* (1846), 17.

29. Lord, *Hugh Hughes*, 125; Hugh Hughes. *Sermons*, 16.

30. Lord, *Hugh Hughes*, 128–29, 192–93, 234.

31. *Welsh Biography On-line*. David Charles Davies (1826–1891).

32. Lord, *Hugh Hughes*, 157–58; Lord, *Arlunwyr Gwlad/Artisan Painters* (Aberystwyth: The National Library of Wales. 1993), 16–17.

33. Gomer M. Roberts, *Y Ddinas Gadarn, Hanes Eglwys Jewin Llundain* (London: Pwyllgor Dathlu Daucanmlwyddiant Eglwys Jewin, 1974), 72.

and Hugh Hughes's contribution included the production of a wood engraving of the new chapel.[34] By 1828 Hugh Hughes, a fervent supporter of the measure to grant full civic rights to Roman Catholics, was in the middle of a fierce debate which divided the membership of the Jewin Crescent chapel, and he was expelled from membership of the church, largely through the influence of John Elias.[35] Despite this action, he continued to be an acceptable portrait painter in Calvinistic Methodist circles. In 1835 he was commissioned to produce a portrait of Lydia Jones, the daughter of Lydia Foulkes who was the sister of Simon Lloyd, Bala, the Methodist cleric and who had been portrayed by him in 1825–6.[36] Prominent Methodists who were his sitters in the following years included the Rev. John Evans, Llwynffortun, another of the first group of south Wales Methodist ministers ordained in 1811. An engraved version of this oil painting of 1839 was produced by Richard Woodman in 1847.[37] In 1841 Hugh Hughes painted the portraits of John Davies, Fronheulog, Llandderfel, a landowner and justice of the peace, and one of those who compiled the Confession of Faith, 1823, and his wife Jennet: these portraits were described as being "among his most accomplished portraits in an academic manner."[38]

Hugh Hughes had moved to Caernarfon by 1835, and William Roos, a native of Amlwch, had already moved there, as in the previous year he had advertised his availability as a portrait painter. Caernarfon developed into an important centre for artisan painters, with several of them competing with Hugh Hughes for commissions from the middle class. William Roos claimed that he had completed a portrait of John Elias in 1839, the same year as Hugh Jones's famous portrait of the renowned preacher. An engraving of this portrait was commissioned in 1840, probably on account of the connection between William Jones, the portrait painter from Chester and the artist's brother, and the publisher Edward Parry. This portrait, the basis for Samuel Bellin's engraving published by Edward Parry in Chester, became a very popular icon in Wales, as also was the one of Christmas

---

34. Lord, *Hugh Hughes*, 159; Lord, *Artisan Painters*, 17, 19.
35. Roberts, *Jewin*, 58–68.
36. Lord, *Hugh Hughes*, 134–35, 229–30.
37. Ibid., 228, 230.
38. Ibid., 233–34; Lord, *Imaging the Nation*, 197.

Evans, the Baptist leader, painted by William Roos in 1835.[39] It is uncertain whether an engraved version of William Roos's portrait of John Elias was based on an oil painting by him, either the alleged one in 1839, another one in 1841 or a copy of Hugh Jones's work. The suggestion has been made that this engraving was the basis of the Staffordshire figure of John Elias, which, together with those of Christmas Evans and John Bryan, the eminent Baptist and Wesleyan Methodist preachers, were extremely popular.[40] William Roos also produced in the 1830s an oil painting based on Hugh Hughes's portrait of 1812, but influenced by Bailey's engraving of 1838.[41]

Another generation of portrait artists was later attracted to the town. Evan Williams, a native of Lledrod, Ceredigion, who had been ordained by the Calvinistic Methodists in 1859, contributed a number of substantial articles on visual art to the influential journal, *Y Traethodydd*.[42] This had been established in 1845 by the Rev. Lewis Edwards, the principal of Bala Theological College, with the intention of improving the tastes of the Welsh people, extend their cultural horizons and assist in the creation of a literary medium which had not previously existed in Wales.[43] In the first of a series of articles which appeared in 1848 and 1849 on the subject "Y Gelfyddyd o Arlunio" [The Art of Painting] he declared that he could not recall reading anything in Welsh on this form of art, or indeed on any other of the main arts, and this amazed him as so many of the Welsh people had distinguished themselves in the arts. He specifically referred to Richard Wilson, and to two individuals residing at the time in Rome, the artist Penry Williams and the sculptor John Gibson, who was, as previously mentioned, a former member of the Pall Mall Sunday school, Liverpool.[44] In 1865, before criticising pre-Raphaelite artists, by declaring that the style of Holman Hunt and

---

39. Lord, *Artisan Painters*, 38–40.

40. Lord, *Popular Iconography*, 52.

41. Lord, *Artisan Painters*, 37–38; National Library of Wales Ms. 9031 E.

42. Ibid., 49; Evan Williams, "Y Gelfyddyd o Arlunio," *Y Traethodydd* 4 (1848) 423–34; 5 (1849) 44–52, 357–69.

43. D. Densil Morgan, *Lewis Edwards* (Cardiff: University of Wales Press, 2009), 105; ibid., 101–4 for beginnings of journal.

44. Williams, *Y Gelfyddyd*, 423.

Madox Brown was completely *cyfeiliornus* [heretical] he declared that artistic standards were to a degree alien to the Welsh people.[45]

In 1848 he had produced a portrait of the Rev. John Jones, Tal-y-sarn, and an engraving of this portrait had proved to be very popular.[46] As a result of public subscriptions he was commissioned to paint a portrait of Ebenezer Thomas, the poet and hymnwriter "Eben Fardd," who had established a preparatory school for candidates for the ministry with the Calvinistic Methodists in 1850 and the portrait was presented to him at the Madog Eisteddfod in 1851.[47] By this time the artist had settled in Caernarfon, and he resided there until his death in 1878. Another important portrait for which he was responsible was the one of the Rev. John Roberts, 'Ieuan Gwyllt' the Calvinistic Methodist minister in Merthyr Tudful and Llanberis, who was a notable musician and the editor of several volumes, including the significant collection of hymns, *Llyfr Tonau Cynulleidfaol* (1859). This portrait was dated 1878, the year of Ieuan Gwyllt's death, and it is therefore probable that the portrait was completed after the sitter's death.[48] The growing popularity of photography, as discussed below, had a considerable effect on the artisan painting tradition. There was an increasing tendency for the commissioning of professional artists, and it is therefore significant in this context that Jerry Barrett, the renowned London-based artist responsible for the famous picture of Florence Nightingale, was invited by the Connexion's leaders to produce a portrait of the Rev.Lewis Edwards. A person present at the unveiling of the portrait was reported to have described the occasion as 'a scene of awful seboni [flattery].'[49] There was also an increasing emphasis on the provision of art education, as illustrated in the career of S. Maurice Jones. Born in 1855, the son of the Rev. John Jones, Calvinistic Methodist minister in Mochdre, Llanllechid, Caernarfon and Capel Mawr, Rhosllannerchrugog, described as one of the giants of the Methodist pulpit and one of the most popular

---

45. Evan Williams, "Sefyllfa Gelfyddyd yng Nghymru," *Y Traethodydd* 20 (1865) 423.

46. Lord, *Artisan Painters*, 43.

47. Ibid., 44; Lord, *Imaging the Nation*, 239; Dyfed Evans, "Darlun neu ddau heb ddod i'r fei," *Y Casglwr* 21 (1983) 3.

48. Lord, *Artisan Painters*, 42, 46–48, 58.

49. Lord, *Popular Iconography*, 69.

and powerful preachers in Wales.⁵⁰ He was an active elder of Moriah, Caernarfon from 1899, Sunday school teacher, President of the Arfon Presbytery and Chairman of the Union of Free Churches of the town. Following a period of instruction at the Caernarfon Art School, he studied in Liverpool under the guidance of William Collingwood, and then, whilst at the South Kensington Art School, attended lectures delivered by John Ruskin at the National Gallery. He published a series of articles in *Y Traethodydd* on the theme of 'Datblygiad Arluniaeth yng Nghymru' [The Development of Art in Wales], and he arranged exhibitions at the National Eisteddfod and in galleries including the Walker Gallery, Liverpool. He was a prominent member of the group of artists who assembled in Betws-y-coed , and he coined the term "Yr Arlunfa Gymreig" [The Welsh Studio] to describe this community. He immensely admired the work of David Cox, one of the artists associated with Betws-y-coed, and especially his picture *The Welsh Funeral*. An indication of S. Maurice Jones's special status was that he was the first Welshman to be elected a fellow of the Royal Cambrian Academy.⁵¹ Published versions of his illustrations include those which frequently appeared in the Calvinistic Methodist periodicals, *Y Drysorfa* and *Trysorfa'r Plant*, the children's publication which at the height of its popularity attained a monthly circulation of 44,000, the highest number for a Welsh periodical.⁵²

The activities and publications of S. Maurice Jones indicate the self-confidence of a Welsh artist in the contemporary art world. A similar self-confidence displayed by the Calvinistic Methodists was also illustrated in the efforts to commemorate their leaders by means of public memorials. An early example of a memorial tablet was the one placed in Heol Dwr chapel, Carmarthen to the Rev. David Charles, made by Daniel Mainwaring. Others were added in this chapel, including one to the Rev. John Wyndham Lewis who was the minister in this chapel from 1870 until 1895.⁵³ In that year, 1895, a memorial tablet to

50. *Y Brython*, 26 July 1923; *Baner ac Amserau Cymru*, 20 November 1886.

51. Lord, *Clarence Whaite and the Welsh Art World: The Betws y Coed Artists' Colony, 1844-1914* (Aberystwyth: The National Library of Wales, 1998), 114, 116, 117, 123, 144, 171.

52. *Y Goleuad*, 18 January 1933; Lord. *Clarence Whaite*, 117; Lord, *Imaging Visual Culture*, 342-43.

53. D. Huw Owen, *Capeli Cymru* (Tal-y-bont: Y Lolfa. 2005), 57-58.

the Rev. Howell Davies, the 'Apostle of Pembrokeshire' was placed in Woodstock chapel.[54]

The sculptor, William Davies (Mynorydd), a native of Merthyr Tudful was responsible for the statue of Thomas Charles unveiled in 1872 in front of the chapel, later named Capel Tegid, Bala.[55] Edward Griffith was commissioned to prepare the statue of Daniel Rowland, and this was unveiled by the Rev. Lewis Edwards besides Capel Gwynfil, Llangeitho in 1883.[56] The sculptor recorded his impressions of the competition to choose a sculptor, and the angry response of his competitors to his success: "The opposing party became disinterested & sought all possible means of throwing the contest into their man's favour by inquiring by letter as to my ability to carry out the commission."[57] Also, his observations on the unveiling at Llangeitho, when he addressed the assembled crowd despite his attempts to be excused: "I had to hold forth but I don't know how I got on, it was reported in Welsh, so I never understood what I had been gassing about, excepting that the people followed it up by cheering me when I had finished, whether they understood me I doubt very much as very little English was understood in the remote parts of Wales at that time."[58]

Two days before this ceremony he handed over at the University College, Aberystwyth the sculptured head which he had produced of Lewis Edwards.[59]

However, the final commission for this work was granted to Goscombe John: this is the sculpture which now stands in front of the College at Bala, and the sculptured head may be seen in front of Penllwyn chapel, Capel Bangor.[60]

---

54. Ibid., 202; Owen Wiliam, *250 o flynyddoedd yn hanes Capel M. C. Wystog, Sir Benfro o 1754-1755 hyd at 2004-2005*. 2005, 38.

55. Lord, *Imaging the Nation*, 278.

56. Ibid., 347; Dafydd Ifans, "Edward Griffith a Cherflun Llangeitho," *Journal of the Historical Society of the Presbyterian Church of Wales*, 9 &10 (1985-86) 69-74.

57. Ifans, "Edward Griffith," 70.

58. Ibid., 73

59. Ibid., 72-73.

60. Lord, *Imaging the* Nation, 348, 352. Peter Lord explained to me that the Penllwyn sculptured head, although by the same sculptor, was slightly different from the Bala statue: for a photograph of the head see Harvey, *Art of Piety*, plate 11.

The Transmission of Biblical Visual Imagery

Another indication of the self-confidence of the Calvinistic Methodists as a denomination was the decision to adopt a Connexional badge and motto. Following discussions between several leaders, the General Assembly agreed at Aberdare in 1885 on the motto "Goleuni y Bywyd" [Light of Life], with a dove, representing the Holy Spirit, alighting through the rays of the sun on an open Bible. The original intention was to include the Welsh wording for the Calvinistic Methodist Church, but this was amended by the General Assembly to a bilingual format, and the eventual design produced by James B. Sly, a commercial engraver from London, displayed the English wording alone. The badge was used for the first time in the *Legal Hand-book* in 1891.[61] In the late-nineteenth century the popularity of pictures which became national icons also reflected a growing sense of self-confidence. Considerable attention was focused on the story of Mary Jones walking to Bala to obtain from the hands of Thomas Charles a copy of the Bible and it has been suggested that there was a possible comparison with Biblical female characters.[62] Engravings of ministers and preachers appeared in various publications, and especially favoured were black and white, and colour prints of John Elias preaching at the Bala *Sasiwn*.[63] The most influential picture of the period was undoubtedly the one of Salem, the Baptist chapel in Merioneth painted by Sydney Curwen Vosper in 1908. It was exhibited at the Royal Academy, London and purchased the following year by Lord Leverhulme for 100 guineas. This picture attracted an exceptionally enthusiastic response by the Welsh people in general, especially as prints of the picture were made available as a result of the commercial enterprise of the Lever Brothers Company.[64] Another extremely popular print was that of the picture in 1912 of the first *Sasiwn* by Hugh Williams, a commercial artist. This reconstruction featured

---

61. Brynley F. Roberts, "Badges and Mottoes," *Journal of the Historical Society of the Presbyterian Church of Wales* 26-27 (2002-2003) 122-33.

62. Lord, *Popular Iconography*, 62.

63. Ibid., 70-71; *Enwogion y Ffydd*, eds. Peter John and Gweirydd ap Rhys (London: William Mackensie. 1880); Davies, David, *Echoes from the Welsh Hills* (London: Passmore and Alabaster, 1883).

64. Williams, Tal, Salem, *Y Llun a'r Llan: Painting and Chapel* (Llandybie: Cyhoeddiadau Barddas, 1991); Lord, "Salem, a National Icon," *Planet* 67 (1988) 14-19; and in Lord, *Gwenllian*, 37-42.

seven individuals including Howell Harris, Daniel Rowland, William Williams, and also George Whitefield.[65]

One consequence of the increasing dependence on professional and commercial artists and craftsmen was that the work of artisan painters was often reviled. Therefore, the pictures produced by the Rev. Robert Hughes, described in 1885 as an "Amateur Artist",[66] represented an exception to contemporary trends. In September 1830, at the age of fourteen, and in the company of drovers, he had walked all the way from Pwllheli to London. In his autobiography he recounted the difficulties experienced by him in London during the next three years. He had secured work in a soap factory largely through the support of his uncle, Griffith Davies, a distinguished mathematician who was elected an F.R.S. in 1832, and whose portrait he painted. He was a member of Jewin Crescent chapel and Robert Hughes described in detail his own harrowing experience of being cross-examined by the three prominent ministers who considered his application to become a member of this church. Having succeeded in convincing them, he received his first communion from the Rev. John Elias.[67] After he had returned to north Wales in 1833, he settled in the Llanaelhaearn area, and took possession of the Uwchlaw'r Ffynnon farm. A regular preacher in local chapels, he joined the Rev. John Jones, Tal-y-sarn in 1840 and 1846 on preaching tours in mid and south Wales, and became an ordained minister in 1848, After he had purchased land to build a chapel, Babell chapel was opened in the village of Llanaelhaearn in 1857, and he served as an unpaid minister for many years. From 1861-2, the production of paintings was his main leisure activity, and a large collection of portraits and landscapes was created in his studio on the farm.[68]

The subjects of most of his portraits were ministers and preachers, with the artist often relying on his memory for the portraits of

---

65. Monica Davies, "Y Sasiwm Gyntaf," *Journal of the Historical Society of the Presbyterian Church of Wales* 6 (1982) 61-63.

66. John Jones, "Ynys Enlli," 111, *Y Traethodydd* 40 (1885) 438; Geraint Jones, *Gŵr Hynod Uwchlaw'r Ffynnon* (Llanrwst: Gwasg Carreg Gwalch. 2008), 68, for a family tree which indicates that the Rev. Dr. John Tudno Williams was a direct descendant of Robert Hughes.

67. *Hunan-gofiant Robert Hughes* (Pwllheli, 1893), 23-28; Roberts, *Y Ddinas Gadarn*, 69-71; Jones, *Gŵr Hynod*, 18-23.

68. Jones, *Gŵr Hynod*, 33-34, 37-39, 55-59.

individuals who had died when he was a young man.⁶⁹ This group of portraits included those of Robert Dafydd, Brynengan and the Rev. Michael Roberts, Pwllheli. A much larger category was based on the portraits of other artists, such as those of the Revs. John Thomas, Liverpool, Dr. Owen Thomas, Liverpool, and Dr. Lewis Edwards, Bala.⁷⁰ Also, it has been suggested that the portrait of the Rev. John Elias was probably based on an engraving of Hugh Jones's oil painting (1839).⁷¹

The Rev. Robert Hughes's portraits of the Calvinistic Methodist giants, the 'men of God,' reflected the standards of his age, and this was also the case with the photographer John Thomas. A native of Cellan, he was a faithful member of the Calvinistic Methodist chapels of Rose Place and Fitzclarence Street, Liverpool, and therefore was closely associated with the same city as Hughes had been in a previous generation. In his memoirs, published in a series of articles in the periodical *Cymru*, between 1895 and 1905, and his unpublished autobiography in the National Library of Wales, John Thomas recalled the period of two years when he worked as the organizer of orders for the photographer Harry James Emmen, before establishing his own photography company, the "Cambrian Gallery".⁷² He remembered several ministers calling to be photographed, including the Revs. Lewis Edwards [Bala], Roger Edwards [Mold] and Robert Hughes [Gaerwen]. He also remembered the visit of the Rev. Henry Rees, and when they inspected the proofs the photographer remarked on the sitter's sullen expression. After persuading the minister to sit for another session, John Thomas was eventually very pleased with the end-product.⁷³ In view of his commitment to the Connexion, it is significant that his first visit to Wales as a photographer was to the General Assembly held at Llanidloes in July 1867. He assembled delegates on a plot of land behind the chapel normally used

---

69. *I Dyddiadur Methodistaidd.* 1893.

70. See Jones. *Gŵr Hynod* for reproductions of the first two portraits mentioned in this sentence.

71. Lord, *Popular Iconography*, 54–55.

72. Emyr Wyn Jones, "John Thomas of the Cambrian Gallery [John Thomas, Yr Oriel Gymreig] 1838–1905." *Journal of the National Library of Wales*, 4, 1956, 385–391; idem., "John Thomas Cambrian Gallery, ei atgofion a'i deithiau," *Journal of the Merioneth Historical and Record Society* 4.3 (1963) 242–73; Iwan Meical Jones, *A Welsh Way of Life* (Talybont: Y Lolfa, 2008); Facsimile, The National Library of Wales, 499.

73. Jones, *John Thomas Cambrian Gallery*, 248–49.

for growing potatoes.[74] Other composite photographs included those of the giants of the Welsh pulpit and the Calvinistic Methodist ministers of Liverpool. Many of his photographs were used for *Cenhadon Hedd*, the extremely popular and regularly published collections of ministerial profiles. Groups of Methodist members frequently photographed included the elders of Nefyn and Moreia, Llanfair Caereinion, the officers of Capel y Ffor, Aber-erch (with some of the individuals perched on the roof) the Tan-y-fron Sunday school, near Llansannan, and the Bible class of Nasareth, Tal-y-bont, Ceredigion.[75] John Thomas also commented on individual members whom he met during his visits to Wales, and those who made an impression on him included Mary Williams, who kept a shop in Corris, who sold elderberry wine- "Home made. To be drunk on the premises": "Yr oedd yn Fethodus o'r hen stamp" [She was a Methodist of the old type].[76] One of the inhabitants of Pentrefoelas was Robert Hughes, an elder in the Rhydlydan chapel (M.C.), who was both an innkeeper and shopkeeper. The photographer commented that some might be surprised that a Methodist elder was an innkeeper. However, if all the elders in the Connexion behaved similarly, many a village and home would be in a better condition, and he added "yr oedd ef yn arfer cydwybod ynghyd â doethineb, yn y dafarn fel yn y Capel" [he would exercise conscience as well as wisdom, in the inn as well as the Chapel].[77]

Shortly before John Thomas's death in 1904 his collection of 3,000 negatives was purchased by O. M. Edwards and his descendants later presented the collection to the National Library of Wales. After 1904 there were important developments in the production of postcards, and *The Revival Series*, which celebrated the 1904/05 Revival proved to be extremely-popular, with the one of Evan Roberts a great favourite. The extensive photographic and postcard collections housed in the Calvinistic Methodist Archive at the National Library of Wales include postcards published during Association and Presbytery meetings, and depict ministers, elders and Sunday school officers and teachers. Many photographs in this collection also record the activities of the

74. Ibid., 250.

75. John Thomas Collection, The National Library of Wales, 1360, 6531, 6589, 6103, 4822.

76. Jones, *John Thomas Cambrian Gallery*, 251.

77. Ibid., 254.

Connexion's Foreign Mission. One of the earliest photographs is the portrait of Gour Das, who had been baptised by the missionary William Pryse when he was a young man in the 1850s, standing in front of the ruins of a chapel in Sylhet following the earthquake of 1897. Nine missionaries, three male and six female, were photographed as they were preparing to leave Liverpool for India in November 1910, and two of them, Laura Evans and Laura Jones, appeared in a photograph of Maulvi Bazaar, in southern Sylhet, in 1911.[78] In the other mission fields, The Revs. Thomas Jones and William Lewis, early missionaries to the Khasi Hills, were photographed, as also was the damage caused in Shillong in 1897, and Khuma, one of the earliest Christians in Mizoram, was also photographed.[79] The Calvinistic Methodist Archive and the John Thomas Photographic Collection contain many photographs illustrating the various 'houses of God' which served as places of worship for members of the Connexion. Many relevant photographs are also held in various public collections, and of particular interest are those that illustrate chapels and distinctive features which have been modified or demolished. Examples of these include photographs of the original Seilo chapel, Aberystwyth (1863); the chapel rebuilt in 1867, including the tower demolished c. 1950 and the façade rebuilt in 1963, but demolished by now with the site presently occupied by the Morlan Centre for Faith and Culture.[80]

Changes in chapel architecture reflect the spiritual aspirations of the Calvinistic Methodist leaders and members. Early chapels of all the Nonconformist denominations were originally simple structures, frequently similar to other buildings, such as barns in rural communities. One of the earliest surviving chapel buildings in Wales is the John Hughes Memorial Chapel, Pontrobert, Montgomeryshire, built in 1800. In the early period it housed a school with John Hughes, a local weaver, one of the teachers. Following his ordination in 1814, he ministered at the chapel, and resided with his wife Ruth in the neighbouring cottage until his death in 1854. The two contributed significantly to

---

78. Aled Gruffudd Jones, "Ffrwyth y Diwygiad, Etifeddiaeth Weledol y Genhadaeth Bresbyteraidd Gymreig ar wastadedd Sylhet, India, 1880-1935," *Journal of the Historical Society of the Presbyterian Church of Wales*, 29-30. 2005-2006, 130, 131, 132.

79. Ednyfed Thomas, *Bryniau'r Glaw* (Caernarfon: Gwasg Pantycelyn, 1988), 66, 67, 82; J. Meirion Lloyd, *Y Bannau Pell* (Caernarfon: Gwasg Pantycelyn, 1989), 51.

80. Howard C. Jones, *Aberystwyth Yesterday* (Barry: Williams, 1980), 92, 93.

Welsh hymnology, with John Hughes composing original hymns, and also recording those hymns recounted to him by Ruth, Ann Griffiths's maid who had memorised the hymns which contained many biblical allusions. The chapel had closed in 1865, when the congregation had moved to a larger chapel in the village. The chapel was sold to a local craftsman, and although again sold, was used as a carpenter's workshop until a national appeal was launched in 1983 to conserve and restore the chapel. The chapel was subsequently restored to its earlier condition before the conversion to a workshop and the Centre for Christian Unity and Renewal for Wales was opened at the Memorial Chapel in 1983.[81] The white-washed Soar y Mynydd chapel in Ceredigion was built in 1822, with building material carried from Aberaeron by carts and on horseback to this site on the bank of the river Camddwy in one of the most remote areas of Wales.

Soar y Mynydd

The chapel and chapel house are under the same roof, and nearby is the stable which would house the horses of the minister and congregation.[82]

---

81. James, E. Wyn. *Rhyfeddaf fyth* (Newtown, 1998); Huw D. Owen, *Capeli Cymru* (Tal-y-bont: Y Lolfa, 2005), 152–53.

82. Gruffydd, W. J. *Tua Soar* (Aberystwyth: Capel Soar y Mynydd, 1994).

The Transmission of Biblical Visual Imagery

A crucial influence in the development of chapel architecture in Wales was the construction of Peniel, Tremadog in 1810. The decision to adopt a plan based upon that of St. Paul's Church, Covent Garden, one of London's finest churches, designed by Inigo Jones, and opened in 1638, has been attributed to William Alexander Maddocks, who was largely responsible for the development of Tremadog in the early years of the nineteenth century.

Peniel, Tremadog

Columns were added in 1849, in accordance with the original plan, and the gallery was extended in 1880 to encircle three sides of the chapel.[83] In time the architectural style of Peniel became a common pattern for many Welsh chapels, with the result that chapels were turned around, and the meeting house became an auditorium. The numerous examples of notable Classical Presbyterian chapels in Wales include Seion, Llanrwst and Bethesda, Mold.[84]

---

83. Anthony Jones, *Welsh Chapels* (Stroud: Sutton, 1996), 31–33, 54, plate 6; Owen, *Capeli Cymru*, 195–96; Richard Haslam, Julian Orbach and Adam Voelkar, eds., *Gwynedd: The Buildings of Wales* (New Haven: Yale University Press, 2009), 80, 256–57.

84. Owen, *Capeli Cymru*, 118–19, 199–200.

Bethesda, Mold

Increased membership resulted in the construction of new chapels, and the extension or rebuilding of many existing chapels. Ministers were often closely involved in this process. The Rev. W. Pierce was the builder, and possibly the designer of the new chapel, Jerusalem "Y Capel Mawr" built in 1838 at Rhosllannerchrugog. It was reported that he would physically work on the new structure by day, and preach in the open air at night.[85] The Rev. William Jones, minister of Jerusalem, Ton Pentre, was apprenticed as a carpenter, and won acclaim not only as a prominent preacher but also as a proficient architect reputed to

---

85. "Jerusalem," Eglwys y Capel Mawr, Rhosllannerchrugog, Llawlyfr y Daucanmlwyddiant 1770–1970, 12–13.

The Transmission of Biblical Visual Imagery

have designed more than 200 chapels.[86] Most of the chapels designed by the Rev. Thomas Thomas, Landore, belonged to the Independents, but some, including Trinity Llanelli; Salem, Pwllheli; Tabernacl, Aberaeron and Armenia, Holyhead were Calvinistic Methodist chapels.[87] The Rev. E. Ambrose Jones, "Emrys ap Iwan", made a significant contribution to the design of Y Tabernacl, Rhuthun, on the basis of his experience on the Continent which he visited during 1874–76. He accepted a call to the church in 1888, and the new chapel was opened on 5 April 1891. The chapel made a considerable impression with its handsome walls, white appearance and spire said to point towards heaven. Ezra Roberts, one of the elders, described the chapel as a palace, temple and workplace to Almighty God . . . a most suitable place in which to worship.[88]

Tabernacl, Ruthun

The concept of the chapel being a temple was also expressed with regard to other chapels, and the Rev. W. E. Prytherch referred in 1888 to

86. Nerys Ann Jones, *Capel y Garn, c.1793–1993* (Bow Street: Capel y Garn. 1993), 13–15, 19–20, 23; E. D. Lewis, *The Rhondda Valleys* (Cardiff: Phoenix House, 1959), 221.

87. Stephen Hughes, "Thomas Thomas, 1817–88: The First National Architect of Wales," *Archaeologica Cambrensis* 152 (2003) 144, 146–47, 150, 152, 158.

88. J. Meirion Lloyd Pugh, ed., *Dathlu Dwbl, Hanes daucanmlwyddiant yr Achos, 1791–1991* (Ruthun: Capel y Tabernacl, Ruthun, 1991).

the important work facing the church of Y Gopa, Pontarddulais, near Swansea, namely the building of a new temple: the present impressive chapel was subsequently built in 1890.[89] The actual process of selecting a name for each chapel, which was then prominently displayed on the exterior front wall, was generally shrouded in mystery, but the personal preference of a minister or influential member may well have been a crucial factor. In some cases, the congregation may well have been given an opportunity to vote on two possible suggestions, and in one recorded instance several names were placed on slips of paper in a hat and the first one taken out was accepted as the name of the chapel.[90] A distinctive feature of chapels in Wales, and especially of Welsh-language chapels was the provision of biblical names. A distinction between those chapels where services were conducted in the Welsh and English languages was illustrated on a long list of chapels in the Cynon Valley. Of the 22 Presbyterian chapels listed, 19 chapels, all originally Welsh-language places of worship, were named "Bethania", "Bethel", "Carmel", "Ebenezer", "Hermon", "Jerusalem", "Libanus", "Moriah", "Nazareth", "Penuel", "Seiloh", "Soar" and "Tabernacl". On the other hand, the four English-language chapels were named "Trinity", "Saint David's", "English Calvinistic Methodist Chapel" and the "Presbyterian Church".[91] The prominent position of the pulpit within the chapel illustrated the Protestant emphasis on preaching the Word of God. Within the John Hughes Memorial Chapel, the pulpit, dating from c. 1835, and standing in the middle of the rear wall, on a low dais, is the central feature. A wooden frame separates the chapel and the neighbouring cottage, and on it there is a hatch-door which was opened to enable John Hughes, despite his failing health, to preach from his bed to the congregation in the chapel.[92]

The pulpit continues, to the present day, to be the dominant element within chapel buildings, even though changes in architectural styles led to an increased elaboration, especially in the urban and industrial centres in the nineteenth century.

89. Owen, *Capeli Cymru*, 151.

90. J. Derfel Rees, *Ar eu Talcennau* (Swansea: Ty John Penry. 1981), 13.

91. Alan Vernon Jones, *Chapels of the Cynon Valley: Capeli Cwm Cynon* (Aberdare: Cynon Valley History Society, 2004), Appendix C, 401–5.

92. Owen, *Capeli Cymru*, 152.

The Transmission of Biblical Visual Imagery

Jerusalem, Bethesda

Jerusalem Chapel, Bethesda, a Grade 1 Cadw listed building, was built in 1842-3 and remodelled in 1872-5 by Richard Davies, Caernarfon, with the intention to provide an amphitheatre setting within the chapel with the seats in the gallery and in the ground floor seats under the gallery steeply raked. The dominant feature however is the polished mahogany pulpit with polished brass rails to steps on each side. There is a projecting triple-curve front with a lavishly carved panel on main half-oval front.[93] The present form of Capel Mawr, Denbigh dates from 1880, when Thomas Gee was the minister, and this remodelled a chapel of 1828 which in turn was a renewal of an earlier building, c, 1790. Facing the *sêt fawr* (elders seat), with its curved enclosing rails, the central, semi octagonal pulpit has flanking stair approaches has a panelled front with pierced decoration, fluted columns and foliated capitals.[94] Moriah, the John Elias Memorial Chapel, Llangefni, built in 1897 and designed by Richard Thomas based on an original design by Owen Morris Roberts, had a rectangular pulpit with bays advanced in steps to the front,

93. CADW Leaflet, Capel Jerusalem, Bethesda, Record no. 18387; Haslam, Orbach and Voelkar. *Gwynedd*, 263, plate 101.

94. CADW Leaflet, Capel Mawr, Denbigh, Record no. 974; W. H. Pritchard. *Dysg i'm Edrych* (Denbigh: Capel Mawr Dinbych. 1993), 15-26, 32-34.

raised by five steps, and facing a rectangular *sêt fawr* with curving angles and side entrances. There are two stages to the pulpit front, with the lower stage having recessed panels with moulded surrounds and the upper stage with carved foliate designs.[95]

William Williams Memorial Chapel, Llandovery

The pulpit in the William Williams Memorial Chapel, Llandovery, built in 1886–8 and designed by John Henry Phillips, Cardiff, is placed on the side in the front of the chapel and in the central location is the communion table, together with four chairs, donated by Christians from

95. CADW Leaflet, Moriah Llangefni, Record no. 5751; Haslam, Orbach and Voelkar, *Gwynedd*, 181–2, plate 103.

the Khasi Hills in response to the national fund appeal. The pulpit was made of Caen stone, and on it were placed five carved panels illustrating the Biblical scenes of the Good Samaritan, the Prodigal Son, and Jesus and the woman of Samaria, together with one of William Williams writing on an antique scroll.[96]

These four Victorian chapels had richly detailed interiors. Richard Davies's intention when remodelling Jerusalem, Bethesda, was to provide an amphitheatre setting within the chapel with the seats in the gallery and in the ground floor seats under the gallery steeply raked. One of the finest features is the ceiling a saucer-domed main circle, with a centre rose flanked by radiating panels with smaller roses.[97] The U-shaped gallery of Capel Mawr, Denbigh is supported on fluted cast iron colonnettes with foliated capitals.[98] The outer part of the central ceiling panel of Moriah, Llangefni contains large, circular floriate bosses and the inner part has panels with floriate decoration.[99] The Memorial Chapel in Llandovery was described in the local newspaper soon after its opening in August 1888 as 'a very beautiful structure' and 'as handsome a structure as a memorial of the poet as heart could wish.' It was then claimed that 'It is remarkable as one of the first, if not actually the first, Welsh Calvinistic places of worship into which works of art have been admitted. The most striking work of art is a magnificent stained-glass window in four large divisions.[100] The four divisions contained representations of King David, the prophet Isaiah, the St. Matthew and Miriam, and the persons commemorated included the musician Ieuan Gwyllt and the hymn-writer Ann Griffiths.[101] Also opened in the same year was the English-language Presbyterian Church at Menai Bridge, designed by R.G.Thomas, the architect of the Baron Hill estate: other buildings designed by him include the now-demolished Howel Harris Memorial Chapel, Trefeca. A stained-glass window depicting four Biblical scenes commemorated Robert Davies, Bodlondeb, who, with his

96. *Williams Pantycelyn Memorial Chapel Centenary Souvenir, 1888-1988.*

97. CADW Leaflet, Capel Jerusalem, Bethesda, Record no. 18387; Haslam, Orbach and Voelkar. *Gwynedd*, 263, Plate 101.

98. CADW Leaflet, Capel Mawr, Denbigh, Record no. 974; Pritchard. *Dysg i'm Edrych*, 15-26, 32-34.

99. CADW Leaflet, Moriah Llangefni, Record no. 5751.

100. *Carmarthen Journal*, 10 August 1888.

101. *Williams Pantycelyn Memorial Chapel Centenary Souvenir, 1888-1988.*

brother Richard Davies, Treborth, Member of Parliament for Anglesey, was one of the principal patrons of the church.

Presbyterian Church, Menai Bridge

The two brothers, together with Richard's wife, Anne, the daughter of the Rev. Henry Rees, Liverpool, and other members of the family were commemorated in the various memorial tablets in the church.[102] A more recent example is the stained glass window installed at the English-language Presbyterian Church ['Presby'], Llanelli in 1988 "in loving memory of those who have given dedicated service to promote the

---

102. *English Presbyterian Church Menai Bridge: Centenary Leaflet, 1876–1976*; Haslam, Orbach, and Voelkar, *Gwynedd*, 198.

Christian witness of Presby in the town of Llanelli." The window comprises 24 sections with Biblical symbols and a combined landscape and townscape of Llanelli' with Biblical texts presented in five languages, including appropriately the Welsh words "Goleuni y Bywyd", referring to the light of the gospel, and the Christian message beamed to street outside.[103] Coloured windows placed in Welsh-language churches include the two memorial windows unveiled at Capel Newydd, Llanelli on 30 August 1848; one of Mary Magdalen washing the feet of Jesus, described as "an act of humility an repentance", and the other of Martha "a symbol of purity and service."[104] At Capel y Crwys, Cardiff, two windows designed by Gareth Morgan portray William Williams and Ann Griffiths: the church previously meeting in Crwys Road had moved in 1988 to this chapel built c.1960 for the Christian Scientists.[105] Also, Berea Newydd, Bangor, the new chapel designed by the Ap Thomas Partnership, Bangor and opened in January 2003, contains coloured windows designed by Gwawr Roberts, one of the members of the church, and created by Meri Jones, Llangollen.[106]

A Biblical text was often presented on an interior wall and one notable example is the wording "Duw Cariad Yw" [God is Love] on the wall behind the pulpit in the Soar-y-Mynydd chapel.[107] In the Presbyterian Church Llanelli the Biblical verse "O Worship the Lord in the Beauty of Holiness", in capitals, was placed on the wall behind the pulpit.[108] Other images featuring biblical texts which were often found inside chapel buildings were Sunday school banners. Illustrations of religious leaders are generally confined to vestries or porches, and a notable exception is the photograph of Evan Roberts which has been placed behind the pulpit of Blaenannerch Presbyterian chapel, near Cardigan, and on a seat in close proximity a plaque records where Evan Roberts was sitting before his profound spiritual experience which was one of the remarkable incidents leading up to the revival of 1904–05.[109]

103. Huw Edwards, *Capeli Llanelli: Our Rich Heritage* (Carmarthen: Carmarthenshire County Council Libraries and Heritage Section, 2009), 517–18.
104. Ibid., 454–55.
105. Owen, *Capeli Cymru*, 51.
106. Ibid., 38–39.
107. Ibid., 179.
108. Edwards, *Capeli Llanelli*, 508.
109. Owen, *Capeli Cymru*, 45.

Blaenannerch, near Cardigan

The uniqueness of this photograph's location emphasises the continuing influence on the Presbyterian Church of Wales, and on Protestant worship generally, of the Calvinist view on visual imagery, whilst at the same time individual ministers and members of the Church have contributed immensely to the visual cultural heritage of Wales.

I wish to acknowledge the co-operation of the staff of the Reading Rooms of the National Library of Wales whilst I was preparing this chapter. I also appreciated the assistance of Martin O'Kane, Peter Lord, and also of Jan Kirschner, whose Diploma thesis, "Contemporary Protestant Liturgical Space, Czech Situation in the Wider Context—An Ecumenical Point of View", submitted in 2009 at the Charles University in Prague whilst he was an Erasmus Exchange student at the Pontifical University, St. Patrick's College, Maynooth, provided valuable information on the Calvinistic influence on religious art and buildings in other European countries.

10

'From "Monastic Family" to Calvinistic Methodist Academy': Trefeca College (1842–1906)

J. GWYNFOR JONES

One issue which is raised among Methodist historians concerning the establishment of Trefeca College in 1842, and which has not received the attention it fully deserves, is whether or not the Association in the South (*Sasiwn y De*) within the Calvinistic Methodist Connexion owned it. It is known that responsibility for the upkeep of the property was solely entrusted to the Brecknockshire Presbytery on behalf of that Association, but the relationship between Trefeca and the rapidly-growing Connexion from that year onwards demands some clarification. Normally, an establishment of this kind would be transferred to the Connexion and its daily administration delegated to the Association in which it is located. The role assumed by that Association in safeguarding its interests during the following years down to 1906, when it was transferred as a theological college to Aberystwyth, reveals a sharp conflict of interest between it and its northern counterpart, and this study is partly intended to trace its main features.

Selina, Countess of Huntingdon, established her college at Trefeca Isaf in 1768, thus laying the basis for another educational establishment to emerge in south Wales for the training of preachers.[1] The owner was Thomas Harris of Tregunter, Howell Harris's older brother, a prosperous London tailor and merchant.[2] The property was closed on the Countess's death in 1791 when the lease expired, and the college was moved to Cheshunt in Hertfordshire in that year. At the time the need for theological education was increasing, decisions having already been taken generations previously by the older nonconformist bodies to provide a standard of education considered appropriate for the Christian ministry in Wales and England. Private schools had already been held by Howell Harris at Trefeca in 1736, Robert Jones, Rhos-lan, at Llangybi, Caernarfonshire in 1766, Evan Richardson at Caernarfon in 1787, Thomas Lloyd at Abergele in 1799 and John Hughes at Wrexham in 1819.[3] The old dissenters, closely bound to their radical traditions of religious and civil liberty and free enquiry in the seventeenth century, set up academies for this purpose, and they became centres which produced generations of preachers from the latter years of that century onwards, the earliest and most notable among them in Wales being Samuel Jones's academy at Brynllywarch in Llangynwyd, Glamorgan, established in 1672.[4] Other academies appeared such as that at Llwyn-llwyd, in the parish of Llanigon, Brecknockshire, where the Carmarthen Presbyterian academy, first established in 1704,[5] was moved for a short period in 1773, and the famous academy set up by Dafydd Dafis, Arian minister at Castellhywel, Cardiganshire.[6] Such

1. For further information on the Countess's involvement with Trefeca see Cook, *Selina, Countess of Huntingdon*; Welch, *Spiritual Pilgrim*; Schlenther, *Queen of the Methodists*; Harding, *The Countess Huntingdon's Connexion*; Davies, "Trevecka 1706–1964," 45–49; Nuttall, *The Significance of Trevecca College 1768–91*.

2. Davies, "Trevecka 1706–1964," 42–43; *DWB*, 342–43.

3. Part of the information which follows is based on W. P. Jones's discussion of the college in his short bilingual volume entitled *Coleg Trefeca/Trevecca College* (Trefeca Committee, 1942), a comparatively short study of its history from its establishment in 1842 to the centenary in 1942. The author was Principal of the Preparatory College at Trefeca and the volume was written to celebrate the occasion. For the background see *Education in Wales/Addysg yng Nghymru 1847–1947* (Welsh Department of Education, Pamphlet no. 2 (London, 1948), 6–7; *DWB*, 152, 382, 507, 856–57.

4. *DWB*, 511–16. He was a native of Denbighshire and was educated at All Souls and Jesus Colleges, Oxford. He was a renowned scholar who was ejected from the living of Llangynwyd in 1662.

5. Roberts, "Nonconformist academies in Wales," 15–35.

6. Jenkins, *Hanes Cymru yn y Ddeunawfed Ganrif*, 59–61.

centres became the strongholds of the eighteenth-century dissenting ministry in days when non-Anglicans were denied places at Oxford and Cambridge. They provided rural communities with an adequately educated and powerful ministry who became the influential leaders of the Victorian nonconformist tradition.[7] In 1807 a Baptist academy was established at Abergavenny, and in 1836 it was moved to Pontypool.[8]

In view of this progress in the educational provision for prospective ministers in dissenting churches it is hardly surprising that the most ambitious of Calvinistic Methodist preachers, many of whom were itinerant and uneducated lay exhorters, felt neglected because of the firm opposition among leading Association ministers to higher education. Lewis Edwards of Pen-llwyn, Cardiganshire, for example, faced opposition in the Woodstock Association (1830) after he had applied to enter London University.[9] Edwards himself, who was highly regarded as a scholar by the Revd Ebenezer Richard (father of Henry Richard, the 'Apostle of Peace') and his brother Thomas who were, at the time, powerful policy makers of the Association, commented that his failure to win their approval was the only time that he had been disappointed with their response. Many years later, in 1875, he remarked as follows:

> Yr oedd Ebenezer Richard a'i frawd [Thomas Richard] yn benderfynol yn fy erbyn, a gwyddai pawb mai hwy oedd y Gymdeithasfa. Ond pan oedd yn ymddangos yn anobeithiol ar fy achos, cododd iachawdwriaeth o blith y blaenoriaid, ac am hyny nid rhyfedd fod genyf barch i'r blaenoriaid hyd heddyw.[10] [Ebenezer Richard and his brother [Thomas Richard] were determined to oppose me, and everyone knew that they were the Association. But when it appeared that my cause was impossible, salvation aros from among the elders, and for that it is not surprising that I have respect for the elders to this day.]

The opposition to Edwards's application was based simply on the belief that education in the art of preaching should rely chiefly on faith

---

7. *DWB*, 299; Jones, *Hanes Annibynwyr Cymru*, 127; Roberts, "Nonconformist academies in Wales," 14-15; Owen, *Ysgolion a Cholegau yr Annibynwyr*, 9-10; Jenkins, *Foundations of Modern Wales*, 196-97, 314-15; Evans, *A History of Wales 1660-1815*, 118-23.

8. Matthews, *From Abergavenny to Cardiff*, 15-24. See also Himbury, *The South Wales Baptist College*, 15-36.

9. Morgan, *Lewis Edwards*, 17-19.

10. Ibid.; *Y Goleuad* 4 September 1875, 9.

and devotion. The Holy Spirit, not theological learning, was regarded by them as the prime requirement in preparing for the ministry.

Before being admitted to London University Lewis Edwards had considered *Seceders* school in Belfast, a theologically conservative Presbyterian college established by the United Secession Church which had broken away from the Church of Scotland. His determination to obtain the benefits of higher education was clearly expressed in a letter to his friend John Matthews (later to become mayor of Aberystwyth) in September 1830: "But let them [i.e. John Elias and Ebenezer Richard] do what they will, I shall never stoop again to flatter any man living, thought he be as despotic as the great Sultan himself . . . I don't want more emolument, more wordly ease, or more respect. My only object is the acquisition of learning. Yes my friend learning I will obtain and that soon."[11]

Similarly, John Elias's application to the Monthly Meeting for permission to further his education at Manchester for half a year in 1790 was rejected since it was considered that "it was the pride of my heart and a desire to be a great preacher, that made me think of going to school... They were afraid that I should be puffed up, and consequently made wholly useless for the work."[12]

For the Methodists formal education was not considered necessary because, in their view, it might affect true spirituality in the preaching process.[13] Many of the laymen who preached were largely illiterate, but several denominational leaders were educated at local schools or self-taught, some even improving their knowledge of English, Hebrew and classics. When it is considered that higher education was not within their reach it is remarkable how well-educated some of these leaders had become. Thomas Jones of Denbigh, for example, obtained classical education at Caerwys and Holywell. He translated William Gurnall's work *The Christian in Compleat Armour* (*Cristion mewn Cyflawn Arfogaeth* (1795–1819) and published his own *magnum opus*, *Diwygwyr, Merthyron, a Chyffeswyr Eglwys Loegr* in 1813.[14] Henry

11. Evans, *Lewis Edwards: Ei Fywyd a'i Waith*, 35–36.

12. Morgan, *John Elias: Life, Letters and Essays*, 37; Owen, *Hunangofiant John Elias*, 63.

13. Watts, *The Dissenters*, II, 71–72, 266–67.

14. For further information on Thomas Jones's literary work, see Jones, *Cofiant y Parch Thomas Jones o Ddinbych*; Jones *Thomas Jones o Ddinbych*.

Rees, who influenced John Jones of Tal-y-sarn to become a Methodist minister, was acclaimed as the most famous preacher of his day, and he contributed articles to *Y Traethodydd* and other religious journals. He was the older brother of the Revd William Rees (Gwilym Hiraethog), equally renowned as a man of letters, preacher, editor and religious leader.

The achievements of Griffith Jones, Llanddowror, and Thomas Charles of Bala, to cite but two of the most famous educationalists of their age, enabled preachers who conducted services in Methodist gatherings to instruct hearers of the Word, many of whom had benefited from the instruction they had received in the Circulating Schools and later Sunday Schools. Charles wished to extend knowledge and understanding of the scriptures, principally in the Welsh language, as he stated in his preface to *Geiriadur Ysgrythyrol*:

> Y mae diffyg llyfrau yn ein hiaith, ar y rhan fwyaf o ganghenau gwybodaeth, wedi peri i mi helaethu ar rai pethau nad oeddwn ar y cyntaf yn bwriadu crybwyll nemawr amdanynt . . . Nid oes dim yn fwy ar fy meddwl, ddydd a nos, na helaethiad gwybodaeth iachusol a defnyddiol ym mhlith fy nghydwladwyr hawddgar ac anwyl.[15]
>
> [The lack of books in our language, on most branches of knowledge, has caused to extend some matters I was not at first intending to mention hardly at all . . . There is nothing more on my mind, day and night, than to extend healthy and useful knowledge among my amiable and dear fellow countrymen.]

The publication of this eminent work was a significant contribution to the 'campaign against illiteracy' which had maintained its philanthropic activities by means of the *Welsh Trust* and the *Society for the Promotion of Christian Knowledge* over many decades in the post-Restoration era in Wales and England.[16] About half a century before Charles's *Geiriadur* appeared Griffith Jones firmly believed that biblical knowledge was far more beneficial to proclaim the gospel than inspired preaching:

15. Charles, *Geiriadur Ysgrythyrol*, I, v.

16. Jones, *The Charity School Movement*, 266–325; Clement, *The S.P.C.K. and Wales*, 26–47; Williams, "Griffith Jones, Llanddowror," 11–29; White, "Popular Schooling and the Welsh Language," 317–41; Jenkins, *Foundations of Modern Wales*, 173–212; Jenkins, "'An Old and Much Honoured Soldier': Griffith Jones, Llanddowror," *Welsh History Review* 11 (1983) 449–68.

> Nid yw yn anhawdd i Araith synnfrwd neu daranllyd ddeffröi a chynhyrfu'r serchiadau naturiol, sef anwydau ysbryd anianol dŷn, i lenwi'r meddwl o ryw gynnwrf neu gilydd ... nes i'r cwbl, fel y mae'n digwydd yn rhy fynych, sychu ymmaith fel y *gwlith boreuol*, neu ddiflannu a chrino fel *planhigyn heb wrâidd iddo*. A phan y bo Crefydd, yn wir, ymmysg y pethau ymma, mae'n sicr na ddichon y cynyrfiadau hyn dywys na dysgu dŷn i rodio *un cam* o Ffordd Dduw yn uniawn, heb fod yn ofalus dan Gyfarwydd-deb y *Goleuni* a roddir gan Ysbryd Duw yn *Athrawiaeth* yr Ysgrythur Lân.[17]
>
> [It is not difficult for an intense or thunderous discourse to awaken and excite the natural affections, namely man's innate spiritual passions, to fill the mind with some agitation or other ... until it all, as happens too frequently, dries away like morning dew or disappears and withers like a plant without root. And when religion, indeed, is among these things, it is certain that these passions cannot guide or teach man to walk one step of God's way justly, without being carefully guided by the Light given by God's spirit in the doctrine of the Holy Scripture.]

Despite his friendship with Howell Harris and Daniel Rowland this Anglican priest opposed Methodism because he considered that acquiring biblical and catechismal knowlege in the vernacular was far more important than high-powered preaching. Exhorters, who were also active as itinerant preachers before a formal ministry was established, were often illiterate. Although their educational standards were hardly lower than that of many Anglican priests supportive of the Methodists Howell Harris refused to accept them as ministers because of that deficiency. Several exhorters, however, served in Griffith Jones's Circulating Schools that were approved by the Association, and evidence shows that their preaching assisted in evangelising the preaching methods of dissenting preachers whose approach was arid and intellectual until the Methodist preachers, in due course, influenced them by making their preaching more emotionally appealing.[18] The Wesleyan Methodists, following the Calvinistic Methodists, also believed that 'scholarship and linguistic proficiency' should not be considered supe-

---

17. Jones, *Llythyr ynghylch y Ddyledswydd o Gateceisio Plant a Phobl Anwybodus* (1749), 13.

18. For further discussion of this theme see Evans, "Ymateb y Methodistiaid i fater addysg y weinidogaeth yn y ddeunawfed ganrif," to appear in *Journal*, 2010; Knox, *Wales and 'Y Goleuad'*, 51–54.

rior to the act of proclaiming the Word of God. Increased pressures, however, led in England to the eventual establishment of the Didsbury and Richmond Wesleyan colleges in 1842 and 1843 respectively.

In Wales of the late eighteenth and early nineteenth centuries, when Calvinistic Methodist societies were growing rapidly, the southern Association began to seek better educational facilities for its preachers. In the Association held at Tŵr-gwyn, near Rhydlewis, on 1 July 1836, delegates of the Monthly Meetings were urged to support the establishment of a college for the Connexion.[19] Moreover, at the Association meeting at Pontypridd in August 1836 it was unanimously recommended 'that a college be established and maintained financially by the Calvinistic Methodists in the Principality of Wales',[20] although it was envisaged that this college would be located in the south. Both Associations in the south and north were expected to contribute annually towards the founding and maintenance of that establishment. The northern Association (*Sasiwn y gogledd*), which assembled at Caernarfon in September 1831, expressed the view that establishing colleges in the southern and northern provinces would be an asset to improve educational standards.[21] A joint-committee was formed between these Associations to discuss the matter, but no final agreement was reached,[22] and in August 1837 a private school for boys was opened at Bala by Dr Lewis Edwards and the Revd David Charles III (1812–1878), Thomas Charles's grandson.[23] In November of that year the southern Association decided to use that school over a period of two years, agreeing to contribute towards its upkeep.[24]

Earlier, in June 1837, however, the Brecknockshire Monthly Meeting was entrusted with maintaining the land and property, the official transfer taking place on 19 December of that year 'for such purposes as the majority of the ministers and elders of the Calvinistic Methodists in the County of Brecon decide in their monthly meetings'. That decision led to greater interest being taken in the southern

19. Jones, *Trevecca*, 65; *Y Drysorfa* 1895, 136.

20. Jones, *Trevecca*, 65; *DWB*, 71–72, 191.

21. Jones, *Trevecca*, 65. For a short resume of activities at Pontypridd see *Y Drysorfa* 1836, 313–14.

22. Edwards, *Athrofa'r Bala*, 16.

23. Ibid., 17.

24. Jones, *Trevecca*, 66.

Association to use Trefeca as a centre.[25] In April 1838 a message was sent by the Talgarth Monthly Meeting to the southern Association urging it to establish a college at Trefeca and to invite Dr Lewis Edwards to 'preside' there.[26] That proposition was not accepted at the time because the connexional courts had not at that stage discussed the college's location.[27]

What were the circumstances at Trefeca at the time? By 1838 Thomas and Gwenno Jones and William James, the last three to reside at Howell Harris's picturesque residence, disparagingly described by the traveller Benjamin Heath Malkin as 'a sort of monastic family',[28] ceased to care for the place and its property.[29] For the sum of £70 they were transferred to the care of the Brecknockshire Monthly Meeting at a time when the southern Association was seeking a site on which to build a theological college. According to an agreement the old residents were given an annual payment of £15 (promised them by the Brecknockshire Monthly Meeting), were allowed to use the land (excepting the garden connected to the college house) and were to receive the rent of nearby houses. A fund was set up to maintain teachers and students at Trefeca independently of the means needed for the upkeep of the premises. The Revd Thomas Phillips of Hay-on-Wye declared as follows in his address: "The committee regard it as an indication of the Divine Will, that Trefecca House and premises, *are now become the property of the Calvinistic Methodists in Wales* . . . it is considered advisable to form a fund for securing permanently the necessary salary of the Tutor, or Tutors, and providing also, as far as necessary, for the maintenance of the Students, independently of the sum requisite for the repairs of the edifice."[30]

In June 1838 the Brecknockshire Monthly Meeting offered to open a school at Trefeca, and the fund was organised to collect for its maintenance, but nothing came of it at the time.[31] In September 1838,

---

25. Ibid.
26. Ibid.
27. Ibid.
28. Malkin, *Scenery, Antiquaries and Biography of South Wales*, 378.
29. Roberts, "Yr olaf o hen bobl Trefeca," *Journal* 1965, 23–27.
30. Jones, *Trevecca*, 68 [My italics].
31. Ibid., 66; Davies, "Trevecca 1706–1964," 18–20.

'From "Monastic Family" to Calvinistic Methodist Academy'

however, the Monthly Meeting at Crai decided to transfer Trefeca's property to the Connexion,[32] and that was finally endorsed in the southern Association held at Aberystwyth in August 1839.[33] The siting of the college was discussed in July 1839,[34] and the Association decided to accept Trefeca for that purpose.[35] A committee was appointed to consider Trefeca as the location for a college and the minutes of its first meeting, held on 9 January 1840 at Carmarthen, included a decision to make the Breconshire Monthly Meeting responsible for the upkeep of the property and ensure that the existing residents be moved to nearby cottages.[36]

Both organisations, the Monthly Meetings and the Association, had become powerful agencies of Calvinistic Methodism well before the close of the eighteenth century. The Association which had emerged from the 'Society of Ministers and Exhorters', was to become the governing body, divided into two regions, north and south, within the Connexion, a corporate entity embracing the Methodist movement in its entirety and binding the movement together. John Wesley used the term from the 1750s onwards to denote the connection between 'religious societies', the first Welsh Association was held in January 1742 at Dugoedydd, Cil-y-cwm, Carmarthenshire, and the Countess of Huntingdon set up her own 'Connexion'.[37] It was this Association which placed Trefeca in the care of the Brecknockshire Monthly Meeting, acting on behalf of the Connexion.

At the Talgarth Association in October 1839 a committee was set up to organise the opening of the college, and the Revd David Charles was appointed one of the two secretaries of the establishment.[38] Another committee, referred to above, held on 9 January 1840

32. Ibid., 67.
33. Ibid., 67.
34. Ibid., 67.
35. Ibid., 67.
36. Roberts, "Yr olaf o hen bobl Trefeca," 23.
37. For the background to the Welsh Calvinstic Methodist denomination see Roberts, *Calvinistic Methodism of Wales*, 62–63; Knox, "Methodistiaeth ac Eglwysyddiaeth," in Roberts, ed., *Corff ac Enaid*, 70–71; Roberts, "Datblygiad Trefn, 1736–1750," in Roberts (ed.), *Hanes Methodistiaeth Galfinaidd Cymru*: I, 168–73; Roberts, "Y Tair Sasiwn gyntaf 1742," *Journal* 1941, 93–96.
38. Jones, *Trevecca*, 67.

at Carmarthen, decided to proceed forthwith:[39] "Ein bod yn dal at y bwriad o sefydlu Athrofa yn Nhrefecca, gan goleddu y gobaith y bydd i Ogledd Cymru ymuno â Chymdeithasfa y Deheu i gynnal un sefydliad i'r holl dywysogaeth."[40] [That we intend to establish a College at Trefeca hoping that North Wales will join with the Association in the South to maintain one establishment for the whole Principality.]

The reason for this decision to locate the college at Trefeca was quite clear—its connections with Howell Harris and the Countess of Huntingdon, and the fact that Harris's successors had transferred the property to the Brecknock Monthly Meeting which was prepared to transfer it to the Connexion.

Clearly, for geographical reasons, the southern Association showed greater enthusiasm for establishing this college. In the minutes of the first committee meeting the following was recorded: "On Enquiry respecting the property it was found to have been legally conveyd to the Breconshire Monthly Meeting & requires only reconveyance to Trustees for the Welch Calvinistic Connexion in S. Wales . . . Resolved that this Committee now request Messrs Watkin's of Brecon [solicitors] to make arrangements with the said old proprietors for their removal to the Cottages, & that they secure the Library, Letters & Manuscripts by placing the same under lock and key."[41] In the second committee meeting on 4 March 1840 it was further recorded that solicitors were in the process of moving the old residents and seeing that the property, including books and archives, were cared for.[42]

It was hoped that the northern Association would join in the celebration designed to open the college. On 4 March 1840 the southern Committee minuted as follows: "That the execution of the Deed conveying the property at Trefeca be delayed with a view to afford opportunity for conference with North Wales on the subject, and that the word 'South' in the Draft now need be left out."[43] That was not possible at the time since a preparatory school had already been established by Dr Lewis Edwards and the Revd David Charles at Bala in August 1837.[44]

39. Ibid.
40. *Y Drysorfa*, January 1895, 34.
41. Roberts, "Yr olaf o hen bobl Trefeca," 23.
42. Ibid. The second Carmarthen committee was held on 4 March 1840.
43. Jones, *Trevecca*, 69.
44. Ibid., 66.

Since the committee, in June 1840, received a letter from the northern Association declaring that it intended to continue its college at Bala, the matter was kept on hold for the time being.[45] In *Y Drysorfa* (1840) David Charles and Benjamin Watkins of Brecon, referring to the history and location of Trefeca, and seeking financial aid to support the teaching staff, the buildings and students, stated that the southern Association had organised the appeal's funding throughout Wales in conjunction with the commemoration of the Methodist movement in Wales, It was expected, however, that if insufficient funds were raised, then open collections would be made in chapels in other parts of the Principality:

> Mae sefydlu Athrofa wedi bod er ys amser bellach ar feddwl nifer mawr o aelodau mwyaf duwiol a chyfrifol y Cyfundeb ... Ystyriant yn arwydd o nawdd Rhagluniaeth, fod yr adeiladaeth helaeth sydd yn Nhrefecca, a'r hyn a berthyn iddo, wedi dyfod yn feddianaeth i'r Trefnyddion Calfinaidd yn Nghymru. Penderfynodd y Cyfundeb bellach fod i'r lle gael ei neillduo i fod yn sefyllfa Athrofa, tuag at roddi manteision dysgeidiaeth i ddynion ieuanc duwiol ... am nad oes ganddynt unrhyw sefydliad o'r fath yn Neheubarth Cymru.[46]
>
> [Establishing a College has been for some time by now on the minds of a large number of the most godly and responsible members of the Connexion ... They consider it a sign of Providential patronage that the extensive building at Treteca and what belongs to it, has become owned by the Calvinistic Methodists in Wales. Further, the Connexion decided that the place is to be set aside as a site for a College, to give scholastic advantages to godly and approved young men...since they do not have any establishment of the kind in South Wales.]

During the dispute a reference to the situation was made in an obituary to Benjamin Watkins, first secretary of the college, in *Y Traethodydd* (1846). He had been enthusiastically in favour of establishing a college at Trefeca: "yr oedd yn un o'r rhai oedd â'r llaw flaenaf yn ffurfiad y cynllun tuag at gael *fund* ddigonol i gynnal y sefydliad. Ymddiriedwyd iddo gan y cyfeisteddfod y gorchwyl o arolygu adgyweiriad adeilad fawr Trefecca, i fod yn lle cymhwys i'r athrofa..."[47] [he

---

45. Ibid., 66.
46. Charles and Watkins, "Athrofa Trefeca," *Y Drysorfa* 1840, 344–45.
47. "Athrofa Trefecca," *Y Traethodydd* 1846, 348.

was one of those prominent in forming the plan for adequate funding to support the establishment. He was entrusted by the committee with the task of supervising the renovation of the main Trefeca building as a suitable place for the college . . .]

In the same number of *Y Traethodydd* the following comment appeared in an essay on Williams of Pantycelyn: "Da genym bod y Methodistiaid wedi prynu ac adgyweirio yr hen "Fonachlog fawr" a adeiledid ganddo i fod yn feddiant i'r enwad, ac at ei wasanaeth, i feithrin gwyr ieuainc mewn dysgeidiaeth at waith y weinidogaeth."[48] [We are glad that the Methodists have purchased and renovated the old 'great monastery' built by him to be owned by the denomination to nurture young men in learning for the work of the ministry.]

Moreover, in an essay on Revd David Charles published in 1893, it was noted as follows when discussing the confrontation between Trefeca and Bala:

> Y diwedd fu, trosglwyddo yr adeilad gan y pump hen frodyr oeddent mewn meddiant o honi, ar delerau neillduol, i Gyfarfod Misol Brycheiniog; a chyn hir trosglwyddwyd y cwbl i Gymdeithasfa y Deheudir.
>
> Nid annaturiol oedd i'r ffaith hon arwain brodyr y Deheudir i fod yn llawn sel a hyder mai Trefecca oedd y lle priodol i'r Athrofa . . .[49]
>
> [In the end the building, previously owned by the five old men, was transferred, on special conditions, to the Brecknockshire Monthly Meeting, and before long all was transferred to the Association in the South.
>
> It was not unexpected that this fact would lead the men of the South to be full of zeal and confidence that Trefeca would be the suitable site for the College.]

These sources did not specifically state that the southern Association owned Trefeca. During discussions on unity at one point and the southern Association's unwillingness to consider a more central site, it was obvious that the Association was determined to maintain its hold on to Trefeca and that it was a matter for both Associations to settle. In a letter to Griffith Harries, a prominent Calvinistic Methodist from Carmarthen, Dr Lewis Edwards wrote: "Do you not think that

---

48. "William Williams o Bant-y-Celyn a'i amserau," *Y Traethodydd* 1846, 234.
49. Evans, "Y Parch David Charles," *Y Traethodydd* 1893, 131.

some compromise may be yet come to? If we fail to agree in a matter of such slight importance, it is useless to talk any more that we are one Connexion."[50]

Association officials proceeded to set up a fund (£10,000) in the churches. A number of delegates were chosen to visit them, and the response was reported to be encouraging, £8,000 having been collected by 1845.[51]

At that time the northern Association decided to release the Revd David Charles to enable him to become Principal of Trefeca College,[52] which was opened earlier on 7 October 1842,[53] and *Y Drysorfa* maintained hopefully that one day a college and one Foreign Mission would be established in the Connexion in the near future.[54] The library contained more than 700 volumes, and further donations were earnestly requested.[55] It was intended to open a preparatory school to teach literature at Trefeca, but that did not materialise, and it was not until 1850 that a school was opened for a similar purpose by John Pugh of Dowlais: "Bod y cyfryw ymgeiswyr am dderbyniad i'r Athrofa ag na fo yn ddewisadwy o ran cyrhaeddiadau mewn dysgeidiaeth, i fyned yn ddioedi i Ysgol Ramadegol y Parch J. Pugh, ond yr un pryd dan ofal y Parch Mr. Charles, ac i drigfanu yn y Coleg."[56] [That the suchlike candidates for acceptance to the College and who are not eligible in ability to go forthwith to Revd J. Pugh's Grammar School, but at the same time in the care of the Revd Mr Charles, and to reside at the College.]

The Association assumed the responsibility for organising the opening ceremony, and the committee co-operated fully for this purpose with the southern Monthly Meetings. Bala college, however, re-

50. Evans, "Y Parch David Charles," *Y Traethodydd* 1893, 132.

51. Jones, *Trevecca*, 70.

52. Ibid., 71.

53. Ibid., 71.

54. Anon., "Agoriad Athrofa Trefecca," *Y Drysorfa* 1842, 351. The last sentence ran as follows: "A diau fod llawer o'r brodyr yn cryf obeithio cael gweled cyn bo hir Un Athrofa, ac Un Genhadaeth Dramor o fewn cylch yr Un Corph." [And doubtless many of the brethren strongly hope to see before long One College, and One Foreign Mission within the sphere of the One Body.]

55. Charles and Lumley, "Llyfrgell Athrofa Trefecca," *Y Drysorfa* 1843, 21–22. The Revd Richard Lumley had been appointed librarian.

56. Walters, "Cymdeithasfa Castellnewydd yn Emlyn," *Y Drysorfa* 1851, 170.

mained independent because the southern Association had refused to move its college there.[57]

In October 1865 it was decided at the Rhymni Association to establish a fund so that the southern Monthly Meetings might contribute to maintain the college and to build the Howell Harris Memorial Chapel to commemorate the centenary of his death.[58] In January 1870 it was decided that the proposal should be accepted and that the chapel should be opened on the anniversary of his death in July three years later.[59] That decision was confirmed at the Tregaron Association in April of the same year,[60] and in the General Assembly at Aberdare in June 1872 it was reported that R. G. Thomas, a Menai Bridge architect, had been appointed to design it and Evan Williams of Bangor to be the contractor.[61]

In the Llandeilo Association in August 1870[62] it was agreed to proceed, and the foundation stone was laid on 4 September 1872 by David Davies, the famous Montgomeryshire industrialist, using a silver trowel presented on the occasion by Mrs Evan Morgan of Birmingham.[63] As planned, the chapel, which cost £2,600 to build, opened its doors on 21 July 1873, the centenary of Harris's death,.[64] This celebration was largely the idea of the Revd Edward Matthews, an ardent supporter of Trefeca. He had been a student there for a short period and had contributed much financially towards the venture as well as supplying and cataloguing books and other literary material for its library.[65] This celebration was designed, not only as a memorable event to commemorate the anniversary of Harris's death but also as a means of revealing an increase

---

57. Jones, *Trevecca*, 73–75.
58. Ibid., 87–88.
59. *Y Goleuad*, 1 January 1870, 5.
60. *Y Goleuad*, 7 May 1870, 10.
61. *Y Goleuad*, 6 July 1872, 4.
62. *Y Goleuad*, 7 May 1870, 10; 6 July 1872, 4.
63. *DWB*, 116.
64. *Y Goleuad*, 14 September 1872, 7; 7 July 1873, 5–6, 8. For a short report on improvements made at Trefeca before the opening ceremony see *Y Goleuad*, 10 May 1873, 5; 26 July 1873, 8.
65. Jones, *Trevecca*, 90–91; Davies, "Trevecca 1706–1964," 20–21; *DWB*, 620. For a list of donations to the Library from 1852 to 1855 see *Report of the Committee of Trevecca College*, 27–29. See also *Contributions towards the Trevecca College Fund*.

in Welsh national consciousness in the years following the Blue Book controversy of 1846–7.⁶⁶ 'A lle y ceir hunanbarch ag egwyddorion crefydd wrth ei wraidd', the editorial to *Y Goleuad* stated, 'gwelir cymwynaswyr dyngarol yn cael eu parchu yn ddyladwy gan eu cyd-ddynion' [And where self-respect for religious principles at its source is found, charitable benefactors are seen being duly respected by their fellow men.]⁶⁷

An effort was again made to unite Trefeca and Bala under one governing body in 1887, Trefeca being the centre for classics and Bala for theology, but the South rejected the move at that time.⁶⁸ This did not hinder *Y Goleuad* from publishing weighty correspondence on the whole affair leading to speculation concerning the future of the two colleges following the appointment of the Revd Owen Prys as Principal of Trefeca to replace the Revd D. Charles Davies on his death in December 1891.⁶⁹ At that time an editorial statement was issued in *Y Goleuad* concerning the proposed union of the colleges which surprisingly suggested that the northern Association was more in favour of uniting both colleges than the south and that an influential group there believed that the *status quo* should be maintained:

> Deuir i deimlo yn fwyfwy mai mantais...fydd uno y ddwy Athrofa, fel ag i sicrhau mwy o athrawon a mwy o ysgoloriaethau. Teimlwn fod y ddau brifathraw yn ddigon rhyddfrydig i roddi yr ystyriaeth ddyladwy 1 bethau o'r fath hyn. O leiaf, gallant wneyd gwasanaeth difesur mewn addfedu barn y wlad, mewn lladd rhagfarn a chreu mwy o frawdgarwch...⁷⁰
>
> [It is felt more and more that it would be an advantage to unite the two Colleges to secure more professors and scholarships. We feel that both principals are sufficiently liberal to give due consideration to things of this kind. At least, they can give immesurable service to ripen opinion of the country to kill prejudice and create more brotherly love.]

66. This is a reference to the Education Reports of 1847, severely criticized in Wales for their adverse comments on its poor educational standards, its nonconformity and its native language. See further, Ieuan Gwynedd Jones. *Mid-Victorian Wales* (Cardiff: University of Wales Press, 1992), 103–165.

67. *Y Goleuad*, 26 July 1873, 5–6, 8.

68. Jones, *Trevecca*, 91–92.

69. *Y Goleuad*, 3 December 1891, 10–11.

70. *Y Goleuad*, 10 December 1891, 8.

When the Revd Owen Prys was appointed Principal in 1892, therefore, the northern Association clearly adopted a more positive approach. Doubtless the appointment strengthened the will in the south to keep Trefeca open for the future: "Bellach, y mae 'dydd claddu' Trefeca yn ymgolli draw yn y pellder" ["Now the 'burial day' of Trefeca has been lost away in the distance",[71] and it was further testified: "ein bod yn parhau o'r farn fod lleshad y Cyfundeb yn gyffredinol, yn sefyllfa bresenol addysg yn Nghymru, yn galw am undeb agosach rhwng y De a'r Gogledd gyda golwg ar addysg ein gweinidogion, a'n bod yn dymuno datgan ein parodrwydd i eistedd mewn cyd-ymgynghoriad â'n brodyr yn y Deheudir ar y mater hwn."[72] [We continue of the opinion that the welfare of the Connexion generally in the present position of education in Wales, calls for closer union between South and North regarding the education of our ministers, and that we wish to state our willingness to sit in consultation with our brethren in the South on this matter.]

One event, however, which exposed the academic reputation established by Trefeca later in the century was the Jubilee celebrations there in September 1892. *Y Goleuad* editorial gladly drew attention to this:

> Gyda golwg ar yr Athrofeydd Cenedlaethol dylid gofalu peidio gwastraffu amser ynddynt gyda myfyrdodau anmherthynasol, achos dylid manteisio gymaint arnynt fel y bydd yr efrydwyr yn hollol barod ar eu mynediad i Drefecca i ymroddi at faterion duwinyddol gyda difrifwch a blas.[73] [Regarding the National Colleges care should be taken not to waste time in them with irrelevant meditations, because so much advantage should be placed on them so that students can be compleletly ready when they enter Trefeca to dedicate themselves to theological matters soberly and with taste.]

The entire Jubilee proceedings were publicised in *Y Goleuad*, including a report on the public meeting, a brief synopsis of the college's history, a variety of memorial speeches, a talk on Howell Harris by the Revd Thomas Levi, Aberystwyth, and a *résumé* of the revivalist's theol-

---

71. Ibid., 12.
72. Ibid., 9.
73. *Y Goleuad*, 22 September 1892, 8.

ogy by the Revd Thomas Rees, Merthyr Tydfil.[74] Also reported was an address by the Revd William James, Aberdare, on the quality of preachers Wales expected from Trefeca in view of the theological crises at the close of the Victorian era. On that occasion James touched upon a matter of major concern:

> There is a great stir and life amongst the young men of our day, and I believe in "Young Wales". They lead the van in politics . . . A new political era has dawned on our country . . . In literature also, there is an unusual activity, and new phases are being developed. The press is getting more and more into the hands of learned and energetic young men who are determined if possible to raise Wales into an honourable position among the nations of the world. We hope soon to see our young divines taking the lead in theology and becoming the true saviours of their country, and as pioneers of the cross leading the Welsh people . . . through the wilderness of the higher criticism and the cloudland of agnosticism, into the promised land of faith and religious certainty.[75]

These words touched upon central issues in late Victorian times which challenged orthodox faith, chiefly the long-term impact of Darwin, higher criticism and the rise of socialism, especially in the densely-populated industrialised areas, problems which the Connexion could not easily solve unless the colleges trained young men of conviction to spread the gospel message.[76] In those words the signs of more testing times were clearly visible.

∾

Trefeca College was fortunate in its Principals. Throughout its existence as a theological college in its original location—extending over a period of sixty-four years—a combination of high academic standards and good management only would ensure the success of its foundation. The appointment of the Revd David Charles, who accepted the post of Tutor in 1842, followed a short period teaching at a school estab-

---

74. Ibid., 9–13.

75. *Y Goleuad*, 29 September 1892, 12; *Jiwbili Coleg Trefecca*, 27.

76. For the background to the social and theological background of Wales in this era see Pope, *Building Jerusalem*; Pope, *Seeking God's Kingdom*; ODN B, 11, 159–60.

lished by Dr Lewis Edwards, his brother-in-law, at Bala in 1837. That school subsequently became the theological college—known as 'yr hen Goleg' ('the old college')—established in that town in 1839. The original school, successful from the outset, claimed to have educated pupils 'in the acquirement of sound learning and general information, and in the cultivation of religious principles'.[77]

The college at Trefeca opened its doors on 7 October 1842. Charles was well-qualified for the post, having been educated at Jesus College, Oxford. He remained at Trefeca for twenty years and in 1863 resigned his post and moved to minister the Calvinistic Methodist church at Abercarn in Monmouthshire. It appears that this move was caused by some mismanagement regarding the appointment of an external examiner for the 1862 college examinations which forced Charles to undertake the task himself despite student objection. This led to his resignation, much to his own regret. His departure was a great loss to Trefeca for the range of his teaching over twenty years at Trefeca was remarkable, namely classics, Hebrew, Mathematics, Greek, Latin, English, Philosophy, Theology and Biblical exegesis. After his move to Abercarn Charles continued to take an active part in higher education matters, thus preparing the way for the establishment of the University College at Aberystwyth in 1872.[78]

The Revd David Charles's departure led to a gap of three years during which time the college was closed because of lack of cooperation with the Association and insufficient funds. He was succeeded by the Revd William Howells, a native of Cowbridge, who obtained his early education at different places, including Cardiff and Chichester. He then entered Cheshunt and Trefeca (1842–1845) and ministered at Swansea, Carmarthen and Liverpool. He came to Trefeca as Principal in September 1865, assisted by the Revd John Harries Jones, a classics scholar educated at Carmarthen grammar school and the Presbyterian College. Further education took Howells to Glasgow, Goettingen and Halle. During his period as Principal at Trefeca he earned a good reputation as a scholar and preacher, and a "man of marked individuality" who, among other things, showed no sympathy for the intonation of the

77. Edwards, *Athrofa'r Bala*, 23–24; Evans, *Lewis Edwards: Ei Fywyd a'i Waith*, 74; Edwards, *Bywyd a Llythyrau Lewis Edwards*, 193–94.

78. Williams, "Rev. David Charles, B.A., B.D., Principal of Trevecca College (1842–1862)," *Journal* 20 (1935) 28–36.

'From "Monastic Family" to Calvinistic Methodist Academy'

"Welsh hwyl", which he considered to be mere "barbarism"![79] His role at Trefeca over a period of thirty-five years, however, prepared the way for the Revd David Charles Davies, a native of Aberystwyth, who eventually, after some delay, took office in 1888.[80] He published a number of articles and studies, including theological commentaries on the epistles to the Ephesians, Romans and St John's first epistle. He conducted a successful Homiletics course, excelling himself as a commentator on preachers and preaching styles:

> Nis gallwn lai na dyfynnu engraifft neu ddwy o'n cof, at yr hyn a ddywedwyd eisoes ar y pwynt hwn: — "y pregethwr goreu yw yr hwn eill wneyd i'r bobl *addoli* dan ei weinidogaeth." "Pregethu yw *siarad â'r bobl* yn y fath fodd naturiol nes eu bod yn awyddus i ateb neu ofyn cwestiwn i'r pregethwr yn ystod y bregeth. Pregethu felly ydoedd eiddo yr Iesu." Eto, " Nid oes gennym hanes ddarfod i ddysgeidiaeth yr Iesu beri i'r bobl *chwerthin* nac *wylo*; eithr hwy a "synnasant wrth ei ddysgeidiaeth Ef."[81]
>
> [I could not but quote an example or two from memory, what has already been said on this point—"the best preacher is he who can make the people worship by means of his ministry." "Preaching is to speak to people in a natural way so that they are keen to answer or ask a question to the preacher during the sermon. Jesus was that kind of preacher." Again, "we do not have any knowledge that Jesus's teaching made the people laugh nor cry; for they were astonished by His teaching."]

Arguably, the most distinguished of the Principals at Trefeca down to 1906 when the college moved to Aberystwyth was the Revd Dr Owen Prys, who surprisingly is given but scant attention by W. P. Jones in his history of the college.[82] Prys was a highly-respected Cardiganshire scholar, born at Pen-llwyn in 1857, an area known for its scholars and litterateurs.[83] As a child he became aware of the deep

---

79. For a short survey of Howell's career at Trefeca, see Williams, "Y Parchedig William Howells," *Y Traethodydd*, 44 (1889), 168–80'; Morgan, "Principal William Howells, Trevecca," *Journal* 20 (1935) 37–43 (here 41–42); ODNB, 28, 513 (unfortunately omits any reference to Trefeca).

80. For D. Charles Davies, see Jones, "Y Prifathraw D. Charles Davies, M.A. yn Nhrefeca," *Y Traethodydd*, 1893, 378–83; DWB, 117, 370; ODNB, 15, 350–51.

81. Job, "Y Prifathro D. Charles Davies, M.A., yn Nhrefecca," *Y Traethodydd*, 1893, 185.

82. Jones, *Trevecca*, 93, 98.

83. For Prys's background and contribution to academic life see Williams,

influence which the 1859 religious revival had on his native county, a spiritual power which also, in due course, had an impact on him. He became a pupil-teacher in the British school at Pen-llwyn before entering Bangor Normal College, and then served briefly as headmaster of Goginan British School. A rapid change of fortune enabled him to enter Peterhouse and later Trinity colleges, Cambridge, where he graduated with first-class honours in the Mental and Moral Sciences Tripos. In 1887 Prys went to Owen's College, Manchester, where, for a year, he assisted in the Philosophy Department and, in 1890, after spending some time broadening his studies chiefly at Leipzig university, he became a tutor at Trefeca. Two years later, in the college's jubilee year, following the death of the Revd David Charles Davies he was appointed tutor at Trefeca with the Revd Edwin Williams, a former student at Trefeca and minister at Aberdare, as his deputy.

The Revd Dr Owen Prys was a studious individual, quietly disposed and known to have devoted himself as a student entirely to his academic studies. It is hardly surprising that when he became Principal he intended to introduce more theology into the curriculum. In the Trefeca report in January 1892 reference was made to the appointment of the Revd J. Young Evans, a native of Dowlais and renowned classical scholar, to the staff. It was further commented that one of the applicants was primarily a theologian which led to a discussion of the need to make the college more theological in its curriculum, but it appeared that there was no clear-thinking on the matter at the time. Prys, however, succeeded in achieving this in due course, initiating courses in theology rather than classical studies, and in 1897 the college became mainly a theological academy. His own specialisms were divinity, philosophy of religion and ethics, studies on which "the doctrine of man", the theme of his Davies Lecture delivered in the General Assembly at Cardiff in 1904, was based. Young Evans's appointment was not planned as part of the campaign to establish one theological college, which was made clear in the college Report of 1905. What it did, in fact, was to strengthen the classical tradition well-rooted there.[84]

"Cyn-brifathro, y Parch. Owen Prys, M.A., D.D.," *Journal*, 20 (1935) 44–51; *Blwyddiadur*, 1936, 207–9; DWB, 806–7; Williams, "Y Prifathro Owen Prys," in W. Morris, ed., *Deg o Enwogion*, 1:45–52.

84. *Y Goleuad*, 11 August 1905, 12.

'From "Monastic Family" to Calvinistic Methodist Academy'

Although Dr Owen Prys was outwardly a reserved person he actively engaged himself in connexional matters, especially after the removal of the college, under his principalship, to Aberystwyth in 1906. During his time at Trefeca he served on several connexional and interdenominational committees, and, together with the Revd E. O. Davies, Llandudno, was regarded as a pioneer of the Ecumenical Movement in Wales. It was during his years at Aberystwyth that he was elected to the Connexion's highest offices as Moderator of the General Assembly in 1910 and the southern Association in 1917. In fact, he was one of the very few elected to the Moderatorship of the General Assembly on two occasions, although, on the second occasion in 1935, the year when the Connexion's bi-centenary was commemorated, he died before he was able to assume office. His contribution to learning and his denomination was duly acknowledged by the University of Wales in 1922 when he was awarded a doctorate of divinity *in honoris causa*.

Despite his profound learning Owen Prys was not a prolific publisher of theological studies but he did deliver memorable lectures in Associations and General Assemblies. As his public delivery on the occasion of opening the college at Aberystwyth clearly revealed, he was well aware of the changing religious climate in Wales of his day and the challenges which it posed. One such challenge in the late 1920s, which created much publicity, was Prys's suspension of the Revd Tom Nefyn Williams, chiefly on doctrinal grounds.[85] He devoted himself diligently to his teaching commitments, thus contributing immensely during his sixteen years at Trefeca to strengthening the college's reputation as a seat of theological teaching and learning.

In March 1904 a new period dawned in the history of Trefeca when David Davies, first baron of Llandinam, grandson of the famous David Davies, the Victorian industrialist and philanthropist, with the support of his immediate family, offered £12,000 towards establishing a college at Aberystwyth on condition that Trefeca and Bala united and one

---

85. Much has been published on this unfortunate episode in the annals of the Connexion. See Morgan, *Rebirth of a Nation*, 199-200; Morgan, *The Span of the Cross*, 123-26; Parri, *Tom Nefyn: Portread*, 36-68; Pope, "Corwynt gwyllt ynteu tyner awel?" *Y Traethodydd* (1997) 150-62.

preparatory college be established to provide suitable students.[86] His decision officially was made known in a letter sent to the Association held at Y Gelli, Ystrad Rhondda on 5 March 1904 and read on 8 March. It is clear from the wording of the letter that this proposal was a sincere effort by a family, closely attached to the Connexion, to further theological teaching and training for the ministry in Wales:

> on behalf of my mother, my sisters, and myself, I wish to say that we shall be very glad to subscribe £12,000 towards the erection of a new college, provided the two following conditions are carried out, viz. (1) That the present colleges of Bala and Trevecca shall be united into one college for the Denomination. (2) That this college shall be situated at Aberystwyth. As far as I can gather the feeling in North and South Wales is running strongly in favour of a united college, and I think Aberystwyth is by far the the most central spot in Wales where such a college might with advantage be built.[87]

By this scheme Davies was aware that closer connections could be established between the new college and the university at Aberystwyth where students of both colleges could attend classes, mix socially together and enrich academic experiences. He hoped that his proposal would be acceptable to both Associations and that a positive step forward might be taken as soon as possible. He attended these Associations and addressed their representatives regarding this proposal. The offer appealed more to the southern Association, but it refused to act on his proposal if the northern Association was determined to establish a preparatory school at Bala for suitable students.[88] At the time the interest in this new plan, however, grew rapidly among delegates of both Associations and Presbyteries. The editorial of *Y Goleuad* in March 1904 commented favourably on the possibility of establishing a new location but drew attention to some practical matters which required close scrutiny, such as the deeds and investments of both colleges and

86. Jones, *Trevecca*, 95; Edwards, *Athrofa'r Bala*, 45: DWB, (1940–1970), 30; ODNB, 15, 348–50; *Who's Who in Wales* (2nd ed. 1933), 33. He was educated at King's College, Cambridge, and became Liberal Member of Parliament for Montgomeryshire (1906–29). He maintained close relations with the Calvinistic Methodist denomination in Wales and his mother, Mary, was the daughter of the Revd Evan Jones of Llandinam.

87. Sent from Plas Dinam on 5 March. *Y Goleuad*, 11 March 1904, 7.

88. *Y Goleuad*, 12 August 1904, 8.

'From "Monastic Family" to Calvinistic Methodist Academy'

the financial implications of building a college at Aberystwyth.[89] It was also argued by some that a preparatory school should still remain at Bala and another established at Trefeca. Consequently, the southern Association quickly appointed a committee of fifteen members to discuss these problems, which included keeping Trefeca open as a preparatory college,[90] and at the Tredegar Association on 2 August 1904 it was recorded that the Revd John Davies, Pandy, a member of the committee, voiced his opinion as follows:

> Mae rhwymedigaeth cyfreithiol a moesol i gadw Trefecca i ddiben addysgol. Cynygiodd perthynasau Howell Harries yr holl feddianau i Gyfarfod Misol Brycheiniog, ar yr amod eu bod yn darparu i gadw ysgol yn Nhrefecca, ac nid oedd dim yn y telerau yn gyfryw nad all y Cyfarfod Misol gymeryd meddiant o'r cwbl eto. Felly os oedd uniad i gymeryd lle, yr oedd efe yn cynyg fod ysgol ragbaratoawl i gael ei chychwyn yn Nhrefecca, a bod hono i fod yn agored i fechgyn na fwriadent fynd i'r weinidogaeth yn gystal ag i bregethwyr ieuainc . . .[91]
>
> [There is a legal binding to keep Trefeca for educational purposes. Howel Harris's relations offered all the possessions to Brecknock Monthly Meeting on condition that they continue to maintain a school, and there is nothing in the conditions as such that the Monthly Meeting cannot possess all of it again. Therefore, if a unity was to take place he proposed that a preparatory school should be opened at Trefeca, and that it was to be opened to young men who had no intention of entering the ministry as well as to young preachers . . .]

Finance, travelling facilities to and from Aberystwyth and student accommodation were to become the main talking points.[92] The Revds Thomas Levi, former minister of Y Tabernacl, in the town, and John Morgan Jones, Pembroke Terrace, Cardiff, a prominent member of the southern Association, were in favour of locating the college at Aberystwyth although Jones would have preferred Cardiff.[93] One factor which surprisingly was not given publicity was the anglicized surroundings of eastern Brecknockshire and the borders which increasingly

89. *Y Goleuad*, 18 March 1904, 8, 11.
90. *Y Goleuad*, 5 August 1904, 3; 12 August 1904, 10; Jones, *Trevecca*, 95.
91. *Y Goleuad*, 2 August 1904, 10.
92. *Y Goleuad*, 29 April 1904, 9.
93. *Y Goleuad*, 18 March 1904, 8, 11; 18 April 1906, 11.

created difficulty for ministerial trainees at Trefeca wishing to conduct services in the Welsh language.

David Davies of Llandinam was present at the Llanrwst Association and spoke to his proposal. Although he was aware of the difficulties he was prepared to pay two-thirds of the total cost on condition that the Connexion agreed to establish one Theological College and one preparatory school only.[94] The proposal to unite the colleges had a history which extended back several years, and at the Llanrwst Association old views and arguments were aired on both sides, the Bala delegates being chiefly concerned about the feasibility of the venture. Davies stated that both colleges at the time shared about 80 students between them, and was convinced that to support one college would be more practical. His intention was to end the competition between colleges sited in two different regions. He argued that uniting the students in one institution would be desirable on geographical and academic grounds, and his inquiries revealed that a college could be built, two-thirds of the cost being borne by him.[95] It was agreed that a committee be convened to investigate the matter further and to report at the Bangor association at the end of August. "If we are going to amalgamate our colleges", the Revd William James of Aberdare stated, "we must amalgamate ourselves first of all", a warning that the Connexion urgently needed to maintain and strengthen its own unity.[96] The views expressed stressed that whatever the outcome careful and full consideration was required before reaching a final decision. It was proposed that a new college, if acceptable, should be residential, scholarships being offered and a preparatory school established at Bala, and Trefeca converted, like Bontnewydd, as a home for orphan children![97] It was also suggested in published correspondence that it should be made a "printing office" or "Book House" for the Connexion to print books such as *Rhodd Mam* (Mother's Gift), the Bible and hymn-tune books.[98] The editor of *Y Goleuad*, who favoured one college, declared that whatever the outcome the equal status

---

94. *Y Goleuad*, 10 June 1904, 7.

95. *Y Goleuad*, 17 June 1904, 4–5.

96. Ibid., 5.

97. *Y Goleuad*, 29 July 1904, 9.

98. *Y Goleuad*, 5 August 1904, 7. John Parry of Chester was the author of *Rhodd Mam I'w Phlentyn*, Llanrwst: O. Evans, 1825. Written in 1811, this was a famous children's catechism used in Sunday Schools for well over a century.

'From "Monastic Family" to Calvinistic Methodist Academy'

of both Associations should be preserved, and that a preparatory school should be established at Bala. If the northern Association insisted on this then, it was stated, the scheme would be "shipwrecked,"[99] a viewpoint unequivocally supported by the Revd. John Morgan Jones.[100] Presbyteries were required to voice their opinions and report to the Tredegar Association on the proposal that a school be established at Trefeca for ministerials and laymen.[101]

Issues were discussed in the northern Association at Bangor in August 1904 and it was decided that if the investigative committee, already appointed by it, was informed that Presbyteries agreed to unite a more formal committee would then be appointed to discuss the matter with the southern Association.[102] Unfortunately, however, the report of the Llanrwst committee, compared to the effective moves made by the southern Association, had not been completed, possibly a ploy to stall proceedings.[103] To prevent further embarrassment it was suggested that both sub-committees should convene to establish the facts so that equality between the Associations could be maintained.[104] Delaying tactics in the north, however, did not ease matters and a letter sent to the southern Association at Aberdulais in October 1904 clarified the situation:

> Ein bod fel Cymdeithasfa yn llawenychu wrth weled parodrwydd ein brodyr yn y De i gydymgynghori a ni ynglyn a'r mater pwysig o gael un Athrofa Dduwinyddol i'r Cyfundeb. Ein bod yn ystyried mai angenrheidiol fydd i ni yn y Gogledd nodi pwyllgor i gyfarfod a'u pwyllgor hwy, fel yr awgrymant; ac os bydd adroddiad y Pwyllgor Ymchwiliadol a benodwyd genym, a barn ein Cyfarfodydd Misol, yn ffafriol i'r Undeb, y byddwn yn apwyntio y cyfryw bwyllgor yn ddioed.[105]
>
> [As an Association we rejoice seeing the readiness of our brethren in the South to discuss with us regarding this important matter of having one Theological College for the Connexion. We consider it essential for us in the North to appoint a committee

99. *Y Goleuad*, 5 August 1904, 3.
100. Ibid., 3.
101. Ibid., 8.
102. *Y Goleuad*, 26 August 1904, 6.
103. Ibid., 8.
104. *Y Goleuad*, 2 September 1904, 9.
105. *Y Goleuad*, 21 October 1904, 6.

to act with their committee, as they suggest, and if the report of the Investigative Committee appointed by us, and the opinion of our Presbyteries are in fact of unity, then we shall appoint such a committee immediately.]

The Investigative Committee submitted its report at the Llanrhaeadr Association in November 1904 in which it estimated that, if no financial aid was forthcoming, a new college would cost £25,000–£30,000. Moreover, in the event of a merger, legal advice was needed regarding the circumstances of the college at Bala.[106] In such uncertain circumstances, on behalf of the Association, the Pwllheli solicitor O. Robyns-Owen sought the advice of J. Bryn Roberts, barrister of Lincoln's Inn and Liberal M.P. for South Caernarfonshire, on matters relating to the legal and constitutional position of Bala college, and he advised against the merger on the grounds that there were no ways of merging the funds of both colleges under new constitutional regulations.[107] He advised that both Associations should seek the advice of the Board of Education in London on these matters, but legal difficulties were not easily resolved and that path appears not to have been followed.

In 1905, however, the intensity of the religious revival largely overshadowed much of the ongoing discussion concerning the union of the two colleges. To move matters forward, in April 1906 David Davies generously offered the Hotel Cambria in Aberystwyth, which he had purchased, to the Connexion so that a united theological college might be established there. "We believe", he stated on behalf of his family, "that the union of the two Colleges in this building would promote economy and greater efficiency in the education of our ministerial students, and would at the same time bring these students into close touch with the life of one of our national university colleges." He then continued: "It is our earnest desire that the two existing colleges should be amalgamated, but in the event of the rejection of this proposal we are still prepared, as an alternative, to offer the building to either of the Associations for a theological College on condition that it will be open for the other Association to join later should it desire to do so. We are assured that

---

106. *Y Goleuad*, 18 November 1904, 12–13.
107. Ibid., 13; *DWB*, 1148; Humphreys, *Gwŷr Enwog Gynt*, 28–39.

the accommodation will be amply sufficient for the needs of a united college, and the building is admirably suited for that purpose."[108]

His enthusiasm for the proposal led him to hope that both Associations would arrange to inspect the building and report on it and come to a satisfactory conclusion. He was also prepared to do what was necessary to accommodate students and staff at the college.[109] This offer was eagerly supported by the southern Association which was prepared to proceed with the venture. The committee had already met on 19 August 1904 and 14 March 1906, and it was decided to invite the northern Association to consider the proposal. If rejected, them its southern counterpart would accept it, so that a final decision could be reached in the June Association.[110]

In the north, however, the principle of union was not unanimously supported, and at the Ruthin Association in late April views were sharply divided. The Caernarfonshire county architect, employed to inspect the building at Aberystwyth, reported that space for student accommodation was inadequate to which Davies responded immediately stating that "any proposal should be measured, not by the maximum standard, but with the conditions now prevailing" at Bala and Trefeca: "and I venture to think that the accomodation at the Hotel Cambria, although it does not come up to the ideal Residential College, as conceived by the Committee, is nevertheless infinitely superior to the condition of things, under which the students now pursue their studies. For instance, I see no reason why several students should not share the same study, or that it is essential that each professor should have a room for himself in the College."[111]

Frequent exchanges occurred at Ruthin and differing views were published in *Y Goleuad*, regarding maintenance costs, the deficit being calculated at between £400 and £1,000. In such circumstances the Revd Isaac Jones of Nantglyn unequivocally stated that the *status quo* should be maintained: "Coleg y Gogledd i ni, a Choleg y De iddynt hwythau" ("A Northern College for us, and a Southern College for them").[112] The

---

108. *Y Goleuad*, 4 April 1906, 5, 13 June 1906, 3. Report of G. Dickens-Lewis, architect, Aberystwyth.

109. *Y Goleuad*, 4 April 1906, 5.

110. *Y Goleuad*, 18 April 1906, 11; 25 April 1906, 8.

111. *Y Goleuad*, 2 May 1906, 6.

112. *Y Goleuad*, 2 May 1906, 7.

Revd H. Barrow Williams, recently retired minister of Seilo chapel, Llandudno, however, argued that the proposal should not be entirely abandoned and that union was the best way forward:

> Dywedwch a fynoch am y De, yn y De y mae dyfodol Methodistiaeth . . . Mae ysbryd yr oes, mi gredaf, yn awgrymu i ni yr hyn y dylem ei wneyd: mae y wlad, mi dybiaf, yn addfed i uno . . .Yr ydym yn cwyno beunydd oherwydd y ddwy Genhadaeth Gartrefol, oblegid dwy Drysorfa y Gweinidogion... Yr ydym yn cario y Symudiad Ymosodol ymlaen yn unol; mae Pwyllgor y Llyfrau yn unol; mae Pwyllgor yr Ysgol Sabbothol yn unol, ac yn fwyaf pwysig o'r oll, y mae gwaith ardderchog y Genhadaeth Dramor yn cael ei gario ymlaen gan ddau haner y Corff. Yr ydym ni ein hunain yn un Cyfundeb, ac yn y cyfeiriad yna y mae oreu i ni symud ymlaen. Ond pan mae cwestiwn pwysicach i ni, mi gredaf, na'r un o'r rhai yna yn dyfod ger bron, sef cwestiwn addysg ein pregethwyr, yr ydym yn suddo yn y fan dan ddylanwad teimladau talaethiol. Dylem ymddyrchafu uwchlaw hynyna, ac edrych ar y cwestiwn; nid pa un fydd y goreu i'r De neu i'r Gogledd . . . ond pa un fydd y goreu i'r Cyfundeb Methodistaidd yn y dyfodol.[113]
>
> [Say whatever you want about the South, the future of Methodism lies with the South . . . the spirit of the age, I believe, suggests to us what we should do: the country, I imagine, is ripe for union . . .We complain daily about the two Home Missions, about two Ministerial Treasuries . . .We maintain the Forward Movement together; the Book Committee is united; the Sunday School Committee is united, and most important of all, the excellent work of the Foreign Mission is continued by the two halves of the *Corff*. We ourselves are one Connexion, and in that direction it is better for us to move onwards. But when a more important question for us, I believe, than any of those is brought before us, namely the question of ministerial education, we sink immediately influenced by regional feelings. We should arise above all this, and look at the question, not which one would be best for the South or the North . . . but which one would be better for the Methodist Connexion in future.]

One of the firmest opponents of the move to Aberystwyth was the Revd T. J. Wheldon, minister of Y Tabernacl, Bangor, who, in a tediously long speech stated that the Hotel Cambria was unsuitable

---

113. Ibid.

'From "Monastic Family" to Calvinistic Methodist Academy'

as a theological college.[114] He was supported by the Revd Evan Jones, Moriah, Caernarfon, another prominent leader of his Connexion who, despite his personal opinion on the matter, declared his high regard for the Davies family of Llandinam.[115] In a letter in May 1906 another correspondent detailed the arguments for and against the merger and referred to four possibilities for the northern Association, namely to join with the south, to await and see how well Trefeca settled at Aberystwyth, to remain at Bala and strengthen its reputation as the best theological college in Wales and set up a preparatory school for the north and south instead of a college at Aberystwyth, and to keep the existing colleges as they were.[116] Whatever the response may have been to these alternatives it was clear that the northern Association needed more time before submitting a final decision by the end of June, as David Davies expected, and an extension was rather grudgingly granted by him until the August Association.[117] "That being so", he declared in his response to the Revd J. Owen Thomas, Secretary of the northern Association, "I am quite prepared to extend this time for a reply . . . but I must ask that a definite decision be arrived at then, as we are anxious to proceed with the alterations at the Cambria as soon as possible."[118] The Revd Thomas Charles Williams of Menai Bridge considered that a majority vote should be rejected and that a respite of three years should be accepted to allow the northern Association to reach a final decision.[119] Leading delegates, the Revds John Williams, Brynsiencyn, John Owen of Chester and H. Barrow Williams, however, were firmly in favour of union.[120] In response to a request for guidance from other denominational college principals, one lengthy reply was obtained from Principal T. Witton Davies of the Baptist College, Bangor, recommending the move to Aberystwyth. He was well aware that university training was necessary to produce the best kind of theological student, and added: "My position is this: Theological students have offered to them the best

114. Y Goleuad, 2 May 1906, 10; DWB, 1015–16.
115. Ibid.; DWB, 461–62.
116. Y Goleuad, 16 May 1906, 9–10.
117. Y Goleuad, 23 May 1906, 4.
118. Ibid., 4.
119. Y Goleuad, 23 May 1906, 9; 13 June 1904, 9.
120. Ibid.,10–11; 30 May 1906, 5.

training in Arts subjects which can be obtained in Wales. Even during the theological course the student has so many advantages offered him in a University Centre, in the way of libraries, special lectures stimulus, that he loses much by being transferred to remote and out of the way places."[121]

In the meantime the southern Association was busily preparing the way for the move to Aberystwyth. At the Nantymoel Association in June a lengthy discussion took place on the submission of Presbyteries, and final plans were made to expedite the move and establish Trefeca as a preparatory school,[122] all of which was unanimously accepted so that they could be presented to the Cardigan Association. *Y Goleuad*, however, published the view of the Brecknockshire Presbytery which, for obvious reasons, wished to keep the college at Trefeca,[123] and an unnamed correspondent maliciously rejected Davies's proposal:

> Mae rhodd Mr Davies yn hudo y dyn anwybodus ac anmhrofiadol i'r domen . . . Onid oes genym ddau College noble wedi eu sylfaenu ar lefydd cysegredig? A cystal a tynu eu hawdurdod nhw i lawr i fildio ar hen domen lygredig o dafarndy! . . . Piti garw na buasai Mr Davies yn cael ar ei galon i roddi y rhodd ardderchog hon i'r Gymdeithas Genhadol Gartrefol yn lle bod ei gweinidogion yn llwgu.[124]
>
> [Mr Davies's gift entices the ignorant and inexperienced man to the dung heap . . . Have we not two noble Colleges established on consecrated ground? And as well as destroying their authority to build on an old corrupt dung heap of a tavern..It's a great pity that Mr Davies had not felt in his heart to give this excellent gift to the Home Mission Society instead of allowing its ministry to famish.]

Correspondence from the southern Association at Pontarddulais in April 1906 reached the northern Association at Newtown in mid-June empowering its committee, in cooperation with the northern committee, to prepare a plan to unite both colleges. If that was rejected by the north then the southern committee would proceed to seek the Presbyterian agreement to it. The meeting with the north was expected

121. *Y Goleuad*, 30 May 1906, 5.
122. *Y Goleuad*, 20 June 1906, 5–6.
123. Ibid., 24.
124. Ibid., 24.

'From "Monastic Family" to Calvinistic Methodist Academy'

as soon as possible hoping that an agreement could be reached.[125] Using its customary delaying tactics the north replied that the Association did not know its own mind at the time and its committee could not move forward since the matter was still being considered by the Presbyteries until the Association in August.[126] In the meantime divergent views were expressed in the press,[127] but it was evident that southern correspondents were, in the main, eager to see the matter finally decided, and that came about in the Cardigan Association in August when it was declared that a theological college would to be established at Aberystwyth with Trefeca as a preparatory school. This was regarded as a major move forward in the education of the Christian ministry.[128]

The Porthmadog Association in August brought matters to a head so far as the north was concerned when it was reported that the Aberystwyth plan had been rejected by the presbyteries nine to five against it. It was recommended that the Association should thank the Davies family for its generosity in providing a new college for the Connexion at Aberystwyth. It also appreciate David Davies's willingness to allow the north to join with the south if and when it was considered appropriate for it to do so, and a letter was sent in reply to that sent by the southern Association. In it, the following statement was made:

> Mewn atebiad ychwanegol i'r genadwri a dderbyniwyd yn Nghymdeithasfa y Drefnewydd yn Mehefin diwethaf oddiwrth y Gymdeithasfa yn y De yn gofyn i ni enwi nifer o frodyr i gyfarfod nifer o frodyr o'r De i baratoi cynllun i uno y ddwy Athrofa, yr hyn na allasem y pryd hwnw oherwydd fod yr achos o uniad y Colegau dan ystyriaeth y Cyfarfodydd Misol a'r Henaduriaethau. Yr ydym yn awr ar ol derbyn llais y Cyfarfodydd Misol a'r Henaduriaethau, yn cael nas gallwn, ar hyn o bryd, weled ein ffordd i uno y Colegau, ac oherwydd hyny fe welir nad oes bellach angen am i'r ddau Bwyllgor gyfarfod.
>
> Dymunwn hefyd, fel Cymdeithasfa, longyfarch ein brodyr yn y De yn galonog ar yr unfrydedd gyda pha un y galluogwyd hwy i ddyfod i benderfyniad ar fater mor bwysig.

---

125. Ibid., 25.
126. Ibid., 27.
127. *Y Goleuad*, 27 June 1906, 9–10; 4 July 1906, 11.
128. *Y Goleuad*, 8 August 1906, 11–12; 15 August 1906, 8.

Yn mhellach, yr ydym o galon yn gobeithio y bydd yr Athrofa yn parhau, ac yn cynyddu fwyfwy mewn effeithiolrwydd.[129]

[In a further reply to the message accepted in the Newtown Association last June from the southern Association asking us to name several brothers to meet a number of brothers from the South to prepare a plan to unite the two Colleges, what we could not do at that time because the matter of uniting the two colleges is being considered by the Monthly meetings and Presbyteries. We now find, having accepted the decision of the Monthly meetings and Presbyteries, that we cannot at this time, see our way clearly to unite the Colleges and consequently we see that there is no need for the two Committees to meet.

As an Association we also wish to congratulate our brothers in the south heartily on their unanimity which has enabled them to reach a decision on such an important matter.

Furthermore, we heartily hope that the College will continue and increase more and more in efficiency.

Thus ended, for the time being, the extensive discussions regarding the union of the two colleges. The proposal to establish a new college at Aberystwyth was accepted by the southern Association on 1 June 1906, and it was decided to open it on 1 October of that year.[130] The preparatory school opened on 24 September with 43 students was largely established to meet the enthusiastic call, following the 1904–5 revival, for a pre-theological centre to educate ministerial students who had not the qualifications to enter the college at Aberystwyth.[131] Its doors were opened on Wednesday 17 October in the same year with 30 students.[132] The college was officially opened on Tuesday and Wednesday 30-31 October, and several celebrations were held, including a preaching festival at Y Tabernacl chapel when the Revds John Williams, Brynsiencyn, and W. E. Prytherch, Trinity chapel, Swansea, were the guest preachers.[133] In his formal address on this occasion Principal Owen Prys drew attention to the development of education at Trefeca and the "Trefecca newydd" established alongside the young University College which

129. *Y Goleuad*, 5 September 1906, 8–11.
130. *Y Goleuad*, 12 September 1906, 8–9.
131. *Y Goleuad*, 17 October 1906, 5.
132. *Y Goleuad*, 31 October 1906, 7.
133. *Y Goleuad*, 7 November 1906, 5–10.

contributed immensely to fostering the academic integrity of the new theological college:

> As I think of that time [when he was at Trefeca], one cannot help noticing the considerable progress which has been made in the education of the ministry . . . We are trying to equip our men; that is the ideal we have set ourselves; to raise . . . the whole status of the ministry so far as education is concerned . . . But there is one still greater responsibility . . . upon the churches . . . and that is, to send us men filled with the Holy Spirit; spiritually-minded men. We want men intellectually strong, but above all things we want men filled with the spirit of God, spiritually -minded men. I thank God for the number of men who offer themselves to the ministry in Wales today.[134]

The relocated "monastic family"—as it was once called—of Howell Harris had, in 1906, become the Calvinistic Methodist theological college of Wales which maintained a high academic profile for almost another century.

---

134. Ibid., 6.

BIBLIOGRAPHY

Printed Sources

Blwyddiadur, Y (1936)
Contributions towards the Trevecca College Fund from the year 1867 to 1880; together with the Contributions towards the Memorial Chapel and the Library. Newport, 1882.
Drysorfa, Y (1840, 1842)
Goleuad, Y (1870–1906)
Jiwbili Coleg Trefecca Medi 20fed a'r 21 ain, 1882. Dolgellau, 1882.
Jones, Griffith. *Llythyr ynghylch y Ddyledswydd o Gateceisio Plant a Phobl Anwybodus.* London, 1749.
Report of the Committee of Trevecca College with a general statement of accounts. Aberystwyth, 1856.
Traethodydd, Y (1846, 1893, 1897, 1997)

Secondary Sources: Volumes

Charles, Thomas. *Geiriadur Ysgrythyrol.* Y Bala: 1805–11
Clement, M. *The S.P.C.K. and Wales, 1699–1740.* London: SPCK, 1954.
Corff ac Enaid: Ysgrifau ar Fethodistiaeth. Edited by Elfed ap N. Roberts. Caernarfon: Pantycelyn, 1988.
Cook, F. *Selina, Countess of Huntingdon.* Edinburgh: Banner of Truth Trust, 2001.
Education in Wales/Addysg yng Nghymru 1847–1947. Pamphlet no. 2. London: Welsh Department of Education, 1948.
Edwards, G. A. *Athrofa'r Bala, 1837–1937.* Y Bala: 1937.
Edwards, T. C. *Bywyd a Llythyrau y Diweddar Barch. Lewis Edwards, M.A., D.D.* Liverpool: Foulkes, 1891.
Evans, E. D. *A History of Wales 1660–1815.* Cardiff: University of Wales Press, 1976.
Evans, Trebor Lloyd. *Lewis Edwards: Ei Fywyd a'i Waith.* Swansea: Penry, 1967.
Hanes Methodistiaeth Galfinaidd Cymru: I Y Deffroad Mawr, edited by Gomer M. Roberts. Caernarfon: Pantycelyn, 1973.
Harding, A. *The Countess of Huntingdon's Connexion.* Oxford University Press, 2003.
Himbury, D. Mervyn. *The South Wales Baptist College, 1807–1957.* Cardiff: South Wales Baptist College, 1957.
Humphreys, E. Morgan. *Gwŷr Enwog Gynt.* I. Aberystwyth: Welsh Book Club, 1950.
Jenkins, G. H. *The Foundations of Modern Wales, 1642–1780.* Oxford University Press, 1987.
Jenkins, R. T. *Hanes Cymru yn y Ddeunawfed Ganrif.* Cardiff: University of Wales Press, 1928.
Jenkins, R. T. et al., editors. *The Dictionary of Welsh Biography 1941–1970*, edited by. London: Honourable Society of Cymmrodorion, 1971.
Jones, Frank Price. *Thomas Jones o Ddinbych, 1756–1820.* Denbigh: Gee, 1956.
Jones, Jonathan. *Cofiant y Parch Thomas Jones o Ddinbych.* Denbigh: Gee, 1897.
Jones, M. G. *The Charity School Movement.* Cambridge: University of Cambridge Press, 1938.

Jones, R. Tudur. *Hanes Annibynwyr Cymru*. Swansea: John Penry Press, 1966.
Jones, W. P. *Coleg Trefeca/Trevecca College*. Trefeca Committee, 1942.
Knox, R. Buick. *Wales and 'Y Goleuad' (1869-1879)*. Caernarfon: Pantycelyn Press, 1969.
Malkin, B. H. *The Scenery, Antiquities and Biography of South Wales*. London: Longman & Rees, 1804.
Lloyd, J. E., and R. T. Jenkins, editors. *The Dictionary of Welsh Biography down to 1940*. London: Honourable Society of Cymmrodorion, 1959.
Matthew, H. G. C., and Brian Harrison, editors. *Oxford Dictionary of National Biography*. 60 vols. Oxford: Oxford University Press, 2004.
Matthews, D. Hugh. *From Abergavenny to Cardiff: History of the South Wales Baptist College, 1806-2006*. Swansea: Ilston, 2007.
Morgan, D. Densil. *Lewis Edwards*. Cardiff: University of Wales Press, 2009.
———. *The Span of the Cross: Christian Religion and Society in Wales 1914-2000*: Cardiff: University of Wales Press, 1999.
Morgan, E. *John Elias: Life, Letters and Essays*. Rev. ed. Edinburgh: Banner of Truth Trust, 1973.
Morgan, K. O. *Rebirth of a Nation: Wales 1880-1980*. Oxford: Oxford University Press, 1982.
Morris, William (ed.). *Deg o Enwogion*. Caernarfon: Pantycelyn Press, 1959.
Nuttall, Geoffrey F. *The Significance of Trevecca College 1768-91*. London: Epworth Press, 1969.
Owen, G. Dyfnallt. *Ysgolion a Cholegau yr Annibynwyr*. Llandysul: Welsh Congregational Union, 1939.
Owen, Goronwy P. *Hunangofiant John Elias*. Bridgend: Welsh Evangelical Movement, 1974.
Parri, Harri. *Tom Nefyn: Portread*. Caernarfon: Pantycelyn, 1999.
Parry, R. Ifor. *Ymneilltuaeth*. Llandysul: Gomer, 1962.
Pope, R. *Building Jerusalem: Nonconformity, Labour and the Social Question in Wales, 1906-1939*. Cardiff: University of Wales Press, 1998.
———. *Seeking God's Kingdom: The Nonconformist Social Gospel in Wales 1906-1939*. Cardiff: University of Wales Press, 1999.
Roberts, John. *The Calvinistic Methodism of Wales*. Caernarfon: Pantycelyn, 1934.
Schlenther, Boyd S. *Queen of the Methodists*. Durham: 1997.
The Welsh Language Before the Industrial Revolution, edited by G. H. Jenkins. Cardiff: University of Wales Press, 1997.
Watts, Michael R. *The Dissenters: II The Expansion of Evangelical Nonconformity*. Oxford: Oxford University Press, 1995.
Welch, Edwin. *Spiritual Pilgrim*. Cardiff: University of Wales Press, 1995.
Who's Who in Wales. 2nd ed. London: Reynolds, 1933.

Articles and Chapters in Books

Anon. "Agoriad Athrofa Trefecca." *Y Drysorfa* 12 (1842) 351.
Anon. "Athrofa Trefecca—y diweddar Mr Benjamin Watkins, Aberhonddu." *Y Traethodydd* 2 (1846) 345-51.

Anon. "William Williams o Bant-y-Celyn a'i amserau." *Y Traethodydd* 1 (1846) 225–39.
Charles, D. and B. Watkins. "Athrofa Trefecca: Cyfarchiad y dirprwywyr." *Y Drysorfa* 10 (1840) 344–45.
Charles, D., and R. Lumley. "Llyfrgell Athrofa Trefecca." *Y Drysorfa*, 13 (1843) 21–22.
Davies, Gareth. "Trevecka 1706–1964." *Brycheiniog* 15 (1971) 41–56.
Evans, E. D. "Ymateb y Methodistiaid i fater addysg y weinidogaeth yn y ddeunawfed ganrif." *Journal* 34 (2010).
Evans, J. "Y Parch David Charles, D.D." *Y Traethodydd* 48 (1893) 264–71.
Jenkins, G. H. " 'An old and much honoured soldier', Griffith Jones, Llanddowror." *Welsh History Review* 11 (1983) 449–68.
Job, J. T. "Y Prifathraw D. Charles Davies, M.A. yn Nhrefecca." *Y Traethodydd* 48 (1893) 181–85.
Jones, W. Morgan. "Y Prifathraw D. Charles Davies, M.A. yn Nhrefecca: II Y Dosbarth Athronyddol." *Y Traethodydd* 48 (1893) 378–83.
Knox, R. Buick. "Methodistiaeth ac Eglwysyddiaeth." In *Corff ac Enaid: Ysgrifau ar Fethodistiaeth*, edited by Elfed ap N. Roberts, 69–78. Caernarfon: Pantycelyn, 1988.
Morgan, J. J. "Principal William Howells, Trevecca." *Journal* 20 (1935) 37-43.
Pope, R. "Corwynt gwyllt ynteu tyner awel?: helynt Tom Nefyn yn y Tymbl." *Y Traethodydd* 152 (1997) 150–62.
Roberts, Gomer M. "Datblygiad Trefn, 1736–1750." In *Hanes Methodistiaeth Galfinaidd Cymru: I Y Deffroad Mawr*, edited by Gomer M. Roberts, 162–203. Caernarfon: Pantycelyn, 1973.
———. "Y tair sasiwn gyntaf 1742." *Journal* 26 (1941) 93–101.
———. "Yr olaf o hen bobl Trefeca." *Journal* 50 (1965) 23–27.
Roberts, H. P. "Nonconformist academies in Wales (1662–1862)." *Transactions of the Honourable Society of Cymmrodorion* (1928-9) 1–98.
Walters, J. "Cymdeithasfa Castellnewydd yn Emlyn." *Y Drysorfa* (1851) 170–71.
White, E. M. "Popular Schooling and the Welsh Language, 1650–1740." In *The Welsh Language before the Industrial Revolution*, edited by G. H. Jenkins, 317–41. Cardiff: University of Wales Press, 1997.
Williams, D. "Cyn-brifathro, y Parch Owen Prys, M.A., D.D." *Journal*, 20 (1935) 44–51.
Williams, D. D. "Rev. David Charles, B.A., B.D., Principal of Trevecca College (1842–1862)." *Journal* 20 (1935) 28–36.
Williams, Glanmor, "Griffith Jones, Llanddowror (1683–1761)." In *Pioneers of Welsh Education*, edited by Charles Gittins, 11–29. Faculty of Education, University of Wales, Swansea, n.d.
Williams, W. "Y Parchedig William Howells." *Y Traethodydd* 44 (1889) 168–80.
Williams, W. R. "Y Prifathro Owen Prys, M.A., D.D., Aberystwyth (1857–1934)." In *Deg o Enwogion*, edited by William Morris, vol. 1, 45–52. Caernarfon: Pantycelyn, 1959.

11

A Chapter in the History of Welsh Theology

D. DENSIL MORGAN

In an early assessment of the influence of the twentieth century's premier Protestant theologian Karl Barth, John McConnachie, a minister in the Church of Scotland, mentions the fact that by the mid-1930s Barth's teaching had made headway not only in his native Scotland and among a vibrant section of the younger English Congregationalists, but also in Wales. In the light of the nation's "strong Calvinistic background and lively religious interest",[1] this was hardly surprising, he wrote. McConnachie mentions no names and it is obvious that his knowledge of Welsh theology was minimal. Some years earlier the Swiss ecumenical statesman Adolf Keller in an even more panoramic study of the earliest impact of Barth mentioned Wales in passing, but apart from a tradition of energetic preaching and religious revivalism he was at a loss to say much more about the theological traditions which would prove conducive to the acceptance of Barth's theology among the Welsh.[2] Their ignorance was hardly wilful. Rather it was the result of

---

1. John McConnachie, 'Der Einfluss Karl Barths in Schottlund und England.' In Ernst Wolf, ed., *Theologische Aufsätze Karl Barth zum 50. Geburtstag* (Munich: Kaiser, 1936), 559-70 [569].

2. Adolf Keller, *Der Weg der dialectischen Theologie durch die kirchliche Welt* (Munich: Kaiser, 1931), 112.

the fact that most of the vigour and breadth of religious life in Wales at the time took place not in English but through the medium of Welsh. As the recipient of this *Festschrift* has made a sterling contribution to biblical studies through his native language and knows something of the Reformed tradition from the inside, it may be useful to say something about modern Welsh theology in general and the impact made by Barth and his followers in particular. In so doing we pay tribute to an esteemed colleague whose long career has upheld the best values of Christian scholarship in Wales.

Religion in Victorian and Edwardian Wales

Although Welsh theology had been influenced since the 1880s by a reverent biblical criticism and a faintly liberalized evangelicalism, it was only after the First World War that a pronounced philosophical idealism and a more blatant liberalism came into the Nonconformist chapels, first by way of a younger generation of able preachers, some of whom had been nurtured at Mansfield College, Oxford, and then by a cohort of gifted seminary teachers who were intent on modernizing Welsh religion according to the norms of the Enlightenment.[3] The University of Wales had been established in 1893, and its theological faculty bore the imprint of Mansfield College's Scottish principal, Andrew M. Fairbairn, who had been employed by the young university to establish the curriculum in divinity. The university movement had begun decades earlier with separate colleges being established in Aberystwyth (1872), Cardiff (1883) and Bangor (1884) all of which prepared candidates for University of London degrees. The theological colleges of the Nonconformist denominations were academically respectable though aimed at producing preachers rather than scholars. St David's College, Lampeter, although technically a university in its own right was in fact a seminary for the Anglican Church. Such had been the contentiousness between Nonconformity and the established church that the incipient University of Wales prevented the new "national colleges" from teaching theology as such, though there was provision for study of the biblical languages and their literature at each. Confessional

---

3. See Robert Pope, *Seeking God's Kingdom: The Nonconformist Social Gospel in Wales, 1906–39* (Cardiff: University of Wales Press), 1999.

A Chapter in the History of Welsh Theology

divinity and ecclesiastical polity would be left to the denominational establishments though the Bible, which was thought to be doctrinally neutral, could be studied by all.

It was not long, however, before most of the seminaries migrated towards the national colleges: the two Bala Congregational colleges amalgamated and moved to Bangor in 1886 with the Llangollen Baptists following in 1892, the Pontypool College relocated to Cardiff in 1893 while the Bala college of the Calvinistic Methodists which was by far the most academically distinguished, ceased providing a general education and became wholly a theological college in 1891 having appointed as its head Wales's foremost biblical theologian, Thomas Charles Edwards (1837–1900). Wales was spared the doctrinal tensions which had wracked Scotland principally because both the Congregationalists and the Baptists, though basically Calvinist in doctrine, were not bound by an official creed, while the doctrinal convictions of the Calvinistic Methodists as enshrined in their 1823 Confession of Faith were sufficiently supple to absorb the broadening movement which had occurred as the century had progressed. In their case creedal controversy would be delayed until the late 1920s.[4] In a speech entitled "Religious Thought in Wales" given to the Presbyterian Council in London in 1888, Thomas Charles Edwards described the changes of the previous half century. Up to the 1840s religion had been deep, he said, rather than broad. For the Nonconformist fathers, "the doctrine of the incarnation had no value or meaning . . . except as the incarnation was a necessary condition of Christ's atoning death, and the idea of any connection between Christ and the race, be it true or be it false, had not occurred to them . . . Theology, in fact, was dying of asphyxia."[5] It was only following the broadening of horizons that occurred after 1845 not least through the influence of the Edinburgh educated Lewis Edwards, the author's father and predecessor as principal at Bala, that the piety of the Calvinistic Methodists had been combined with patristic learning and classical culture to create a more rounded faith: "A stream of fresh air poured in when the younger generation of theological students began to read and ponder over Coleridge's *Aids to Reflection* . . . Augustine's *City of God*,

---

4. D. Densil Morgan, *The Span of the Cross: Christian Religion and Society in Wales, 1914–2000* (Cardiff: University of Wales Press, 1999), 107–30.

5. 'Religious Thought in Wales.' In D. D. Williams, ed., *Thomas Charles Edwards* (Liverpool: National Eisteddfod Society, 1921), 103–12 [105].

Anselm's *Cur Deus Homo*, Hooker's First and Fifth Books, Locke . . . Kant . . . and Milton's *Paradise Lost*, with which students were urged to saturate their minds."[6]

Such a blend of culture, learning, doctrinal breadth and piety needed to be created anew in each generation: "the circulating blood of theology needs constantly to be oxygenized by contact with the broad human conceptions that create and inspire and govern literature and the age . . . We are aware of the dangers of knowledge, but we think the dangers of ignorance to be greater."[7]

The Wales of 1888, alas, was markedly different from that of 1860 to say nothing of 1845. The industrialization which has transformed the economic fate of the south Wales valleys making its iron production and coalfields the most profitable in the world had introduced new problems and different values, and although evangelical Nonconformity had kept up with these changes, the churches could take nothing for granted. The English language, which was advancing rapidly, was a secularizing force, while the establishment of compulsory state provided elementary education in 1870 would weaken the hold of the all-age Sunday schools, previously such a potent means of inculcating biblical truths and puritan values into the populace at large. Organized religion was still widely popular and massively influential. In a population of 1,750,000 in 1891, as many as 315,450 were communicant members of the four principal Nonconformist denominations, the Calvinistic Methodists, the Congregationalists, the Baptists and the Wesleyan Methodists, with 460,000 Sunday school scholars and just as many "listeners", namely unconfirmed adults who were faithful to the services and ripe for conversion.[8] Easter communicants in the parish churches and cathedrals of the four dioceses of a rejuvenated Anglican Church, those of St David's, Llandaff, Bangor and St Asaph, were 105,500 in 1891, while the Church's Sunday Schools catered for 142,000 scholars.[9] The chapels were centres of a teeming cultural and social life including Bands of Hope, temperance societies, literary meetings, debating clubs

---

6. Ibid., 106.

7. Ibid., 107.

8. See John Williams, ed., *Digest of Welsh Historical Statistics*, vol. 2 (Cardiff: Welsh Office, 1985), 267–328.

9. Ibid., 257–66.

and choirs which gave Nonconformity the status of a vibrant alternative society to that of the public house in both rural and industrial Wales.

As elsewhere, changes in theology reflected the transformation of the country's intellectual environment. The pace of change had been slower in Wales due to the prevalence of Welsh, still spoken by well over half of the population, its culture being the repository of traditional faith. Darwinism, evolutionary theory, speculative philosophy especially Hegelian idealism championed by Henry Jones, Wales' foremost philosopher, professor in Bangor and to become in 1894 Edward Caird's successor at Glasgow, was a mainstay of the new university, while biblical criticism, never radical, was already becoming staple fare. Although Thomas Charles Edwards was optimistic that current Nonconformity could meet the challenge of the hour, he realized what was at stake. "The greatest danger that besets religion in Wales today is plain", he stated. "The sense of sin is not keen."[10] Primarily a biblical exegete as evidenced by his two substantial New Testament commentaries,[11] his own theology was that blend of centrist evangelicalism and kenoticism which had become fashionable in the late Victorian era, and was expressed with verve, ability and substantial patristic learning in his treatise *The God-Man* (1895). As the founding principal of University College Aberystwyth, he was intimately acquainted with current trends. "In the present condition of things in Wales, you have a people actually weary of contending systems," he claimed, "keenly alive, at the same time, to the fascination of new ideas, political and scientific, and, for this reason, in danger of drifting away from theological truth altogether."[12] Wales had been well served in the past by its preachers, many of whom were men of power and grace. What it needed now was "a great theologian who will draw from the fountain of truth in the Word of God a theology which shall be more divine than Arminianism, more human than Calvinism, and more Christian than either because it combines them in the broader and deeper truth concerning the Person of Christ which underlies both."[13]

10. Edwards, "Religious Thought in Wales," 109.

11. See Thomas Charles Edwards, *A Commentary on the First Epistle to the Corinthians* (London: Hodder & Stoughton, 1885); Edwards, *The Epistle to the Hebrews* (London: Hodder & Stoughton, 1888).

12. Edwards, "Religious Thought in Wales," 110–11.

13. Ibid., 112.

Such an ambition would not be fulfilled. By the Edwardian period Wales did, however, produce a generation of skilled thinkers who introduced a liberalized doctrine into the churches. Along with Edwards, one of the brightest stars of the Calvinistic Methodist Connexion was J. Puleston Jones (1862-1925) whose essays on the atonement displayed the influence of a cautious Hegelian idealism while his volume on the doctrine of inspiration, *Until the Day Dawns* (1909) was Quaker-like in its championing of a subjective view of the theme. A much more traditionalist stance was taken by the popular J. Cynddylan Jones (1840-1930) whose four-volume systematic theology *Cysondeb y Ffydd* ("The Consistency of Faith") (1907-15), although much indebted to the work of the American Presbyterian W. G. T. Shedd, displayed a highly attenuated form of Calvinism. Scholastic orthodoxy was represented in Wales by the erudite R. S. Thomas (1848-1923) who had learned his theology at the feet of Charles and Archibald Hodge at Princeton during the 1870s. Though he upheld the Princeton doctrine of scriptural inerrancy, his Calvinism was frankly revisionist: he rejected the eternal decrees outright and was wary of Chalcedon's two-nature Christology for downplaying Christ's full humanity. Even Thomas felt that the orthodox formulations needed to be re-worked in the light of current thought.[14] A reverent, evangelical biblical criticism much in the style of Scotland's Andrew Bruce Davidson[15] and William Robertson Smith had become the Calvinistic Methodist norm, a fact affirmed by the appointment of Llewelyn Ioan Evans, fresh from the inerrancy controversies among the American Presbyterians, to the New Testament chair in the Bala College in 1892.

For Evans, it was not so much the text of scripture that was infallible but its message, that Christ had died to save sinners. One looked in vain for detailed historical accuracy or support for scientific hypotheses in the Bible. In order to be understood, scripture needed to be interpreted according to the canons of modern historical criticism and if this meant that the creation accounts in Genesis were mythological, that the book of Isaiah was a composite document, that Jonah swallowed by the fish or Daniel and the lion's den were allegorical rather than factual, then so

---

14. D. Densil Morgan, *Bywyd a Gwaith R. S. Thomas, Abercynon (1848-1923)* (Bangor: Canolfan Uwch Efrydiau Crefydd yng Nghymru, 2005).

15. Alan P. F. Sell, *Defending and Declaring the Faith: Some Scottish Examples, 1860-1920* (Exeter: Paternoster, 1987), 89-117.

be it. In the New Testament, however, the miraculous element belonged to the essence of Jesus' teaching, while the resurrection occurred within rather than beyond history and as such criticism needed to take this into account.[16] By the 1890s ideas such as these had come into the main stream. Even such a staunch traditionalist as Josiah Thomas could say, from the chair of the North Wales Calvinistic Methodist Association in 1897, that God was not inextricably linked "to the idea that Moses wrote every word of the Pentateuch as it has come down to us."[17] It was the Baptists, however, who were most enthusiastic in accepting the new standards in biblical studies. Less wedded to dogmatic theology as such, they were more heavily Biblicist than their fellow Nonconformists. A reverent, "believing" criticism was assimilated painlessly, with T. Witton Davies (1851–1923), the first holder of the Hebrew chair at the new university college of Bangor and Silas Morris (1862–1923), another accomplished Old Testament scholar and principal of the city's Baptist college, doing much to ensure its wholesale acceptance in the churches at large. According to R. Tudur Jones, "The radical higher critics made little headway in Wales up until 1914. The weight of opinion . . . was with the moderates."[18]

The Triumph of Theological Liberalism

It was with the Congregationalists, however, that liberal theology impacted most heavily upon Wales. Impatience with inherited doctrinal formulae had characterized such key nineteenth century Independent leaders as John Roberts, Llanbryn-mair, and Michael D. Jones, the pugnacious principal of what would become the Bala-Bangor College, but it was with David Adams (1845–1923), minister of Grove Street Welsh church in Liverpool, that Hegelianism would replace moderate Calvinism as the systematic basis of denominational thought. An early alumnus of Aberystwyth, he did more then anyone to popularize Hegelian terminology and introduce the concept of evolution, a

16. See D. Densil Morgan, *Wales and the Word: Historic Perspectives on Welsh Identity and Religion* (Cardiff: University of Wales Press, 2008), 55–87.

17. "Adroddiad Cymdeithasfa Corwen" "A Report from the Corwen Association," *Y Goleuad*, 12 May 1897, 10.

18. R. Tudur Jones, *Faith and the Crisis of a Nation: Wales, 1890–1914*, trans. Sylvia Prys Jones, ed. Robert Pope (Cardiff: University of Wales Press, 2004), 270.

theology of immanence and the idea of the Absolute into Welsh religion. His notorious treatise *Datblygiad yn ei berthynas â'r Cwymp, yr Ymgnawdoliad a'r Atgyfodiad* (1893) ("Evolution in its relation to the Fall, the Incarnation and the Resurrection") was a wholesale reconstruction of orthodox theology according to an alien philosophical scheme. For Adams God was not a transcendent divine being but an abstract life spirit which infused all things. Sin was not so much rebellion against God as humanity's struggle against the effects of its primitive past. Far from being the incarnation of the eternal Word, Christ was the perfect example of human kind animated by the divine whose death had no unique atoning qualities but exemplified the clash between residual evolutionary imperfection and the Absolute's striving for synthesis and perfection. The miraculous categories of the New Testament were metaphorical rather than literal, while the supernatural modes of traditional faith needed to be reinterpreted according to the scientific laws of cause and effect. Adams' subsequent publications such as *Paul yng Ngoleuni Iesu* (1897) ("Paul in the Light of Jesus"), *Yr Hen a'r Newydd mewn Diwinyddiaeth* (1907) ("The Old and New in Theology") and *Yr Eglwys a Gwareiddiad Diweddar* (1914) ("The Church and Recent Civilization") merely reiterated his basic assumptions while his commentary on the Epistle to the Galatians (1908) was so infused by his preconceptions that anything genuinely Pauline virtually disappeared: "David Adams' philosophical bias was so overwhelming . . . [that] he turned the teaching of justification by faith completely on its head."[19]

Adams was neither an able exegete nor an original thinker. Even such a radical modernist as Thomas Rees admitted that "[h]is tendency was to face the problems of theology as a philosopher rather than a theologian, and reason from a few general suppositions rather than traverse slowly and carefully through the detailed history of the experience and doctrines of religion."[20] In short, "he was no theologian at all."[21] His significance, though, was immense. If his ideas had been considered alien in 1893, by 1913, when he ascended to the chair of the Union of Welsh Independents, his views were becoming the norm. "Adams", accord-

---

19. Tudur Jones, *Faith and the Crisis of a Nation*, 259.

20. Thomas Rees, "Dylanwad David Adams ar Ddiwinyddiaeth Cymru" ("The Influence of David Adams on Welsh Theology"), in E. Keri Evans and W. Pari Huws, *Cofiant y Parchg David Adams* (Liverpool: Hughes and Sons, 1924), 179-98 [183].

21. Rees, "Dylanwad David Adams ar Ddiwinyddiaeth Cymru," 183.

ing to R. Tudur Jones, the historian of Welsh Congregationalism, "had graduated from being a heretic into one of the denomination's oracles."[22] It was left to liberal theologians of the stature of Miall Edwards, Thomas Rees and John Morgan Jones to supply the sophistication which Adams lacked, by which time many ordinary ministers had deemed it no longer necessary to preach on sin, redemption and faith through the cross, but on Christ as the ultimate ideal and on human beings' potential for perfectability. Widespread theological change would register fully after the Great War.

If Adams provided the Congregationalists with a conceptual basis for their liberalism, it was left to three exceptionally gifted Mansfield trained theologians to endow that liberalism with substance. Thomas Rees (1869–1926), D. Miall Edwards (1873–1941) and John Morgan Jones (1873–1946) had studied in the University of Wales, Rees and Jones in Cardiff and Edwards at Bangor, before joining a glittering generation of students destined for positions of authority within British Nonconformity.[23] Already open to the newest intellectual trends, the influence of Andrew M. Fairbairn, Mansfield's principal, would be seminal for Thomas Rees, though the Ritschlian theology of values espoused by Fairbairn's pupil, Alfred Garvie, would be important for John Morgan Jones while his personal indebtedness to Adolf von Harnack, with whom he studied in Berlin in 1900, would be even more pronounced. Rees, who had been born in a poverty stricken home in Pembrokeshire and had been both a farm labourer and a coal miner before embarking on a ministerial career, had been appointed to the chair in Christian Doctrine at the Brecon Memorial College straight ftrom Mansfield where he had graduated with a first in Oxford's honours school of theology in 1899. After ten years service in Brecon, he accepted the principalship of the Bala-Bangor College. His major published works, *Duw, ei Fodolaeth a'i Natur* ("God, his Existence and Nature") (1910) and his English language volume *The Holy Spirit in Thought and Experience* (1914) bear the clear imprint of Fairbairn's Hegelianism, while his editorship of the weighty *Geiriadur Beiblaidd* ("Biblical Dictionary"), published under the auspices of the University of Wales'

---

22. R. Tudur Jones, *Yr Undeb: Hanes Undeb yr Annibynwyr Cymraeg, 1872–1972* (Swansea: Gwasg John Penry, 1975), 199.

23. See Elaine Kaye, *Mansfield College, Oxford: Its Origin, History and Significance* (Oxford: Oxford University Press, 1996), 111–33.

theological guild in 1926 and the benchmark for scholarly liberalism, crowned his career. Rees's theology was immanentist and idealist, with the Trinity being a modalist expression of God's inner nature while the Holy Spirit brought the historical Jesus's moral influence alive. "I used to chaff him with being a Sabellian", quipped Miall Edwards, "and he would retort by calling me a Samosatene or even an Arian! I think we were orthodox in spirit and intention, though somewhat heterodox in form."[24] A much more powerful thinker than David Adams and the bearer of direct influence over generations of ministerial students, he reinforced the prevailing norm that the only way forward for religion in Wales was through a progressive and escalating liberalism. "Rees's danger', according to Robert Pope, 'was to allow the philosophy of the period with its emphasis on unity and reason to destroy the doctrine [of the Holy Spirit]'s traditional purpose and meaning."[25]

John Morgan Jones was Rees's closest Mansfield friend, his colleague as professor of Church History at Bala-Bangor and his successor as principal. He combined an even more radical theological stance with a clear and attractive prose style. "Although he taught history and was a pupil of Adolf von Harnack, the greatest church historian of his generation," wrote R. Tudur Jones, "his heart was in the study of the New Testament, and in discussing it he revealed himself to be the most daring of the Welsh Modernists."[26] Books such as *Paul of Tarsus: the Apostle and his Message* (1915), *Y Testament Newydd, ei Hanes a'i Amcan* ("The New Testament, Its History and Aim") (1930), his commentary *Y Bedwaredd Efengyl* ("The Fourth Gospel") (1931) and his handbook *Dysgeidiaeth Iesu Grist* ("The Teaching of Jesus Christ") (1937) showed how far the liberal consensus had evolved. If Thomas Rees had departed the scene before the Barthian renewal occurred,[27] it was left to John

---

24. D. Miall Edwards, "Dr Thomas Rees of Bangor," *The Welsh Outlook* (1926) 182–85[184].

25. Robert Pope, *Codi Muriau Dinas Duw; Anghydffurfiaeth ac Anghydffurfwyr Cymru'r Ugeinfed Ganrif* (Bangor: Canolfan Uwchefrydiau Crefydd yng Nghymru, 2005), 238; for an appraisal of Rees's social theology see Pope, *Seeking God's Kingdom*, 56–67.

26. R. Tudur Jones, *Congregationalism in Wales*, ed. Robert Pope (Cardiff: University of Wales Press, 2004), 235.

27. See T. Eirug Davies, ed., *Y Prifathro Thomas Rees: ei Fywyd a'i Waith* (Llandysul: Gwasg Gomer, 1939).

Morgan Jones to plead the cause of radical liberalism when J. E. Daniel emerged to challenge its ascendency in the late 1920s and 30s.

Of these three Congregational scholars it was Miall Edwards who proved most plausible in combining the new emphases with Nonconformity's historical faith. Reared in the radical Dissent of Merionethshire and named after Edward Miall, leader of the anti-establishment Liberation Society, he too took first class honours in theology at Mansfield and, after nine years in the pastorate, was appointed Rees's successor as professor of Christian Doctrine at Brecon. According to R. Tudur Jones, "[h]e was anxious to express the faith once given to the saints in a manner that would be meaningful to his contemporaries . . . [while] his personal godliness as well as his deep reverence for the classic theologians of the church is evident on every page that he wrote."[28] Nevertheless, "[i]t was with the thought of David Miall Edwards that popular Welsh theology lurched to the left."[29] He was convinced that the gospel faith could only contend with the intellectual realities of the day by conceding that God was immanent within creation, that the supernatural categories of the New Testament needed to be restated in naturalist terms, and that Christ's unique deity should be understood not ontologically but in terms of the quality of his experience of God's benign fatherhood. As such, "[h]is work marks a dramatic turning point in the history of Welsh theology."[30] His able treatises *The Philosophy of Religion* (1929) and *Christianity and Philosophy* (1932) forged for him a reputation as a competent philosophical theologian beyond Wales,[31] but it was as both a creative thinker and a popularizer that he affected common thought most readily. His volume *Crefydd a Bywyd* ("Religion and Life") (1915) was a winsome assessment of contemporary religious needs characterized by "an understanding of the gospel in the terms of philosophical idealism, the doctrine of God's immanence, and the social implications of the Ritschlian interpretation of the Kingdom of God."[32] It was his accomplished systematic theology

28. Tudur Jones, *Faith and the Crisis of a Nation*, 240.

29. Ibid., 237.

30. Ibid., 240.

31. See Sell, *The Philosophy of Religion, 1875-1980* (Bristol: Thoemmes, 1996), 30–31, 96–97.

32. Pope, *Seeking God's Kingdom*, 40; for assessments of his theology see ibid., 38–55, and Tudur Jones, *Faith and the Crisis of a Nation*, 237–40.

Bannau'r Ffydd ("The Pinnacles of Faith") (1929), however, which drew the fire of J. E. Daniel, the most striking of the young Welsh Barthians, and so created a new epoch in the nation's theological development.

By the mid-1920s pronounced liberalism had found a home for itself in all four of the major Nonconformist denominations. The Wesleyan scholars Tecwyn Evans and E. Tegla Davies, the Baptists Herbert Morgan and J. Gwili Jenkins as well as Calvinistic Methodists of the stamp of D. Francis Roberts and Griffith Arthur Edwards, now shared with the more radical Congregationalists in the new consensus: that the key to a valid theology was not an authoritative objective revelation but the fact of religious experience, that any concept of revelation needed to be in accord with enlightened rationality, that the theory of evolution had been proven to be a religious as well as a biological fact, and that there was an ontological continuity between humankind and God.[33] "Theology", according to Philip Josiah Jones, a minister in Presbyterian Church of Wales, writing in 1927 was "an attempt on the part of men to give articulation to religious experience", while "[m]odern theology can be most satisfactoraly gauged by taking as the point of our departure the movement commonly known as Philosophical Idealism of the absolute type."[34] In surveying the history of Welsh theology since the mid-nineteenth century, he delighted in the fact that traditional formulations of the faith were fast disappearing and that a radical Nonconformity was taking its place. "Fall from innocence into sin [within the new scheme] is a fall upwards and onwards", he claimed, "and every stage of sin contributes to the ultimate realization of perfect goodness."[35] Christ was not so much the divine saviour but the archetype of human perfectibility. "Atonement is, according to this teaching, a cosmic process", whereas the resurrection of the body could only be rationally interpreted in terms of the immortality of the soul, "the loss of self by death implies the finding of self in the larger life of union in God."[36] "Whatever may be the actual implications of this challenging and attractive teaching", he continued blithely, "there can be but no

---

33. See, for instance, G. A. Edwards and J. Morgan Jones, *Traethodau'r Deyrnas: Diwinyddiaeth yng Nghymru* (Wrexham: Hughes and Son, 1924).

34. Philip J. Jones, "Theology in Wales during the last eighty years," *The Treasury* 15 (1927) 8–10, 43–5[8].

35. Ibid., 9.

36. Ibid.,10.

A Chapter in the History of Welsh Theology

doubt that it gives rise to questions of great importance for theology",[37] which no doubt was the case. It seemed that, for some young preachers, philosophical idealism had all but swallowed Christian faith whole. "Hegelianism," he stated, with neither irony nor incongruity, "is the most potent vindication of Christianity and Christian doctrines which has as yet been offered to human intelligence."[38] Time was ripe for a counter movement, and in Wales it was provided not by the conservative evangelicals, but by the more substantial and innovative thought of Karl Barth.[39]

J. D. Vernon Lewis, E. Keri Evans, and J. E. Daniel

Even during its heyday not all Welsh Independents were enamoured of radical liberalism, and it was through the offices of the Congregational biblical scholar J. D. Vernon Lewis (1879–1970) that Barth's reputation was first consolidated in Wales. Like his colleagues Rees, J. M. Jones and Miall Edwards, he had proceeded from the University of Wales to Mansfield College, Oxford, also graduating with first class honours in the theology schools, and thence, in 1908-9, to the University of Leipzig. His first intimation of Barth had occurred in the early 1920s following discussion with a contemporary of his, a professor at Halle, who had conveyed to him the "thrill of surprise" which the *Römerbrief* had created among continental biblical scholars. Lewis published his assessment in July 1927 in *Yr Efrydydd* ("The Student"), a monthly review published by the Student Christian Movement, based on his own reading of the third German edition of the Romans commentary, the composite volume of essays *Das Wort Gottes und die Theologie* (1924) and assorted papers which had appeared on the pages of *Zwischen den Zeiten*, the journal of the "Crisis Theologians", during the previous few years. His approval of Barth's exegesis was hearty and his relief at the advent of a new method of reading the Bible was palpable. "For those of us who have been raised on and satiated in the mode of

---

37. Ibid., 9.
38. Ibid., 43.
39. For the impact on Barth on English (and Welsh) Nonconformist thought, see Alan P. F. Sell, *Nonconformist Theology in the Twentieth Century* (Milton Keynes: Paternoster, 2006), 25–32.

exposition represented by the *International Critical Commentary*", he wrote, "which reached its deadening, dry-boned pinnacle of dullness in the publication of W. C. Allen's barren commentary on Matthew, turning to Barth's volume is like leaving the parched stagnation of the desert for a land of abundance, vitality and delectability."[40] Lewis's two articles described the background and content of Barth's thought to date and mentioned the response and secondary literature which it had generated in German and Dutch. What was significant for the Welshman was not only that it had signalled a new epoch in Protestant theology but that it had arisen from a pastoral context within the Swiss Reformed churches: 'Its home is Switzerland, though it has spread now to Germany, Holland and Italy'.[41] The parallels between Swiss Calvinism and Welsh Nonconformity were striking: both countries tended to be marginalized by the mainstream while their ecclesiastical traditions put a premium on the exposition of the Word. Given the overwhelmingly Calvinist nature of Welsh religion, Barth's message was one which was likely to appeal.

This being so, it is not surprising that it was not an essay but a sermon which Lewis chose to translate. The text of "Wele—yn awr!" ('Behold - now!') was 2 Cor 6:1–2, namely the final address in *Komm, Schöpfer Geist!*, the volume of sermons authored jointly by Barth and Eduard Thurneysen, his ministerial colleague from his years as a village pastor in Safenwil, canton Aargau,[42] which been published in 1924. The Welsh version appeared in the Congregationalists' weekly newspaper *Y Tyst* ("The Witness") on 3 May 1928.[43] This, it seems, was the first of Barth's work to appear in Britain, preceding the American Douglas Horton's translation of *Das Wort Gottes und die Theologie*, which became *The Word of God and the Word of Man*, by a few months. The response it generated was remarkable. Throughout that spring and summer a stream of letters, comments and supplementary articles

---

40. J. D. Vernon Lewis, "Diwinyddiaeth Karl Barth" ("The Theology of Karl Barth"), *Yr Efrydydd* 3 (1926–1927), 254–58, 281–87[254].

41. Ibid., 281.

42. See Eberhard Busch, *Karl Barth: His Life from Letters and Autobiographical Texts*, trans. John Bowden (London: SCM, 1976), 60–125.

43. "Pregethu'r Cyfandir: trosiad J. D. Vernon Lewis o bregeth Karl Barth" ("Continental Theology: A Translation by J. D. Vernon Lewis of a Sermon by Karl Barth"), *Y Tyst*, 3 May 1928, 6–7.

A Chapter in the History of Welsh Theology

from Presbyterians, Methodists as well as Congregationalists, appeared in *Y Tyst* which were, in the main, appreciative of the sermon's thrust and desirous of knowing more of its author and the new movement in continental theology. There followed two short articles by E. Keri Evans, who had been two decades earlier professor of philosophy at Bangor but since the religious revival of 1904–1905, which had affected him profoundly, minister of Priory Street Congregational Church in Carmarthen.[44] His "Karl Barth—the prophet", of 16 August 1928, and "Karl Barth—the philosopher and theologian", published a week later, added nothing new to Lewis's account or to the essays already published in the theological journals by Adolf Keller, H. R. Mackintosh and John McConnachie,[45] but they did show the interest that Barth was generating within Wales. The fact that Evans published a further positive assessment in the conservative evangelical journal *Yr Efengylydd* ("The Evangelist") in 1930,[46] illustrated the nature of the response. Liberalism was at last being challenged not by obscurantists or blinkered pietists but by those who had partaken most deeply of scholarly modernism itself.

It was not the biblical scholar and preacher Vernon Lewis, or the former professional philosopher E. Keri Evans, who did most to facilitate the reception of Barth's thought during this initial phase in Wales, but the theologian and seminary professor John Edward Daniel (1902–1962). Daniel, the son of a Yale-educated Welsh Congregational minister, had come down from Jesus College, Oxford, in 1925 with firsts in Classical Moderations, Greats and Theology, and was appointed fellow and tutor at Bala-Bangor, the Congregationalists' theological college in Bangor, at the age of 23. Following Thomas Rees's death a year later, he was promoted to a full professorship. A generational change was about to occur, while Daniel's acumen as a theologian of extraordinary depth was soon to be revealed. He would become, by common consent, the ablest dogmatician of his generation and a devastating critic

---

44. An autobiography, first published in Welsh in 1938, which charts his religious development appeared as *My Spiritual Pilgrimage: From Philosophy to Faith* (London: James Clarke, 1961).

45. See D. Densil Morgan, *Barth in Britain: The Reception of the Theology of Karl Barth in Great Britain, 1924–1968* (London: Continuum, 2010), chapters 1 and 2.

46. E. Keri Evans, "Cenadwri Karl Barth" ("The Message of Karl Barth"), *Yr Efengylydd* (1931), 6–7.

of the prevailing Ritschlianism of the Congregational establishment.[47] His review of *The Word of God and the Word of Man* (1928) indicates puzzlement rather than commitment. Despite its strong christocentricism, its refreshing emphasis on the strangeness of revelation and the telling nature of its critique of liberalism, for Daniel the volume was too rhetorical and strident, too one-sided in its emphasis on God's transcendence, for its underlying theology to be ultimately satisfying: "As a protest against all types of superficial evolutionary doctrine, every sort of Pelagianism and Titanism, and especially as an expression, despite itself, of a passionate experience of God, this work will endure."[48] But Daniel's curiosity had been aroused, his interest had been engaged and he would soon find himself jettisoning his scruples and championing Barth's theology unreservedly.

This became obvious in his assessment of what was the most elegant (though belated) apologia for theological liberalism to appear in Welsh, D. Miall Edwards's *Bannau'r Ffydd* ("The Pinnacles of Faith"). Edwards, like Daniel, was, as we have seen, a Congregational seminary professor, at the Memorial College in Brecon, and his volume took the form of a systematic theology whose integrating theme was humankind's innate capacity for God. For Edwards the touchstone of all valid theology was its ability to reflect upon the experience of transcendence. Christianity, he claimed, begins with salvation interpreted as the believer's experience of the divine; it advances through Christology interpreted as Jesus of Nazareth's sense of sonship in relation to the Father; and concludes with a doctrine of God as the ground of all existence. "It is apparent", he wrote, "that we are working on the assumption that experience is the key to doctrine."[49] His systematic theology reflected this progression; rather than beginning with the doctrine of God and the Trinity in the fashion of the older dogmatics, he began with the doctrine of salvation and thence moved on. So subjective was this principle that few truths remained inviolate: "If in the future 'evolution' produces one whose authority in the realm of the spiritual is higher than Jesus Christ,

---

47. See D.Densil Morgan, *Torri'r Seiliau Sicr: Detholiad o Ysgrifau J.E.Daniel* (Llandysul: Gwasg Gomer, 1993), passim.

48. J. E. Daniel, "Gair Duw a Gair Dyn" ("The Word of God and the Word of Man"), *Yr Efrydydd* 5 (1929), 251–5[255].

49. D. Miall Edwards, *Bannau'r Ffydd* (Wrexham: Hughes and Son, 1929), xiii.

I would be obliged to pledge my most absolute loyalty to him."[50] It was not the Christ of apostolic testimony which was absolute any longer but an individual's "authority in the realm of the spiritual" (even other than that of Jesus of Nazareth).

Daniel's response to his colleague's work was devastating. In an extended review in the students' journal *Yr Efrydydd*, he took Edwards to task on every single point: the axiomatic status of "the modern mind" in religious questions, the use of experience as the sole criterion for truth, and the attempt to do theology on the basis of human perception rather than on God's objective revelation of himself as attested in scripture. In an understandable though wholly misguided attempt to be relevant, what the Brecon professor had done was to shear God of his radical otherness and make him nothing but a projection of the religious spirit of mankind. Such errors, he claimed, had already "led to the theological and spiritual bankruptcy of Protestantism."[51] Daniel continued by challenging Edwards's adoptionist Christology and his truncated theory of atonement. If Jesus of Nazareth was a man whose particular attribute lay in his exquisite experience of the divine, anything resembling an objective salvation would be rendered impossible: "The modernists' Christ could not perform an objective redemption even if they believed such a thing existed", he exclaimed.[52] Yet man, as sinner, needed to be redeemed. What he required was not an example—Edwards's "expert . . . in the realm of the spiritual"—but a saviour who was actually divine: "For me atonement is something which is wrought for us, independently, a fountain opened *before* we drink from its waters."[53] Despite its pious talk of Jesus's fellowship with the Father and his experience of the divine, what liberal theology did, claimed Daniel, was to posit an unbridgeable ontological divide between the Father and the Son which rendered true salvation impossible. On the basis of Edwards's theology the church could no longer claim that *God* in Christ had reconciled the world to himself. Despite its elegance, attractiveness and undoubted appeal, this was in fact a theology of despair. For the sake of its present doctrinal integrity and its future spiritual health, Welsh Nonconformity

50. Edwards, *Bannau'r Ffydd*, 374.

51. J. E. Daniel, "Diwinyddiaeth Cymru" ("Wales's Theology"), *Yr Efrydydd* 5 (1929) 118–22, 173–75, 197–203 [174].

52. Ibid., 197.

53. Ibid., 198.

should, "with the undivided tradition of the Church, reject the concept of experience and return once more to the concept of revelation."[54] What was needed, exhorted the Bangor professor, was a restatement of classic orthodoxy according to a rejuvenated theology of the Word of God.

It was clear by now that Daniel had not only made Barth's spirited polemic against Protestant liberalism his own, but that he was interacting creatively with the Swiss theologian's more systematic thought. The *Christliche Dogmatik 1: Die Lehr vom Worte Gottes*, precursor of the *Church Dogmatics* and Barth's so called "false start," had been published in 1927. Daniel's heavily annotated copy, dated 1929, shows that the Barthian dogmatics had arrived in north Wales by that time and was serving as a basis for the Welshman's evolving doctrinal convictions. A widely reported paper on ecclesiology and its link with the gospel which he delivered to the annual conference of the Union of Welsh Independents in 1930[55] enhanced his growing reputation as a theological *enfant terrible* while his handbook on the Pauline theology *Dysgeidiaeth yr Apostol Paul* ("The Teaching of the Apostle Paul") (1933), written in a popular style though explicitly from the standpoint of "the new traditionalism,"[56] not only lent heavily on the *Christliche Dogmatik* and an equally heavily annotated copy of Barth's sixth edition of the *Römerbrief* (1929) but distilled all the principal themes of the orthodox Protestant reawakening of the period. In lucid prose laced with powerful if homely illustrations, Daniel (as both a seminary teacher and a highly effective pulpit orator) succeeded in making the new emphases known among the Congregationalists of the early 1930s. By this time the whole of Welsh Nonconformity, still the largest Christian body in the land, was being affected by the Barthian trend.[57]

---

54. Ibid., 121.

55. J. E. Daniel, "Eglwys Crist yn hanfodol i Efengyl Crist" ("The Church of Christ Essential to the Gospel of Christ"), *Adroddiad Undeb Caernarfon* (Swansea: Llyfrfa'r Annibynwyr, 1930), 107–11.

56. J. E. Daniel, *Dysgeidiaeth yr Apostol Paul* (Swansea: Llyfrfa'r Annibynwyr, 1933), iii.

57. Cf. Morgan, *Wales and the Word*, 121–41; cf. Keith Robbins, *England, Ireland, Scotland, Wales: The Christian Church, 1900–2000* (Oxford: Oxford University Press, 2008), 249–50.

Barth and Welsh Presbyterianism

If the initial response had occurred among the Welsh Congregationalists, it did not go unheeded among the Presbyterians. Indeed there was one who was so struck by the work of Barth that he decided to go to the continent to find out for himself.

Ivor Oswy Davies (1906–64) had graduated in philosophy at Bangor before proceeding to Jesus College, Oxford in 1927, and had been drawn to what he called the "modern theological movement in Germany" while training for the ministry at the Presbyterian Church's theological college at Aberystwyth in 1930–2. A graduate thesis written during his pastoral year at the Bala seminary a year later indicated his mastery of the current trends within continental theology at the time. "Today we find a new post-war theological movement in Germany", he noted, "which was intent on retreating from the direction which Protestantism had been taken by Kant and Schleiermacher and returning to the classic doctrines of Luther and Calvin."[58] Whereas Kant's philosophy had posited an unbridgeable gap between reality and knowledge, and Schleiermacher's romanticism had made experience the criterion of all valid piety, by affirming the concept of a divinely authenticated revelation the new theologians had vaulted the Kantian divide and restored an element of objectivity to Protestant theology once more. "The value of revelation is not that the human spirit stumbles across some new vision", he wrote, "but that God actively impinges upon human consciousness, and coercively reveals himself to his creatures,—it is God discovering man, rather than man discovering God."[59]

Whereas by 1933 Anglophone theology was becoming slowly more conscious of the work of the younger German language theologians, Davies's sources were in the original, Barth's *Christliche Dogmatik* (1927), Rudolf Bultmann's *Jesus* (1929) and, more especially, Emil Brunner's second edition of *Der Mittler* (The Mediator) (1932). His treatment of Schleiermacher was already influenced by the thought of "the dialectical school", whose work "might be characterized as a throwing down of the gauntlet of a Neo-Calvinistic theology, as constituting

---

58. Ivor Oswy Davies, "Schleiermacher in Relation to the Modern Theological Movement in Germany," 3, Davies MSS, Bangor University Archive.

59. Ibid., 41.

the essential nature and truth of Christian Faith."[60] Following his critique of the still prevalent Protestant liberalism, he described the new theology as being biblical, dialectical, revolutionary and existentialist. Although he was not yet wholly convinced of its validity—its still all too blatant Kantianism, its supra-rational character and "the incognito of the historical Jesus"[61] caused Davies consternation—its attraction was in its radical nature and uncompromising stance. Its practitioners were not ashamed of the gospel: "In this lies the immense value and importance of their work for our own time," he claimed: "They have certainly indicated, at least roughly for us, the way we must traverse if the distinctiveness and solitary supremacy of the faith as absolute and final, is to be effectively maintained."[62]

The winter semester of 1933–4 had found Davies in Zürich attending the classes of Emil Brunner. It was initially Brunner whose writings had impressed him most, and in his first article on continental church life in *Y Goleuad* ("The Light"), the Presbyterian Church of Wales's weekly, he shared his impressions of meeting with and learning directly from his Swiss teacher: "He faces each problem from the standpoint of Christianity, that is from the standpoint of his doctrinal convictions, those of 'the Dialectical Theology.'"[63] Yet it was not Brunner but Barth who was destined to have the most lasting effect, and in April 1934 Davies crossed the border into Germany and made for Bonn. "Professor Barth plays a dual role in the life of German Protestantism today", he stated, first as the leader of the theological movement which challenged the preconceptions of the older liberalism, and secondly as a leader of the Confessing Church. Hitler, of course, had come to power in January 1933 and throughout the first year of his regime the Aryan "German Christian" movement was gaining influence within the state churches while anti-Jewish legislation was being enforced. The Confessing Church, led by the Lutheran pastor Martin Niemöller, was proving to be an unexpectedly effective means of challenging Nazi ideology within the new Reich.[64] "This church has claimed during the

60. Ibid., 56.
61. Ibid., 73.
62. Ibid., 77.
63. Ivor Oswy Davies, "Adlais o'r Swistir," *Y Goleuad*, 17 January 1934, 8–9[8].
64. See E. H. Robertson, *Christians against Hitler* (London: SCM, 1962); A. C. Cochrane, *The Church's Confession under Hitler*. Philadelphia: Westminster Press,

last few weeks that it is the one *true* Protestant church in wholesale opposition to [Reichbishop Ludwig] Müller's church. The latter is, to a great extent, *a paper church*, only supported by a few ministers and laymen from among the 'German Christians' . . . The great majority of the people stand with the opposition as members of the Confessing Church."[65]

Davies's reports became vitally important in informing the Welsh religious public of the gravity of political and religious developments in Germany at the time.[66] When the situation became critical it was he, more than anyone else, who kept his church informed of the fate of the German Confessing Church and its members.

> The 'German Christians' hold to the view that the 'historic moment' of the national revolution (which began nearly two years ago) is *an independent source of revelation to them as a German people*, side by side with God's Word in the Bible. Contrary to this Barth and the Confessing Church state absolutely and unconditionally that *God has given his revelation to his church once and for all in the incarnation of our Lord Jesus Christ*. It is very difficult for us to realize how hard it is for a German who is also a committed Christian to think clearly about the meaning of Christianity when so much propaganda in the press, on the wireless, from the platform, in the schools and universities as well as through movements especially formed for that purpose, deify nationalism and loyalty to the state.[67]

In the rest of the article he described Barth's background and theological development, his personal characteristics and relationship to his students, his method of teaching in the 7 a.m. lecture four times a week which always began with a scripture reading and the singing of a hymn, and in the more informal "open evening" at home each Wednesday, and his unembellished though powerful preaching in the university's Castle Church: "What is its secret? Perhaps the absence of any apologetic note. The gospel which he has to proclaim is a miracle; this is his underlying

---

1962; Klaus Scholder, *The Churches and the Third Reich, Vol. 2, Rome and Barmen* (London: SCM,1985).

65. Ivor Oswy Davies, "Karl Barth: y dyn," *Y Goleuad*, 24 November 1934, 2–3.

66. I have discussed Davies's role in Barth reception in Wales in *Cedyrn Canrif: Crefydd a Chymdeithas yng Nghymru'r Ugeinfed Ganrif* (Cardiff: University of Wales Press, 2001), 132–57.

67. Davies, "Karl Barth: y dyn," 2.

conviction; he proclaims it thus quite unassumingly allowing it to speak for itself."[68] Yet it was his teacher's closing words at the last "open house" of the summer semester which had impressed themselves on the young Welshman before returning home: "I would urge you to do one thing", he had said, "that is—take your theology seriously." In the uncertain future which lay ahead, faith in God's free and gracious sovereignty was the only anchor. God alone would usher in his Kingdom, it was their responsibility to stay faithful to him.[69]

Davies's sojourn on the continent took him to the heart of the German Church Struggle. Not only had he witnessed the tense drama of Barth's dismissal from the university in December 1934,[70] but he had experienced the camaraderie of his professor's Wednesday evening Bible class on the Gospel of Luke at his home during the spring of 1935. He was also present at the conference of the Confessing Church, held in Bremen in November 1934. Barth preached what was, for the Welshman, a tremendously moving sermon on Jesus asleep in the boat while the disciples were in fear as the storm raged. The boat, of course, was God's church in the land of Martin Luther, the storm was Nazi oppression and they, the faithful, were the disciples. Barth then led his congregation in prayer: "God is our refuge and strength, a very present help in trouble. Therefore we will not fear, though the earth be removed and though the mountains be carried into the midst of the sea . . ." Davies felt that he was witnessing one of the latter day acts of the apostles and martyrs. "So long as I live", he noted, "I will remember that hour."[71] It is hardly surprising that Ivor Oswy Davies's championing of the Barthian theology in Wales would thereafter be infinitely more than an academic preference.

---

68. Ibid., 2.

69. Ibid., 3.

70. This is related in his article "Karl Barth," *Y Dysorfa* 112 (1942), 44–49; see D. Densil Morgan, *The SPCK Introduction to Karl Barth* (London: SPCK, 2010), 48–49.

71. Davies, "Karl Barth," 49; for the text of the sermon see Kurt I. Johansen ed., *The Word in This World: Two Sermons by Karl Barth* (Vancouver, BC: Regent College, 2007).

Barth Reception in the Shadow of the War

If Ivor Oswy Davies functioned as an observer and interpreter of current events, it was J. E. Daniel who did most to infuse Barthianism into the bloodstream of Welsh Nonconformist theology. His 1933 handbook on the Pauline theology *Dysgeidiaeth yr Apostol Paul* ("The Teaching of the Apostle Paul") was radically different from what Welsh readers had been used to when considering the life and mission of the great apostle from Tarsus: "Always remember that it was not through studying the moral and religious experience of Jesus of Nazareth in the manner of T. R. Glover's *Jesus of History* that made Paul a Christian but an overwhelming conviction that he was the messiah."[72] Daniel had spent a semester in Marburg with the radical New Testament scholar Rudolf Bultmann in 1929 and the experience had clearly left its mark. He had little to say either about the psychology of St Paul or about the personality of Jesus. Christ's significance was that he was the divine saviour who had been sent by the Father to be the saviour of the world: "It is true that Paul nowhere calls Jesus God; his Jewish heritage would never allow him to do so, but he says unequivocally that it is on the godward side of the line separating God from man that Jesus's essence is to be found."[73] It was in his divine sovereignty and vicarious sacrifice that Christ's uniqueness lay: "Despite the fashion of many teachers to dispense with the wrath of God, it's obvious enough in Paul."[74] The essence of Pauline religion and the Christian gospel as construed by Paul was not that men and women were naturally open to God, but that God, unbidden, had come to them. "Let the mind of the philosopher or the scientist search the mysteries of their own psyche or the secrets of the universe", he wrote, "yet they will never come across God. There is no human net whose mesh is small enough to catch him." Revelation was the only way in which the transcendent God could ever be known by man: "Imagine a castle, stronger even than Harlech castle, a castle which resisted every siege, a castle which no raider or marauder ever succeeded in conquering. You seek entrance to that castle. It is surrounded by a deep moat, its base is washed by the sea waves and it is situated on a rocky cliff. How

---

72. Daniel, *Dysgeidiaeth yr Apostol Paul*, 101.
73. Ibid.
74. Ibid., 86.

can you ever gain your wish? You must first have the permission of the castle's inhabitants, that they lower the drawbridge so that you can cross the moat and enter in."[75]

Daniel was not alone. More and more Welsh preachers were being attracted by Barth and his message. In a thoughtful series of essays in the Methodist monthly *Yr Eurgrawn* ("The Periodical") in 1935, George Breeze, a Wesleyan preacher, described the essence of Barth's thought. Mentioning his concept of revelation and God as the transcendent "Other", he was especially taken by his Christology. "There is little doubt that Barth and Brunner would consider our current interest in the Jesus of history as an attempt to know Christ after the flesh",[76] he claimed. Yet the Christ of the New Testament was, above all, the resurrected Lord: "Biblical criticism as an historical science can only reveal Christ "after the flesh." It is the gracious privilege of faith alone to perceive Christ as the revelation of God."[77] For a jaded minister in need of both spiritual refreshment and a vital message to preach, Barth had been a Godsend: "Although I cannot follow him in all he says, I must admit that no other religious thinker has ever had such an influence upon me. He has forced me to reconsider God for myself, reconsider him not in terms of Calvinism but of the divine revelation in scripture."[78] Similar sentiments were voiced by T. Ivon Jones, a Calvinistic Methodist minister in the heart of the North Wales slate quarry district a year later. It was Barth who had reminded evangelical Protestants what the gospel was all about and that the preaching of the Word was not only a privilege but a tremendous force for the salvation of the world.[79]

By the mid-1930s, Barth's reputation had been firmly established within international theology as a whole. His expulsion from Germany and return to his home city of Basle, Switzerland, in the summer of 1935 had coincided with Oswy Davies's ordination to the ministry of the Presbyterian Church of Wales. Davies contributed a succinct précis of Barth's theology to date in *Y Goleuad* in September 1937, as well as an

75. Ibid., 74.
76. George E. Breeze, "Karl Barth: y dyn a'i genadwri," *Yr Eurgrawn* 127 (1935) 13–16, 63–6, 85–9, 144–8, 187–92, 247–51 [189].
77. Ibid., 191.
78. Ibid., 14.
79. T. Ivon Jones, "Pregethu'r Gair yn ôl Karl Barth," *Y Traethodydd* N.S. 5 (1936) 18–27.

assessment of its author's significance: "The *emphasis* within Christian theology in each Protestant church throughout the world has changed during the last ten years", he claimed, and it was due to Barth and his colleagues that this had come about.[80] The renewal of the German church under the Word of God had already begun before Hitler had come to power, he stated, but: "[T]oday a host of young theologians in Germany are in leadership positions within the Confessing Church in direct response to the work of Karl Barth. The debt which German Protestantism owes him is immeasurable; Barth's strong personality and his definite and undeviating leadership, from the beginning of 1933 to his forced expulsion in mid-1935, not only made "opposition" a possibility but kept it alive as well."[81]

Yet it was not Barth's political role which Davies emphasized, but his doctrinal stance. The key conviction concerning God's revelation of himself in Christ, witnessed to in scripture and coming ever alive in the preaching of the gospel, had become a startling imperative, even for preachers!

> There is no doubt that Barth's standpoint has met a need which many had perceived for a long time. We felt that we had to accept the new and scientific way of treating the Bible and its literature,—but the theology of Modernism, even when at its best, had failed to satisfy. Then came Barth to show us where we had gone astray. The *theological content* of the Bible as revelation, as the *Word of God*, was something which the net of the scientific method of treating the text could never catch,—it was essential to look at Scripture from God's side as both Speaker and Executor, and listen to his message. The testimony of the prophets and the apostles to the Word must *become* God's living and powerful Word *to us, anew*, constantly, every day.[82]

The one objective criterion of theology was the Word, God's specific and unique revelation of himself: "There is no standard outside of revelation with which to judge God's truth." Unlike philosophy, theology was not a free science but one which functioned within its own sphere, that of the church, and under a discipline, that of the Christian

---

80. Ivor Oswy Davies, "Mudiad Karl Barth," *Y Goleuad*, 22 September 1937, 9–10 [9].

81. Davies, "Mudiad Karl Barth," 10.

82. Ibid.

life: "Love of Christ, obedience to his will, and consecration to his service,—such are the conditions of interpreting the Word."[83] Yet this revelation was not impersonal and bare, rather it was clothed in the gospel and in the form of Christ. "We must put God, the Creator, the Lord, and the Redeemer, once more in the centre," he claimed, "That is the message of Barth."[84]

As the Second World War approached the teaching, doctrines and presuppositions of the new theology had not only gained a hearing but had found a niche within Welsh Nonconformist circles. Its practitioners were gaining influence within their respective denominations and their profile was being raised ever higher. J. D. Vernon Lewis's appointment as professor of Christian Doctrine at the Brecon Memorial College in 1934 in succession to D. Miall Edwards illustrated the nature of the development. In lecture rooms and, more importantly (given the still considerable popular influence of chapel religion), in pulpits, the older liberalism was yielding to the new orthodoxy. Ivor Oswy Davies's reputation as a leading representative of the Barthian position was registered as having a salutary influence on his denomination. In an address to its English assembly in June 1938, only a few months before Neville Chamberlain's last attempt at appeasing Hitler at Munich, the note he struck was uncompromisingly positive. His subject was "God in History." Whereas by any secular standard, humankind could glean little of comfort from the present situation, yet the church would reign triumphant whatever was about to occur. "We interpret this well-nigh uninterpretable phenomenon called "history" by faith, not by sight", he claimed:

> Although there is much in the past, present and future, we do *not* know, yet, we speak authoritatively and dogmatically, about the deepest, ultimate and eternal *meaning* of what men call "world-history", in virtue of the revealed Word of God, the Lord Jesus Christ, as the Lord of History, and of Eternity. That God, the Father of Jesus, is *in* history, cannot be logically proven,—it can only be believed. The more we obey His Lordship in our own lives, the stronger shall our conviction of His Lordship in the world, and its history, become. The Kingdom or Lordship

---

83. Ibid.
84. Ibid.

A Chapter in the History of Welsh Theology

of God as at hand, *today*; "repent ye, and believe this divine proclamation."[85]

According to the R. Buick Knox: "In a conference where the tone of many speeches was gloomy, Davies spoke of Christ's Kingdom as present in the world as judgement and redemption; he said that God could use the encircling darkness, as He had done on the Cross, to bring His light to view."[86] The effect this had on his congregation was considerable, and it suggested that the new emphases had something supremely pertinent to say to the Welsh churches at the time. On the eve of war, this was a message to which Welsh Christians could assuredly respond.[87]

---

85. Ivor Oswy Davies, "God in History," 1–8[3], Ivor Oswy Davies MSS, Bangor University Archive.

86. R. Buick Knox, *Voices from the Past: A History of the English Conference of the Presbyterian Church of Wales, 1889–1938* (Llandysul: Gomer, 1969), 54.

87. For the story in the wider context see Morgan, *Barth Reception in Britain*, passim.

12

Divine Election: An Exercise in Bridge-Building

STEPHEN N. WILLIAMS

In a text on missiology which may well be destined to assume the status of a contemporary classic in some circles, Christopher Wright remarks that "between election in the Hebrew Scriptures of Jesus and election in the formulations of theological systems there sometimes seems to be a great gulf fixed. Few and narrow are the bridges from one to the other."[1] The *prima facie* justification for this averment is not hard to detect; election in the Old Testament is centred on the historical vocation of Israel, while election in theological systems has typically focussed on the post-mortem salvation destiny of believers, in contrast to unbelievers. But is the justification more than *prima facie*? And, even if it is, is it nonetheless possible to construct a modest bridge, one which nevertheless bears the weight of serious biblical and theological traffic? It is worth ruminating on the possible design of such a bridge, provisionally granting that the justification for Chris Wright's statement is more than *prima facie*.

---

1. Christopher J. H. Wright. *The Mission of God: Unlocking the Bible's Grand Narrative* (Nottingham: Inter-Varsity, 2006), 262.

My former colleague, John Tudno Williams, possesses the excellence of a double distinction, in that he is expert in both Old and New Testaments. However, this qualification comes at a price. For it means that the capacity for getting frustrated at systematic theologians is liable to double accordingly. I trust that the personal graciousness extended over the years by John Tudno towards one who plies his trade under the sign of 'Systematic Theology' will be extended just a little while longer, over the course of this essay. I hope to show that things are, or, at least, need not be, in such a bad shape as Chris Wright assumes.

A Question of Privilege

Election is of interest not just to biblical and systematic theologians, but also to missiologists. Surely none has been more globally influential for some time now than Lesslie Newbigin. A solid account of his work argues the case for identifying the doctrine of election as the theological core of his missiology.[2] "Newbigin's interpretation of the significance of election stands apart. Rarely, if ever, has anyone else given it the prominence which it has in his mission theology, and for no one else does it hold so foundational a place in the rationale for mission."[3] Whether or not we judge that the author overplays his hand here just a little, there is no doubt that he is near the mark. As Newbigin put it in one of his principal works, the doctrine of election "permeates and controls the whole Bible."[4] As far as he is concerned, election is even a kind of necessity, as far as God's *modus operandi* is concerned. Why is it a necessity? For three reasons.

Firstly, there is a the anthropological requirement: "the nature and destiny of humanity" calls for it. God wants to indicate the nature of human destiny to his creatures in the world by inaugurating and establishing patterns of anticipation and exemplification within the socio-

---

2. George Hunsberger. *Bearing the Witness of the Spirit: Lesslie Newbigin's Theology of Cultural Plurality* (Grand Rapids: Eerdmans, 1998).

3. Ibid., 82–83.

4. Newbigin, *The Open Secret* (London: SPCK, 1978), 75. Of this work Hunsberger remarks that "amongst the mission theologies written in this century, Newbigin's *The Open Secret* stands unique in at least this one important respect: it alone weaves a comprehensive purpose around 'election' as the central and dominant thread" (*Bearing the Witness*, 66).

historical nexus of inter-personal relationships. That is, the elect must show forth the secret of true humanization and so lead the way for the world to follow. Secondly, election is required by the doctrine of God. God is personal and is known in a personal relationship. Therefore, he acts in relation to human beings in their particular histories, space and time, so that they might make their appropriate personal response to his personal activity. This also is revealed through the elect. Thirdly, the way of election is a soteriological requirement. "Salvation means 'wholeness', which must include the restoration of social justice and interpersonal relationships. The method of election means that I cannot be made whole apart from my neighbour, on whom I have depended for the message of God's reign . . . The humility required to receive the message from another corresponds to the humility by which the grace of God must be received as a free gift."[5]

What is striking about these arguments is that they fall short of their aim, which is to explain why election is actually necessary. They do show that, in order for God to fulfil his purposes, it may be necessary for him to act in history. At a stretch, they may even open out the possibility that God's operations in history are *fittingly* undertaken in the form of electing activity towards a particular people. But only at a stretch and only as a possibility; that is the very most that is indicated. We remain puzzled as to why Newbigin makes the election of a particular people a *necessary* vehicle in the saving economy of God—why *historical* action should be particularly *electing* action.

We acquire a clue about what impelled Newbigin to take the direction which he took when we observe that he repeatedly emphasizes in his writings that election is not a privilege but a responsibility. "God chooses men and women for the service of his mission. To be a Christian is to be part of a chosen company—chosen, not for privilege, but for responsibility."[6] Again: the people of Israel were 'bearers—not exclusive beneficiaries' of a blessing to the nations; 'again and again it had to be said that election is for responsibility, not for privilege.'"[7] This is as true in relation to the Church as it was in relation to Israel. "We have to guard against the perversion which regards election as the con-

---

5. Hunsberger, *Bearing the Witness*, 103. All three points are summarised on this page.

6. Newbigin, *The Open Secret*, 19.

7. Ibid., 34.

Divine Election

ferring of a privileged status."[8] I have lifted all these statements from *The Open Secret*, but the same note is struck in, for example, *The Gospel in a Pluralist Society*: "As the story unfolds [in Scripture], it becomes clear that to be God's chosen people means not privilege but suffering, reproach, humiliation."[9] Newbigin's doctrine of election is an attempt to close a gap between Israel and the nations, or between the church and extra-ecclesial communities, a gap opened up by what he regards as an unhealthy and misguided understanding of election. What he aspires to correct is the false contrast, familiarly peddled in systematic theology, between the elected and the rejected. Newbigin maintains that election is not a soteric privilege, standing in contrast to the exclusion of the rejected non-elect. What God wants to do in Israel (and the Church) is to demonstrate in history the kind of religious and social relationships that should mark the life of humankind. Election is the revelation of a universal design. In his eagerness to ward off distortions of the biblical view of election, Newbigin presses the distinction between privilege and responsibility and, in his eagerness to focus our eyes on God's universal designs achieved through historical action, he argues for the necessity of election as the form of God's action in history.

So much for the impetus behind talk of election as necessity, but, logically, we are no further along; Newbigin's argument still does not satisfy. It remains unclear why *one people* in particular should be the vehicle for this demonstration. Why does God not reveal the secret of humanization by calling all the peoples of the earth to demonstrate it? To repeat: Newbigin's reasoning enables us to understand why God must act in history, but not why he must act outstandingly in one particular history. But our allusion to the underlying rationale for his position, far from relieving the problem, compounds it. For we have now encountered another and a different set of statements that slightly puzzle. Newbigin consistently insists that election is not a privilege but a responsibility. It is an insistence which surely rings strange on the ear of a non-professional, non-scholarly reader of Scripture which is, nevertheless, reasonably attuned to the tones of Testaments Old and New. It may indeed be the case that the contrast between election and non-election has been wrongly drawn in much systematic theology. It may indeed be the case that election entails responsibility at its very

8. Ibid., 86.
9. Newbigin. *The Gospel in a Pluralist Society* (London: SPCK, 1989), 84.

core. But, in any ordinary sense of that word, how can we escape the belief that election entails "privilege"?

It is interesting that H. H. Rowley's study of sixty years ago, *The Biblical Doctrine of Election*, continues to exert such a direct or indirect influence on some missiological writing.[10] Rowley is the biblical scholar credited with bringing to the fore the biblical understanding of election as election for service. The gulf between biblical and systematic theology on election, to which Chris Wright alluded, is displayed early in Rowley's work with his announcement: "At the outset it must be made clear that I do not propose to deal with the theological question of predestination to salvation or damnation, to heaven or to hell."[11] Rowley was, of course quite right as far as the Old Testament was concerned; it is not directly about the post-mortem destiny of individuals. "In the thought of the Old Testament," said Rowley, "it is always election to service, and it is held to be forfeited when it has no relation to that service."[12] However, Rowley did not deny privilege. "Election is for service. This is not to ignore the fact that it carries with it privilege. For in the service of God is man's supreme privilege and honour."[13] So service and privilege are not baldly contrasted, although it is true that Rowley also observed that "honour is but incidental to election whereas service is fundamental."[14]

My objective here is not to get bogged down in semantic questions at the expense of substantive ones.[15] But a justifiable reaction to a faulty understanding of a given subject easily slides into over-reaction; it ap-

10. Hunsberger's account documents this at several points: see, e.g., *Bearing the Witness*, 88. The very first footnote in the main body of Chris Wright's book follows on from a very complimentary reference to an even earlier work produced by Rowley on *The Missionary Message of the Old Testament*: see *The Mission of God*, 24n.1.

11. Rowley, *The Biblical Doctrine of Election*, 16.

12. Ibid., 94.

13. Ibid., 45.

14. Ibid., 122. The contrast between "honour" and "service" is expressed elsewhere in the chapter from which these words are taken, "Election without Covenant."

15. However, it remains profitable to read Rowley carefully here in light of missiological contributions which throw up the question of election and privilege in the train of Newbigin's work, and that of others. E.g., notice his remark on the twelve disciples: "They were not picked out for privilege *from the mass of men in whom God had no interest*. They were chosen and called for service" (*The Biblical Doctrine of Election*, 170). The italics are mine. It appears to me that Rowley used language more carefully than did Newbigin.

Divine Election

pears to be an abiding characteristic of vast tracts of intellectual history that, in rightly affirming what we affirm, we wrongly reject what we reject. Time and time again, Leibniz' words prove to be correct when we generalize them and apply the spirit of his remark: "Most philosophical schools are largely right in what they assert, but not so much in what they deny."[16] It is an insight appropriately placarded over the construction of a bridge such as I am attempting to design here.

Privilege and Presence

In the Old Testament, there is election within election. For example, the tribes of Judah and of Levi are peculiar recipients and beneficiaries of election. Let us grant that the Old Testament language of election, as it applies either to Israel or to any group, institution or figure within Israel, does not have as its direct reference the post-mortem fate of individuals. There is nonetheless a vast territory lying between the areas marked: 'Service and responsibility towards others', on the one hand, and "The post-mortem destiny of the few," on the other. It is the old, old theological and intellectual story: *tertium datur*. And it is into this area (inadequately marked for our purposes) that we shall make a brief reconnaissance. The area in question can be described as: "Communion with the living God." At all the general levels of election in the Old Testament, whatever the instrumental necessity of election in God's hands for carrying out his historical purposes for humanity via Israel, election does also carry the peculiar privilege of communion, except when God chooses non-Israelite nations for purposes of immediate judgment against Israel. If the Lord is our life (Deut 30:20), there is no higher privilege than the privilege of service; but, more than that, if he is truly our life and truly God of the living, the privilege in question cannot be stripped of all eschatological clothing.[17]

If we turn, firstly, to Judah, we find that its pre-Davidic history is full of interest. At the dedication of the tabernacle in the desert,

---

16. Quoted in G. MacDonald Ross, *Leibniz* (Oxford: Oxford University Press, 1984), 75.

17. I do not, however, want to insist on the widest possible scope for the word "life" in this Deuteronomic text. Quotations in this essay are consistently from the New International Version of the Bible only because nothing in my argument hangs on the precise rendering of the texts.

"the one who brought his offering on the first day was Nahshon son of Amminadab of the tribe of Judah" (Num 7:12), a "tribal leader," as he is described in 1 Chronicles (2:10). When, shortly afterwards, the people of Israel resumes its march after being on pause since the book of Exodus, it is Judah and Nahshon that lead the way (Num 10:14). The tribe first named in the book of Numbers to help Eleazar and Joshua in land distribution is Judah (34:19) and, in the book of Joshua itself, after the case of the Trans-Jordanians has been sorted out, it is the allotment to Judah that heads up the list and dominates it (15:1–63). In the dreadful civil conflict that witnessed the isolation of the Benjaminites, God commands that Judah must be the first to go and fight against them (Judg 20:18). All this is recorded before the book of Ruth discloses to us her relationship with David after she married Nahshon's grandson, Boaz (4:20–21).

Now it must be granted that the personal piety and fidelity of some of the tribal members of Judah may account for at least a measure of tribal privilege on this occasion or that; Caleb, in his day, was the stalwart exemplar of the best in the piety of this tribe. But the overriding factor, when we consider the privilege attaching to the tribe of Judah, is independent, divine sovereign choice, culminating in David himself. And David could only be amazed at his election. "The Lord God of Israel chose me from my whole family, and from my father's sons he was pleased to make me king over all Israel" (1 Chron 28:4). Personal, tribal and national privilege alike fill him with awe: "But who am I, and who are my people, that we should be able to give as generously as this?" a gift for the building of the temple (1 Chron 29:14). It is a truism that the Psalms testify to David's communion with God. If we revert to Newbigin's language of "necessity," and take the long view of biblical history from a Christian perspective, we shall indeed grant that it was necessary for Israel to have on its throne the type of him who was to come, even though our talk of necessity must be modified to take into account that strand in the Old Testament witness which indicts the demand for monarchy as a case of Israelite infidelity towards Yahweh, the king. It was presumably necessary for the people to possess an inspiring psalmist, too. But David received far more than the privilege of assigned responsibility as monarch and singer. Election is about a depth of personal communion possible for its humble recipient. If you are elect as an instrument with responsibility in the service of God, you are also a person who attains privilege in communion with God.

We now turn to Levi. Here, again, we may speak of necessity, if we wish. Proper order in a multi-tribal society is only maintained if responsibilities are tribally allocated. Someone, and so some tribe, had to perform the duties surrounding priesthood and a particular clan (the Aaronic) was accorded peculiar priestly access to Yahweh within that order. Of course, the priestly function is a representative one on behalf of the nation, but the privilege of representation is immense. "When I struck down all the firstborn in Egypt, I set them apart for myself. And I have taken the Levites in place of all the firstborn sons of Israel," the Lord tells the people in the book of Numbers, a book which, from near its beginning, heavily underlines the position of the Levites. The Levites are spared the privilege of land in Canaan because they have the greater privilege of the Lord as their inheritance. The book of Joshua witnesses the implementation of this arrangement which includes a remarkable reference to Joshua's own humble retirement in the land on par with other members of his tribe and with all other tribes save the Levite, as he settles down in Timnath-Sereh, the spot allocated to him by his fellow-Israelites (19:50). Even before Joshua is named as the one who divided up the land, Eleazar the priest is mentioned (19:51).

In no book after the book of Joshua are we more reminded of Joshua's description of territorial allocation than in the prophetic book of Ezekiel. Ezekiel himself was a priest. His prophecy concludes with the description of the allocation of land, divided amongst all the tribes, but with a special portion to be offered to the Lord and this is the 'sacred portion for the priests' (Ezek 48:10). The central portion of this special portion is the sanctuary of the Lord himself and reserved for the faithful Zadokites (48:11). But the other Levites still have the best of the land which remains, a portion especially "holy to the Lord" (48:14). It is true that specific faithfulness is rewarded here, namely, that of the Zadokites. But it is also true that tribal membership of Levi is, *ipso facto*, a special privilege. It is not that this privilege issues in a felicitous guarantee of the welfare of every member of the tribe. On the contrary, throughout the Old Testament, the greater the privilege, the greater the penalty for unfaithfulness.[18] But the Levites have been put

---

18. Witness the outcome Korah's rebellion; Korah was a Levite, although some Reubenites were also involved in the dissension, see Numbers 16:1–50.

in the position of being able to exhibit a peculiar kind of faithfulness. Where you are in the land and what you do in the temple not only signifies but also seals a spiritual communion, privilege and possibility. Whatever orderly necessities attach to the socio-religious organization of Israel, the reality of communion is a privilege of grace. The geography of Ezekiel's closing chapters is deeply interesting in this respect.[19] Comparison with the geographical descriptions of tribal allocations in Numbers 34 and Joshua reveals that borders have drastically shifted around, as though to provide an idealized description.[20] (Incidentally, this suggests that we have to be careful in interpreting Ezekiel's prophecy as though he himself, or his redactors, expected its literal fulfilment or, to be more precise, expected fulfilment in the strict literal form in which he couched his prophecy.) The territorial definitions appear to indicate an hierarchical principle embedded in the prophetic mind of someone well able to distinguish between the individual and the tribe or family when it comes to emphasising individual, as opposed to collective, responsibility and penalty in the case of sin. At all events, the privilege of communion with God is assumed and it is a privilege granted in sheer sovereign choice.

It is easy to forget the religious wealth packed into the belief that God is the living God. Not for nothing did an Old Testament theology of an earlier day—that of Edmond Jacob—begin with the account of God as living.[21] "Let me see your glory," Moses said, stirred by an impulse which went far beyond the passion to serve (Exod 33:18). Tertullian interpreted with charming fancifulness the significance of Moses' encounter with God: Moses saw the hind region of God, but Tertullian's Latin translation, rendering this as *posterior*, lured him into exploiting the *double entendre*—Moses did indeed see God in "posterior" times, in later times, *in temporibus posterioribus*.[22] When did Moses later see God? At the mount of Transfiguration, of course, in the company of

---

19. Here I decisively part company with James Barr, who finds nothing stirring in these chapters: see *The Concept of Biblical Theology: An Old Testament Perspective* (Minneapolis: Fortress, 1999), 166.

20. Examples include the relative positions of Judah and Benjamin and the southward movement of Issachar and Zebulun.

21. E. Jacob, *Theology of the Old Testament* (London: Hodder & Stoughton, 1958), Part One, I.

22. Tertullian, *Adversus Marcionem* (Oxford: Clarendon, 1972), vol. 2, 4:22.

Elijah, Jesus being God in incarnate form! We may permit ourselves to smile at Tertullian just as long as we moderate our countenance in simultaneous recollection of the words of Jesus, spoken in response to the Sadducean attack on belief in the resurrection: God is not God of the dead, but of the living (Mark 12:17 and parallels). The faithful elect have the privilege not only of temporal service, but of eternal communion. Of this rock we must build our bridge.

On from Israel

The first five books of the New Testament—the Gospels and Acts—are to be read as a continuation of the Old Testament history of Israel. In these books, as in the New Testament as a whole, we should undoubtedly appropriate the theme of election in its continuity with the Old Testament treatment. Failure to do this has made shipwreck of much in systematic and popular theology and, worst of all, tortured sensitive souls. The book of Hebrews, for example, has generated bewildered consternation: how can saved and sanctified believers possibly fall away from grace?[23] In truth, although it may seem cavalier to say so, there is surely nothing particularly puzzling here, as long as we read the letter in the light of the Hebrew Scriptures. Israelites, saved from Egypt and sanctified in the wilderness, include both the faithful and the unfaithful, alike commanded to persevere and capable of fatal disobedience. Read in terms of the corporate election of the OT, Hebrews presents no puzzle in its account of the saved and sanctified falling away and forfeiting grace, for that was, to a depressingly large extent, the story familiar to all readers of the Old Testament. It is a problem only when we individualise salvation and sanctification in a way that the book does not.[24] Similarly, Romans 9-11 has been read with bewildered consternation on account of what looks to some eyes like God's dastardly decree of the unconditional reprobation of Esau. How can the arbitrary choice of Jacob for salvation and Esau for perdition express or be squared with

---

23. While the biblical vocabulary of election tempts us to suppose that this is not a prominent theme in Hebrews, in reality, the people of God in that letter is always the elect.

24. I have stated this without nuance, but, in any comprehensive treatment, it is a statement which should certainly be modified to take into account significant questions that have been standardly raised in systematic theology.

either divine mercy or divine justice? But Paul is not occupied at this juncture with the question of personal destiny. Of Esau's personal post-mortem fate, or that of his descendants, we hear nothing. Further, elect Gentiles, at the opposite end from Esau on the spectrum of privilege, are warned that they may fall away as surely as those elect Israelites who refused the message of the gospel (11:17–24). To the extent that systematic theologians (or biblical scholars) have mapped questions of personal destiny onto biblical materials that do not deal with it, the biblical depiction of election has indeed been lost from sight.

However, although this is true as far as it goes, it is certainly one-sided and certainly not that simple. The New Testament language that we translate in terms of "calling" or "election" or "predestination" or other ways—and it is by no means assumed here that all the underlying Greek terms are cognate—can certainly include reference to post-mortem life eternal. Indeed, Jacob himself, like grandfather Abraham and father Isaac, will feast at the eschatological banquet. Believers in Jesus Christ are elect not simply to temporal service, in continuity with the Old Testament people of God, but elect also to the consummation and reward of service, to risen life on the new earth. That is indisputable. What is mistaken is not the belief that election is to life eternal along with temporal service. What is mistaken are inferences drawn from this. It is often assumed that the opposite of election to the temporal-eternal nexus of earthly service and eschatological life is the exclusion of those who are not elect from both temporal service and eternal life. However, biblical logic does not work that way. It is true that Esau and his house are not elect to temporal service; it is also true that Jacob's election to temporal service goes beyond that and entails a positive eschatological destiny, when he faithfully follows the way of Yahweh. But all this does not entail that Esau and his house are, considered as individuals, subjects of post-mortem perdition. The New Testament, like the Old, simply leaves certain questions unaddressed. If we ask about the post-mortem destinies of those who are not hearers of the Word, whether in the Old or in the New Testaments, we find ourselves in some contentious and uncertain areas of exegesis and making inferences one way or another which, admittedly, we may regard as soundly warranted, yielding a fairly strong presumption this way or that. But theologians have often erred in deducing from New Testament election what they believe that its opposite must be - the passing over of some individuals or their positive ordination to a particular post-mortem destiny.

Indeed, we must not unjustly extend the scope of the accusation of error. If the election of Israel in the Old Testament includes felicitous eternal consequences for faithful Israelites, and if the election of the church of Jews and Gentiles, in the New, correspondingly—and more clearly—embraces the same felicitous eternal consequences for faithful followers of Christ, then we have established *some* sort of distinction of the kind that beckons us in the direction of the classical systematic-theological discussions of election and predestination.[25] From the standpoint of what we might term "biblical theology"—here understood as a theology expressed more or less explicitly in the canon of the Old and New Testament Scriptures, taken in their unity—it is not so much that systematic theological discussions of election have fastened on entirely the wrong set of questions. They have, in a measure, fastened on a set of questions directly introduced by the text, as we shall illustrate in a moment. The problem, rather, is that mistaken logic has too often compounded the problem of an exegesis which does not read the New properly in the light of the Old Testament.

Classical theological questions in relation to election are, after all, invited on the very surface of the biblical text. We may illustrate this from Luke's account of the history of the early church. In the course of his narrative, Luke remarks that, when the Gentiles heard the word of God 'they were glad and honoured the word of the Lord, and all who were appointed for eternal life believed' (Acts 13:48). Here, I have followed the practice adopted in this essay of quoting the New International Version. However, there are proposals to render the Greek differently, including taking *tetagmenoi* in the Middle voice, so that Luke's converts are really said to be disposing or setting themselves responsively to believe.[26] But, even if we are prepared to concede this possibility, nothing, for my purposes, hangs on a dogmatic interpreta-

---

25. I am not simply lumping together indiscriminately the words "election" and "predestination" or refusing to distinguish between the meaning and semantic range of the underlying Greek words. We are dealing with those cases where there is an overlap relevant to God's effective activity in calling and guiding people to eternal life.

26. For a quick summary of the options here and a plausible remark on the relation of this Lukan text to what Luke says elsewhere in both Luke and Acts, see William J. Larkin, *Acts* (Downers Grove, IL: InterVarsity, 1995), 287.

tion of this particular text either for an account of Luke's theology in general or a wider account of predestination or election in the New Testament. The point that I wish to make is valid even if we draw on different texts or portions in the New Testament to make it.

It is this. On the one hand, we cannot get away from New Testament reference to the life of the world to come as the terminus of election or predestination. On the other, it is instructive to ask what Luke takes to be the opposite of foreordination to life. It is instructive without prejudice to the precise interpretation of this text, because what is indicated can be validated from elsewhere even if we follow an alternative translation and interpretation of Acts 13:48. The text, as traditionally read, is significantly instructive on the question: "What is the opposite of appointment to life?" We understand the meaning of words when we understand their opposites or their contrasts.[27] In asking about "opposites," clearly, we must beware of foisting onto Luke, or onto anyone in Scripture, an alien linguistic mode of speech or logical mode of thought. But the question as I raise it here is rooted in the text itself. Prior to these words, Luke has recorded the opposition of the Jews to Paul and Barnabas. Consequently, Paul responds as follows: "We had to speak the word of God to you first. Since you reject it and do not consider yourselves worthy of eternal life, we now turn to the Gentiles. For this is what the Lord has commanded us: "I have made you a light for the Gentiles, that you may bring salvation to the ends of the earth." When the Gentiles heard this, they were glad and honoured the word of the Lord; and all who were appointed for eternal life believed."

What is contrasted is not divine appointment unto life with divine appointment (or passing over) unto death. Rather, divine appointment to life is contrasted with culpable rejection of life. The course of the narrative in Acts, in deep continuity with Luke's Gospel, not to mention other Gospels and the Old Testament, reveals the same thing: the opposite of foreordination to eternal life is not foreordination to eternal death. The opposite is wilful, culpable and responsible rejection of an opportunity that could and should have been taken. If the ministry of Jesus lays bare the human heart by laying bare the Israelite heart, the Gospel records of it illustrate most perspicuously how human fault comes from within when we forfeit eternal life. More particularly,

---

27. Obviously, I do not have all words in mind here—plenty of words (like 'lake,' 'green,' 'London') have no opposites.

the Gospel narratives and Acts seamlessly join with Paul (especially in Romans 9–11) to indicate how Gentile inclusion in the people of God is the fruit of Israel's rejection of the Gospel. This is not to say that everything in Acts and in the Gospels (including John) can be flattened out as though they and Paul are always emphasizing exactly the same thing. And it is certainly not to advance supersessionism: the Church does not replace Israel; it is the community of believing Gentiles grafted on to the people of God that is Israel, when believing Israelites are joined by the Gentiles. But the text in Acts on which I have fastened indicates how Luke is interested in predestination in the context of the historical phenomenon of Gentile belief in its religious contrast and temporal succession to Jewish unbelief. If space and time allowed, it would be interesting and profitable to pursue further the question of the extent to which New Testament interest in election or predestination outside the Gospels is connected with the specific question of Gentiles entering into the Jewish inheritance. Our point here, however, is to draw attention to what it is that Luke contrasts with divine appointment to life in that stark statement of outcomes which he sets before us in the relevant passage in Acts.

What theologians are often doing is paying the penalty for the failure to interpret statements about election or predestination in the context of the biblical narrative. When theological concepts are abstracted from biblical narrative, the opposite of foreordination to eternal life appears to be an antecedent decision on the part of God either to 'pass over' some people in an election which embraces eternal life, or to actively ordain their perdition. Now, let us be quite fair. It is often the case of course, that when theologians stipulate the opposite of an election which embraces eternal life, they are not doing so just on the basis of a logical inference from texts which speak positively about election. On the contrary, appeal is usually made to texts which, it is alleged, explicitly teach the darker side of divine determination. Romans 9, for example, is prominent here, with respect to what is said about Pharaoh and not just about Esau. I certainly grant that the case in question is offered on these grounds and on other, wider, theological grounds. If it is no part of my objective here to try to offer an exegesis of all the relevant texts, it is no part of my intention either to dismiss the importance of doing so. But I suspect that I shall be forgiven for not attempting to resolve exegetical debates on the question of election in the course of a single essay.

My interest is a limited interest in bridges. *To the extent that* systematic theologians have sought to derive propositions about ordination to destruction from the putative logic of affirmations about ordination to eternal life, they have often abandoned the contrasts that Scripture presents in favour of conceptual alternatives wrested from the context of the biblical narrative. And is it not the narrative which supremely displays, in Scripture, the relation of God to humans? The intelligibility of some of the more concise propositions in the Bible—on election or on anything else—depends on our grasp of the narrative which explains the meaning of those propositions, just as those propositions (for want of a better word) clarify the import of the narrative. It is not basically the theological discernment that divine election can pertain to eternal life, as well as to service, that creates that gulf with the biblical world which Chris Wright laments. It is the extraction of the operations of theological logic from the storied form of thought that we meet in the world of Scripture, both Hebrew and Christian.

If we are urging methodological theological attention to narrative, in order to build bridges with the biblical world, we are scarcely doing anything novel. On the contrary, this sort of proposal has been around for a while.[28] However, in attending to those aspects of the doctrine of election that properly arise from both Testaments and from classical theologies alike, it is not necessary to rely on biblical narrative to rescue systematic theology from its captivity to theologically misleading forms of thought. As far as I can tell, theologians have yet to take properly on board a set of observations made by Charles Simeon in respect of the Calvinist-Arminian controversy which was raging especially fiercely some years before he made them, at the beginning of the nineteenth century. Reputed a moderate Calvinist evangelical, who turned out to be hugely influential, especially in the Church of England, Simeon declared himself to be "no friend to systematizers in Theology."[29] But

28. In a *Festschrift*, I am presumably allowed the remark that my own doctoral studies, completed in the year that I joined John Tudno Williams on the staff of United Theological College in Aberystwyth, were undertaken under the directorship of Hans Frei.

29. Those interested in references and a fuller treatment will find them in Stephen N. Williams, "Observations on the Future of System," especially 42–45, in A. T. B.

preachers do not have to be their friends. For the responsibility of the preacher is rightly to apply to individual lives those truths found in Scripture, not to reconcile those truths conceptually to each other. The truth of apparently contrary texts (those to which Calvinists and Arminians respectively appealed) may lie, not exclusively in either, nor yet in a confused mixture of both, but in the proper and seasonable application of them both; or, to use the language of St. Paul, "in rightly dividing the word of truth." Beliefs conceptually hard to reconcile may nevertheless be existentially joined, shaping and coherently integrating the life of discipleship. Prayer and action are sites which reveal this process for, in prayer, the Arminian confesses complete dependence on God and, in action, the Calvinist acknowledges complete responsibility before God.

In saying this, Simeon did not appeal to the significance of narrative. His intuition was that the biblical witness is concerned with relating this or that truth to the life of faith or to the phenomenon of unbelief, whereas systematic theologians struggle to relate the truths to each other. Simeon held that the outcome of the latter (systematic) operation was, in unfortunate effect, the theological expulsion of some aspect of biblical truth because it did not fit the theological system. On the other hand, the outcome of the former (basically homiletic) operation was, to good effect, the practical application of all aspects of biblical truth, heedless of what makes for a system. Simeon's position is not beyond dispute. But his instincts are surely commendable. Wittgenstein's conviction that the meaning of a concept is to be understood according to how it shapes a form of life, is well known. Simeon was arguing, in effect, precisely that: we understand a truth only when we understand how it integrates life in one way or another and not when we understand its abstracted relationship to another putative truth. It goes without saying that I am stating all this very crudely. Nevertheless, it is interesting that Wittgenstein insisted that his own modes of thought were Hebraic.[30]

Attention to the narrative of election; attention to the responsibilities of application; attention to the relation of concepts to life—all this

---

McGowan, ed., *Always Reforming: Explorations in Systematic Theology* (Leicester: Apollos, 2006).

30. M. O'C. Drury, "Conversations with Wittgenstein," in Rush Rhees, ed., *Ludwig Wittgenstein: Personal Recollections* (Oxford: Blackwell. 1981), 175.

gives systematic theology plenty to attend to in an attempt to reconnect biblical election with traditional doctrinal preoccupations. But the logic of election in the Hebrew and Christian Scriptures is susceptible of treatment that provides another plank for our bridge and this directs our thought to the bridge that connects heaven and earth. I conclude this essay with reference to the connection between election and incarnation.

The Logic of Incarnation and the Logic of Election

Divine election is often perceived as an offence because it seems like a case of divine favouritism. The employer in Jesus' parable might have thought that he had a self-evident right to do as he wished with his own money (Matt 20:15) but we are frequently not disposed to concede that God can do as he wishes with his own world. At least, that is so when something important is at stake, as it undoubtedly is on any biblical or theological understanding of election. Election apparently compounds a wider problem familiarly experienced in relation to divine exclusivism, as it is often presented in traditional modes of Christian thought. Exclusivism is centred, of course, in Christology. Incarnation, with all its soteriological effects, seems like a clear case of divine exclusivism one way or another. Are we really to say that the beneficiaries of the favour of a God who is called a God of love, are especially those who inhabited Palestine in the first century and those who have since then heard and believed their witness?

In response, we must say that everything depends on perspective. We are familiar with those trick diagrams which depict one thing from one point of view, another from another point of view; viewers see different pictures in the one identical configuration before them. (Wittgenstein's celebrated duck-rabbit is an obvious example.) On the perspective explicitly afforded to us by the biblical writings, the charges of exclusivism or favouritism which embrace election in connection with incarnation show only that their proponents have grasped rather firmly the wrong end of the stick.

Suppose that there is a God who loves his creation and suppose that the creation has gone awry. What would appear to be the supreme demonstration of love so long as evil remains and creation remains?

The answer can be stated in various ways, but we might opt for the phrase: "saving identification." It would appear that love is supremely demonstrated when God gets as close to his creatures as he possibly can, in order to effect their salvation.[31] But what would that involve? Human beings are inhabitants of a particular space and time; they live once and they die once on this planet. Of course, there are world-views that maintain otherwise, particularly those that are expressed in oriental philosophies or religions. But biblical and secular perspectives coincide at this point, in the doctrine or assumption that humans live only once on this earth.

Suppose, then, that God has the capacity for incarnation and so for identification with the human creature, and accordingly plans saving action within human history. Then incarnation in particular space and time is required. Incarnation is not theophany, which is, in principle, repeatable. Incarnation is not mere indwelling, which as a bare concept, suggests the possibility of many possible human receptacles. Incarnation is the particular action of the one through whom all things were created when he enters earthly space and time, entering a world designed by a God powerful enough to design and effect an entry, a world designed specifically so that incarnation would be possible. If it is the case that being human means living once and dying once in a particular space and time, and if it is the case that the Son of God assumes humanity, then, of necessity, he lives once and dies once in a particular space and time. This is the opposite of a limitation on God's saving concern. On the contrary, it is its expression. Purposeful love towards humanity, getting as close as possible to the human race by becoming human, requires the particularity of space and time.[32]

---

31. It should be noted that I am not assuming an "exemplarist" understanding of atonement in order for this argument to work.

32. The thought experiment of multiple incarnations will not get us very far, quite apart from the fact that multiple incarnations would prove precisely that God had *not* assumed our human uni-spatial and uni-temporal form. We should be saying, in principle, that a first-century Palestinian Jew could also be a second-century Chinaman and third-century Welshman etc. It would scarcely solve the problem of making God more universally available in incarnate form, as, even on this hypothesis, if God incarnate were to be in the world at all *times*, he would still be absent at those times from most *spaces*, on the assumption that you can only be embodied in one place at a time. For some discussion of the logic of particularity, see Stephen N Williams, "On Religion and Revelation," in *Books & Culture* 12.6 (2006), and John Caputo's response in the same issue.

But true humanity requires attachment not just to particular place and time, but also to a particular history. There is a requirement of lineal descent, of belonging to clan or tribe or nation or people-group. The traditional affirmation that Jesus Christ was conceived of a virgin has brought well-known problems in its train, but it was a belief never meant to deny the human biological descent of Jesus Christ, only to deny that such descent could be traced in the normal way, through both biological parents. And, biology aside, Jesus could not be inserted into the human world without being inserted into a human history. The historical background of Jesus Christ is immediately and proximately that he belonged to the people of Israel.[33] Israel was a people that believed in the one God who created heaven and earth, giver of the law and ultimate author of messianic expectation. From a biblical point of view, these were not beliefs, values and hopes which happened to arise in a group of people, upon which they might happily stumble or which were rationally self-evident. If there was incarnation, there had to be preparation—particular moulding and calling—that is to say, an election. If incarnation was fitting or necessary for salvation, then election was necessary for incarnation. We earlier discussed Lesslie Newbigin on the necessity of election. Its deepest necessity (a conviction which Newbigin actually upheld) lies in its necessity to secure the incarnation which God has designed to secure human salvation. It is from within this perspective that the questions of exclusivism and inclusivism must be addressed, together with everything which they bring in their train. But we have surely secured the principle that election is not an exclusionary device. If we were to adumbrate that principle, we should be found uniting the biblical and theological worlds, casting in the mode of "the logic of election" the ways of God depicted in the biblical narrative. If adumbration did not bear us away too far on the wings of exercise in theological logic, the construction of our bridge would be furthered. Indeed, perhaps we should be found laying its very foundation.

An essay such as this. painting with broad brush strokes, is bound to invite the charge of excessive and impressionistic generalization. Granted, its argument will carry little conviction unless it is nailed down in meticulous biblical exegesis, on the one hand, and rigorous theological analysis, on the other. But, in the absence of an opportunity to do

---

33. Though see Luke 3:38, which traces Jesus' line back beyond Abraham to Adam.

this, it seems worth flagging up synthetic possibilities—synthetic, that is, in relation to biblical disciplines and systematic theology. Synthesis is not for the sake of the academic community; it is in order to encourage the life of the church. That is more important than delivering the polished product that satisfies the demands of the academy, although the academy has some right to require satisfaction on its own terms. In a *Festschrift* which honors a churchman, as well as a scholar, who himself has built bridges between two worlds too often apart—those of the church and of the academy—it seems appropriate enough at least to construct a signpost pointing in the direction of a bridge over the waters of election, which is perhaps the realistic way to look at the exercise attempted in this essay. These are waters in which biblical and theological fishermen should harmoniously spread their nets from En Gedi to En Eglaim, united in the task of fetching in the kingdom haul (Ezek 47:1–12; Rev 22:1–2).

Index of Persons

Aageson, James W., 105, 111
Aaron, John, 164, 165
Achtemeier, Paul, 65
Ackroyd, Peter R., 27
Adams, David, 233–34, 235, 236
Adams, Edward, 68
Adeney, W. F., 131
Aled, Siôn, 151
Allen, W. C., 240
Alter, Robert, 30, 55
Anselm, 230
Ap Gwilym, Gwynn, 143
Ap Rhys, Gweirydd, 175
Arn, Win, 83
Ascough, Richard S., 110
Ashley, Timothy R., 7
Ashton, Margaret, 163
Augustine, 58, 229
Augustus, 112, 117

Bailey, Mr., 166, 171
Balch, David L., 112, 113
Balz, Horst, 90, 94
Barclay, William, 93
Barr, James, 26, 262
Barrett, C. Kingsley, 132, 133–34, 136
Barrett, Jerry, 172
Bartchy, S. Scott, 114
Barth, Karl, 18, 227, 239, 240, 241, 242, 244, 245, 246, 247, 248, 250, 251, 253
Barton, John, 47, 50, 51, 53

Bassler, Jouette M., 105, 112, 113, 115, 118
Battle, Michael, 61, 73
Beale, Gregory, 63, 70
Beardwood, Herbert, 4, 5
Becker, J. Christian, 72
Beetham, Christopher A., 101–2
Bellin, Samuel, 170
Bennett, W. H., 131
Beutler, J., 94
Bicknell, E. J., 32, 33
Birch, B.C., 52
Black, Matthew, 132, 136, 140
Blair, Edward P., 90
Blenkinsopp, J., 45, 50
Bontrager, G. Edwin, 83
Borg, Marcus J., 41
Bowen, Geraint, 144
Brackney, William H., 83
Brash, W. Bardsley, 124, 125, 127, 136
Brawley, R., 125
Breeze, George, 250
Brettler, Marc, 30
Breytenbach, Cilliers, 64, 68
Bright, John, 48
Brown, Ford Madox, 172
Brown, R. E., 34
Brown, W. P., 30
Brunner, Emil, 245, 246, 250
Bryan, John, 171
Bultmann, Rudolf, 245, 249
Burt, R., 166
Busch, Eberhard, 240

Index of Persons

'Cadrawd' (Thomas Christopher Evans), 143
Caesar, 118
Caird, Edward, 231
Caird, George B., 90
Calvin, John, 37, 38–39, 43, 162–64, 245
Campbell, William S., 15, 58, 120
Caputo, 271
Carr, David, 28
Causse, A., 48
Chamberlain, Neville, 252
Charles, David, I, (1762–1834), 160, 173
Charles, David, II, (1803–1880), 168–69
Charles, David, III, (1812–1878), 197, 199, 200, 201, 202, 203, 207–8
Charles, Eliza, 169
Charles, Sarah, 169
Charles, Thomas, 17, 165, 166, 167, 168, 174, 175, 195, 197
Chesterton, G. K., 133
Childs, B. S., 44, 46, 51, 55
Clarke, Andrew, 107, 108, 109, 111, 114
Clements, R. E., 48, 125, 131
Clifford, John, 9
Cochrane, A. C., 246
Coleridge, S. T., 229
Colfe, Abraham, 3–4
Collingwood, William, 173
Collyer, J., 166
Cook, F., 192
Corley, Kathleen, 110
Corrie, G. E., 163
Cox, David, 173
Cross, Anthony R., 7
Curran, Charles, 20

D'Angelo, Mary Rose, 105, 117, 118
Dafis, Dafydd, 192
Dafydd, Robert, 164, 177
Daniel, John Edward, 18, 238, 241–44, 149–50
Darwin, Charles, 207
Das, Gour, 179

Davidson, A. B., 232
Davidson, Robert, 31, 34, 35
Davies, A., 45
Davies, Anne, 188
Davies, Cynthia, 159
Davies, David, 175
Davies, David, industrialist, 204
Davies, David, 211–12, 241, 216–17, 219, 220, 221
Davies, David Charles, 169, 205, 209, 210
Davies, E. O., 211
Davies, E. Tegla, 238
Davies, Eryl W., 14, 45, 48, 50, 51, 55
Davies, Gareth, 192, 198, 204
Davies, Griffith, 176
Davies, Howell, 174
Davies, Ivor Oswy, 18, 245–48, 249, 250–253
Davies, Jennet, 170
Davies, John, 213
Davies, John J. P., 170
Davies, Mary, 212
Davies, Monica, 176
Davies, P. R., 25
Davies, Richard, 185
Davies, Richard, of Treborth, 188
Davies, Robert, 169
Davies, Robert, of Bodlondeb, 187
Davies, Saunders, 159
Davies, T. Eirug, 236
Davies, T. Witton, 219, 233
Davies, Tudor, 159, 160–61
Davies, W. D., 75
Davies, W. H., 6
Davies, William, 166, 174
Derrida, Jacques, 108
Dicken, E. W. Trueman, 56
Dickens-Lewis, G., 217
Dillistone, F. W., 7, 130
Dinkler, Erich, 72, 73
Dix, Gregory, 135
Doane, W. H., 151
Dodd, C. H., 64, 130
Donfried, Karl P., 115
Douglas, Mary, 48
Drury, M. O'C., 269

Index of Persons

Duncan, Leland Lewis, 4
Dunn, James D. G., 65, 130

Edwards, D. Miall, 18, 235, 236, 237–38, 239, 242–44, 252
Edwards, G. A., 197, 208, 212, 238
Edwards, Huw, 189
Edwards, John Robert, 3
Edwards, Lewis, 18, 171, 172, 174, 177, 193–94, 197, 198, 200, 202, 208, 229
Edwards, O. M., 178
Edwards, Roger, 177
Edwards, Thomas Charles, 229, 231, 232
Ehrensperger, Kathy, 15, 107, 114
Eichrodt, W., 46, 51
Eisenbaum, Pamela, 59
Elias, John, 166, 170, 171, 176, 177, 194
Elliott, Neil, 112, 118, 119
Elmslie, W. A. L., 129
Emmen, Harry James, 177
Enoch, S. Ifor, 6, 11
Epsztein, L., 48
Estienne, Robert, 23
Euripides, 141
Evans, C. F., 27
Evans, Christmas, 171
Evans, Craig A., 83
Evans, David Gwyn, 6
Evans, Dyfed, 172
Evans, E. D., 193, 196
Evans, E. Herber, 154
Evans, E. Keri, 234, 241
Evans, J. Young, 210
Evans, John (1723–1817), 166
Evans, John, printer, 168
Evans, John, biographer, 202, 203
Evans, John, of Llwynffortun, 170
Evans, Laura, 179
Evans, Llewelyn Ioan, 232
Evans, Margaret Ann, 6
Evans, Owen E., 1, 7–8, 16, 18, ch. 7
Evans, Ruth, 180
Evans, Tecwyn, 238
Evans, Trebor Lloyd, 194, 208

Fairbairn, A. M., 228, 235
Fatum, Lone, 113
Fewell, D. N., 54
Fiorenza, Elisabeth Schüssler, 42, 105
Fitzgerald, John T., 64
Forsyth, P. T., 9
Foulkes, Lydia, 171
Fowl, Stephen E., 59
Fredriksen, Paula, 58, 74
Frei, Hans, 268

Garland, D., 136
Garlick, Kenneth B., 125
Garvie, A. E., 235
Gaventa, Beverly Roberts, 90
Gee, Thomas, 185
George, A. Raymond, 125
Georgi, Dieter, 66
Gerth, H. H., 48
Gerstenberger, E. S., 56
Gibbs, Eddie, 83
Gibson, John, 165, 171
Gibson, Solomon, 165
Giessen, H., 90
Gilbert, W. S., 12
Glancy, Jennifer, 117
Glover, T. R., 249
Glyn, John, 3
Gomes, Peter J., 41
Goodspeed, Edgar J., 82, 93
Goodwin, Mark J., 118
Gowan, D. E., 125
Griffith, Edward, 174
Griffith, Huw, 167
Griffiths, Ann, 148, 149, 180, 187, 189
Griffiths, Evan, 151
Grifiths, Rhidian, 150, 155
Gruffydd, W. J., 180
Guinness, Os, 83
Gunn, D. M., 54
Gurnall, William, 194

Haacker, Klaus, 65
Hadrian, 117
Hagner, D. A., 130
Hammarskjold, Dag, 9
Handel, G. F., 12

Index of Persons

Harding, A., 192
Harnack, Adolf von, 235, 236
Harrelson, W., 45
Harries, Griffith, 202
Harris, Howel(l), 9, 146, 176, 192, 196, 198, 200, 204, 206, 213, 223
Harris, Thomas, 192
Harvey, John, 162, 164
Haslam, Richard, 181, 185, 186, 188
Hawkins, John, 39
Hayes, Haf Tudno, 7
Heckel, Ulrich, 60
Hempel, J., 47, 50
Herzer, Jens, 109, 114, 115, 116, 117
Himbury, D. Mervyn, 193
Hitler, Adolf, 246, 251, 252
Hodge, Archibald, 232
Hodge, Charles, 232
Holladay, Carl R., 101
Holmberg, Bengt, 59
Hooker, Morna D., 125
Hooker, Richard, 230
'Hopcyn' (L. J. Hopkin James), 143
Horrell, David, 105, 106
Horton, Douglas, 240
Howard, James H., 102
Howells, William, 208
Hughes, D. G. Lloyd, 167
Hughed, Garfield H., 144
Hughes, Henry, 164
Hughes, Hugh, 17, 164, 165, 166, 167–70, 171
Hughes, J. G. Moelwyn, 153
Hughes, John, 192
Hughes, John, weaver, 179–180
Hughes, Robert, 2, 176, 177
Hughes, Robert, of Gaerwen, 177
Hughes, Robert, innkeeper, 178
Hughes, Ruth, 179
Hughes, Stephen, 183
Hulme, Basil, 10
Humphreys, E. Morgan, 216
Hunsberger, George, 255, 256, 258
Hunt, Holman, 171
Huws, W. Pari, 234

Ifans, Dafydd, 174

Jacob, Edmond, 262
James, E. Wyn, 180
James, William, 198
James, William, of Aberdare, 207, 214
Janzen, W., 45
Jenkins, David, 5
Jenkins, Geraint H., 163, 195
Jenkins, J. Gwili, 238
Jenkins, Kathryn, 147, 155, 160
Jenkins, R. T., 2, 10, 193
Jeremias, J., 135
Jewett, Robert, 68, 71, 72, 73, 76
Job, J. T., 158
Johansen, Kurt I., 248
John, Goscombe, 174
John, Peter, 175
Jones, Alan Vernon, 184
Jones, Aled Gruffudd, 179
Jones, Anthony, 181
Jones, D. Gwenallt, 155
Jones, David, 154
Jones, E. Ambrose, 183
Jones, Edward (1761–1836), 146
Jones, Edward, 166
Jones, Emyr Wyn, 177
Jones, Evan, 212
Jones, Evan, of Caernarfon, 219
Jones, Gareth Lloyd, 14
Jones, Geraint, 2, 176, 177
Jones, Glyn Tudwal, 7
Jones, Griffith, 17, 195–96
Jones, Gwenno, 198
Jones, Gwilym H., 6
Jones, Henry, 231
Jones, Howard C., 179.
Jones, Hugh, 171
Jones, Ieuan Gwynedd, 205
Jones, Ieuan S., 150
Jones, Inigo, 181
Jones, Isaac, 217
Jones, Iwan Meical, 177
Jones, J. Cynddylan, 232
Jones, J. Gwynfor, 17–18
Jones, J. Puleston, 232
Jones, John, 172, 176, 195
Jones, John (1796–1857), 172

Index of Persons

Jones, John Gwilym, 149, 158
Jones, John Harries, 208
Jones, J. Morgan, Presbyterian, 164, 213, 215
Jones, John Morgan, Congregationalist, 235, 236–37, 238, 239
Jones, Jonathan, 194
Jones, Laura, 179
Jones, Lydia, 170
Jones, M. G., 195
Jones, Mary, 175
Jones, Meri, 189
Jones, Michael D., 233
Jones, Morgan D., 159
Jones, Nerys Ann, 183
Jones, Philip Josiah, 238–39
Jones, R. Tudur, 193, 233, 234, 235, 236, 237
Jones, Richard, 151
Jones, Robert, 164, 192
Jones, S. Morris, 17, 164, 165, 172–73
Jones, Samuel, 192
Jones, Sylvia Prys, 233
Jones, T. Ivon, 250
Jones, Thomas, 198
Jones, Thomas, of Berriew, 10, 179
Jones, Thomas, of Denbigh, 166, 194
Jones, W. P., 192, 197, 198, 199, 203, 204, 205, 209, 212, 213
Jones, W. Morgan, 209
Jones, William, 170,
Jones, William, of Ton Pentre, 182
Jordan, E. K. H., 9
Josephus, 97

Kaiser, W. C., 45
Kant, I., 230, 245
Käsemann, Ernst, 60, 105
Kaye, Elaine, 130, 131, 235
Keck, Leander, 82
Keller, Adolf, 227, 241
Keown, Mark J., 93
Kim, Seyoon, 63
Kimbrough, S. T., 48
Kirschner, Jan, 190
Klopfenstein, M., 46
Knight, D. A., 51

Knowles, Vincent, 141
Knox, R. Buick, 6, 199, 253
Kohl, Margaret, 48
Kraftchick, S. J., 63, 64

Lacey, W. K., 112
Lambrecht, Jan, 63
Land, Darin H., 98
Lang, B., 48
Larkin, William J., 265
Larsen, Timothy, 125, 130, 131
Lee, Jae Won, 66
Leeds, Frederick, 4
Leibniz, G. W., 259
Leverhulme, Lord, 175
Levi, Thomas, 206, 213
Levy, T., 48
Lewis, E. D., 183
Lewis, J. D. Vernon, 18, 239–41, 252
Lewis, John Wyndham, 173
Lewis, Thomas, 153
Lewis, William, missionary, 179
Lewis, William, weaver, 152-3
Lidgett, John Scott, 9
Lim, Kar-Yong, 114
Linder, M. W., 125
Livingstone, E. A., 7
Lloyd, Mrs., 166
Lloyd, D. Tecwyn, 156, 157–58
Lloyd, J. Meirion, 179
Lloyd, Mair, 2
Lloyd, Mary, 166
Lloyd, Simon, 170
Lloyd, Thomas, 192
Locke, John, 230
Longenecker, Richard N., 85
Lopez, Davina, 60
Lord, Peter, 162, 165, 166, 167, 168, 169, 170, 171, 172, 173, 174, 175, 177, 190
Luff, Alan, 146
Lumley, Richard, 203
Luther, Martin, 37, 245, 248

McCartney, Paul, 3
McConnachie, John, 227, 241
McCormick, R. A., 20

Index of Persons

MacDonald, Margaret Y., 104, 106, 113
McDonald, Lee M., 82
McGavran, Donals, 82–83
McGowan, A. T. B., 269
McKim, Donald K., 125, 130, 131, 132, 136
Mackintosh, H. R., 241
MacPherson, D. Neal, 83
Maddocks, William Alexander, 181
Mainwaring, Daniel, 173
Malina, B. J., 48
Malkin, Benjamin Heath, 198
Malphurs, Aubrey, 83
Manning, Bernard Lord, 144
Manson, T. W., 16, 18, ch. 7
Marshall, I. Howard, 105, 106, 107, 108, 109, 111, 115, 117
Martin, Ralph P., 62, 72, 85, 125
Martindale, D., 48
Matthews, D. Hugh, 193
Matthews, Edward, 204
Matthews, John, 194
Mazar, A., 48
Mead, Loren D., 83
Meecham, H. G., 138, 139
Meeks, Wayne A., 108
Megahey, Alan, 61
Mein, A., 45
Menken, Martin J. J., 101
Miall, Edward, 237
Milburn, Geoffrey E., 124
Mills, M. E., 45
Milton, John, 230
Mitchell, H. G., 45
Mitton, C. Leslie, 136
Morgan, D. Densil, 18, 171, 193, 211, 229, 232, 233, 241, 242, 244, 247, 248
Morgan, Derec Llwyd, 146
Morgan, Dyfnallt, 146
Morgan, E., 194
Morgan, Mrs. Evan, 204
Morgan, Gareth, 189
Morgan, Herbert, 238
Morgan, J. J., 209
Morgan, K. O., 211
Morgan, William, 164

Morgan-Guy, John, 162
Morgans, Delyth G., 146
Morris, Silas, 233
Moyise, S., 57
Muilenburg, James, 53
Müller, Ludwig, 247

Newbigin, J. E. Lesslie, 18, 255–58, 260, 272
Newborough, Lord, 169
Nicholas, W. Rhys, 151, 154, 159
Niemöller, Martin, 246
Nightingale, Florence, 172
Nowell, Alexander, 163
Nussbaum, Martha, 47
Nuttall, Geoffrey F., 192

O'Kane, Martin, 162, 190
Oman, John, 129
Omanson, Roger L., 99
Orbach, Julian, 181, 185, 186, 188
Osiek, Carolyn, 112, 113
Owen, D. Huw, 17, 173, 180, 181, 184, 189
Owen, Daniel, 156
Owen, G, Dyfnallt, 193
Owen, Jimmy, 150
Owen, John, 3
Owen, John, of Chester, 219
Owen, Robert, 169

Pailin, David A., 125
Painter, J., 132
Parri, Harri, 211
Parry, Edward, 170
Parry, John, 214
Parry-Williams, T. H., 149
Peake, A. S., 130–31
Peake, Leslie S., 131
Peirce, W., 182
Perdue, L. G., 52
Peters, George, 83
Phillips, A., 45
Phillips, John Henry, 186
Phillips, Thomas, 198
Pick, E., 166
Pillar, Edward, 118

Index of Persons

Pleins, J. D., 47, 48, 49
Pliny the Younger, 82
Pointer, Roy D., 83
Pope, Robert, 207, 211, 229, 233, 236, 237
Porter, Stanley, 73, 82
Powell, W. Eifion, 11
Preston, Ronald H., 140
Pritchard, Rhys, 143, 148
Pritchard, W. H., 185
Prys, Edmund, 143, 150
Prys, Owen, 18, 205–6, 209–11, 222
Pryse, William, 179
Prytherch, W. E., 183, 222
Pugh, J. Meirion Lloyd, 183
Pugh, John, 203

Rad, G. von, 56
Reckwitz, Andreas, 64
Rees, Henry, 177, 188, 194–5
Rees, J. Derfel, 184
Rees, Thomas, 207
Rees, Thomas, (1869–1926) 234–36, 241
Rees, William, 195
Rehkopf, Friedrich, 135
Reumann, John, 93
Rhees, Rush, 269
Rhys, Morgan, 149
Richard, Ebenezer, 193, 194
Richard, Henry, 193
Richard, Thomas, 193
Richards, Pernille, 4
Richardson, Evan, 192
Robbins, Anna M., 7
Robbins, Keith, 244
Roberts, Brynley F., 16, 175
Roberts, D. Francis, 238
Roberts, Elfed ap Nefydd, 11–12, 199
Roberts, Evan, 178, 189
Roberts, Ezra, 183
Roberts, Gomer M., 169, 170, 176, 198, 199, 200
Roberts, Gwawr, 189
Roberts, H. P., 192, 193
Roberts, J. Bryn, 216
Roberts, John, 166, 167
Roberts, John, 'Ieuan Gwyllt', 172
Roberts, John, of Llanbryn-mair, 233
Roberts, John (1880–1959), 199
Roberts, John (1910–1984), 152
Roberts, Michael, 167, 177
Roberts, Owen Morris, 185
Robertson, E. H., 246
Robyns-Owen, O., 216
Rodd, Cyril S., 37, 45, 46, 47, 49, 136
Rogerson, J. W., 48
Rollins, Wayne G., 92
Roos, William, 166, 170, 171
Ross, G. MacDonald, 259
Rowland, Daniel, 176, 196
Rowley, H. H., 18, 125, 126, 132, 140, 258
Runcie, Robert, 10
Ruskin, John, 173
Ryan, John, 148

Saunders, Erasmus, 144
Saunderson, Robert, 166
Schleiermacher, F. D. E., 245
Schlenther, Boyd S., 192
Schlier, Heinrich, 105
Schmidt, W. H., 45
Schneider, Gerhard, 90, 94
Scholder, Klaus, 247
Schottroff, Luise, 105, 106
Schürmann, Heinz, 135
Schütz, John H., 73. 76., 106
Schweizer, Eduard, 106
Scott, C. A. Anderson, 129
Scott, James C., 118
Selina, Countess of Huntingdon, 191–2, 200
Sell, Alan P. F., 7, 131, 232, 237, 239
Shedd, W. G. T., 232
Showalter, Nathan D., 83
Simeon, Charles, 268–69
Skinner, John, 129
Sly, James B., 175
Smith, D. L., 48
Smith, J. M. Powis, 45
Smith, William Robertson, 232
Snaith, Norman, 55, 125
Söding, Thomas, 115, 116, 117

281

Index of Persons

Stendahl, K., 53, 62
Streeter, B. H., 135
Stringfellow, Thornton, 40
Sullivan, Arthur, 12

Talbert, Charles H., 97
Taylor, Elizabeth Alice, 127, 134
Taylor, Vincent, 16, ch. 7
Tertullian, 262, 263
Thatcher, Margaret, 10
Theudas, 97
Thomas Aquinas, 32
Thomas, Ebenezer, 172
Thomas, Ednyfed, 179
Thomas, J. Owen, 219
Thomas, John (1742–1818), 147
Thomas, John, 166, 177
Thomas, John, photographer, 177–78
Thomas, Josiah, 233
Thomas, Owen, 177
Thomas, Peter M., 151
Thomas, R. G., 187, 204
Thomas, R. S., 232
Thomas, Richard, 185
Thomas, Thomas, 183
Thurneysen, Eduard, 240
Towner, Philip H., 106
Townsend, Henry, 9
Trajan, 82
Trickett, Kenneth, 156
Trites, Allison A., 8, 15, 83, 84, 87, 91, 94, 95, 96, 97
Tsevat, M., 46
Tucker, G. M., 56
Tutu, Desmond, 73
Twain, Mark, 35–36, 39–40

Voelkar, Adam, 181, 185, 186, 188
Volf, Miroslav, 59, 73
Vosper, Sydney Curwen, 175

Wagner, C. Peter, 83
Wallace, J. E., 3
Walters, J., 203
Warren, Rich, 83
Washington, George, 40
Waterhouse, E. S., 127

Watkins, Benjamin, 201
Watson, Richard, 156
Watts, Isaac, 151, 169
Watts, Michael R., 194
Weber, Max, 47, 48, 106
Welch, Edwin, 192
Weld, Wayne, 83
Wenham, G. J., 45
Wheldon, T. J., 218
White, Eryn M., 145, 195
Whitefield, George, 176
Whitehorn, R. D., 9
Whiteley, Denys, 5
Wilkinson, John T., 131
Wiliam, Owen, 174
William, Dafydd, 148
William, Thomas, 153
Williams, Arthur, 159
Williams, Arthur Tudno, 1, 2–3, 7
Williams, D., 209
Williams, D. D., 208, 229
Williams, David J., 87
Williams, Edwin, 210
Williams, Evan, 171, 172
Williams, Evan, of Bangor, 204
Williams, Glanmor, 163, 195
Williams, H. Barrow, 218, 219
Williams, Hugh, 175
Williams, Ina, 1, 6, 7, 10
Williams, J. Edward, 158
Williams, J. Gwyn, 163
Williams, J. J., 150
Williams, John, 230
Williams, John, of Brynsiencyn, 219, 222
Williams, John Tudno, Sr., 2
Williams, John Tudno, 1–13, 17, 19, 77, 81, 104, 130, 142, 176, 228, 255, 268, 273
Williams, Mary, 178
Williams, Penry, 171
Williams, Primrose, 1
Williams, Rheinallt Nantlais, 6, 11
Williams, Rowan, 147
Williams, Stephen Nantlais, 18–19, 268, 271
Williams, Tal, 175

Index of Persons

Williams, Thomas, 153
Williams, Thomas Charles, 219
Williams, Tom Nefyn, 211
Williams, W., 209
Williams, W. Nantlais, 151, 154, 158
Williams, William, 146, 147, 157, 176, 187, 189, 202
Williams, William Richard, 5, 210
Williams, Tomos Gwyn Tudno, 7
Wilson, R. R., 48
Wilson, Richard, 171
Wilson, Robert S., 7
Wittgenstein, Ludwig, 269
Wolf, Ernst, 227
Wolff, Christian, 63
Wolff, H. W., 48
Wooden, R. Glenn, 7
Woodman, Richard, 170
Wright, Christopher J. H., 46, 49, 254, 255, 258
Wright, G. E., 48
Zuck, Roy B., 96
Zwingli, Unrich, 37

Index of Subjects

Acadia Divinity College, 8, 81
Accrington Grammar School, 127
All Souls College Oxford, 192
Arminianism, 231, 268–69
artisan painters, 176

Bala-Bangor Independent College, 6,
    229, 233, 235, 236, 242, 244
Bala Presbyterian Seminary, 245
Bala Theological College, 5, 202, 203,
    205, 208, 211–16, 217, 218, 229
Bangor Baptist College, 233
Bangor Normal College, 210
Bangor University College, 228, 231,
    233, 235, 241, 245
baptism, 156
Baptists, 125, 229, 230, 233, 238
Barthianism, 239–53
Bible
    and hymns, ch. 8
    and systematic theology, ch. 12
    authority of, 42
    canonicity, 23–25
    characteristics of, 22–23
    criticism, 250
    diversity of, 27–28, 30
    ethics of Old Testament, ch. 3
    historical-critical method, 47–53,
        57
    history and cultural setting, 25–27
    inerrancy, 232
    interpretation of, 28–43, 232–33,
        234, 239–40, 252, 268–69

literary-critical method, 53–57
visual imagery of, ch. 9
Blue Book controversy, 205
Bonn University, 246, 248
British Academy, 129, 131
British Council of Churches, 10

Calvinism, 156, 231, 232, 233, 240, 250,
    268–69
Calvinistic Methodist Connexion: see
    Presbyterian Church of Wales
Caneuon Ffydd, 146
Cardiff University College, 228, 235
carols, 143
Centre for Christian Unity and
    Renewal, 180
chapel architecture, 179–90
chapel names, 184
chapels, illustrations of, 180–83, 185–
    86, 188, 190
Charles University, Prague, 190
Christian identity, 58–60
Christology, 231, 232, 234, 237, 238,
    242–43, 270–72
Christ's College Cambridge, 129
Church
    as the "house of God", ch. 6
    office in the, 104–11, 114
    polity, 156
church growth
    and collegiality, 93–95
    and prayerfulness, 91–93
    and relationships, 89–91

284

Index of Subjects

church growth (*continued*)
    as qualitative, 86–88
    Christocentricity of, 85–86, 103
    costliness of, 88–89
    Paul and Luke on, 95–102
Church of England, 145, 228, 230
Church of Scotland, 10, 194
Circulating Schools, 195
Colfe's Grammar School, 3–5
communion service, 152
Confessing Church, 247, 248, 251
Congregationalists, 183, 227, 229, 230, 233–39, 241, 242–43, 244, 245
Corrymela Community, 9–10

Darwinism, 231
Didsbury Wesleyan College, 197
Dissenting academies, 192–93
Drew University, 132

election, ch. 12
eternal life, 264–68
evolutionary theory, 231, 233–34, 238
experience, 242–44

Free Church Federal Council, 9–10

German Christians, 247
Global Anglican Future Conference, 20
Great Awakening, 146

Halle University, 239
halsingod, 143–44
Handsworth Methodist College, Birmingham, 136
Hartley Victoria Methodist College, Manchester, 124, 126, 131, 136, 137, 138
Holy Spirit, 236
Hotel Cambria, Aberystwyth, 216–17, 218
Hymns, ch. 8

idolatry, 162–63, 164
immanentism, 234, 237
Independents: see Congregationalists

Jesus College Oxford, 1, 5, 192, 208, 241, 245
Judaism and Christianity, ch. 4

King's College Cambridge, 212

Lancashire Independent College, 131
Leipzig University, 210, 239
liberalism, 228, 233–39, 241, 243, 244, 246, 252
Liverpool Institute High School, 3
Llangollen Baptist College, 229

Manchester Free Church Council, 131
Mansfield College Oxford, 130, 228, 235, 236, 237, 239
Marburg University, 249
Memorial College Brecon, 235, 237, 242, 243, 252
Memorial College Swansea, 6
Methodist Church, 127–28, 137
Methodist societies, 142, 144, 145, 146
missiology, 255, 258
missions, 10–11, 179, 218, 220

National Gallery, 173
National Library of Wales, 124, 178, 190
Northern Ireland, 61
New Testament scholarship, ch. 7

Old Testament ethics, ch. 3
ordination, 6
Owen's College Manchester, 210

paraphrases, 151-2
peace, ch. 4
Peterhouse Cambridge, 210
philosophical idealism, 228, 231, 232, 237, 238–39
Pine Hill Divinity Hall, Nova Scotia, 131
Pontifical University, Maynooth, 190
Pontypool Baptist College, 229
preaching, 208–9, 251
Presbyterian Church of England, 125, 129, 130, 131

285

Index of Subjects

Presbyterian Church of Ireland, 10
Presbyterian Church of Wales, 1, 2, 5, 10–11, 81, ch. 9, ch. 10, 230, 232, 245–48, 250
Presbyterian College Carmarthen, 208
Princeton Theological Seminary, 232
privilege, 255–63
psalms, 150–51, 153

reconciliation, ch. 4
responsibility, 256–58, 269
revelation, 249–50, 251, 252
Richmond College London, 127, 197
Roman imperial thought, 111–14, 117–18, 120
Royal Society, 176

St. David's College Lampeter, 5, 228
St. Paul's, Covent Garden, London, 181
Second Vatican Council, 20
seiat, 145, 146, 148, 153
service, 258
slavery, 39–41
social action, 156–57, 160–61
social responsibility, ch. 4
Society for Old Testament Study, 131
South Africa, 61
Strasbourg University, 131
Student Christian Movement, 239
Studiorum Novi Testamenti Societas, 132
Sunday Schools, 195, 218, 230
synopsis of chapters, 14–19

Trefeca College, 191–92, 198–214, 217, 218, 220, 221
Trinity, 236, 242
Tynemouth Municipal High School, 129

Union of Welsh Independents, 234, 244
United Secession Church, 194
United Theological College Aberystwyth, 5, 6, 7, 11, 12–13, 81, 124, 222–23, 245
University College Aberystwyth, 6, 8, 174, 222, 228, 231, 233
University of Cambridge, 130, 131, 193
University of Chicago, 130
University of Dublin, 128, 131
University of Durham, 131, 132
University of Edinburgh, 229
University of Glasgow, 128, 129, 130, 131, 231
University of Leeds, 128
University of London, 127, 128, 193, 194, 228
University of Manchester, 124, 130, 131, 132–33, 136, 137, 138–40, 141: and see Owen's College
University of Oxford, 128, 193
University of St. Andrews, 130
University of Wales, 5–6, 11, 81, 239
usury, 36–39

visual arts, 164–79

Wesley College Headingley, Leeds, 125–26, 127, 128, 133, 137
Wesleyan Methodists, 196–97, 230, 238, 241, 250
Westminster College Cambridge, 129

Yale University, 241

Zurich University, 246

www.ingramcontent.com/pod-product-compliance
Lightning Source LLC
Chambersburg PA
CBHW071236230426
43668CB00011B/1460